Home
Environments

Human Behavior and Environment

ADVANCES IN THEORY AND RESEARCH

Home Environments

EDITED BY

IRWIN ALTMAN

AND

CAROL M. WERNER

University of Utah
Salt Lake City, Utah

PLENUM PRESS • NEW YORK AND LONDON

Library of Congress Cataloging in Publication Data

Main entry under title:

Home environments.

(Human behavior and environment; v. 8)
Includes bibliographies and index.
1. Architecture—United States—Human factors. 2. Architecture—Environmental
aspects—United States. I. Altman, Irwin. II. Werner, Carol M. III. Series.
BF353.H85 vol. 8   155.9 s [155.9′45]   85-12272
[NA2542.4]
ISBN 0-306-41976-9

©1985 Plenum Press, New York
A Division of Plenum Publishing Corporation
233 Spring Street, New York, N.Y. 10013

Printed in the United States of America

Articles Planned for Volume 9
NEIGHBORHOOD AND COMMUNITY ENVIRONMENTS
Editors: Irwin Altman and Abraham Wandersman

Islands in the Stream: Neighborhood in the Political
Economy of Urban Areas
DAVID BARTELT, DAVID ELESH, IRA GOLDSTEIN,
GEORGE LEON, AND WILLIAM YANCEY

Resident Participation in Neighborhood Rehabilitation
in Practice
ARZA CHURCHMAN

Neighborhood Preservation: Equity and Integrity in
the Urban Frontier
DAVID GOLDFIELD

The Symbolic Ecology of Suburbia: The Territoriality of
Individual and Collective Identities
ALBERT HUNTER

Culture and Environment in Neighborhood Conflict
SALLY ENGLE MERRY

Architectural Design and Neighborhood Formation
GEORGE RAND AND BERGE ARAN

The Neighborhood, Personal Identity, and Group Affiliations
LEANNE RIVLIN

The Sociocultural Context of Neighborhood and
Community Planning
WILLEM VAN VLIET AND JACK BURGERS

Toxic Wastes and the Community
ABRAHAM WANDERSMAN AND MICHAEL EDELSTEIN

Contributors

IRWIN ALTMAN • Office of the Vice President for Academic Affairs, University of Utah, Salt Lake City, Utah

JAMES R. ANDERSON • School of Architecture and Housing Research and Development Program, University of Illinois, Urbana, Illinois

SIDNEY BROWER • School of Social Work and Community Planning, University of Maryland, Baltimore, Maryland

GERALD J. CONTI • MSE Library, The Johns Hopkins University, Baltimore, Maryland

JAMES S. DUNCAN • Department of Geography, Syracuse University, Syracuse, New York

KIMBERLY DOVEY • Department of Architecture, Royal Melbourne Institute of Technology, Melbourne, Victoria, Australia

GRAEME J. HARDIE • National Institute for Personnel Research, Braamfontein, Republic of South Africa

ELIZABETH D. HUTTMAN • Department of Sociology and Social Services, California State University, Hayward, California

PERLA KOROSEC-SERFATY • Institut de Psychologie, Université Louis Pasteur, Strasbourg, France

RODERICK J. LAWRENCE • Université de Genève, Genève, Switzerland

DIANA OXLEY • Department of Psychology, University of Utah, Salt Lake City, Utah

AMOS RAPOPORT • Department of Architecture, University of Wisconsin, Milwaukee, Wisconsin

DAVID G. SAILE • School of Architecture and Urban Design, University of Kansas, Lawrence, Kansas

SUSAN SAEGERT • Program in Environmental Psychology, City University of New York Graduate Center, New York, New York

SALLY A. SHUMAKER • Behavioral Medicine Branch, DECA/NHLBI, The National Institutes of Health, Bethesda, Maryland

RALPH B. TAYLOR • Department of Criminal Justice, Temple University, Philadelphia, Pennsylvania

SUE WEIDEMANN • Department of Landscape Architecture and Housing Research and Development Program, University of Illinois, Urbana, Illinois

CAROL M. WERNER • Department of Psychology, University of Utah, Salt Lake City, Utah

Preface

The present volume in the series focuses on homes, residences, and dwellings. Although many fields have had a long-standing interest in different aspects of home environments, the topic has recently come to the forefront in the interdisciplinary environment and behavior field. Researchers and theorists from many disciplines have begun to meet regularly, share ideas and perspectives, and move the investigation of psychological, social, and behavioral aspects of home environments to the central arena of environment and behavior studies. This volume attempts to provide a representative—though not comprehensive—sampling of contemporary perspectives on the study of home environments.

As in previous volumes, the authors are drawn from a variety of disciplines, including environmental design fields of architecture and planning, and from the social science fields of psychology, sociology, anthropology, and history. This diversity of authors and perspectives makes salient the principle that the study of homes in relation to behavior requires the contributions of many disciplines. Moreover, the chapters in this volume reflect an array of research and theoretical viewpoints, different scales of home environments (e.g., objects and areas, the home as a whole, the home as embedded in neighborhood and communities, etc.), design and policy issues, and, necessarily, a comparative and cross-cultural perspective.

Home environments are at the core of human life in most cultures, and it is hoped that the contributions to this volume display the excitement, potential, and importance of research and theory on homes.

Volume 9 of this series will be coedited by Abraham Wandersman and Irwin Altman, and will deal with the topic of community and neighborhood environments.

IRWIN ALTMAN

Contents

CHAPTER 1

TEMPORAL ASPECTS OF HOMES: A TRANSACTIONAL
PERSPECTIVE

CAROL M. WERNER
IRWIN ALTMAN
DIANA OXLEY

CHAPTER 2

HOME AND HOMELESSNESS

KIMBERLY DOVEY

CHAPTER 3

EXPERIENCE AND USE OF THE DWELLING

PERLA KOROSEC-SERFATY

CHAPTER 4

THE RITUAL ESTABLISHMENT OF HOME

DAVID G. SAILE

CHAPTER 5

A MORE HUMANE HISTORY OF HOMES:
RESEARCH METHOD AND APPLICATION

RODERICK J. LAWRENCE

CHAPTER 6

THE HOUSE AS SYMBOL OF SOCIAL STRUCTURE: NOTES ON
THE LANGUAGE OF OBJECTS AMONG COLLECTIVISTIC GROUPS

JAMES S. DUNCAN

CHAPTER 9

CONTINUITY AND CHANGE IN THE TSWANA'S HOUSE
AND SETTLEMENT FORM

GRAEME J. HARDIE

CHAPTER 10

UNDERSTANDING MOBILITY IN AMERICA:
CONFLICTS BETWEEN STABILITY AND CHANGE

SALLY A. SHUMAKER
GERALD J. CONTI

CHAPTER 7

A CONCEPTUAL FRAMEWORK FOR RESIDENTIAL SATISFACTION

SUE WEIDEMANN
JAMES R. ANDERSON

CHAPTER 8

HOME AND NEAR-HOME TERRITORIES

RALPH B. TAYLOR
SIDNEY BROWER

CHAPTER 11

THINKING ABOUT HOME ENVIRONMENTS:
A CONCEPTUAL FRAMEWORK

AMOS RAPOPORT

CHAPTER 12

THE ROLE OF HOUSING IN THE EXPERIENCE OF DWELLING

SUSAN SAEGERT

CHAPTER 13

TRANSNATIONAL HOUSING POLICIES:
COMMON PROBLEMS AND SOLUTIONS

ELIZABETH D. HUTTMAN

Introduction

There is a growing number of researchers from a variety of disciplines whose topic of study is home environments. The field is growing, but it is not young, and it has reached a stage in its development where it is appropriate to assemble a volume that samples what has been accomplished so far. Thus, the purpose of this volume is to describe the state of the art in the study of homes and to provide a glimpse of what the future holds for theory, research, and application in this area. It is difficult to draw a representative sample of perspectives, levels of analyses, topical foci, disciplines, and the like in such a rapidly expanding and diverse field, and we are aware that some important topics have been omitted. What we do have is an exciting collection of chapters from many disciplines and countries, with each contribution representing unique but complementary approaches to the study of homes.

It is not surprising that research and interest in this area are burgeoning. First, people in every society usually have some type of residence. Although their form and permanence vary widely from one group to another, homes are more or less a universal. Second, in many societies, homes are one of the most important places. Homes offer physical amenities that sustain and support the residents, and they are often essential to the very survival of their occupants. Furthermore, homes are important centers for the development and manifestation of central psychological meanings. Individuals develop identities and regulate privacy in homes; families establish, grow, and bond themselves into a unit in homes and often bond themselves to the larger society through their homes. Thus, homes are the repository of central and essential psychological and cultural processes. A final reason for this interest in homes is that there is a well-established body of information available about homes in many cultures, and this core knowledge facilitates as well as stimulates additional theory and research. Prior work is being accepted as well as scrutinized, and this is leading to healthy challenges and new developments as well as continuations in many areas.

Some of the challenges facing theoreticians and researchers in this area emerge as themes in the present volume. One such challenge involves the interdisciplinary nature of the field. Homes have attracted researchers from every social science discipline, the arts and humanities, and the environmental design fields. Anthropology, psychology, sociology, geography, gerontology, history, economics, interior design, and architecture are among the disciplines represented in the study of homes. Indeed, one challenge facing those interested in homes is to nurture cross-disciplinary contact, so that each field enriches and complements the others.

The chapters in this volume incorporate a diversity of research methodologies, perspectives, and philosophical assumptions, often within a single chapter. Indeed, diversified approaches are probably necessary to comprehend fully such a central and complex setting as the home. For example, the phenemological perspective is represented in the chapters by Dovey (Chapter 2) and Korosec-Serfaty (Chapter 3). Dovey is an architect, and Korosec-Serfaty is a psychologist, and their chapters contain elements of their parent fields and other disciplines. An anthropological approach is contributed by Duncan (Chapter 6), Hardie (Chapter 9), Saile (Chapter 4), and others; however, these authors also represent the perspectives of geography (Duncan) and architecture (Saile). A historical view dominates the works by Lawrence (Chapter 5) and Shumaker and Conti (Chapter 10) in part because of Lawrence and Conti's backgrounds as historians; but this emphasis is complemented in the one chapter by Lawrence's architectural background, and in the other by Shumaker's psychological background. The chapters by Werner, Altman, and Oxley (all psychologists) (Chapter 1), Weidemann and Anderson (a psychologist and an architect, respectively) (Chapter 7), and Taylor and Brower (Chapter 8) (a psychologist and a city planner) all have a strong psychological flavor, but these authors, too, have drawn from their own and other disciplines. And finally, a sociopolitical view is included in the chapters by Huttman (a sociologist) (Chapter 13), Saegert (a psychologist) (Chapter 12), and Rapoport (an anthropologist and city planner) (Chapter 11). These authors draw on a diversity of disciplinary material to examine the broad cultural, political, and sociological contexts of home environments.

In spite of this diversity of perspectives and levels of analysis, the chapters contain a number of common topical and theoretical themes. For example, most of the chapters address the fundamental question of the meaning of home, albeit at varying degrees of specificity and differing levels of analysis. The analysis of this issue is simultaneously simple (a home is a residence invested with psychological meaning) and complex (How does this psychological investment happen? When does it happen? What happens when it does not happen? etc.). Although many of the chapters provide insights into this issue, the question continues to fascinate the field.

In addressing this fundamental question, many of the authors have focused on similar theoretical content or topical areas. For example, the psychological or phenomenological experience of dwelling emerges as a central feature of the chapters by Dovey, Korosec-Serfaty, Taylor and Brower, Saile, Saegert, and Shumaker, among others. Although their methods and units of analysis differ, each of these authors provides a better understanding of what it feels like to be "at home." Another common theme of several chapters is the psychological response to the dwelling. Such topics as the choice of housing, the consequences of the absence of choice, and satisfaction with housing are central to chapters by Weidemann and Anderson, Rapoport, Saegert, and Shumaker and Conti. Such psychological or evaluative responses to homes provide yet another view of the meaning of home.

On a broader scale are chapters that focus at the group level covering such topics as the role of the home in the development of familial relationships, the role of the home in practices that bond the resident to the larger society, and the home in relationship to the neighborhood, community, and entire country (e.g., chapters by Werner *et al.*, Lawrence, Korosec-Serfaty, Hardie, Duncan, Taylor and Brower, and Saile). For example, Hardie's discussion of expressive space among the Tswana of South Africa illustrates how the home is a central part of the residents' lives, their families, and their culture. In this and other examples, the home supports and sustains familial and cultural relationships, while simultaneously representing them. Thus, the meaning of home derives in part from these familial and cultural relationships.

Another theme shared by several chapters is how the meaning of home is related to larger societal forces. For example, Saegert, Dovey, and Huttman each discuss (though from different perspectives and data bases) the disjunction between house-as-dwelling and house-as-economic-commodity. In these and other chapters, the authors explore how individuals can be buffeted by bureaucratic and/or political influences, and how these experiences affect and are affected by the sense of home.

Another theme shared by several chapters is that homes in different cultures have different forms and functions and that a thorough understanding of homes requires a cross-cultural perspective. Some of the chapters span many cultures (Dovey, Saile, Werner *et al.*), others focus on homes in industrialized nations (Huttman, Saegert, Weidemann and Anderson, Taylor and Brower), and others focus on homes in developing nations (Hardie, Duncan).

One of the most important themes in several chapters is how the authors deal with change and temporal qualities of homes. For example, Werner *et al.* proposed a framework of key temporal qualities of homes and applied this framework to homes in different cultures. Other chapters examined how home use and meaning has changed over time, either across generations (e.g., Lawrence, Shumaker and Conti, Dovey) or within a single generation (e.g., Huttman). Others (e.g., Duncan, Hardie) consider both change and continuity and describe what aspects of homes have and have not been affected by rapid Westernization of traditional cultures.

The chapters in the volume have similarities and differences in environmental scale, or unit of analysis. Some chapters focus almost exclusively on the home and its rooms and objects as the unit of analysis; others operate at both the micro- and "meso-" levels, that is, they consider the home in its larger social or environmental context (e.g., neighborhood, city); others incorporate micro-, meso-, and macrolevel elements in their approach (e.g., including homes as part of large social movements, large housing units, etc.). Because this theme is common to all of the chapters, we have chosen to organize the flow of chapters according to their focus on smaller to larger scale aspects of home environments. The ordering is based on our subjective assessment of the importance given by authors to different levels of analysis; hence the arrangement of chapters is imperfect.

The first several chapters focus almost exclusively on the home and its interior; the next series of chapters takes a broader view and examines the neighborhood and country in relation to homes; the final chapters emphasize broad societal forces such as housing services, political pressures, and so on in relation to homes.

The rich substance of the topic of home environments, the relevance of this environmental setting to most people and cultures, the diversity and breadth of perspectives brought to bear on the study of homes from many disciplines, and the potential design implications of work in this field portend a promising and challenging future for continued research and theory on home environments.

IRWIN ALTMAN
CAROL M. WERNER

1

Temporal Aspects of Homes

A TRANSACTIONAL PERSPECTIVE

CAROL M. WERNER, IRWIN ALTMAN, AND DIANA OXLEY

There are many ways of studying homes, each focusing on a different aspect, such as physical qualities, satisfaction, use patterns, and phenomenological experiences. Our thesis is that, central to any of these aspects of homes, and therefore integral to the distinction between *house* and *home*, are the temporal qualities of linear and cyclical time and their subordinate qualities of salience, scale, pace, and rhythm. The goal of this chapter is to propose a general framework that describes these key temporal qualities in the context of a broader transactional orientation. The chapter has four major sections: (1) a description of the transactional world view and of the home as a transactional unity; (2) a discussion of the proposed temporal framework bolstered by examples from a variety of societies; (3) two case studies that demonstrate the application of the framework; and (4) potential research and practical implications of the model.

TRANSACTIONAL PERSPECTIVE

The proposed framework is derived from a transactional perspective in which events are treated as holistic unities comprised of three

CAROL M. WERNER • Department of Psychology, University of Utah, Salt Lake City, Utah 84112. IRWIN ALTMAN • Office of the Vice President for Academic Affairs, University of Utah, Salt Lake City, Utah 84112. DIANA OXLEY • Department of Psychology, University of Utah, Salt Lake City, Utah 84112.

major aspects: people/psychological processes; environmental properties; and temporal qualities (Altman & Rogoff, 1986). Two key assumptions in this perspective are that people and their environments are an
integral and inseparable unit; they cannot be defined separately, and
indeed are mutually defining. Second, temporal qualities are intrinsic to
people–environment relationships, so that homes are conceived of as a
dynamic confluence of people, places, and psychological processes.

   The transactional view has been explored by philosophers (Dewey
& Bentley, 1949; Pepper, 1942) and has been adopted by some psychologists, especially those in environmental psychology (see Altman &
Rogoff, 1986; Barker, 1968; Ittelson, 1973; Proshansky, 1976; Wicker,
1979, 1986). Our conception of the home as a transactional unity is

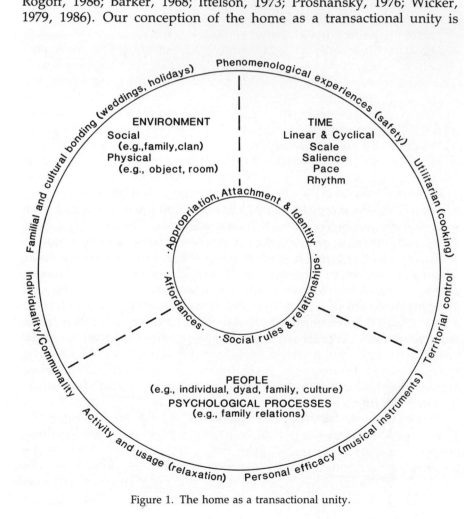

Figure 1. The home as a transactional unity.

diagrammed in Figure 1. Transactional processes in homes occur at the level of action and at the level of meaning; they can be events, activities, meanings, evaluations, or any other psychological process. A few such processes are illustrated in the circumference of the diagram in Figure 1; many more could be added. The model is meant to apply to transactions involving diverse peoples and relationships (e.g., in the diagram, *people* can refer to an individual or a group), at many levels of environmental scale (e.g., the physical environment can refer to an object, place, room, or entire home; the social environment can refer to individuals, families, or groups). Person, environment, and time are identified separately in Figure 1; for ease of description, however, their inherent inseparability is depicted by the presence of dashed rather than solid lines.

Before exploring in detail the temporal qualities of homes, we will first describe the smaller circle in Figure 1, which portrays three general processes by which people can be linked to homes: (1) social rules and social relationships; (2) affordances; and (3) appropriation practices. As will be seen, these processes can only be understood as dynamic transactions involving people, place, and time. Note that these processes span the three aspects of the transactional whole to represent the binding of all three into a unity.

SOCIAL RULES AND SOCIAL RELATIONSHIPS

The category of social rules and relationships encompasses a broad range of dynamic interpersonal processes that occur in homes, including social and cultural norms and rules, affective, emotional, and evaluative bonds, and cultural rituals and practices. These concepts have been summarized nicely by Rapoport (1977, 1982), who defined *environment* as a complex and systematic organization of *space, time, meaning,* and *communication*. These four facets occur simultaneously in a variety of configurations. For example, arrangements of homes around a center or plaza versus row arrangements are likely to reflect and foster different forms of communication between neighbors, different temporal flows of interaction, and different types of interpersonal relationships. Similarly, organization and use of space inside the house support different kinds of communications and meanings for residents.

Social rules describe what behaviors are appropriate and expected in settings at particular times, thereby giving meaning to the settings, people, and their behaviors (Argyle, 1976, 1979; Rapoport, 1982). In all societies, social norms and roles dictate how homes should be used, the times and places for entering, entertaining, sleeping, and eating as well as a myriad of other behaviors and symbolic practices (Gauvain, Altman, & Fahim, 1983; Haumont, 1976; Laumann & House, 1972; Lawrence, 1979, 1982b; Morris & Winter, 1975). Social norms and roles are also reflected in the very designs and configurations of residences, the types and locations of furniture and objects, and the like (Altman, 1977; Altman & Gauvain, 1981; Laumann & House, 1972; Pratt, 1981).

Persons are also linked to their homes by affective and emotional bonds; social relationships are manifested in spatial, psychological, and interpersonal terms, as people use objects and areas in the home to engage in social interaction, mutual succorance, and the like. According to interviews with residents (Csikszentmihalyi & Rochberg-Halton, 1981; Horwitz & Tognoli, 1982; Korosec-Serfaty, 1985; Lawrence, 1982a), the home can also be a symbolic representation of those relationships, as it becomes associated with memories of past interactions and ties between people.

The home also reflects cultural values regarding personal and social identities. For example, the home often symbolizes the establishment of a new household and is frequently involved in wedding rituals such as building a new home or transferring ownership of an existing home to the newlyweds. Or, newlyweds' residences often reflect familial links, such as in matrilocal compounds, and communal living arrangements (Kitahara, 1974; Murdock & Wilson, 1972; Whyte, 1979). In some situations, a wedding may not take place unless the couple can inherit a family farm, thereby providing them with economic resources and a place to live (Hajnal, 1965; Matras, 1973); in others, the family's matrilocal or patrilocal residence determines which family name the children will use (Whyte, 1979). The home can also reflect the very structure of the family, such as in traditional Turkish families, where a son replaces his father as head of the family when the aging father moves into the son's home (Duben, 1982; Kagitcibasi, 1982). In these and other rituals and traditions, the home is integral to and reflects a variety of social and cultural values regarding individual and family identities.

AFFORDANCES

The term *affordance* was coined by Gibson (1979) and indicates that objects and environments are perceived according to the meanings, actions, and behaviors they imply, rather than according to their specific physical characteristics. For example, a chair is not perceived as something with discrete physical characteristics, but as something to sit in. Thus, the emphasis in this linkage is on utilitarian functions and their psychological significance. The home is the locus of many utilitarian activities (personal hygiene, sleeping, cooking and eating, etc.) that lend unique psychological meanings to its objects and places.

Places in the home may serve varied functions at different times of a day or year or even in different historical periods. Thus, the affordance qualities of a home can change with circumstances, architecture, culture, and history. When the affordance functions change, the perceivers' experience of the environment can also vary, such as when the kitchen in Australian homes became integral to the house (Lawrence, Chapter 5, this volume).

APPROPRIATION, ATTACHMENT, AND IDENTITY

Appropriation, attachment, and identity refer collectively to the idea that people invest places with meaning and significance and act in ways that reflect their bonding and linkage with places. At a general level, *appropriation* means that the person is transformed in the process of appropriating the environment. Appropriation can take diverse forms, including taking control over, becoming familiar with, investing with meaning, cultivating and caring for, and displaying identity and belonging with a place or object (Korosec-Serfaty, 1976). The term *appropriation* also connotes mastery or efficacy, such as when people exercise territorial control, and regulate use by others (Altman, 1975, 1977) or gain efficacy through having and using possessions (Furby, 1978; Greenbaum & Greenbaum, 1981). Similarly, the ideas of place attachment and place identity suggest that when people attach psychological, social, and cultural significance to objects and spaces, they thereby bond themselves and the environment into a unity (Gerson, Stueve, & Fischer, 1977; Relph, 1976; Stokols & Shumaker, 1981).

The concepts of *social rules and relationships, affordances,* and *appropriation* reflect the transactional unity of people and environment. The home is an important repository within which these phenomena are manifested and, indeed, the home is partly described by and gains meaning in terms of these phenomena. Similarly, these phenomena are understood partly in terms of the home as an intrinsic aspect of their meaning. Thus, places and processes are inseparable and mutually defining aspects of one another.

And finally, although we have not stressed the temporal component, time is integral to these processes. First, these processes must be seen as occurring over and in time. Second, the processes are *time bound,* by which we mean that their meaning, nature, and probability of enactment can change with the resident's own changing life stage, and their meaning, nature, and occurrence can change with social and cultural changes, that is, from one historical period to another.

TEMPORAL QUALITIES OF HOMES

By our definition, homes intrinsically contain temporal qualities; they reflect dynamic, flowing, and changing relationships between peoples and environments. These relationships have histories and futures as well as a present, they involve change and stability, recurrence, and rhythm. Figure 2 presents a framework of temporal qualities of homes that is based on the work of others who have described psychological aspects of time (Lynch, 1972; McGrath & Rotchford, 1983; Rakowski, 1979; Tuan, 1977).

LINEAR TIME

One major dimension of the present framework is the distinction between linear (past, present, and future) and cyclical, or spiraling, recurrent temporal features of homes. Within each of these general qualities are subordinate properties: *salience,* or the relative emphasis on past, present, or future times; *scale,* or temporal breadth and scope; *pace,* or the density or rapidity of events; and *rhythm,* or the regularity of the pace or pattern of events. Although various writers have identified other temporal qualities, we have selected these constructs because they consistently seem to be reflected in descriptions of home use and meaning.

According to McGrath and Rotchford (1983), whereas philosophers have debated whether time is purely linear or purely cyclical, psychologists have tended to assume that it has both qualities. Linear time, and its associated continuum of past/present/future, contains two important qualities: the first property is the dynamic, flowing, changing, and ongoing aspect of events; the second quality is continuity. Flow and change are explicit aspects of the three person–environment linkages that we described earlier; thus people are linked to homes through dynamic changing processes. Furthermore, people and their relationships grow and change, and these changes are reflected in the use of and association with their homes. And, as was mentioned earlier, these changes occur at the social as well as at the individual levels.

However, no less important is the notion that familiarity and continuity also give meaning to and link people to places. "In time a new house ceases to make little demands on our attention, it is as comfortable and unobtrusive as an old pair of slippers" (Tuan, 1977, p. 184).

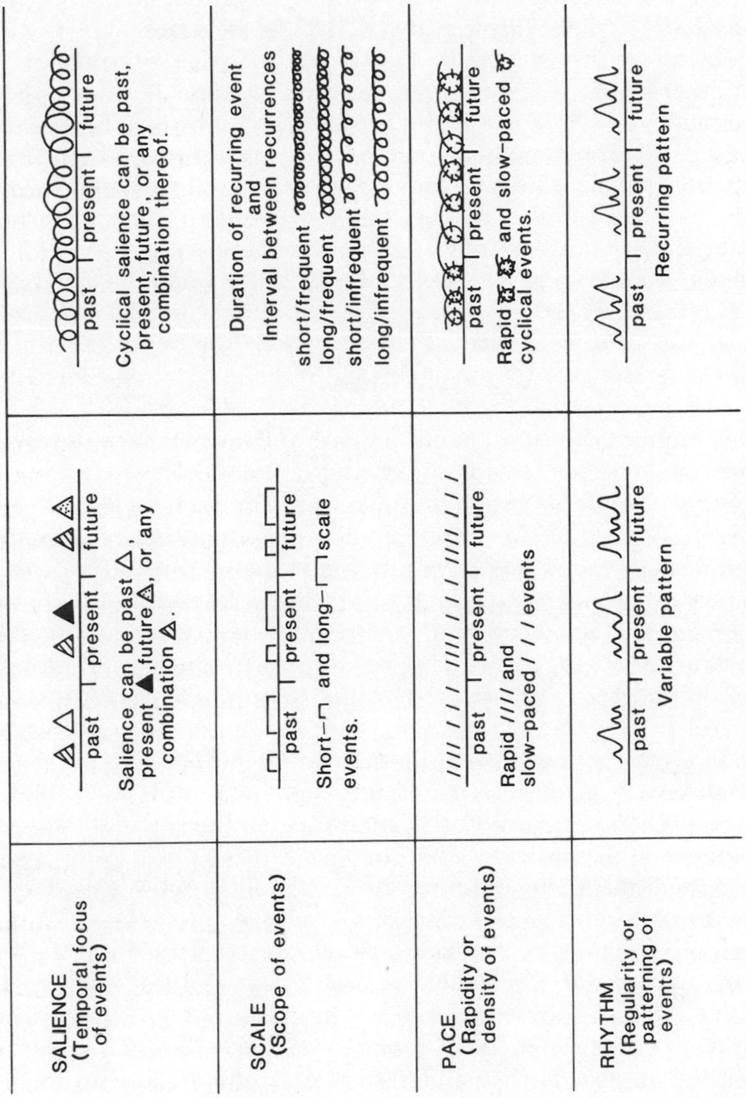

Figure 2. Temporal dimensions of homes.

Relph's (1976) concept of *inside* also suggests that continuity and the accumulation of memories are an essential quality of homes.

The home is a place of continuity across the past, present, and future in many societies at the level of the individual, family, or group. For example, Hardie (1981; Chapter 9, this volume) describes the living arrangements of the Tswana people of South Africa, who believe that the spirits of family ancestors reside in their courtyards and protect the family from evil. The family cannot move to a new homestead without making special arrangements to move the spirits as well. Thus, the past lives in the present (indeed, the Tswana think of these ancestors as being in the present rather than in the past), and the home is a repository for the history of the family.

Similar unions of persons, places, and linear temporal qualities occur in several societies. For example, in traditional Chinese families, it is customary for couples to visit a family shrine in the home as part of the wedding ceremony in order to obtain the ancestors' permission to marry (Fried & Fried, 1980). On the Greek island of Nisos (Kenna, 1976), daughters inherit the family home as part of their marriage dowry. The daughter who was named after the grandmother who lived in the house is the one who inherits the home, "so the same name will be heard in the house" (Kenna, 1976, p. 26). In this way, continuity is achieved through formal procedures by which the home is transferred from one generation to the next. The Tikopians of the Solomon Islands (Fried & Fried, 1980) maintained continuity in an even more concrete way. Before missionaries discouraged the practice, those who died were buried under the floorboards of the home, so that they could remain with their family and protect them. The dying would discuss the burial with the family and speak of being with them even after death.

Continuity is also evident among people who move from one residence to another, such as nomads, migrants, and retirees. Although the environment of nomadic peoples changes as frequently as they move, many of them maintain continuity by consistently using particular furniture arrangements, tent orientations, and positions relative to others in a group as well as by practicing rituals for reestablishing the home (Altman & Gauvain, 1981; Forde, 1950; Lowie, 1954; Tanner 1979; Nabokov, 1982). Efforts to maintain continuity have also been noted among people who voluntarily change residences. Work by Lawrence (1982a, 1983) indicates that preferences for present and future home styles, decoration patterns, and the like often show continuity with previous home styles. The elderly in the United States frequently crowd their retirement apartments with furniture and memorabilia in order to bring their memories with them (Csikszentmihalyi & Rochberg-Halton, 1981; Howell, 1980).

The effort to maintain continuity also occurs when people are forcibly relocated. For example, Gauvain, Altman, and Fahim (1983) analyzed the relocation of 50,000 Egyptian Nubians who moved when the Aswan Dam was built in 1963–1964. Gauvain *et al.* described how the people attempted to reestablish their linkages to homes by replicating decorating practices and modifying the design of homes. (See also Karpat, 1976, for a discussion of house design in squatter settlements).

Future-oriented qualities of rituals and ritual objects in homes are often quite explicit. Thus, among ancient Romans, particular house gods were honored because of their believed ability to protect and guarantee the family's future (Orr, 1980). Similarly, among the nomadic tribes of northwest Australia, each tribal subgroup is responsible for a territory or home range. An essential feature of the territories are rocks on which are painted figures depicting different species of plants and animals. Annual ceremonies are held to "freshen" or repaint the figures in order to assure the prosperity of the plants or animals, thereby assuring the tribe's future hunting and gathering success (Blundell, 1980).

In summary, the property of linear time deals with past, present, and future aspects of person–environment relationships. Although meanings and actions can be predominantly related to the past, present, or future taken singly, it is often the case that an act, ritual, or object associated with one temporal referent blends into another, that is, past-oriented actions or objects often bring the past into the present and sometimes ensure that the past and present will continue into the future. Although these examples have stressed continuity, change is also an essential aspect of person–home transactions, and the mechanisms by which individuals and cultures balance continuity and change are an equally important topic of study.

CYCLICAL TIME

The second overarching dimension of our framework involves cyclical properties of person–environment events in homes. Cyclical features of homes refer to repetitive and recurring activities and meanings, with cycles potentially recurring daily, weekly, monthly, annually, or in some other regular or semiregular fashion. Thus, Lynch (1972) referred to the rhythmic repetition of events, "a heartbeat, breathing, sleeping and waking, hunger, the cycles of sun and moon, the seasons, waves, tides, clocks" (p. 65). In a more poetic and phenomenological vein, Eliade (1959) used the concept of *sacred time* to describe religious or quasi-religious events that involved a reactualization, reliving, and repetition of earlier sacred events through the performance of a unique and new event.

For some societies the concept of cyclical time is literal; in others cyclical time incorporates a linear conception as well, such that what occurred before does not literally ever recur in identical form. Thus, in the Judeo-Christian value system there is a blending of cyclical and linear time, and for the great preponderance of Western society, the idea of *spiraling recurrence* is more accurate than the idea of *identical recurrence*. The idea of spiraling recurrence is depicted in Figure 2 through irregularly patterned spirals.

Examples of cyclical/spiraling events in homes are evident in a broad variety of writings. Bachelard (1964), Korosec-Serfaty (1985), and others (e.g., Pétonnet, 1973; Saile, Chapter 4, this volume) refer to daily practices that are part of the rhythms of homes, for example, affordances such as eating and work cycles, and appropriation routines that involve certain places in homes. All of these result in the home and its activities, places, and associated cognitions being unified in a recurring and cyclical pattern.

In addition to daily rhythms, many authors have described the home in relation to seasonal cycles and rhythms. For example, Tuan (1977) dealt with how people in different societies occupy and use different homes at different times of the year. Pétonnet (1973) described surveillance zones that seemed to fit into daily as well as seasonal cycles. The residents whom she observed would work in open windows or sit at certain focal points at regular times of day, but these surveillance activities were only apparent during warm weather. Seasonal cyclicity is also evident in the celebration of annual or seasonal holidays such as religious and cultural holidays (Thanksgiving, Christmas, Chanukah), and family rituals (birthdays or anniversaries) (Rakowski, 1979).

Another aspect of cyclical/spiraling time has been called *entrainment* (McGrath & Rotchford, 1983) or *synchronicity* (Lynch, 1972). Entrainment is the process of adapting asynchronous cycles (e.g., of different lengths) to one another, or accomodating recurring activities to a dominant cycle, such as when people migrate or vary their living patterns to adapt to seasonal availability of food (Hardie, Chapter 9, this volume; Lowie, 1954; Tuan, 1977), or in modern times, when daily homebound cycles are adapted to the work schedule. Michelson (1975, 1977) studied time budgeting and activity patterns in and around the home and found that residence location, commuting patterns, and commercial utilization are interrelated. He even suggested (1982) that houses be built close to work sites or have access to work sites and that shopping centers be provided enroute, thereby facilitating the entrainment of the home-based cycle to the work-based cycle.

Pétonnet (1973) also noted several instances in which daily routines seemed to be entrained to a larger cycle. In her observations of French public housing residents, the men's cycle was adapted to the work cycle, the children's to the school cycle, and the women's to both of these and to those of their neighbors and the larger society (e.g., the work hours of social service agencies). Furthermore, these patterns operated within a larger seasonal cycle, as women stayed indoors in cool weather and opened their homes or stayed outdoors more in warm weather. Thus, entrainment involved temporal cycles embedded hierarchically within one another, with personal cycles woven into the hierarchy.

These two overarching features of our framework—linear and cyclical/spiraling time—can be described in terms of four other dimensions: temporal salience, scale, pace, and rhythm (see Figure 2).

TEMPORAL SALIENCE

Salience refers to the temporal focus of a person–environment transaction. The term derives from the concept of *time orientation* that means that one's thoughts, actions, or feelings can be directed toward the past, present, or future (Hoornaert, 1973; Rakowski, 1979). An object is past salient if it reminds one or is associated with actions relevant to some past experience or transaction. It is future salient if it prompts future actions or refers to symbolic, cognitive, or affective aspects of some future event. And a place, object, or event in the home is present salient if its focus is primarily in the immediate present. Objects, places, activities, and events in the home can contain two or more foci simultaneously.

Salience is relevant to both linear and cyclical/spiraling time. Csikszentmihalyi and Rochberg-Halton (1981) elicited descriptions of objects in homes, and frequently found references to past, present, and future linear salience. Respondents described the history of an object, (e.g., how it had been acquired and used) as well as its future (e.g., plans to pass it on to their children). These authors did not inquire about nonsignificant objects; however, implicit in their discussions is the notion that temporal salience is related to the importance or meanings of things, that is, the richer and more important the history and present of an object and the more significant the future plans for it, the more central it is to the person.

The salience of an object or place in homes is not fixed; salience can rise or fall at different times, making the concept of temporal salience a dynamic one. An object might not be noticed for years, or one of its meanings or plans for action might lay dormant until circumstances combine to bring that object or meaning to the fore. Csikszentmihalyi and Rochberg-Halton's interviews imply that a person's psychological experience regarding a place or object depends upon which meanings are associated with it at any particular time.

Salience in cyclical/spiraling time also refers to the temporal focus of meanings and actions. Spiraling time refers to recurrences, and as a ritual or act is performed, the participants can be reminded of certain past, present, or future relationships, activities, beliefs, values, and events. Blundell (1980) described the annual freshening ceremony of Australian aborigines as bonding the people to their clans, to their ancestors, and to their descendants, that is, to social relationships in the present, the past, and the future. Hoebel (1960) described the annual reunion of the Cheyenne tribe into a single living unit as an event that bonded individuals to the past, present, and future.

Note that cyclical salience is also a dynamic concept, with activities and rituals often simultaneously conveying more than one temporal referent. For example, many groups harvest and store certain kinds of foods at certain times of the year, depending on seasonal availability (Bolton, 1979; Forde, 1950; Hyde, 1959; Korosec-Serfaty, 1984; Tanner, 1979). The activities can be both present and future salient, because they are current and because they are designed to assure the future well-being of the family or group. The activities can also be implicitly past and future salient when the participants are aware that the present activities fit into a total historical, cultural, and lifelong cyclical pattern of gathering and processing of food.

TEMPORAL SCALE

The concept of *scale* is typically used in architecture to refer to variations in the size or scope of an environment. In a similar way, temporal scale refers to the temporal scope of an event. Scale is an intrinsic part of events; their onset or duration cannot be imposed or defined independently of the events themselves. In linear time, as depicted in Figure 2, brief or small-scale events can be termed *incidents*, for example, an accident, a trip to the store, entertaining in one's home. Lengthy or large-scale events can be termed *stages*, and they include long and complex combinations of peoples, places, and relationships, for example, a friendship or old age. Work on environmental autobiographies (Cooper-Marcus, 1978; Horwitz, Klein, Paxson, & Rivlin, 1978; Rowles, 1980) indicates that scale is an inherent part of people's memories of their homes and other environments. Some places reminded people of specific incidents such as birthday parties and holidays; others brought to mind periods or stages in their lives, such as early marriage, or childhood.

The concept of scale is implicit in the idea of life stages, and the home is also often involved in rites of passage or transitions from one stage to another. The primary example of this, of course, is marriage, which represents a new household composition or the establishment of a new household (Bartels, 1969; Gregor, 1974; Hoebel, 1960; Kagitcibasi, 1982; Kenna, 1976; Murdock & Wilson, 1972; Ottenberg, 1970; Timur, 1981).

Other rites of passage are also celebrated in the home. For example, the Cree Indians celebrate a child's first steps with a "walking-out" ceremony that symbolizes the child's future role in maintaining the family home (Tanner, 1979). The Macha Galla of Ethiopia celebrate a child's early years with a ritualistic walk around the house in order to introduce and bind the child to the home where she or he will live (Bartels, 1969). In ancient Pompeii, an adolescent celebrated the transition into adulthood by dedicating an amulet to one of the household gods (Orr, 1980). And a number of societies and groups have rituals associated with death. Ancient Scandinavians would carry the corpse out through a particular door of the home (Doxtater, 1981); Navajo Indians of the American Southwest would burn a home if the resident died in it (see Gauvain, Altman, & Fahim, 1983). Such ceremonies helped purify the home after death and hastened the entry of the deceased into the afterlife. In addition, these actions and rituals serve to provide definitive temporal boundaries or demarcations to life stages. In these examples, the home is integral to and symbolizes an important transitional event in people's lives.

The concept of scale is also evident in cyclical or spiraling time. Cyclical events consist of both the length of the interval between recurrences and the durations of the events themselves (Figure 2). There can be short intervals between recurrences, such as in daily or weekly practices in homes, for example, affordance-related activities of hygiene, and eating; customs or social relationships such as regular prayer and religious activities; family meetings and discussions; or time-linked appropriation of different rooms and objects. There can be relatively long intervals between events as well, such as annual celebrations of birthdays and holidays. Similarly, the recurrent events can be brief (e.g., a family prayer at the dinner table), or lengthy (e.g., a several-day celebration of religious or cultural holidays).

As with linear scale, cyclical scale is, in our framework, defined in terms of intervening activities and events. That is, although the interval between recurrent events can be indexed as the "amount of chronological or clock time that passes," our perspective suggests that it is appropriate to index intervals in terms of the numbers and kinds of intervening events. Similarly, the duration of the recurring events should be measured as a coherent behavior sequence rather than according to an externally imposed time period that is unitized in terms of minutes, hours, days, or weeks.

There are any number of cyclical events that vary in their duration and interval length. For example, annual seasonal cycles are commonly associated with agricultural or preindustrial societies but can also have significance for other societies through annual holidays, family gatherings, and rituals (Rakowski, 1979). What determines the cycle length and activity duration is complex. In some cases, cycle length is influenced by the physical maturation of residents, by environmental constraints such as the day/night cycle, and seasonal or lunar changes. The Christian Christmas holiday season is an annual event held on the same calendar date; yet it can involve events spanning several days or even a month (Werner, Oxley, & Altman, 1983). The Christian Easter is also held annually, but the date varies because it follows a lunar calendar. Here, too, the duration of the celebration can vary; some people celebrate the entire Lenten period; others celebrate Easter week, Good Friday, or only Easter Sunday, and so forth. In other cases, home-related rituals occur periodically when "the time is right" and last until some phenomenological experience is achieved. For example, Hoebel (1960) mentioned three major Cheyenne Indian ceremonies, any one of which could mark the annual regathering of the tribe into a communal living unit. Zuni house-blessing rituals, described in detail later, are held annually, but the exact date varies from year to year and is not known until specified by the religious leaders.

TEMPORAL PACE

Pace refers to the relative rapidity or density of experiences, meanings, perceptions, and activities. Activities or experiences (whether ongoing, recollected, or anticipated) can have a rapid pace, with details and events moving quickly, or they can have a slow, gradual pace, with events unfolding in an unhurried fashion. The immediate events surrounding wedding ceremonies in many societies are often fast paced, whereas periods of extended mourning can be slower paced. Certain areas in the home can often come to be associated with activities of different paces. Consider, for example, the Western home, in which the kitchen is often a busy fast-paced area, whereas the bedroom is more relaxed and slow paced. Furthermore, the pace of an area can vary from time to time, such as when a kitchen is variably fast and slow paced, depending on the family's ongoing activities. When these paces vary on a recurrent basis, we speak of cyclical/spiraling pace, such as when the pace of activities in the kitchen increases and decreases as mealtimes approach and pass. Cyclical/spiraling pace will be illustrated in more detail later in the descriptions of Zuni Shalako house-blessing ceremonies and French residents' seasonal harvesting activities.

TEMPORAL RHYTHM

Rhythm refers to regularly occurring patterns and sequences of behaviors, feelings, and experiences within events. Patterns and sequences can involve variability in activities or the paces of activities, participants, or any other aspect of the events. For example, in a single day, activities can flow at fast and slow paces, different people can come and go, staying variable lengths of time, and so on. These variations would lend a particular pattern of activities and experiences to the day. When such patterns are repeated on a regular and predictable basis, we speak of a rhythm in the home. Patterns can be composed of many aspects, and this complexity is represented abstractly in Figure 2 as nonrecurrent and recurrent sequences and configurations of events and activities.[1]

According to phenomenologically oriented writers (Bachelard, 1964; Dovey, Chapter 2, this volume; Korosec-Serfaty, 1984; Pétonnet, 1973; Seamon, 1982), it is the sequential and recurrent repetition of actions and meanings and the regular involvement of people, places, and processes that create a sense of rhythm, and the sense of regular rhythm that in turn gives one a sense of home. A number of authors have stressed that the home is a rhythmic place and that the development of rhythmic patterns contributes to the transformation from a house to a

[1]The height, or amplitude, of these curves has been defined as "the degree of change within a cycle" (Lynch, 1972, p. 77) and could refer to changes in activity rates during the harvest season, changes in the amount of social contact during the Christmas season, and so forth. We might have drawn curves of slightly different heights to indicate that these recurrent events are not necessarily identical but can vary in amplitude from occurrence to occurrence. An additional kind of change that might be conveyed by amplitude is change in psychological experience, or the psychological intensity of an event. We have found little discussion of the relation between time and psychological significance but intend to explore this idea further.

home (e.g., Lawrence, Chapter 5, this volume; Saile, Chapter 4, this volume). Rowles (1980, 1981a,b) examined daily patterns and rhythms and learned that many elderly residents of a small town had regularly established routines that lent a varied activity pattern or rhythm to their days. Many would rise at a particular time, sit at a particular window of their home during a specified period to watch regular passersby, call their friends, raise the shades, and wave to neighbors. They spoke of these activities as recurring on a systematic and regular basis from day to day and as being favorite and special aspects of their daily routines.

The unities of the home illustrated in Figures 1 and 2 and in the text are quite extensive and not easily grasped through a single analysis. The model we have proposed is deceptively simple in that it contains a relatively small number of separate elements, that is, three kinds of dynamic person–environment linkages (affordances; social rules and social relationships; appropriation, attachment, and identity), and several temporal qualities through which the linkages operate or exist (linear and cyclical qualities coupled with salience, scale, pace, and rhythm). However, the framework is complex and implies an almost bewildering array of research topics, levels of analysis, and points of entry into the study of homes. That is, each of the properties is multifaceted (e.g., appropriation can take many forms; linear scale includes short- and long-duration events as well as life stages and life-stage demarcations, etc.), and events often involve many properties simultaneously. For clarity of exposition, we have treated the properties separately; however, the model is meant to apply to transactions at many levels of scale, involving all possible combinations of people, place and time. In particular, it is important to recognize that the temporal qualities do not occur independently of one another. Events contain salience, scale, pace, and rhythm, and although one could examine these qualities separately, events are only fully comprehended when the four are examined simultaneously.

One can use the framework detailed in this chapter to examine different aspects of transactional unities in homes, to focus theory and research on practical designs, to identify gaps in one's own thinking or in a body of literature, and generally to guide research and theory. In the next section, we will explore the model's usefulness by undertaking two case studies. That is, we will describe aspects of home use in two very different societies, using our concepts of person–environment linkages and the eight temporal qualities as a framework for our presentation. These intensive analyses also illustrate how the holistic model can be applied to single groups, thereby complementing our previous strategy of demonstrating that many societies share these transactional features.

ATTICS AND CELLARS IN RURAL FRANCE

Korosec-Serfaty's (1984) analysis of French residents' experiences and uses of their attics and cellars illustrates how our framework can be used to portray the transactional nature of homes. Based on intensive interviews with residents, she found that behaviors, activities, meanings, beliefs, and attitudes in and about their homes' cellars and attics are congruent with our earlier classification of person–environment transactional unities. For example, cellars and attics were described as having affordance features, in that people stored and did things in them that were functional and important in everyday life. Firewood and coal were stored in the cellars; cheeses and wines were prepared and kept in the cellars; fodder and hay for animals were pitched into and stored in the attics; children played in the attics; women did their laundry and ironing in the cellars, and so forth.

Korosec-Serfaty's interviews also revealed that there were transactions associated with social relationships. For example, the attic often involved play relationships between siblings and friends, and evoked memories in older people of childhood relationships and romances, family history, cultural and religious affiliations. Respondents also sometimes referred to gender-linked activities associated with these places, such as cheesemaking by women and wine preparation by men, thereby making salient the homes as a locus of social bonds, rules, and norms.

Finally, cellars and attics in rural France also seemed to reflect appropriation, attachment, and identity. The preparation and storage of food in attics and cellars often gave people a sense of control and order, lent a feeling of security, shelter, and privacy, and made the future more predictable. Even the tendency to store unusable or infrequently used things in attics and cellars was associated with a sense of belongingness—to the past, present, and to an indefinite future in which one might need an object. These and related activities and meanings yielded a sense of identity, attachment, and appropriation to the home and to these particular places in homes.

Korosec-Serfaty's analysis also revealed strong temporal qualities of attics and cellars. Linear aspects of time were vivid in the minds and actions of residents, and the salience of past, present, and future objects and events was frequently reported. For example, many residents noted how books, photographs, diaries, collections, items of clothing, and pieces of furniture tripped off recollections of the past: their childhood, parents and grandparents, and events and activities in their lives. Furthermore, some people remembered attics and cellars as places of hiding and safety in World War II, evoking memories of relationships and cultural events of that period. In these past-salient references, one also sees the temporal quality of scale. Thus, an object or place sometimes referred to a small-scale incident, such as a pair of shoes that tripped off memories of a wedding day. More often, people reported larger scale events or stages in their lives; for example, baby clothing and photographs often keyed off recollections of childhood in general, not specific incidents. The temporal concepts of pace and rhythmic patterns did not appear in past-salient aspects of cellars and attics, either because they were less vivid in past-temporal references or because they were not elicited in Korosec-Serfaty's analysis.

Respondents also described present and future linear referents. For example, cellars often were salient in present activities, as people reported going there one or more times a day to get foodstuffs, do laundry, or to obtain privacy. Furthermore, as might be expected, most present-salient examples involved small-scale events, that is, specific activities and limited periods of action. In present-salient cases, the pace and pattern of activities were usually explicit, in contrast to past-salient reports. Thus, the performance of household chores reflected a more defined pace and systematic pattern of events than did general recollections of the past.

Attics and cellars also had future-salient qualities. People reported that certain items, such as photographs, diaries, clocks, and heirlooms, were being kept as inheritances, to be passed on to their children and grandchildren. In some cases, items were to be used in a specific future event, such as a wedding, thereby reflecting a small temporal scale. In most cases, however, the scale of the future temporal period was larger; for example, a clock was to be used by one's heirs throughout their lives.

An object or activity sometimes involved several temporal referents simultaneously. For example, family heirlooms occasionally evoked past and future orientations, as an object reminded people of their parents or grandparents, and at the same time was described as something to be passed on to subsequent generations.

Attics and cellars also had cyclical/spiraling temporal qualities, although these usually related to affordance activities, not to meanings and feelings, and to present- and future-oriented events, not to past events. For example, cheesemaking, food preparation, and winemaking were described as occurring during certain seasons, weeks, or times of day, with such work being salient to both the present and future. Thus, people went to the cellar for food supplies on a recurring and regular basis to meet present needs, and they prepared wine and cheese or pitched hay and fodder into the attic for future needs.

These and other cyclical activities also varied in temporal scale. Some recurred annually or seasonally, with a long interval between the cyclical events, for example, storing hay, whereas other events recurred almost daily, such as doing laundry and ironing. A second facet of temporal scale in our framework is the duration of a cycle. Thus storage of hay and fodder requires more time to complete than does doing laundry or ironing, yielding differences in the length of a recurring cycle. So, the data reflect how one must take into consideration both the length of spiraling events and the interval between events.

Korosec-Serfaty's respondents did not appear to emphasize pace or rhythm of events associated with attics and cellars—as hurried or unhurried, following a certain cadence and sequence, and so forth. However, one can readily imagine that laundering, cheesemaking, or wine preparation have aspects of hurriedness or slowness as well as systematic rhythms and sequential patterns of activity. Indeed, many such activities can probably be treated as behavior settings (Barker, 1968) in which specified programs, patterns, and sequences of behaviors are enacted by participants. For example, the storing of hay involves cutting, drying, bailing, or gathering, and hauling and placement in the attic. These activities occur in a certain sequence, pace, and rhythm, with various actors playing out managerial, support, and laboring roles in different phases of the process.

In summary, Korosec-Serfaty's data illustrate how linear and cyclical features of time are an intrinsic aspect of affordance-, social relationship-, and appropriation-related phenomena that occur in attics and cellars, as are the temporal dimensions of salience, scale, pace, and rhythm. On the other hand, not all combinations of psychological/environmental/temporal qualities appeared in the data. For example, we found no instances of cyclical past-, present-, or future-salient aspects of social relationships or appropriations and attachments, whereas there were many references to linear features of social relationships. In contrast, there were many examples of cyclical activities associated with affordances, for example, cheesemaking, wine preparation, and food storage. Future research may be necessary to ascertain whether these gaps are a function of data collection or actual qualities of attics and cellars.

HOUSE-BLESSING CEREMONIES: PUEBLO OF ZUNI

The Pueblo Indians live in tightly knit and compact communities in the southwestern United States. In portions of some Pueblo communities, homes are terraced in stepwise fashion, sometimes being four and five stories high. Although terraced homes are still found in Pueblo communities, it is common nowadays to build freestanding, separate dwellings. In spite of changes over the years in their physical design, homes have a central place in Pueblo culture and appear to exhibit a transactional unity of the type described throughout this chapter. Because of our own experience and because of the availability of extensive literature on the subject, we will focus on the homes of the Zuni people, one of several Pueblo Indian cultures (Bunzel, 1932; Cushing, 1974; Parsons, 1939; Saile, 1977; Stevenson, 1904).

The religion and cosmology of the Zuni people are so rich, complex, and pervasive in everyday life that we cannot even begin to describe their many facets. Although we do an injustice to cultural and religious beliefs and practices in effecting any separation of one feature from the others, we will focus on the home as a single but essential feature of Zuni culture.

The home is a sacred place in Zuni. It is a "living" thing, is blessed and consecrated, is a location for communication with the spirit world and with God, is a place for religious observances, and is a setting within which occupants reside, live, eat, and raise children. The central place of the home in Zuni culture is made salient through an elaborate annual ceremony in which as many as eight new homes are blessed and consecrated. This ceremony, the Shalako, is part of a larger winter solstice observance (Shalako is actually the culmination of year-long events) and is highlighted by a 24-hour period of religious activities associated with the blessing of the new homes. The ceremonies involve special dances, prayers, and activities throughout the community and in the homes being blessed. Central to the 24-hour ceremonies are the Shalako figures. These elaborately decorated 10-feet-tall masked figures are manned by carefully selected members of the community who train for a year to assume their religious roles.

The various ceremonies and prayers during the Shalako ceremony involve social relationships, affordances, and appropriation and identity. For example, social relationships are manifested in the custom of feeding all who come to the Shalako houses, including strangers and those outside the community, thereby symbolizing friendship and bonds with all people. And part of the ceremony involves symbolic feeding of the spirits of ancestors who are believed to come up the Zuni River for the ceremony in order to reestablish social bonds with their families. The coming together of relatives, friends, community members, and strangers in the Shalako House further symbolizes the social relationships and bonding of people with one another.

Zuni values emphasize communality over individuality, and the processes of attachment, identity, and appropriation reflect this communal tone. Although we have treated them separately, appropriation and attachment qualities of homes merge with social relationships in the Shalako example. Rituals, prayers, and activities simultaneously bond people to the home itself, the clan (familial subdivisions within the tribe), community, ancestors, and spirits and gods. For example, residents and the house are attached to the clan by virtue of the fact that the home is built cooperatively with clan members. In addition, it is richly decorated for the Shalako ceremony with rugs, jewelry, shawls, and other materials given by the clan members. The community is entertained and fed in the house, symbolizing that the home, its residents, and the clan are linked to the larger society. In addition, identical events occur simultaneously in several new homes during Shalako, yielding a broad bond to the community and the religious value system. Finally, the Shalako ceremony occurs throughout the village as well as in particular homes, thereby further bonding the community together.

Affordances, or utilitarian aspects of the home, are displayed throughout the Shalako house-blessing ceremonies, particularly in relation to food production and preparation. For example, the symbol of corn is prevalent, and dancers and ceremonial figures are sprinkled with cornmeal or corn pollen, prayers are made with corn kernels, and seeds are planted in the floor of the home. Food appears in other rituals associated with health and well-being, and in prayers for rain and other aspects of agricultural productivity.

The Shalako ceremony and the larger temporal events within which it is embedded unify psychological and social processes and homes in a transactional whole. Although the main Shalako ceremony occurs in a 24-hour period, it is embedded in a longer time frame that extends several days after and several weeks before the 24-hour ceremonies. Moreover, even these events are part of a year-long series of activities that are initiated almost immediately following the completion of the Shalako activities. Thus, events surrounding Shalako occur from one winter solstice to another, although the scale, pace, and rhythm of events change throughout the year. The year-long events are very complex and involve cycles of activities within larger cycles, rituals and practices that vary in duration of cycles and intervals between cycles and differences in the pace and rhythm of temporal events.

The annual cycle begins with the naming of the households that will be blessed at the next Shalako observance and the appointment of the "impersonators" or Shalako dancers who will be central to the ceremonies a year hence and who will impersonate or represent the rain god. Soon after their appointment, the impersonators begin a lengthy period of learning prayers, chants, rituals, and dances under the tutelage of the elders and religious leaders of their clans. Throughout the year they participate in daily, monthly, and other recurrent and cyclical religious activities associated with their special roles—daily offerings of prayer to the rising sun, evening prayers at the river, monthly prayer activities at holy places in the surrounding countryside, and the like.

By virtue of their religious, historical, and cultural training and extensive contact with their mentors and community the impersonators and those around them are embedded simultaneously in a blend of past-, present-, and future-salient cyclical events. The religion and culture of the Zuni people are brought to the fore in the process of learning history, religious prayers, and rituals, dancing, and so forth. Thus the past is learned for its own sake but is also brought into the present on a regular basis, and in a way that extends into the future, that is, the impending Shalako ceremonies and the long-term future of the homes and occupants that will be blessed.

The impersonators also work throughout the year for the household who will entertain them at the time of the Shalako ceremonies—bringing in wood, working in the fields, building the house to be blessed, and the like. These affordance and social activities lend present- and future-salient temporal orientations to their activities. Over a long time scale, therefore, a variety of smaller scale cycles of activity come to be associated with the Shalako ceremony.

Several weeks before the Shalako ceremony two of the impersonators begin a complex period of counting down toward the main ceremony. Their activities involve daily rituals and prayers, for instance counting off the days remaining before Shalako by means of a string with knots symbolizing the days. Here again, a number of small-scale, recurring cycles are woven into the longer year-long cycle. These cycles and the durations between them are short, yielding a quickening pace and quickly recurring cyclical events. Eight days before Shalako, sacred clown figures appear in the evening, visit throughout the community, announce the coming of Shalako, and begin a retreat. Four days before the ceremony another group of sacred figures appears. They signal the impending events and engage in various ritual activities. In the intervening days, more and more activities, rituals, and religious events occur, thereby quickening the pace, telescoping the temporal scale, and creating an atmosphere of excitement.

The 24-hour Shalako ceremony begins in the late afternoon, when the Shalako figures appear in the distance on the south bank of the Zuni River. For the next few hours various figures, including the impersonators, leave the Shalako masks at the riverfront and go to all parts of the village to announce the impending arrival of the figures, plant prayer sticks under the threshold of the homes to be blessed, and sprinkle cornmeal, seeds, and other materials at the threshold and around the home.

In the next phase of the ceremony, when it becomes dark, the Shalako figures are led by their clan members, who chant and sing along the way, to the homes to which they have been assigned. When they reach a home, the clan members surround the Shalako figure and sing and pray at the threshold, following which the figure enters the home. Clan members, villagers, and visitors are assembled in the home to watch the next phases of the ceremony. There is then a period during which a group of male singers chants and prays, which is followed by a lengthy ceremony in which the impersonators, who have temporarily emerged from the Shalako masks, chant from memory the history of the Zuni people from their origin to the present time. In this historical recounting, the past is salient but is linked to the present as the history of the people is updated, made a continuous and unending stream, and taught anew to the assemblage of infants, children, adults, and elderly members of the community. The oral recitation also includes future-oriented prayers for the health of the residents of the home, for many children who will live to old age, for rain and good crops, and so forth. Simultaneously, there are repeated references to spirits and gods of the past, ancestors, and important historical events.

The linking of past and present occurs in a variety of forms throughout the Shalako ceremonies. For example, following the oral history recitation, women bring large tubs of food into the house (much of the food is supplied by members of the community). The Shalako impersonators take a sample from each tub and carry the food to the Zuni River, where they feed the spirits of the ancestors who have come up the river from a distant place to participate in the Shalako ceremony. Thus, past and present are salient and fuse in this part of the celebration.

The Shalako ceremony is interrupted near midnight by a meal to which all are invited. Members of the community, Indians from other tribes, and non-Indians, many of whom are strangers, are entertained with politeness and grace, in spite of the labor and expense required. The activity is present salient and involves social relationships with a variety of people. The mealtime event also alters the pace and rhythm of the ceremonies by demarcating sharply the earlier events from the forthcoming dramatic dance of the Shalako figures.

After midnight, the people reassemble in the house to be blessed, and the Shalako dance begins. Following a period of chanting by the men's group and additional prayers and rituals, the 10-foot Shalako figures dance for several hours until morning. The dance is stylized and repetitive and follows a certain pattern and pace. Sometimes a second impersonator joins the dance. Periodically, the Shalako dancer returns to a corner of the room and is surrounded by assistants who hold up blankets to hide the fact that the impersonators are changing places in the figure. This recurring cycle of dancing and switching of dancers occurs over several hours until dawn. Attention by observers appears to be unswerving and patient. The repetitive dance process, like the preceding and remaining chants, creates a sense of fusion of past, present, and future in a way that defies total description. One is completely caught up in the event, and one suspects that participation on several occasions produces a phenomenological blending of past, present, and future, or a form of timelessness that has been often used to describe Zuni and other Pueblo cultures (e.g., Tuan, 1977).

On the following day, the Shalako figures participate in a new cycle of events—the race of the Shalakos. The figures reassemble at the river, thereby completing the cycle from the time of their first appearance in the village. They then participate in a complicated series of events, part of which involves racing to the river one by one in order to demonstrate their "strength" and burying prayer sticks in designated holes in the ground. This part of the ceremony, although the culmination of the 24-hour period, is not the end of the year-long celebration. For several days thereafter, the sacred clowns and other figures continue the celebration, dancing and playing in the plaza and throughout the community, and engaging in ritual activities in the designated house.

The Shalako ceremony and its year-long events are primarily cyclical rather than linear because they recur year after year. They also reflect past, present, and future salience, singly and in combination, and involve affordances, attachments and identities, and social relationships. Moreover, the Shalako activities display variations in pace and rhythm, with slower paced events occurring throughout the year, with a buildup to the rapidly paced 24-hour period of prayer, dancing, and ritual activity. Furthermore, the Shalako observance reflects a myriad of differences in temporal scale. Embedded within the large-scale, year-long events are a series of small-scale subevents, for example, the assembly at the river, the march to the houses to be blessed, the chanting of the men's groups, the recitation of the history of the Zuni people, the meal, the Shalako dancing, the race at the river, and the celebrations that follow in subsequent days. As the year progresses, the scale of events, that is, the intervals between activities and the durations of the activities themselves, become telescoped and accelerated in pace as they lead up to the 24-hour period. Following the 24-hour ceremonies the scale lengthens for several days and the pace slows, signifying the ending of one cycle of events and the beginning of another.

It is through this array of events that new homes, which serve as symbols of all homes in the community, become rooted in a transactional unity with the people, culture, and natural environment.

IMPLICATIONS FOR FUTURE RESEARCH

This chapter illustrated how homes can be viewed as transactional unities wherein phenomena are treated as dynamic confluences of people, processes, environments, and temporal qualities. In particular, we have focused on temporal qualities of homes in terms of a number of selected dimensions: linear and cyclical time and temporal salience, scale, pace, and rhythm.

This temporal framework, applied to homes in a variety of societies and contexts, has implications for future research and theory. First and foremost, our analysis suggests that a home can profitably be treated as a holistic transactional unity. Instead of researching and theorizing about the separate physical, psychological, and interpersonal qualities of homes, a transactional approach calls for an examination of homes as integrated unities of physical, psychological, and temporal features. Concepts of social relationships, appropriation and attachment, to name a few, need to be studied simultaneously in relation to their physical and temporal aspects. The home, therefore, is defined by, incorporates, and gains meaning through the psychological and interpersonal events that occur in it. Similarly, psychological and social processes require incorporation of physical and temporal qualities into their very definition. These processes occur in physical settings, and understanding them requires inclusion of the nature of the settings into the definition and conceptualization of the processes. Neither the physical settings of the homes nor the psychological and social processes with which they are associated can be disentangled from one another.

The focus of this chapter has been on temporal qualities; therefore, the basic prescription is that temporal features of transactional unities be incorporated into research and theory. That is, the focus should be on dynamic processes, rather than on the static aspects of homes. This view suggests that the researcher or practitioner should study the processes involved in making a home, the uses and activities of the home, the relationships that grow and change there, the relations among the person–environment linkages and psychological experiences, and so forth.

Furthermore, the focus should be on the specific temporal qualities that we have detailed. How time relates to meaning and the development of person–environment bonds is an empirical question, and many hypotheses could be tested: Are both a past and a future essential to feeling at home? How much time and what kinds of activities and meanings must transpire in the process of establishing a home? Relative to others, are people who engage in a greater variety of transactions differently bonded to their environments? Does the psychological experience of the transaction moderate the nature of the person–environment bonds, for example, does the pleasure or displeasure with which one appropriates through decorating, or does one's satisfaction with the results of decorating affect the meaning of a home? Are rhythms an essential quality of viable home living? Do significant and nonsignificant objects and events differ in their temporal depth (that is, the extent of their temporal associations)? Observations, questionnaires, and interviews can be used to explore linear and cyclical aspects of the present, memories of the past, and expectations for the future in terms of the subordinate dimensions of salience, scale, rhythm, and pace. Furthermore, as shown in the case examples of attics and cellars and the Zuni Shalako ceremony, these temporal properties should be viewed in combinations rather than as separate independent qualities.

Temporal qualities of homes have typically not been the focus of systematic research but have emerged as incidental aspects. For example, although several authors speak of the rhythms of the home and anecdotes from a few residents attest to the importance of rhythms in home life, there has been little systematic research on this aspect of temporality or how it relates to meaning. Similarly, although scale was evident in many descriptions of objects and homes, few authors proposed how scale links with meaning.

In sum, although we found many examples of time-linked practices and activities in homes, few of the accounts invited systematic attention to the range and scope of temporal dimensions or to the linkage of these to uses and attitudes in homes. Some authors did stress the importance of time and person–environment bonds (e.g., Csikszentmihalyi & Rochberg-Halton, 1981; Furby, 1978; Korosec-Serfaty, 1985; Lawrence, 1982a, 1983), but many others simply described temporally based practices, leaving their significance to the reader's inferences. Research is needed to examine these complex interrelationships among the aspects of the transactional model.

Temporal issues also need to be examined in terms of individual and cultural differences. For example, whereas Furby (1978) and Howell (1980) felt that people needed to represent their memories in their possessions, others (Csikszentmihalyi & Rochberg-Halton, 1981; Rakowski, 1979; Tognoli, 1980) argued that there are large individual differences in the extent to which this is true. And on the surface there also appear to be wide variations in societies in respect to home-linked qualities. These variations need to be examined in a systematic and comparative way, in terms of their similarities and differences and universal and idiosyncratic qualities.

A final area of research and theory concerns further development and elaboration of our conceptual framework. The model is based on evidence selected in a nonsystematic way from different societies and different scales of persons and environments. Furthermore, neither we nor the authors who described practices and rituals in homes can be sure that the interpretation made of them represents accurately their use and meaning to the residents; thus support for the framework is tentative, and the model may not have broad generality. Although it would have been useful, we were unable to find sufficient and accurately interpretable information about any single society to fit the entire framework. Only additional research, specifically designed to test the model, will permit an evaluation of its full utility. Our analyses of French attics and cellars and the Zuni Shalako ceremony involved application of the model to many facets of single groups, but even this was on a limited basis and may have contained biased interpretations.

Moreover, the framework is incomplete. We examined only three general categories of person–environment linkages (social relationships, attachment and appropriation, affordances), and we are aware that these could be expanded and distinguished and that other kinds of linkages might be identified. In addition, there are many other temporal qualities of homes that may be explored in future research and theory. Although our examination of the literature on homes suggests that the temporal dimensions of our framework (linear and cyclical/spiraling time, salience, scale, pace, and rhythm) were the most evident and pervasive, they represent only a few temporal qualities that may be relevant to home environments.

Lynch (1972), McGrath and Rotchford (1983), and others (Gibson 1975; Rakowski, 1979) have identified other temporal features of person–environment transactions that may also warrant attention. For example, although Lynch used concepts similar to aspects of the present model, he also introduced the properties of amplitude (the degree of change within cycles) and regularity (the degree to which behavioral patterns remain stable and unchanging). In contrast, Rakowski (1979) and Hoornaert (1973) stressed people's psychological experiences of time. Rakowski focused on future-time perspective, examining differences in psychological outlook by groups as as function of their future-time perspective. Hoornaert was also interested in time perspective, examining in detail its various aspects (e.g., extension, density) and distinguishing it from other psychological experiences of time (estimation, orientation, calculation). So, there are undoubtedly a variety of temporal features of person–environment transactions that may require attention beyond the few employed in the present framework.

In summary, we have proposed a transactional framework of homes that includes several temporal person–environment linkages. Our analysis suggests that a transactional approach can be applied to the understanding of homes in many societies. Most importantly, we proposed that future research could profitably use this framework to examine in a systematic way the home as a transactional relationship of people, processes, places, and time.

Acknowledgments

We are indebted to the following colleagues for their comments on earlier versions of the chapter: Barbara B. Brown, Kimberly Dovey, Perla Korosec-Serfaty, Roderick Lawrence, Joseph McGrath, Seymour Parker, Barbara Rogoff, Charles P. Shimp, and Dan Stokols. We are also indebted to Floyd O'Neil, American West Center, University of Utah, for arranging and accompanying I. A. on a visit to Zuni for the 1983 Shalako. We are especially thankful to the people of Zuni who permitted I. A. to observe Shalako, and we are most appreciative of the hospitality shown by Alex Boone and his family, relatives, and friends. Their warmth and graciousness will be long remembered.

REFERENCES

Altman, I. *The environment and social behavior: Privacy, personal space, territory, and crowding.* Monterey, Calif.: Brooks/Cole, 1975. (Reprinted by Irvington Publishing Co., New York, 1981.)

Altman, I. Privacy regulation: Culturally universal or culturally specific? *Journal of Social Issues,* 1977, *33,* 66–84.

Altman, I., & Gauvain, M. A cross-cultural and dialectic analysis of homes. In L. Liben, A. Patterson, & N. Newcombe (Eds.), *Spatial representation and behavior across the life span.* New York: Academic Press, 1981, pp. 283–319.

Altman, I., & Rogoff, B. World views in psychology: Trait, interactionist, organismic, and transactionalist approaches. In D. Stokols & I. Altman (Eds.), *Handbook of environmental psychology.* New York: Wiley, 1986.

Argyle, M. Personality and social behaviour. In R. Harre (Ed.), *Personality.* Oxford, England: Blackwells, 1976, pp. 145–188.

Argyle, M. Sequencing in social behavior as a function of the situation. In G. P. Ginsburg

(Ed.), *Emerging strategies in social psychological research*. New York: Wiley, 1979, pp. 11–37.

Bachelard, G. *The poetics of space*. New York: Orion Press, 1964.

Barker, R. G. *Ecological psychology: Concepts and methods for studying the environment of human behavior*. Stanford, Calif.: Stanford University Press, 1968.

Bartels, L. Birth customs and birth songs of the Macha Galla. *Ethnology*, 1969, *8*, 406–422.

Blundell, V. Hunter-gatherer territoriality: Ideology and behavior in northwest Australia. *Ethnohistory*, 1980, *27*(2), 103–117.

Bolton, R. Guinea pigs, protein, and ritual. *Ethnology*, 1979, *18*, 229–252.

Bunzel, R. L. Zuni katcinas. *Bureau of American Ethnology, 47th Annual Report*. Washington, D.C.: United States Government Printing Office, 1932, pp. 837–959.

Cooper-Marcus, C. Remembrance of landscapes past. *Landscape*, 1978, *22*(3), 34–43.

Csikszentmihalyi, M., & Rochberg-Halton, E. *The meaning of things: Domestic symbols and the self*. Cambridge, England: Cambridge University Press, 1981.

Cushing, F. H. *Zuni breadstuff*. New York: Museum of the American Indian, Heye Foundation, 1974.

Dewey, J., & Bentley, A. F. *Knowing and the known*. Boston, Mass.: Beacon, 1949.

Doxtater, D. C. *Thursday at a crossroads: The symbolism, structure, and politics of "center" in the old Scandinavian farm culture*. Unpublished doctoral dissertation, University of Michigan, 1981.

Duben, A. The significance of family and kinship in urban Turkey. In C. Kagitcibasi (Ed.), *Sex roles, family, and community in Turkey*. Bloomington: Indiana University Turkish Studies, 1982, pp. 73–99.

Eliade, M. *The sacred and the profane: The nature of religion*. Chicago: Harcourt, Bruce, and World, 1959.

Forde, C. D. *Habitat, economy and society: A geographical introduction to ethnology* (8th ed.). New York: E. P. Dutton, 1950. (First published in 1934.)

Fried, M. N., & Fried, M. H. *Transitions: Four rituals in eight cultures*. New York: Norton, 1980.

Furby, L. Possessions: Toward a theory of their meaning and function throughout the life cycle. In P. B. Baltes (Ed.), *Life-span development and behavior* (Vol. 1). New York: Academic Press, 1978, pp. 297–336.

Gauvain, M., Altman, I., & Fahim, H. Homes and social change: A cross-cultural analysis. In N. R. Feimer & S. Geller (Eds.), *Environmental psychology: Directions and perspectives*. New York: Praeger, 1983, pp. 180–218.

Gerson, K., Stueve, C. A., & Fischer, C. S. Attachment to place. In C. Fischer *et al.* (Eds.), *Networks and places: Social relations in the urban setting*. New York: Free Press, 1977, pp. 139–157.

Gibson, J. J. Events are perceivable, but time is not. In J. R. Fraser & N. Lawrence (Eds.), *The study of time II*. Proceedings of the Second Conference of the International Society for the Study of Time. New York: Springer-Verlag, 1975, pp. 295–301.

Gibson, J. J. *An ecological approach to visual perception*. Boston: Houghton Mifflin, 1979.

Greenbaum, P. E., & Greenbaum, S. D. Territorial personalization: Group identity and social interaction in a Slavic-American neighborhood. *Environment and Behavior*, 1981, *13*, 574–589.

Gregor, T. A. Publicity, privacy, and Mehinacu marriage. *Ethnology*, 1974, *13*, 333–350.

Hajnal, J. European marriage patterns in perspective. In D. V. Glass & D. E. C. Eversley (Eds.), *Population in history: Essays in historical demography*. Chicago: Aldine, 1965, pp. 101–143.

Hardie, G. J. *Tswana design of house and settlement: Continuity and change in expressive space.* Unpublished doctoral dissertation, Boston University, 1981.

Haumont, N. Home appropriation practices. In P. Korosec-Serfaty (Ed.), *Appropriation of space.* Proceedings of the Third International Architectural Psychology Conference at Louis Pasteur University, Strasbourg, France, 1976, pp. 226–279.

Hoebel, E. A. *The Cheyennes: Indians of the Great Plains.* New York: Holt, Rinehart & Winston, 1960.

Hoornaert, J. Time perspective: Theoretical and methodological considerations. *Psychologica Belgica,* 1973, *13,* 265–294.

Horwitz, J., & Tognoli, J. Role of home in adult development: Women and men living alone describe their residential histories. *Family Relations,* 1982, *31,* 335–341.

Horwitz, J., Klein, S., Paxson, L., & Rivlin, L. (Eds.). Environmental autobiography. *Childhood City Newsletter* (No. 14), December 1978.

Howell, S. Environments as hypotheses in human aging research. In L. W. Poon (Ed.), *Aging in the 1980's: Psychological issues.* Washington, D.C.: American Psychological Association, 1980, pp. 424–432.

Hyde, G. E. *Indians of the High Plains: From the prehistoric period to the coming of the Europeans.* Norman: University of Oklahoma Press, 1959.

Ittelson, W. H. Environment perception and contemporary conceptual theory. In W. H. Ittelson (Ed.), *Environment and cognition.* New York: Seminar Press, 1973, pp. 1–19.

Kagitcibasi, C. Introduction. In C. Kagitcibasi (Ed.), *Sex roles, family, and community in Turkey.* Bloomington: Indiana University Turkish Studies, 1982, pp. 1–32.

Karpat, K. H. *The Gecekondu: Rural migration and urbanization.* Cambridge, England: Cambridge University Press, 1976.

Kenna, M. E. Houses, fields, and graves: Property and ritual obligation on a Greek island. *Ethnology,* 1976, *15,* 21–34.

Kitahara, M. Living quarter arrangements in polygamy and circumcision and segregation of males at puberty. *Ethnology,* 1974, *13,* 401–413.

Korosec-Serfaty, P. (Ed.). *Appropriation of space.* Proceedings of the Third International Architectural Psychology Conference at Louis Pasteur University, Strasbourg, France, 1976.

Korosec-Serfaty, P. The home, from attic to cellar. *Journal of Environmental Psychology,* 1984, *4,* 303–321.

Laumann, E. O., & House, J. S. Living room styles and social attributes: The patterning of material artifacts in a modern urban community. In E. O. Laumann, P. M. Siegel, & R. W. Hodges (Eds.), *The logic of social hierarchies.* Chicago: Markham, 1972, pp. 189–203.

Lawrence, R. J. The organization of domestic space. *Ekistics,* 1979, March/April, *275,* 135–139.

Lawrence, R. J. A psychological-spatial approach for architectural design and research. *Journal of Environmental Psychology,* 1982, *2,* 37–51. (a)

Lawrence, R. J. Domestic space and society: A cross-cultural study. *Society for Comparative Study of Society and History,* 1982, 104–130. (b)

Lawrence, R. J. Ontological and methodological principles for psycho-social analyses of home interiors. Paper presented at the international symposium Psychological Approaches to Home Interiors, Italian National Science Foundation, Rome, 1983.

Lowie, R. H. *Indians of the plains.* New York: McGraw-Hill, 1954.

Lynch, K. *What time is this place?* Cambridge, Mass.: M.I.T. Press, 1972.

Matras, J. *Populations and societies.* Englewood Cliffs, N.J.: Prentice-Hall, 1973.

McGrath, J. E., & Rotchford, N. L. Time and behavior in organizations. In B. Staw & L.

Cummings (Eds.), *Research in organizational behavior* (Vol. 5). Greenwich, Conn.: JAI Press, 1983, pp. 57–101.

Michelson, W. The time-budget. In W. Michelson (Ed.), *Behavioral research methods in environmental design*. Stroudsburg, Penn.: Dowden, Hutchinson, & Ross, 1975, pp. 180–234.

Michelson, W. *Environmental choice, human behavior, and residential satisfaction*. New York: Oxford University Press, 1977.

Michelson, W. H. *Everyday contingencies on behavior for mothers: In and out of the labor force*. Paper presented at the Second Annual Irvine Symposium on Environmental Psychology, University of California at Irvine, April 1982.

Morris, E. W., & Winter, M. A theory of family housing adjustment. *Journal of Marriage and the Family*, 1975, *37*, 79–88.

Murdock, G. P., & Wilson, S. F. Settlement patterns and community organization: Cross-cultural codes 3. *Ethnology*, 1972, *11*, 154–295.

Nabokov, P. *American Indian architecture*. Lecture given at the University of Utah in November 1982.

Orr, D. G. Roman domestic religion: The archaeology of Roman popular art. In R. B. Browne (Ed.), *Rituals and ceremonies in popular culture*. Bowling Green, Ohio: Bowling Green University Popular Press, 1980, pp. 88–103.

Ottenberg, S. Personal shrines at Afikpo. *Ethnology*, 1970, *9*, 26–51.

Parsons, E. C. *Pueblo Indian religion* (Vol. 2). Chicago, Ill.: University of Chicago Press, 1939.

Pepper, S. C. *World hypotheses: A study in evidence*. Berkeley, Calif.: University of California Press, 1942.

Pétonnet, C. *Those people: The subculture of a housing project*. Westport, Conn.: Greenwood Press, 1973.

Pratt, G. The house as an expression of social worlds. In J. S. Duncan (Ed.), *Housing and identity: Cross-cultural perspectives*. London: Croom Helm, 1981, pp. 135–180.

Proshansky, H. M. Environmental psychology: A methodological orientation. In H. M. Proshansky, W. H. Ittelson, & L. G. Rivlin (Eds.), *Environmental psychology: People and their physical settings*. New York: Holt, Rinehart & Winston, 1976, pp. 59–69.

Rakowski, W. Future time perspective in later adulthood: Review and research directions. *Experimental Aging Research*, 1979, *5*, 43–88.

Rapoport, A. *Human aspects of urban form*. Oxford, England: Pergammon Press, 1977.

Rapoport, A. *The meaning of the built environment*. Beverly Hills, Calif.: Sage, 1982.

Relph, E. *Place and placelessness*. London: Pion, 1976.

Rowles, G. D. Growing old "inside": Aging and attachment to place in an Appalachian community. In D. Datan & N. Lohmann (Eds.), *Transitions of aging*. New York: Academic Press, 1980, pp. 153–70.

Rowles, G. D. Geographical perspectives on human development. *Human Development*, 1981, *24*, 67–76. (a)

Rowles, G. D. The surveillance zone as meaningful space for the aged. *The Gerontologist*, 1981, *21*, 304–311. (b)

Saile, D. G. Building rituals and spatial concepts in the Pueblo Indian world: Making a house. *Architectural Association Quarterly*, 1977, *9*(2), 72–81.

Seamon, D. The phenomenological contribution to environmental psychology. *Journal of Environmental Psychology*, 1982, *2*, 119–140.

Stevenson, M. C. The Zuni Indians: Their mythology, esoteric societies, and ceremonies. *Bureau of American Ethnology, 23rd Annual Report, 1901–1902*. Washington, D.C.: Smithsonian Institution, 1904, pp. 1–608.

Stokols, D., & Shumaker, S. A. People in places: A transactional view of settings. In J. H.
    Harvey (Ed.), *Cognition, social behavior and the environment*. Hillsdale, N.J.: Erlbaum,
    1981, pp. 441–488.
Tanner, A. *Bringing home animals. Religious ideology and mode of production of the Mistassini
    Cree hunters*. New York: St. Martin's Press, 1979.
Timur, S. Determinants of family structure in Turkey. In N. Abadan-Unat (Ed.), *Women in
    Turkish society*. Leiden, The Netherlands: J. Brill, 1981, pp. 59–73.
Tognoli, J. Male friendship and intimacy across the life span. *Family Relations*, 1980, *29*,
    273–279.
Tuan, Y. *Space and place: The perspective of experience*. Minneapolis: University of Minnesota
    Press, 1977.
Werner, C. M., Oxley, D., & Altman, I. *Christmas Street*. Paper presented at the Environ-
    mental Design and Research Association Convention, Lincoln, Neb., April 1983.
    (Available from the authors at the Department of Psychology, University of Utah, Salt
    Lake City, Utah 84112).
Whyte, M. K. Revolutionary social change and patrilocal residence in China. *Ethnology*,
    1979, *18*, 211–228.
Wicker, A. W. *An introduction to ecological psychology*. Monterey, Calif.: Brooks/Cole, 1979.
Wicker, A. W. An expanded conceptual framework for analyzing behavior settings. In D.
    Stokols & I. Altman (Eds.), *Handbook of environmental psychology*. New York: Wiley
    (1986).

2

Home and Homelessness

KIMBERLY DOVEY

INTRODUCTION

*The phenomenon of home . . . used to be an overwhelming and
inexchangeable something to which we were subordinate and
from which our way of life was oriented and directed. . . . Home
nowadays is a distorted and perverted phenomenon. It is
identical to a house; it can be anywhere. It is subordinate to us,
easily measureable in numbers of money value. It can be
exchanged like a pair of shoes.*

—Vycinas, 1961, pp. 84–85

The concept of *home* has been receiving increasing attention in the modern world. There are those, such as Vycinas, who lament the passing of a time when deep connections with the home place were unavoidable. Others work to replicate, invent, package, and sell the images of home for an increasingly nostalgic public who perhaps shares this sense of loss. And there are those of us who seek to explore and understand the meanings of this intangible and difficult concept.

I want to begin this essay by distinguishing between the concepts of *house* and *home*. The use of a phrase such as *home ownership* treats house and home as synonymous terms. Although the meaning in this case is clear, in other usages it becomes more ambiguous. For instance the statement *I don't have a home* may mean either that the speaker lacks

KIMBERLY DOVEY • Department of Architecture, Royal Melbourne Institute of Technology, Melbourne, Victoria, Australia 3001.

access to a dwelling place or that the dwelling place does not carry the meaning and experience of *home*. The focus in this essay is on these experiential aspects of *home* that distinguish it from *house*. Although a house is an object, a part of the environment, home is best conceived of as a kind of relationship between people and their environment. It is an emotionally based and meaningful relationship between dwellers and their dwelling places. Concomitant with this distinction is the assumption that the concept of the "housing problem" is not identical to that of "homelessness." Indeed, the housing problem can be, and often is, solved in a manner that creates homelessness. For the purposes of this essay the term *home* is intended to refer to this relationship or experiential phenomenon rather than the house, place, or building that may or may not represent its current manifestation in built form.

The first part of the essay constitutes an outline of what I see as our current understanding of the phenomenon of *home*. There are three themes or approaches to this understanding that have been used to organize this section. The first consists of various kinds of "order" through which we are oriented in the world. The second is the processes of "identification" through which we connect with our world in a meaningful way. The third theme is that of "dialectic processes" that describe an essential dynamism in the process of becoming at home.

In the second part of the essay I turn over the coin to examine some aspects of *homelessness*—processes and conditions that can erode the experience of home and paralyze its emergence in the modern world. I conclude with some brief comments on how these understandings may be applied in the design professions. These applications have both limits and opportunities. They are limited because the current problems of homelessness are deeply rooted in cultural, technological, social, and economic conditions of modern society. The opportunity lies in the chance for a radical shift in the ways that we conceptualize environmental change and the designer's role within it—a shift that may flow from an enhanced understanding of the experience of home and the processes of both its erosion and emergence.

The theoretical approach in this essay is phenomenological. Such an approach is suggested by the intangible nature of the concept in question. Although we might study the *house* as a discrete variable, *home* is not an empirical variable whose meaning we might define in advance of careful measurement and explanation. As a consequence, understanding in this area is plagued with a lack of verifiability that many will find frustrating. My aim, however, is not to produce specific cause–effect relationships or explanations; it is rather to deepen our understanding of an intrinsically intangible phenomenon. My sources are several. First, I draw heavily on the literature of phenomenological philosophy and geography. Second, the cross-cultural studies of anthropological fieldwork offer an insight into the forms and experiences of home in the traditional world. Third, the world of literature reveals important and clear explications of the experience of home and the processes of its emergence.

PROPERTIES OF HOME

I have argued that *home* is distinguished from *house* in that the former is a relationship, an experienced meaning. My aim in this first part is to explicate some properties of this relationship and aspects of its meaning. I do not mean to imply that these properties are necessary nor sufficient for the experience of home; rather they offer us hints at a structure underlying this intangible concept.

HOME AS ORDER

The first of these properties is *order*, by which is meant simply "patterning" in environmental experience and behavior. Being at home is a mode of being whereby we are oriented within a spatial, temporal, and sociocultural order that we understand.

Spatial Order

One of the most important contributions of the phenomenological approach to environmental experience has been a thorough reinterpretation of the concept of *space* that parallels the distinction between *house* and *home*. At the heart of this reinterpretation is an important distinction between *conceptual space* and *lived space* (Bollnow, 1967). Conceptual space is abstract, geometric, and objectively measured, a kind of context or ether within which places, people, and things exist. Lived space, by contrast, is the preconceptual and meaningful spatial experience of what phenomenologists call "being-in-the-world" (Heidegger, 1962). Whereas conceptual space is an abstract homogeneous continuum, lived space is a concrete and meaning-centered bodily experience. The most sophisticated argument for the priority of lived space is that of Merleau-Ponty (1962, p. 243) who argues that

> Space is not the setting (real or logical) in which things are arranged, but the means whereby the positing of things becomes possible. . . . [It is] a certain

possession of the world by my body, a gearing of my body to the world . . . a
pact . . . which gives me the enjoyment of space and gives to things their
direct power over my body.

The concept of home is deeply rooted in this "gearing" of our bodies to
the world. There are three kinds of structures that are important here.
First is the triaxial structure of the human body and the fundamental
distinctions between up/down, front/rear, and left/right (Dovey, 1979;
Needham, 1973; Straus, 1966). Gravity is an ever present part of this
structure of being-in-the-world that sets the vertical dimension apart,
both practically and symbolically from the horizontal. Second, there is
the structure of our actions in space—grasping, sitting, walking, manipulating, looking, hearing, smelling (Norburg-Schulz, 1971; Piaget, 1955).
Third, there is the structure of the world, which, although it may differ
enormously in its geography, retains a structure whereby we live out
our lives on a roughly horizontal surface between earth and sky (Heidegger, 1971). Home finds its roots if not its forms in these universal
structures of environmental experience and action. Although universal,
these structures are not so much determinant as they are limiting structures. The links with architectural form will hopefully become clearer as
I proceed, but they are by no means determinant nor simple.

Thus the human body stands vertically on a horizontal plane with
certain spatial abilities and limits. This is Norburg-Schulz's (1971) model
of existential space, a vertical axis piercing a horizontal plane. The underlying structure of home as spatial order lies in its role as a center of
our spatial world with a sense of verticality and horizontal access. This
center that we inhabit is also infused with other kinds of order that
separate it off from the surrounding world. Home is a sacred place
(Eliade, 1959), a secure place (Rainwater, 1966), a place of certainty and
of stability. It is a principle by which we order our existence in space
(Dovey, 1978). Home is demarcated territory with both physical and
symbolic boundaries that ensure that dwellers can control access and
behavior within. Although this center is clearly distinguished from its
surroundings, it is also strongly oriented within it. This orientation is to
the compass points, the celestial bodies, the surrounding geography,
and the access routes. To be at home is to know where you are; it means
to inhabit a secure center and to be oriented in space. A certain ambiguity in the phenomenon of home becomes apparent at this point because
home as territory also involves a kind of home range that can include
neighborhood, town, and landscape. Yet this larger home is also a kind
of ordered center within which we are oriented and distinguished from
the larger and stranger surroundings.

Temporal Order

Home as order is not only spatial orientation but also temporal orientation. Home is a kind of origin, we go "back" home even when our arrival is in the future. The home environment is one thoroughly imbued with the familiarity of past experience. It is the environment we inhabit day after day until it becomes taken for granted and is unselfconscious. This sense of familiarity is rooted in bodily routines, a place where, according to Seamon (1979, p. 80), space becomes a "field of pre-reflective actions grounded in the body." When we wander through the dark in our home, we do not need to see where the furniture and light switches are; we can "feel" them. The home environment is predictable. Although when we are away from home we need to be alert and adaptable, at home we can relax within the stability of routine behavior and experience.

Home as temporal order and familiarity includes not only direct experience of places over time but also familiarity with certain spatial patterns from other places in past experience. Home thus has strong roots in the experiences of childhood where the visual images of home were formed. It has been suggested that there are connections between such experiences and the environmental attitudes and preferences later expressed in adult life (Cooper Marcus, 1978). Home as temporal order is not dependent on aesthetic attraction; it may be more accurate to say that the homes of our past set the ground for our very perceptions of attractiveness and ugliness.

In yet another way, home as temporal order can extend to a familiarity with the past processes through which the forms of the environment have come into being. The experience of wood for instance connects with our experiences of climbing trees, sawing, chopping, nailing, and carving. We are familiar with its strength that we see reflected in its size and with its growth patterns reflected in the grain. The materials and forms will of course differ much from place to place, but a knowledge of how the places in which we dwell came into being provides a sense of home even when we were not engaged in the construction (Feuerstein, 1965).

The dichotomy of *insideness* versus *outsideness* is increasingly used to categorize relationships between people and places (Appleyard, 1979a; Relph, 1976). In this sense, home is an experience of complete insideness that can only develop over time. The order that constitutes the experience of home often looks like chaos to an outsider. Indeed, many people are more at home among their own "disorder" than within someone else's "order." Herein lies an important dilemma in the attempt to understand the concept of home. Because the insider's temporal order stems largely from the personal routines and cycles repeated through extended periods of time, it may remain invisible to the outsider who sees only the resultant spatial form. Furthermore, this temporal order may be so imbued with familiarity that it becomes taken for granted and is unselfconscious for the insider. Thus both insider and outsider are faced with difficulties in achieving a depth of understanding.

Sociocultural Order

This discussion of home as spatiotemporal order has thus far largely omitted any mention of environmental form. This is because the forms in which this order becomes manifest are primarily sociocultural. Given the basic limits of the structure of the body and the world in space and time, there remain infinite variations in the forms of dwellings. Cultural beliefs and social practices represent the ordering system that selects from among these possibilities and shapes the broad range of formal manifestations of home within any sociocultural context (Benedict, 1946). Thus, the particular patterns and rituals of environmental experience and behavior are largely sociocultural phenomena. The phenomenon of homes comes to be embodied in this ordered structure that is at once spatial, temporal, and sociocultural.

Consider the activity of eating for instance, which, although common to all people, differs markedly in its spatial and temporal manifestations according to cultural patterns. Spatially, Westerners eat while seated in chairs, Indians sit on the floor, and ancient Romans ate lying down. And there are differences with regard to where one eats, with whom, and who sits where. Temporally, certain cyclic routines and rituals are followed (Lawrence, 1982, p. 27) with regard to when meals are consumed, who eats first, and when feasts are held. Certain spatiotemporal categories, such as the *Sunday dinner* or the *breakfast room*, emerge within each culture. As patterns of experience and behavior stabilize over time, so do the spatial arrangements and environmental props that support and evoke those experiences. Patterns of dining, talking, sleeping, studying, and watching television form the bulk of the assumptions that go without saying in housing design. These are patterns that orient us in space, in time, and in the sociocultural context.

The notion of home as social order is at once extremely flexible and yet conservative. It is flexible inasmuch as it is embodied not in a house or building but in the patterning of experience and behavior. It is a way of relating to the environment that may be transposed from place to place, and in this way the meanings of home may be reevoked if the patterns are recreated. For instance the !Kung bushmen of the Kalahari Desert create a new home every night with just a fire to mark the center and a small windbreak or symbolic entry. These are enough to evoke a complex schema of spatial meanings that orients everyone in relation to the fire (Marshall, 1973). This flexibility also extends to the ability to adapt one's "home" to changing social circumstances. The adolescent who rejects the family home, for instance, may not be rejecting "at homeness" so much as reordering a spatial schema to center on a new "home"—a subcultural group and its preferred places. Although the particular spatial patterns may be sociocultural, the sense of connectedness may be more personal. It is a very old tradition that lovers can transcend a dependence on place; their love can elevate any place they happen to be into a home. People who are thoroughly immersed in an activity that they love can convey a sense of home to that place. Thus *home* may be the relationship between an intellectual and a set of ideas, a pianist and a piano, a cook and a kitchen, a gardener and a garden, a sportsperson and a playing field. This is not to say that the setting for such activities is not important—indeed, it is often crucial—however, the place is elevated into a home by virtue of allowing such homelike activities to take place.

The conservative aspect of home as sociocultural order lies in the all pervasiveness and taken-for-grantedness of this order. Everyday discourse and social practices rarely question the spatial context within which they are located and concretized. Bourdieu (1977, Chapter 2) argues that the house is the principal locus for the embodying of the basic categories of the world—the taxonomies of people, things, and practices. For Bourdieu the basic schemes of perception, thought, and action are embodied in the home, which is privileged through being the location of the earliest learning processes. The house is thus a kind of "book" that is read by the body through its interactions. "As an acquired system of generative schemes," he argues, "the habitus engenders all the thoughts, all the perceptions, and all the actions consistent with those conditions and no others" (p. 95). Through being deeply rooted in the past, home also carries with it considerable inertia to change. Social hierarchy, injustice, and outmoded sex roles are difficult to question when they are embodied in, and evoked by, the taken-for-granted world of spatial patterning.

HOME AS IDENTITY

Home then is a highly complex system of ordered relations with place, an order that orients us in space, in time, and in society. Yet the phenomenon of home is more than the experience of being oriented within a familiar order; it also means to be identified with the place in which we dwell. Although home as order has a strong cognitive element, home as identity is primarily affective and emotional, reflecting the adage *home is where the heart is*. Identity implies a certain bonding or mergence of person and place such that the place takes its identity from the dweller and the dweller takes his or her identity from the place. There is an integrity, a connectedness between the dweller and dwelling. Home as order and as identity are strongly interrelated; yet whereas order is concerned with "where" we are at home, identity broaches the questions of "who" we are, as expressed in the home, and "how" we are at home.

Spatial Identity

There are now many interpretations of built form as the representation of identity in space. Complexities in the field have expanded as important differences are shown to occur across cultures (Rapoport, 1981), classes (Gans, 1974), subcultural groups (Pratt, 1981), and stages of the life cycle (Csikszentmihalyi & Rochberg-Halton, 1981). Debate in the field suggests a primary opposition between social and individual interpretations of identity. The social perspective tends to interpret the home as a "statement" of identity expressed through a shared symbolic language (Appleyard, 1979b; Goffman, 1971). In this situation the home may indeed represent a socially desired identity rather than any depth of character. Rakoff (1977) has argued that although the meaning of the house is privately experienced and may be deeply felt, it is collectively determined in Western society by an individualistic ideology. Individual interpretations often argue for a deeper connection between the home and the human spirit. Jung has argued that self-expression in built form is one way in which the self archetype becomes manifest. He has described the construction of his own house as a "concretization of the individuation process" (Jung, 1967, p. 252), an approach that has been developed by Cooper (1974) and others.

The debate of individualistic versus social interpretations of house identity is both rife and productive (Duncan, 1981). My view is that the personal and the social are inextricably interwoven; that representation of identity in the home stems from both social structure and our quest for personal identification within it. The home is both a "statement" and a "mirror," developing both socially and individually, reflecting both collective ideology and authentic personal experience.

If the meaning of home as identity is both collective and personal, it is also in a sense universal. One of the strongest themes here is the house/body metaphor (Bachelard, 1969). The house is commonly experienced as a symbolic body with concomitant distinctions between up/down and front/rear. And just as the body boundary defines the distinction between self and other, so the metaphoric body defines the boundary between home and away-from-home. When this metaphoric body is burglarized or raided, there is often a strong and lingering feeling among the inhabitants of having been personally contaminated.[1] The traditional world abounds with examples of houses that embody representations of the body. The Dogon (Griale & Dieterlen, 1964) and the Tamberma (Blier, 1981) of West Africa inhabit houses where there are direct correlations between parts of the body and parts of the house. Houses of both the Dogon and the Kabyles of North Africa (Bourdieu, 1962) have forms that are symbolic representations of sexual union. For the Tukano of the Amazon the hearth is a symbolic uterus (Reichel-Dolmatoff, 1971). If the home embodies a connection with our microcosmic home, the body, then it also can embody a representation of the macrocosm. For the Atoni of Indonesia (Cunningham, 1973), a triadic view of a sky covering an earth composed of sea and dry land is symbolized in the house by an attic (sky) that covers an inner room (dry land) and a veranda (sea). The house plan is symbolically conceived like a mandala, with cardinal points at the periphery and the hearth at the center. The hearth fire is considered to be the fire of the earth, in symbolic opposition to the sun, the fire of the sky. Sun and hearth are represented in two ridge poles of the house that are tied together with rope, a symbolic connection of microcosm and macrocosm (Cunningham, 1973, p. 222). There is evidence that this kind of symbolism, whereby the meanings of body, house, and world are gathered in the form of the house, is widespread in the indigenous world (Critchlow, 1975; Gardiner, 1975; Rykwert, 1972; Saile, 1977).

Home as identity is not just a matter of the representation of a self-image of a world view; it also entails an important component that is supplied by the site itself. We not only give a sense of identity to the place we call home, but we also draw our identity from that of the place. Since the beginnings of agriculture, humans have endowed places with an earth spirit (Eliade, 1963). This is the chthonian realm of the Greeks and what the Romans called the *genius loci* or "spirit of place." Heideg-

[1]Empirical evidence on this issue is scarce but anecdotal evidence abounds. See "Emotional impact of burglary as serious as robbery, study finds," *Law Enforcement Assistance Association Newsletter*, 1978, 7(4), 5–6; and D. Hickie, Fortress suburbia. *The National Times* (Australia), 1984(682), 12–16.

ger (1966) speaks of what he calls *autochthony* or *rootedness* in place as a basic condition for the development of authentic human existence. The Greek term *autochthonic* meant "sprung from the land itself." The sense of identity embodied in the phenomenon of home has an important component of autochthony. Another way to describe this is as "indigenous," the etymology of which means "to be born within." Home in this sense is something that grows in a place rather than being imposed from without. It grows both from the particular personal and social circumstances of the dwellers but also from the environmental context of the place itself, its *genius loci*. Thus home has a key element of uniqueness, it is place based.

Temporal Identity

Home is a place where our identity is continually evoked through connections with the past. Although temporal order is primarily concerned with familiarity, temporal identity is a means of establishing who we are by where we have come from. The role of the physical environment in this regard is that of a kind of mnemonic anchor. Consider the following description of the experience of the Lepchas of the Himalayas:

> Every piece of land is meaningful for them, for every piece, unless it be the home of a supernatural, is, has been, or will be cultivated. Every piece of land, every step they take reminds them of the past and the present, of their own work and struggles and those of their neighbors; the houses and fences they have helped to build, the land they have helped to clear and weed and harvest, the places where they have played as children or, later, met for amorous encounter. . . . They see the record of their lives and of the lives of their ancestors, and of the lives to come of their children. (Gorer, 1967, p. 81)

Our experience in the world carries its own meanings, and the places in which these experiences occur become inbued with those meanings. The physical environment plays a very important but little-recognized role whereby it enables us to concretize the memory through association. "The emotion felt among human beings," Tuan says (1974, p. 241), "finds expression and anchorage in things and places. It can be said to create things and places to the extent that, in its glow, they acquire extra meaning." Tuan uses the phrase *fields of care* to refer to the connections with place that grow over long periods of time through everyday dwelling and care. The Kaluli of New Guinea see the present landscape as a kind of living history embodying the spirit of past lives and events:

> Each person knows the streams and landmarks of his longhouse territory, and these recall the people he worked with and shared with there. This growth of young trees, that patch of weeds with a burned house post, this

huge Ilaha tree that dominates the crest of a ridge, reflect the contexts and
personalities of his life. (Schieffelin, 1976, p. 182)

During the important Gisaro ceremony, songs are improvised that trace
a path through the landscape, using place-names to evoke grief and
sorrow. The audience has intimate memories thrown at them in the
form of the place-names wherein the memories are anchored. The aim is
to evoke sorrow for lost relatives and ancestors and also for a lost past.
In such a way the sense of connectedness with the past is periodically
renewed. The role of the environment as a mnemonic anchor enables us
to participate in an interaction between present and past, between experience and memory. The memories reflected in the home environment
help to create our current experience of home, and those experiences
serve in turn to preserve, evoke, and even revise the memory.

Home as temporal identity is not limited to connections with the
past but extends into a connectedness with the future. I noted earlier
that home is a center of security, of possessed territory, a place of freedom where our own order can become manifest, secure from the im-
positions of others. This aspect of home as a place of autonomy is also
fundamentally linked to home as identity; it gives a connection into the
future. Home suggests a certain dynamic adaptability. It allows for both
the *representation* and the *growth* of identity. Growth of identity is more
than the search for a form that reflects a static self-image; it is dynamic
and may indeed actively resist equilibrium (Allport, 1955). The growth
of identity requires a certain freedom of interaction between present and
future, between our experiences and dreams. Knowing that we have the
power to remain in a place and change it permits us to act upon and
build our dreams.

HOME AS CONNECTEDNESS

The themes of home as order and identity that I have presented
thus far are summarized in Figure 1. Home is a schema of relationships
that brings order, integrity, and meaning to experience in place—a series of connections between person and world:

- *Connectedness with people*: both through the patterns of sociocultural order and through the role of the home place in the symboliza-
  tion and representation of identity
- *Connectedness with the place*: first, through being oriented in it; and
  second, through the ways in which we put down roots and draw
  an indigenous sense of identity from each unique place
- *Connectedness with the past*: through having memory anchored in

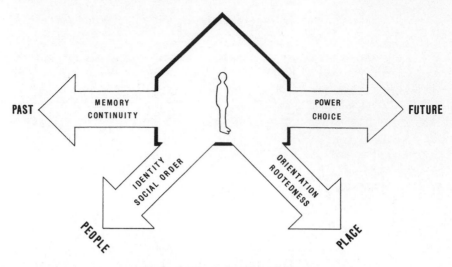

Figure 1. Home as connectedness.

the forms of the home place and from the experience of familiarity
and continuity that this engenders
- *Connectedness with the future*: when power and autonomy permit
  dreams and hopes to inform environmental change

Home then is an integrative schema that is at once a bonding of
person and place and a set of connections between the experience of
dwelling and the wider spatial, temporal, and sociocultural context
within which it emerges. Home orients us and connects us with the
past, the future, the physical environment, and our social world.

DIALECTICS OF HOME

The picture of the phenomenon of home presented here has one
critical weakness—it is too static. It does not convey an understanding
of the dynamic processes through which the order, identity, and connectedness of home come into being. These processes are fundamentally dialectical. My use of the term *dialectic* here is similar to that adopted by Altman and Gauvain (1981) with three defining characteristics: a
tension between binary opposites, an essential unity in that the poles
are mutually defining, and a dynamism that lends their interaction a
certain progression. Unlike the house, the meaning of home is not self-
contained but emerges from its dialectical interaction along a series of
binary oppositions that are summarized in Figure 2. Once again, these

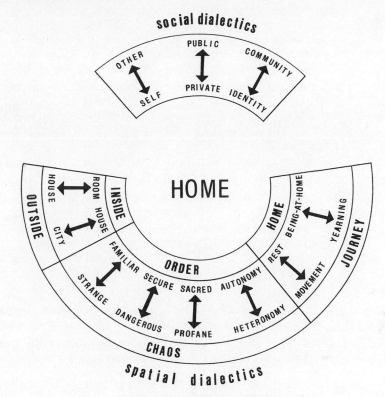

Figure 2. The dialectics of home.

dialectical oppositions may be divided into those that are primarily spatial and those that are primarily sociocultural.

Spatial Dialectics

The spatial dialectics are derived primarily from the opposition of home and journey. We participate in this dialectic through movement in time. Home is a place of rest from which we move outward and return, a place of nurture where our energies and spirits are regenerated before the next journey (Seamon, 1979). Buttimer (1980, p. 169) uses the phrase *lived reciprocity* to describe this dialectic: "like breathing in and out, most life forms need a home and horizons of reach outward." The experience of each pole of the dialectic implies and engenders the other. The journey is opposed to the dwelling as the road is opposed to the hearth; the one grows out of the other (Jager, 1975).

Several of the properties of home outlined earlier also participate in this spatial dialectic. It is a dialectic between inside and outside. It is through an understanding of this dialectic that we can understand the ambiguities in our use of the word *home* when we use it to refer to a room, a house, a town, a city, and a nation. Home can be a room inside a house, a house within a neighborhood, a neighborhood within a city, and a city within a nation. At each level the meaning of home gains in intensity and depth from the dialectical interaction between the two poles of experience—the place and its context at a larger scale.

Yet the dialectics of home involve more than inside versus outside. Home is a place of security within an insecure world, a place of certainty within doubt, a familiar place in a strange world, a sacred place in a profane world (Dovey, 1978). It is a place of autonomy and power in an increasingly heteronomous world where others make the rules. These oppositions can be subsumed under the rubric of order/chaos. Home certainly has the properties of order as argued earlier; yet it is only through the dialectical interaction that its meaning develops. Home as mere order and identity can well become a prison, a hermetically sealed world devoid of chance. To experience the meaning of home is to experience this dialectic. In the words of the poet Auden (1966), home is "not a windowless grave, but a place I may go both in and out of." A world of total order is a world of comfort, yet without the friction that keeps our experiences alive. Order too has no meaning without chaos.

The dialectic processes of home and journey can help us to understand the meanings that are attached to the ambiguous areas at the interface, such as the threshold, porch, front garden, and window seat. To be at the interface is empathically to participate in the dialectic, to be at home yet with a sense of reach, to have a refuge and a prospect (Appleton, 1975). The sense of home is heightened when we are warm in bed yet can hear the rain on the roof and the wind whistling under the eaves. The contrast between inside and outside accentuates the meaning of being inside; the sense of cold outside makes warmth meaningful. The unfamiliar and insecure world may threaten, but it is at the interface between it and the ordered center that we find all new experience, and hence the excitement and aventure of life. To live fully one must both journey out and return. Yet, like all true dialectics, that of home and journey is not merely cyclical but rather is dynamic or spiral. In the traditional Hegelian sense, if home is the thesis and journey its antithesis, then the synthesis is a deepened experience of the phenomenon of home. Finally, it is important to recognize that the dialectic between home and journey is also a dialectic between two kinds of experiences of home, between that of being-at-home and that of yearning-for-home.

Yearning-for-home is "about" being-at-home; it occupies a different level of logical type (Olsson, 1981). Whereas being-at-home is unself-conscious and taken for granted, the experience of yearning is idealized and self-conscious. The two experiences should not be confused.

Social Dialectics

The importance of the representation of social identity to the concept of home was outlined earlier. This property, too, is dialectical because it participates in the negotiation and representation of identity through the oppositions of self/other, identity/community, and private/public. We participate in these dialectics as we engage with the spatial dialectic of home and journey: we journey from the private individual world out into the public communal realm. Altman and Gauvain (1981) argue that our engagement in these dialectics are cross-culturally reflected in dwelling forms, especially in the realm of the threshold and house front, the interface between home and journey. Altman's (1975) model of privacy, as a dialectical boundary control mechanism, is pertinent here. The phenomenon of privacy, like that of home, is not so much a place as a dialectical process of being in contact and being out of contact with others. And there are links to the property of autonomy in the phenomenon of home. "Privacy mechanisms," Altman argues, "define the limits and boundaries of the self. When the permeability of those boundaries is under the control of a person, a sense of individuality develops" (p. 50). From another direction, the symbolic interactionist perspective argues that identity emerges through a process of taking the role of a "generalized other" and changing ourselves in response to how we imagine we are seen (Mead, 1934). Inasmuch as the home is a social symbol of our identity, we participate in this self/other dialectic of imagining how we are perceived through the symbolism of our home.

Dialectics of Appropriation

Perhaps the most important dialectic related to the concept of home is that of *appropriation*. This is a very difficult yet fundamentally important notion because it goes to the heart of the concept of home as a mode of being-in-the-world. I use the term *appropriation* in the general sense of its etymological root, the Latin *appropriare*, "to make one's own." For Heidegger (1962), appropriation is a dialectic process through which we take aspects of our world into our being and are in turn taken by our world. It involves both a "caring" for a place and a "taking" of that place into our own being (Relph, 1981). The caring aspect is not just utilitarian but involves a sparing and preserving of the world in its own right (Heidegger, 1971). The second part of the dialectic is the taking and incorporation of the world into our sense of identity. It is through our engagement with the world, our dwelling, embodying both caring and taking, that the world discloses itself. As we open ourselves to the world of things and places we bring them meaning, and at the same time these things and places lend meaning to our sense of identity. Appropriation is rooted therefore in action, in the dialectical practices of everyday life through which we appropriate aspects of the world as anchors for self-identity. The dialectic of appropriation embodies the emergence of environmental meaning through interaction. It is the dialectic between personal change and environmental change, the process through which we change our environment and we are in turn changed by environmental experience.

An understanding of the concept of home involves an understanding of dialectical processes and changing transactions over time. The trap is to regard the problem in static terms or consider one side of the dialectic and disregard the other. The house is static, but home is fundamentally dynamic and process oriented. There is no sense of home unless there is also a journeying. Without community there is no identity; without a public realm there is no privacy. And in a sense, without homelessness, we would not be concerned with what home means.

BECOMING-AT-HOME

In order to draw together and exemplify some of the themes presented previously, I want to consider two passages from literature that show how the process of becoming at home may be manifest in our culture. The first of these is a passage from Steinbeck's *Cannery Row* where a group of "homeless" men in Monterey, California, appropriate an old warehouse.

> The Palace Flophouse was no sudden development. Indeed when Mack and Hazel and Eddie and Hughie and Jones moved into it, they looked upon it as little more than shelter from the wind and the rain, as a place to go when everything else had closed or when their welcome was thin and sere with overuse. Then the Palace was only a long bare room, lit dimly by two small windows, walled with unpainted wood smelling strongly of fishmeal. They had not loved it then. But Mack knew that some kind of organization was necessary particularly among such a group of ravening individualists. . .with a piece of chalk [he] drew five oblongs on the floor, each seven feet long and four feet wide, and in each square he wrote a name. These were the simulated beds. Each man had property rights inviolable in his space. He could

legally fight a man who encroached on his square. The rest of the room was property common to all. That was in the first days when Mack and the boys sat on the floor, played cards hunkered down, and slept on the hard boards. (Steinbeck, 1954, p. 23)

This is the beginning, there is nothing more than rough shelter, design excellence is far from their consideration. The building is an envelope keeping out the rain; they have a house but not a home. They bring with them certain spatial patterns—sleeping on the floor, sitting while playing cards. They create territorial rules with certain agreed-upon signs to demarcate territory, a place for each individual with a certain freedom of control over it. The passage proceeds:

Perhaps, save for an accident of weather, they might always have lived that way. However, an unprecedented rainfall which went on for over a month changed all that. House ridden, the boys grew tired of squatting on the floor. Their eyes became outraged by the bare board walls. Because it sheltered them the house grew dear to them. And it had the charm of never knowing the entrance of an outraged landlord. For Lee Chong never came near it. Then one afternoon Hughie came in with an army cot which had a torn canvas. He spent two hours sewing up the rip with fishing line. And that night the others lying on the floor in their squares watched Hughie ooze gracefully into his cot—they heard him sigh with abysmal comfort and he was asleep and snoring before anyone else. The next day Mack puffed up the hill carrying a rusty set of springs he had found on a scrap iron dump. The apathy was broken then. The boys outdid one another in beautifying the Palace Flophouse until after a few months it was, if anything, overfurnished. There were old carpets on the floor, chairs with and without seats. Mack had a wicker chaise longue painted bright red. There were tables, a grandfather clock without dial, face or works. The walls were whitewashed which made it almost light and airy. Pictures began to appear—mostly calendars showing improbable luscious blondes holding bottles of coca cola. . . . A bundle of gilded cattails stood in one corner and a sheaf of peacock feathers was nailed to the wall beside the grandfather clock. (pp. 23–24)

Here time brings changes. What began as a refuge also becomes a prison. Trapped within its drabness they are motivated to improve it. They could have adapted, and without the rain perhaps they would have, but they exercised a choice. Their feelings for the place grew with time, with familiarity, with sustained shelter, and when they experienced its security from the landlord. Their furnishing of it was contagious, first a cot, then springs, then a chaise longue, a clock, posters, and aesthetic objects. Notice how, in this case, there is a progression from the personal to the communal and from the functional to the aesthetic.

They were some time in acquiring a stove and when they did find what they wanted, a silver scrolled monster with floriated warming ovens and a front like a nickel plated tulip garden, they had trouble getting it. . . . It took them three days to carry it to Cannery Row a distance of five miles, and they camped beside it at night. But once installed in the Palace Flophouse it was the glory and the hearth and the center. Its nickel flowers and foliage shone with a cheery light. It was the gold tooth of the Palace. Fired up it warmed the big room. Its oven was wonderful and you could fry an egg on its shiny black lids. With the great stove came pride, and with pride, the Palace became home. Eddie planted morning glories to run over the door and Hazel acquired some rather rare fuschia bushes planted in five-gallon cans which made the entrance formal and a little cluttered. Mack and the boys loved the Palace and they even cleaned it a little sometimes. In their minds they sneered at unsettled people who had no house to go to and occasionally in their pride they brought a guest home for a day or two. (pp. 24–25)

Finally comes the heart and the hearth, a center of warmth and a symbol of group cohesion that required their collective efforts. And the decorating efforts took a third step with the outside plants reflecting a sense of permanence and a commitment to the future. The connections and the order had been established. It was a center of security, of shelter, of warmth. It gained meaning through time and activity, through familiarity and through their joint efforts. The men gained power through privacy and territory that engendered commitment and a connection to the future. The caring was contagious. Finally they even cleaned it—a purity ritual. There was a sense of identity both of each man to his territory but of the group to the whole place. There was a transition from the individual to the communal, from house to home, from a very functional and rational attitude to one of love, care, and concern.

A second example comes from the autobiography of Margaret Mead (1972) who describes her struggles to establish a sense of home throughout a life of travel and of a tower office she acquired in the New York museum where she worked:

It was just like the room I had at the farm and the kind of room I had always chosen in each rented house we lived in. Among other advantages, there were two stairways leading up to the tower . . . this meant that one could creep down one stairway while someone whom one did not want to meet— in my childhood, my mother or the person who was It in a game, or later, a too solicitous elderly curator—was coming up the other. . . . Only a few years before I came to the museum, that office had been the bedroom of the building superintendent's apartment in which he had lived with his family. He used to stand in the doorway and tell me how all his children had been born in that room. . . . For those of us who worked in the tower there was no endless hall lined with storage cases to walk along and no limits like those set by the large handsome offices downstairs. At first my office seemed large and bare. . . . I hung tapa-patterned cotton curtains at the window, spread Samoan mats on the floor, and on the wall hung a map of the world on which . . . to plot our future field trips. . . . Since the late 1920's, I have had no permanent house to go back to, only a series of rented apartments. . . . So the office in the museum became the successor to the rooms in which I had grown up. . . . Up in the tower, with two flights of stairs between me and the milling crowds below, I feel as safe from intrusion and loss as once I did at home in my third floor room where the night wind whistled through the closed shutters and the sparrows racketed in the ivy outside my windows every dawn. For all my years of travelling, I have always had somewhere to return to, somewhere where everything is just where I put it away twenty, thirty or forty years ago. (Mead, 1972, pp. 13–16)

In this passage we once again encounter a range of the principles of "home" discussed earlier. Mead has a sense of the past history of the place, there is a structural similarity with her own childhood home, and she brings to it certain objects that evoke memories of the past. The tower has a sense of verticality and centeredness unlike the "endless" corridors below. There is a sense of separation from the "milling crowds." There is a sense of security, power, and control—power to control the dialectics of interaction and power to ensure that her own spatial order would survive the journeys of 40 years. And there is an overriding sense of the dialectics of home and journey, the home as her place of stability, order, and identity throughout a life of travel.

It is not my intention that these examples be seen as an idealized description of the process of becoming-at-home but rather as particular examples of how that process might become manifest in a particular sociocultural context. Indeed, it is of the essence of home and the processes of its emergence that its forms are unique. Home is what emerges out of the dwelling activities, the appropriations and the opportunities available in each particular circumstance. It is an insider's experience, and it is always unique. Although the basic themes remain the same, the manifestations are situation specific. It is also important to reiterate that the phenomenon of home is essentially intangible. There is no precise point at which a house becomes a home, and none of the properties that I have outlined previously are necessary nor sufficient for the experience of home. Rather, like fibers in a rope, each property lends strength to the meaning of home.

PROPERTIES OF HOMELESSNESS

I want to turn now to the problem of homelessness. The approach here is somewhat different in that rather than examining the experience of being homeless I will explore and outline some of the processes, properties, and conditions that have eroded the traditional sense of home and that paralyze its reemergence. These properties can be categorized into six general categories; however, as with the properties of home, there is much overlap, and there are many interrelationships.

RATIONALISM AND TECHNOLOGY

Rationalism is an attitude that permeates much current thinking about human–environment relationships (Relph, 1981). It is an attitude stemming from the Cartesian dualism of body and mind, whereby the physical world is held at arms length for our contemplation. Thus, it is regarded as separate from ourselves and objectively real. Such an attitude has discrete benefits, both in the realm of objective knowledge about our world and in terms of its technological by-products. Yet when allowed to monopolize our experience and discourse, rationalism serves to erode the experience of home both through its forms of knowledge and discourse, and through its technologies.

The rational attitude is biased toward the tangible. Yet the phenomenon of home, as I have argued, is an intangible relationship between people and the places in which they dwell; it is not visible nor accurately measureable. Reason responds to intangibility by reducing terms such as *home* to precise and bounded definitions. Rationally considered, a home becomes reduced to a house—the meaning and experience of home as a relationship becomes confused with the object through which it is currently manifest. Furthermore, the discourse of design knowledge and decision making also assumes an objective stance. Design programs, for instance, are generally written in quantitative terms of measured space and numbers of plumbing fixtures.

A major strength of the rational attitude is that its technological by-products make possible relations with the built environment that were until recently impossible. These include an enhanced ability to change the environment through planning and construction techniques, to control it through lighting and heating, and to expand it through cars, telephones, and television. However, this technology has also played an important part in eroding our sense of home in that many of the sociospatial patterns that were traditionally embodied in everyday life at home have been undercut by rapid advances in technology. Consider, for example, the case of the hearth fire. Beyond its traditional functions of cooking and heating, there is widespread cross-cultural evidence that certain intangible meanings are associated with the hearth fire: as a symbol of home (Raglan, 1966), a sacred center (Eliade, 1959), an anchor for social order (Marshall, 1973), and a place of reverie (Bachelard, 1964). The technologies of heating, however, coupled with a rationalistic attitude, have undercut these meanings and led to the widespread disappearance of the fireplace from many homes. The immediately obvious advantages of technological change, in this case improved efficiency and cleanliness, can serve initially to mask the loss of intangible meanings.

An important component of the rationalistic attitude is that it implicitly gives priority to the abstract conceptual modes of "space" as opposed to the meaning-centered mode of "lived space." Thus space is viewed in terms of square meters, of measured geometric areas and volumes. Such an attitude is, of course, often necessary to the processes of environmental discourse and change. Relph (1981) has pointed out the interesting dilemma that, although there is widespread condemnation of modern rationalistic environments, there is also a widespread appreciation of the comforts and efficiencies that rationality brings. We are, it seems, simultaneously rational and nostalgic. Nostalgia, which was originally the name of the "disease" of homesickness (Starobinski, 1966), is an interesting synonym for the generalized sense of homelessness that, it is often argued, pervades modern culture (Berger, Berger, & Kellner, 1973; MacCannell, 1976). The problem, however, is that the rationalism comes first; nostalgia or homesickness stems from the loss of intangibles that the rationalism and its technologies bring. One result of this nostalgia, stemming from the loss of intangibles, is their replacement with inauthentic substitutes, such as fireplaces that do not work or are never used—elements of home that stand as mere signs and remnants of a lost meaning. The question of authenticity in the built environment is closely related to that of homelessness, and I have discussed it in more detail elsewhere (Dovey, 1985).

My argument here is not that a rational attitude is a wrong one, but rather that it carries no monopoly on truth or progress (Feyerabend, 1975). It might usefully be seen as a tool for changing the world in ways that are meaningful instead of eroding those meanings through its hidden assumptions. Paradoxically, given our current understanding of these issues, there are good *reasons* to oppose the monopoly of rationalism.

COMMODITIZATION

Paralleling the distinction between house and home is a distinction between the house as property and the home as appropriated territory. In the modern world, the house is a commodity involving substantial economic commitment. It is an investment of economic resources that yields profit and power. As such, the house has become increasingly similar to other products—being bought and sold, used and discarded like a car or washing machine. Home, on the other hand, involves a commitment not of money but of time and emotion. It is the place where we invest dreams, hopes, and care. Although we can buy the props and freedom that make such an investment possible and secure, the phenomenon of home itself cannot be bought or commoditized. Home is a relationship that is created and evolved over time; it is not consumed like the products of economic process. The house is a tool for the achievement of the experience of home. Yet the increasing commoditization of the house engenders a confusion between house and home because it is the image of home that is bought and sold in the marketplace. The belief on the part of both producers and consumers that the home is the house trivializes the concept of home and treats it as an object to be instantly consumed. The qualities of a house that contribute to the experience of home may, of course, be encouraged by market forces. The economic value of certain intangibles are increasingly exploited as they become scarcer. A recent housing development in San Francisco is advertized as "townhomes on a legendary site . . . reminiscent of [a] bygone era," a "commons" with a "sense of place." The town*homes* have "woodburning fireplaces" and "windowseats tucked in corners," offering "a warm retreat amidst urban activity and excitement."[2] The image being sold (if not the reality) is close to that which I have outlined earlier—connections to the past, to other people, and to the place, a sense of center with an inside/outside dialectic. The promise of the experience of home is carefully packaged for the very few at an average price per unit of over half a million dollars.

Commoditization has its main eroding effect not in the quality of house form but in the quality of the relationship of the dweller with the dwelling. The house as a piece of property implies a legal relationship between the owner and the place, a relationship embodying certain legal freedoms. Home as appropriation, on the other hand, implies a relationship that is rooted in the experiences of everyday life over a long period of time. It requires adaptability, control, freedom, and security of tenure. A contradiction emerges here under conditions of absentee ownership or rental. Housing rental creates a split between the dwelling experiences through which home emerges and the longer term legal freedoms of ownership. If the owner is personally identified with the house, then a clash of identities may well emerge when the dwellers attempt to appropriate it. If the owner regards the house as a mere rational investment, then his or her interest in maintaining its commodity value may similarly paralyze the processes of appropriation. In

---

[2]All quotes are from the sales brochure *Golden Gateway Commons*, available from the Sales Office, 660 Davis St., San Francisco, Calif., 94111.

either case, the legal relationship that embodies the freedom and security necessary for the emergence of home takes precedence over the dwelling experiences of the users. The issue of ownership and rental is not simple; there is great demand for rental housing, and a sense of home often emerges under such conditions. Yet the rationalistic idea that problems of housing and dwelling might be solved without addressing issues of ownership is incommensurable with our understanding of the phenomenon of home.

BUREAUCRACY

The influence of bureaucratic organization on the phenomenon of home can be understood as a property of the institutional framework of housing design and management. Bureaucracy thus infects the design of housing (through design, planning, and regulatory organizations), the production of housing (through governmental authorities and development corporations), and the management of housing in use. Weber (1978) has argued that the following properties are characteristic of bureaucratic organization: (a) organization is hierarchical with official jurisdiction over rule-bound procedures; (b) there is a focus on written rather than verbal discourse; (c) procedures are enacted by experts using specialized and technical languages of discourse; and (d) the aims of the organization are speed, precision, unambiguity, and objectivity.

According to Weber, the nature of bureaucracy

> develops the more perfectly the more the bureaucracy is 'dehumanized,' the more completely it succeeds in eliminating from official business love, hatred, and all purely personal, irrational, and emotional elements which escape calculation. (p. 90)

Crozier (1964) similarly identifies bureaucracy with hierarchy, dependence on higher authority, rationalism, and impersonal rules. The more that the production, control, and maintenance of home environments is dependent upon bureaucratic organization, then the more this organization both erodes and paralyzes the emergence of the experience of home. Intangible qualities of identification and meaning, slow changes over time, local control, adaptability, and complex dialectic interactions cannot be dealt within a bureaucratic context.

One important effect of bureaucratic organization is that procedures generally become biased toward those operating them, increasing the tendency for the goals of the organization to be subverted by personal power struggles within the organization. As power is centralized, Crozier argues, "the power to make decisions . . . will tend to grow farther and farther away from the field where those rules will be carried out" (p. 189). This can lead, in the case of housing programs, to a phenomenon where the dwellers become "invisible" (Grenell, 1972). Although bureaucratic programs may stem from a genuine desire to improve housing for the maximum number of people, the process begins from a fixed idea or stereotype of who the dwellers are and what "good" housing is.

Bureaucratic structures and processes, like those of home, can be understood as a kind of order and identity; yet this order and identity are diametrically opposed to those of "becoming-at-home." Whereas home is the kind of order that flows upward from the opportunities and problems of each *unique* place and context, bureaucratic order flows downward. A centralized order is imposed across diverse particular cases according to *typical* situations and contexts (Crozier, 1964, pp. 183–184). Likewise, bureaucratic organization has its own identity that, in the case of housing programs, becomes stamped upon the landscape at the expense of the diverse identifications of the dwellers. Housing becomes symbolic of the organization that produces it, spatially regular and temporally regulated places that may not be easily adapted to the uniqueness of each situation or to changes that occur over time. The complexities of the experience of home and the role of the dweller in achieving it are beyond the capabilities of bureaucratic structures to deal with.

SCALE AND SPEED

The scale at which environmental and housing problems are framed and tackled and the speed at which environmental change is implemented are two properties that are closely linked to those outlined previously, and they contribute to the erosion of the experience of home. Bureaucratic organization, for instance, develops to ensure the remote control necessary to implement large-scale programs. Big problems would seem to demand big solutions. Housing, however, is not so much a big problem as it is a large collection of small ones—many people with a desire for shelter, roots, security, and identity, yet with a multitude of dreams, forms, and social patterns within which this might be realized.

The speed of environmental change erodes the sense of home inasmuch as it threatens temporal identity. When identity is anchored in places, a certain continuity is required in order for dwellers to assimilate changes and to accommodate their sense of identity to the new images as they emerge. Being intangible, qualities of home are often only identified when they are lost. Large, swift changes in the home environment can destroy these qualities that might have been salvaged if the changes had been smaller, slower, and more adaptable.

Traditional cities and villages for which our culture is so often nostalgic were not produced from master plans but grew piecemeal over a long period of time, responding to circumstances at a local level. The phenomenon of home, too, grows piecemeal rather than being created complete. Swiftly implemented large developments may lend the impression of solving large-scale problems, yet they do so at the expense of the adaptability and identification possible when we understand the processes by which houses can grow as families grow—as economic resources permit and as needs arise.

THE EROSION OF COMMUNAL SPACE

Another change that has subtly eroded the sense of home is the decline of communally shared open space. The usage and control of streets, squares, and open spaces that form the context of the house were freely negotiated traditionally and appropriated by people through their participation in the community (Aries, 1977; Sennett, 1977). Beginning in the 18th century important changes came about in the relation of the family home to the spatial, political, and social life of the city. Concommitant with the separation of the work place from the home, the state extended its control and surveillance into every domain of city life, eradicating interstitial spaces that were previously beyond the state's sphere of influence (Wright & Rabinow, 1982). As a result, communally shared space has become increasingly managed and regulated by state authorities. Thus its use and transformation must be deferred by the user group to these higher authorities. This remote control of shared open space has political, social, and personal consequences. Politically, it reinforces the jurisdiction of existing power groups and denies the role of shared space as the place of political freedom (Arendt, 1958). Socially, it limits behavior in public to a purified and rule-bound set of activities.

The public realm has become a place where it is difficult if not impossible to enact personal or collective appropriations. It is a place where "they" are responsible for control and maintenance of a rule-bound status quo. At the personal level, this loss of a shared common place as a context of the home brings a subtle yet profound erosion of the dialectics of home/journey and private/public. The home becomes the sole area of personal control and security; its boundary hardens, semiprivate edge areas disappear, informal appropriation and surveillance across the interface weaken, and crime proliferates (Newman, 1972). The dialectical movement between home and reach, private and public, loses its sense of transition. From a place of complete control and security, we cross a boundary of locked doors, barred windows, and security systems to confront a world that is someone else's responsibility. Shut off from this world the home has become an isolated world unto itself, a cocoon of security and comfort severed from its deeper connections with the urban fabric. "The urban conglomerate," Aries (1978, p. 233) argues, "has become a mass of small islands . . . all separated from one another by a great void. The interstitial space has vanished." As the communally shared realm has been eroded, so the private realm has expanded to fill the void, leading to an inordinate demand on the home to fulfill all of one's needs. Herein lies a dilemma—without the broader sense of home extending into community life, the experience of home contracts and loses meaning; yet at the same time increased demands are placed upon this depleted experience of home.

PROFESSIONALISM

Strong forces within the architectural profession mitigate against the emergence of a sense of home. Design professions are strongly peer-group oriented, and the designer's reputation is determined more by the visual images of buildings in professional journals than by the experience of the users. The relationship between the designer and the place designed is characterized by a process of creative identification not unlike that described earlier as a property of becoming-at-home. Thus, a personal relationship and connectedness between the designer and the image of the place emerges. This highly personal relationship, together with its assumptions of professional superiority, tends to paralyze the emergence of similar yet deeper relationships between dweller and place. Because designers receive their kudos from the image of their products as judged by their peers, they have an interest in keeping these fine-tuned symbols free from contamination by the dwellers. The problem here, even when the dwellers share the values of the designer, is that whereas the designer's concern is with the image, the experience of home is dynamic and action based—it is an experience of "living in" rather than "looking at" buildings. I am not trying to deny the designer's role as creative form giver; I am merely trying to draw attention to the ways in which it may be antithetical to the processes of becoming-at-home. A home cannot be someone else's work of art.

BECOMING HOMELESS

The previously mentioned properties have been characteristic of many approaches to housing problems throughout this century. Examples here include most of what began with the modern movement in Europe (Boudon, 1979) and was exported under the guise of urban renewal to the United States (Gans, 1968) and the Third World (Detier, 1973; Turner & Fichter, 1972). The dream of the modern movement in architecture and planning was that technology and industrialized housing would be able to provide high-quality housing for everyone, mass-produced in high-rise blocks set in a garden landscape. Housing was regarded rationally in terms of universal requirements, applicable internationally and cross-culturally. The house was conceived as a "machine-for-living-in," a piece of technology.

The result, we have since learned, was homelessness. The stripped aesthetic of modernism destroyed continuity with the styles of the past and with regional traditions. The scale and speed of the developments instantly transformed the landscape, wiping out the anchored memories of the former dwellers. Little room was left for the expression or development of personal identity; indeed, the very powerful institutional and bureaucratic identity of housing "projects" was a key element in their failure (Newman, 1972). Standards of housing were considered entirely from a rational point of view, in terms of square meters and plumbing requirements. Existing elements of home, such as social networks, were not recognized nor preserved, resulting in severe social and psychological disruption (Fried, 1963; Gans, 1968). Housing was treated as a commodity (Turner, 1972), a product to be provided for people who would have little choice in terms of design or location. Furthermore, bureaucratic management of housing in use has ensured that the lack of user control and the paralysis of personal identification has endured. Despite the promise of landscaped open space and "streets-in-the-sky," these public places have become some of the most dangerous ones in our cities. It is ironic that many of these housing schemes received lavish praise from the design professions in advance of being condemned and even demolished as a result of their extreme social inadequacy. These housing processes and schemes represent the most extreme example of the consequences of not distinguishing between house and home and of ignoring the intangibles of home. Despite solving the "housing problem" as stated, they were an excellent recipe for homelessness.

IMPLICATIONS FOR FUTURE RESEARCH

I will conclude this essay with some brief suggestions as to where I think an understanding of the concepts of *home* and *homelessness* might lead in relation to research and practice in environmental design. There are four directions that I see as useful in this regard.

The first of these relates to the development and application of design patterns or guidelines that embody understandings of the experience of home. Clearly, this kind of knowledge is most available for spatiotemporal patterns that are embodied in a sociocultural order. The aim of this approach is to build a bridge between environmental design research and practice, and much of such work has been done (Alexander, Ishikawa, & Silverstein, 1977; Cooper Marcus & Sarkissian, 1985; Zeisel, 1977). Although such guidelines tend to be primarily formal and spatial, they could usefully be extended to encompass the temporal processes of "becoming-at-home." Patterns could be developed to guide not only the forms of environmental change but also the processes of design and change, embodying an understanding of issues such as the speed of change, the preservation of temporal connections with the built environment and processes of appropriation. There is, however, an important caveat on the use of design guidelines. Based as they are on a sociocultural context, their possible misuse in a multicultural society remains an ever-present problem (Dovey, 1981).

The second direction is that of participatory design. Although the aspects of sociocultural order and identification can be embodied in guidelines, those of a more personal order and identification cannot. Being the representation and embodiment of the order and identity of the dweller or group of dwellers, the experience of home requires their active participation in the design process. This is not only because dwellers all too often have their desires ignored, but also because the opportunity for environmental change is an opportunity for an enhanced sense of home. Participation can be as important for the opportunities it opens up as it is for the mistakes it avoids. Although there is a clear link between participatory design and the experience of home, implementing such a process is no simple matter in the modern context. Techniques of participatory design are scarcely taught in design schools, and the effects of participatory design are not well understood by researchers. The participatory approach therefore offers significant opportunities for research and practice in environmental design.

The third direction of importance for research and practice is that of understanding and undercutting the properties of homelessness outlined in the second part of this essay. Each of these properties represents an aspect of the context within which designers operate in the modern world—the context within which design problems are defined, explored, and solved. This is at once a political, sociocultural, economic, professional, philosophical, intellectual, and bureaucratic context. And like the unself-conscious aspects of the experience of home this context is largely taken for granted. The task is to bring these properties of homelessness into the light: to highlight the issue of scale when problems are unsolvably large; to pressure bureaucracies into adaptability; to talk about the intangibles of life and breathe a certain reality into them before they are lost. This role has a clear political component to it inasmuch as it is an issue of whether the built environment is to represent the order ("home") of centralized power structures or the order of the diverse identifications and adaptations of the dwellers.

Finally, a change in attitude and understanding is required of designers. This involves an enhanced understanding and a celebration of the experience of home and the processes of becoming-at-home that exist in every place and every community. The goal here is not only to create a sense of home but rather to recognize and preserve it in its myriad of processes and forms. Its processes are seldom visible, and its forms are not always beautiful; yet beneath them lie the seeds of a deeper sense of home, struggling to flower.

Acknowledgments

I would like to thank Sandra Gifford and Roderick Lawrence for their critiques of earlier drafts of this essay.

REFERENCES

Alexander, C., Ishikawa, S., & Silverstein, M. *A pattern language: Towns, buildings, construction.* New York: Oxford University Press, 1977.

Allport, G. *Becoming: Basic considerations for a psychology of personality.* New Haven: Yale University Press, 1955.

Altman, I. *The environment and social behavior.* Monterey, Calif.: Brooks/Cole, 1975.

Altman, I., & Gauvain, M. A cross-cultural and dialectical analysis of homes. In L. S. Liben, A. H. Patterson, & N. Newcombe (Eds.), *Spatial representation and behavior across the life span.* New York: Academic Press, 1981, pp. 283–320.

Appleton, J. *The experiment of landscape.* London: Wiley, 1975.

Appleyard, D. *Inside vs. outside: The distortions of distance* (Working Paper No. 307). Berkeley: Institute of Urban & Regional Development, 1979. (a)

Appleyard, D. Home. *Architectural Association Quarterly*, 1979, 11(2), 4–20. (b)

Arendt, H. *The human condition.* Chicago: University of Chicago Press, 1958.

Aries, P. The family and the city, *Daedelus*, 1977, 106, 227–235.

Auden, W. H. *About the house.* London: Faber & Faber, 1966.

Bachelard, G. *The psychoanalysis of fire.* Boston: Beacon, 1964.

Benedict, R. *Patterns of culture.* New York: Mentor, 1946.

Berger, P., Berger, B., & Kellner, H. *The homeless mind.* Harmondsworth, England: Penguin, 1973.

Blier, S. *The architecture of the Tamberma*. Unpublished doctoral dissertation, Columbia University, 1981.

Bollnow, O. F. Lived-space. In N. Lawrence & D. O'Connor (Eds.), *Readings in existential phenomenology*. Englewood Cliffs, N.J.: Prentice-Hall, 1967, pp. 178–186.

Boudon, P. *Lived-in architecture: LeCorbusier's Pessac revisited*. Cambridge, Mass.: M.I.T. Press, 1979.

Bourdieu, P. *The Algerians*. Boston: Beacon, 1962.

Bourdieu, P. *Outline of a theory of practice*. New York: Cambridge University Press, 1977.

Buttimer, A. Home, reach and the sense of place. In A. Buttimer & D. Seamon (Eds.), *The human experience of space and place*. London: Croom Helm, 1980, pp. 166–187.

Cooper, C. The house as a symbol of self. In J. Lang, C. Burnett, W. Moleski, & D. Vachon (Eds.), *Designing for human behavior*. Stroudsburg, Penn.: Dowden, Hutchinson & Ross, 1974, pp. 130–146.

Cooper Marcus, C. Remembrance of landscapes past. *Landscape*, 1978, 22(3), 34–43.

Cooper Marcus, C., & Sarkissian, W. *Housing as if people mattered*. Berkeley: University of California Press, 1985.

Critchlow, K. Niike: The siting of a Japanese rural house. In P. Oliver (Ed.), *Shelter, sign and symbol*. London: Barrie & Jenkins, 1975, pp. 219–226.

Crozier, M. *The bureaucratic phenomenon*. Chicago: University of Chicago Press, 1964.

Csikszentmihalyi, M., & Rochberg-Halton, E. *The meaning of things: Domestic symbols of the self*. New York: Cambridge University Press, 1981.

Cunningham, C. E. Order in the Atoni house. In R. Needham (Ed.), *Right and left: Essays on dual symbolic classification*. Chicago: University of Chicago Press, 1973, 204–238.

Detier, J. Evolution of concepts of housing, urbanism and country planning in a developing country: Morocco, 1900–1972. In L. C. Brown (Ed.), *From medina to metropolis*. Princeton: Darwin Press, 1973, pp. 197–242.

Dovey, K. Home: An ordering principle in space. *Landscape*, 1978, 22(2), 27–30.

Dovey, K. *The dwelling experience: Towards a phenomenology of architecture* (Research Rep. No. 55). Melbourne, Victoria: University of Melbourne, Faculty of Architectural Building and Town and Regulation Planning, 1979.

Dovey, K. Dilemmas of environmental epistemology: Design patterns and participation. In A. Osterberg, C. Tiernan, & R. Findlay (Eds.), *Design research interactions*. Ames: EDRA 12 Proceedings, 1981, pp. 77–83.

Dovey, K. The quest for authenticity and the replication of environmental meaning. In D. Seamon & R. Mugerauer (Eds.), *Dwelling, place and environment*. The Hague: Martinus Nijhof, 1985.

Duncan, J. (Ed.). *Housing and identity*. New York: Holmes & Meier, 1981.

Eliade, M. *The sacred and the profane*. New York: Harcourt, Brace & World, 1959.

Eliade, M. *Patterns in comparative religion*. New York: Meridian, 1963.

Feuerstein, G. Unpremeditated architecture. *Landscape*, 1965, *13*(3), 33–37.

Feyerabend, P. *Against method: Outline of an anarchistic theory of knowledge*. London: Verso, 1975.

Fried, M. Grieving for a lost home. In L. J. Duhl (Ed.), *The urban condition*. New York: Basic Books, 1963, pp. 151–171.

Gans, H. *People and plans: Essays on urban problems and solutions*. New York: Basic Books, 1968.

Gans, H. *Popular culture and high culture*. New York: Basic Books, 1974.

Gardiner, P. *The evolution of the house*. Hertfordshire, England: Paladin, 1975.

Goffman, E. *The presentation of self in everyday life*. Harmondsworth: Penguin, 1971.

Gorer, G. *Himalayan village: An account of the Lepchas of Sikkim*. London: Nelson, 1967.

Grenell, P. Planning for invisible people: Some consequences of bureaucratic values and practices. In J.F. C. Turner & R. Fichter (Eds.), *Freedom to build*. New York: Macmillan, 1972, pp. 95–121.

Griale, M., & Dieterlen, G. The Dogon. In D. Forde (Ed.), *African worlds*. London: Oxford University Press, 1964, pp. 83–110.

Heidegger, M. *Being and time*. New York: Harper & Row, 1962.

Heidegger, M. *Discourse on thinking*. New York: Harper & Row, 1966.

Heidegger, M. *Poetry, language, thought*. New York: Harper & Row, 1971.

Jager, B. Theorizing, journeying, dwelling. In A. Giorgi, C. Fisher, & E. Murray (Eds.), *Duquesne studies in phenomenological psychology* (Vol. 2). Pittsburg: Duquesne University Press, 1975, pp. 235–260.

Jung, G. C. *Memories, dreams, and reflections*. London: Fontana, 1967.

Lawrence, R. Domestic space and society: A cross-cultural study. *Comparative Studies in Society and History*, 1982, 24(1), 104–130.

MacCannell, D. *The tourist: A new theory of the leisure class*. New York: Schocken, 1976.

Marshall, L. Each side of the fire. In M. Douglas (Ed.), *Rules and meanings: The anthropology of everyday knowledge*. Harmondsworth: Penguin, 1973, pp. 95–97.

Mead, G. H. *Mind, self and society*. Chicago: University of Chicago Press, 1934.

Mead, M. *Blackberry winter: My earlier years*. New York: Morrow, 1972.

Merleau-Ponty, M. *Phenomenology of perception*. London: Routledge & Kegan Paul, 1962.

Needham, R. (Ed.). *Right and left: Essays in dual symbolic classification*. Chicago: University of Chicago Press, 1973.

Newman, O. *Defensible space: Crime prevention through urban design*. New York: Macmillan, 1972.

Norburg-Schulz, C. *Existence, space and architecture*. New York: Praeger, 1971.

Olsson, G. On yearning for home. In D. Pocock (Ed.), *Humanistic geography and literature*. London: Croom Helm, 1981, pp. 121–129.

Pratt, G. The house as an expression of social worlds. In J. Duncan (Ed.), *Housing and identity*. New York: Holmes & Meier, 1981, pp. 135–179.

Rainwater, L. Fear and the house as haven in the lower class. *Journal of the American Institute of Planners*, 1966, 32, 23–31.

Rakoff, R. Ideology in everyday life: The meaning of the house. *Politics and Society*, 1977, 7, 85–104.

Raglan, L. *The temple and the house*. London: Routledge & Kegan Paul, 1966.

Rapoport, A. Identity in cross-cultural perspective. In J. Duncan (Ed.), *Housing and identity*. New York: Holmes & Meier, 1981, pp. 6–35.

Reichel-Dolmatoff, G. *Amazonian cosmos*. Chicago: University of Chicago Press, 1971.

Relph, E. *Place and placelessness*. London: Pion, 1976.

Relph, E. *Rational landscapes and humanistic geography*. New York: Barnes & Noble, 1981.

Rykwert, J. *On Adam's house in paradise*. New York: Museum of Modern Art, 1972.

Saile, D. Making a house: Building rituals and spatial concepts in the Pueblo Indian world, *Architectural Association Quarterly*, 1977, 9(2/3), 72–81.

Seamon, D. *A geography of the lifeworld*. London: Croom Helm, 1979.

Sennett, R. *The fall of public man*. London: Cambridge University Press, 1977.

Schieffelin, E. L. *The sorrow of the lonely and the burning of the dancers*. New York: St. Martin's Press, 1976.

Starobinski, J. The idea of nostalgia. *Diogenes*, 1966, 54, 81–103.

Steinbeck, J. *Cannery Row*. New York: Bantam, 1954.

Straus, E. W. The upright posture. In M. Natanson (Ed.), *Essays in phenomenology*. The Hague: Martinus Nijhof, 1966, pp. 164–192.

Tuan, Y. Space and place: A humanist perspective. *Progress in Geography*, 1974, *6*, 211–253.

Turner, J. Housing as a verb. In J. Turner & R. Fichter (Eds.), *Freedom to build*. New York: Macmillan, 1972, 148–175.

Turner, J., & Fichter, R. *Freedom to build: Dweller control of the housing process*. New York: Macmillan, 1972.

Vycinas, V. *Earth and gods: An introduction to the philosophy of Martin Heidegger*. The Hague: Martinus Nijhof, 1961.

Weber, M. Essay on bureaucracy. In F. E. Rourke (Ed.), *Bureaucratic power in national politics*. Boston/Toronto: Little, Brown & Co., 1978, pp. 85–96.

Wright, G., & Rabinow, P. Spatialization of power, *Skyline*, March, 1982, pp. 14–15.

Zeisel, J. *Low rise housing for older people*. Washington: H.U.D. Publication, 1977.

3

Experience and Use of the Dwelling

PERLA KOROSEC-SERFATY

INTRODUCTION

Researchers and theoreticians from a wide variety of disciplines have studied the meaning of home. Some have focused on visible behaviors such as personalization and marking (Boudon, 1969; Hansen & Altman, 1976; Haumont & Raymond, 1975; Jacquier & Jeantet, 1976; Leroy, Bedos, & Berthelot, 1971), whereas others have focused on historical aspects such as demographic and economic factors or successive conceptions of the ideal social order (Barbey, 1980; Gauldie, 1974; Guerrand, 1967; Murard & Zylberman, 1976). Still others have examined how dwellings reflect culture (Clerc, 1967; Heller, 1979; Korosec-Serfaty, 1979; Mauss, 1950; Verret, 1979). Underlying many of these perspectives is an interest in the subjective experience of dwelling, and those with such a focus generally share a vision of the dweller as an acting subject who confers meaning upon the world but also as an individual acted upon by the world of which she or he is a part. These approaches are influenced in various degrees by the theoretical explorations into meaning that are pursued at the interface between sociology, psychology, and linguistics (de Certeau, Giard, & Mayol, 1980; Rochberg-Halton, 1984)

PERLA KOROSEC-SERFATY • Institut de Psychologie, Université Louis Pasteur, 12 rue Goethe, 67000 Strasbourg, France. This chapter has been translated from the French by Viviane Eskenazi.

and at the interface between psychoanalysis and philosophy, especially the philosophical movement of phenomenology. The focus in this chapter will be on the phenomenological view of dwelling, or how the relationship to home is experienced by the dweller.

A BRIEF INTRODUCTION TO PHENOMENOLOGY

Our purpose here is certainly a limited one. We intend to introduce the reader to those few "watchwords" that are agreed upon by phenomenologists, without engaging in a detailed analysis of what separates Husserl (1959, 1961, 1962, 1963) from Heidegger (1958, 1964), or Heidegger from Sartre (1943), even if, for the philosopher, these differences represent much more than mere academic quarrels.

We then intend to introduce some thoughts on dwelling from the phenomenological perspective. One finds partial justification for this project in the fact that phenomenology is, from the outset, concerned with the *question* of space, which is dealt with in various degrees, explicitly or implicitly, in the work of phenomenologists. But it should be kept in mind that it is above all a question. This excludes any idea of a finished doctrine, and, as will be shown, *space, place, dwelling,* and *being* elicit questions rather than certainties.

Phenomenology is "animated" by a few fundamental intentions that, it should be emphasized, are closely intertwined and represent the various expressions of a single endeavor. The key phrase is *return to the things themselves* (Husserl, 1962, p. 8), which refers to the need to recover the attention directed at our primal experience. It has a corollary that is a given conception of personality and consciousness. Consciousness is viewed as oriented toward things, that is, it does not exist in a vacuum but only in relation to something else. Phenomenology, then, describes those concrete phenomena that constitute the experience of the *incarnate subject*, meaning that the person's apprehension of the world is rooted and articulated in his or her own spatiality. Lastly, because experience is by definition multifaceted, the phenomenological activity is undergirded by the quest for unity of meaning in the subject. By this quest, phenomenology claims to be a science. We will now examine four key aspects: return-to-things, spatiality, intentionality, and affectivity, historicity, and sociality.

RETURN-TO-THINGS

The common foundation that has given impetus to the phenomenological movement is embodied in the Husserlian phrase *return to the things themselves* as stated (Husserl, 1959, p. 8). Indeed to return to things themselves is to return to that world which precedes knowledge, of which knowledge always *speaks* and in relation to which any scientific schematization is an abstract and derivative sign language, as is geography in relation to the countryside in which we have learnt beforehand what a forest, a prairie, or a river is. (Merleau-Ponty, 1967, p. 9)

Thus, phenomenology must think through our relationship to the "life world" of first experiences, prior to any representation.

SPATIALITY

At the same time, it is necessary to understand the fundamental, primary spatiality of the thinking subject, that is to say, to understand the meaning and the importance of the existence of a body-as-self, a living body, a lived body in contrast with the body as an object of science, for instance. The spatiality of the life world is a correlate of one's corporeality, and it is the subject's spatiality that makes it possible to understand an *inhabited* space rather than its representation: the subject-as-*dweller* by her or his very need to exist, "spatializes," that is, finds shelter, arranges places for the sphere of her or his possessions, makes *room* for the different institutions of her or his life-in-society (i.e., communal life), and so forth (Villéla-Petit, 1981).

INTENTIONALITY

To the phrase *return to the things themselves*, to the notions of spatiality of the life world and of the thinking subject, it is necessary to add the notion of *intentionality*, which describes the relationship of man-in-the-world as a relationship creating meaning. Things and events exist before and after the subject may have any experience of them. They acquire their meaning, value, and strength insofar as the subject, his or her action, and his or her impulses are oriented toward them. Furthermore, things and events also acquire meaning from the perceptual field to which they belong and that is perceived as open and changing ceaselessly. The things and events around us constitute "a whole that we process in this or that way, with which we act and that motivates us" (Graumann, 1979, p. 4). This is why Sartre believes that situation and motivation are one and the same.

AFFECTIVITY, HISTORICITY, AND SOCIALITY

Finally, phenomenology is situated between three poles—those of affectivity, historicity, and sociality. By *affectivity* I refer to the investments of the subject in the "positive" appropriation of space (e.g., through play) or the "negative" appropriation of space (e.g., through pillage) (Korosec-Serfaty, 1973, 1975). By *historicity*, I refer to the time component in the embodied subject's relationship with the world through personal perceptions, memories, anticipations, or, to use Husserlian terminology, the retentions and protensions that constitute intentionality. Finally, by sociality I mean the analysis of work and language, that is, communication. My experience of space depends on what I can "make" of it, that is, on the nature of the actions I can perform on it. Similarly, places are marked by the words that designate their accessibility, the way they can be used, and their positive or negative qualities as a function of the cultural context I am in.

THE PHENOMENOLOGICAL "METHOD"

Phenomenology has been *practiced* chiefly in three of its aspects: the phenomenological description, the eidetic approach, and the hermeneutic approach. These three aspects do not completely capture the essence of the phenomenological method, but they are the most widely explored. This essay partakes of these three aspects, and it is intended as a contribution to the phenomenology of dwelling rather than with the intention of going through what some authors describe as "the steps of the phenomenological method" (Spiegelberg, 1960, p. 659).

Phenomenological *description* aims at retrieving through thought the original soil of experience, the life world that is assumed by our representations and by scientific knowledge. Take the experience of fire. Before I ever heard any explanation about the phenomenon of combustion, I had already experienced fire in different situations in my own life. I had experienced its heat, its brightness, and its destructive, or purifying, character. Phenomenological description thus seeks to intuitively discern the various appearances of things for the subject. For example, the description of fire necessarily aims as grasping the various affective states or significant orientations that, in various situations, represent my encounters with fire.

It is through these various modalities of appearance that the essential (or "ideal") meaning of fire is constituted for me. This means that any description derives from the intention (called *eidetic approach*) to find out what is intrinsic to the phenomenon and therefore to eliminate what is contingent and incidental. Besides, in attempting to uncover the essential elements of a phenomenon, it also seeks to describe the relationships and their articulations.

Thus, the eidetic method, by asking what makes a phenomenon what it is, raises the question of its meaning or rather, of what makes sense in the phenomenon. It is precisely the uncovering of meaning that is the purpose of *hermeneutics*, which aims to reach the single or multiple meanings hidden beyond what is immediately given. Hermeneutics necessarily is based on the idea that phenomena and human experiences are not immediately accessible and therefore call for an interpretive reading. This is why language, for hermeneutics, is more than an elective field. This is especially true of the work of Heidegger (1958) who undertakes a kind of phenomenology of words. His undertaking, arduous as it may be, is particularly important for us because it deals primarily with dwelling.

LANDMARKS FOR THE HERMENEUTICS OF DWELLING

Heidegger's hermeneutics asserts that the being's primal spatiality is antecedent to the formation of any concept or knowledge of space as it is studied in science (e.g., in geometry), for space is neither a separate entity nor an external object.

The built thing is no longer viewed as an instrument, and, therefore, the question of the activity related to the built thing, that is, the action of building, arises. This activity then appears as subordinated to the meaning expressed by the root of the Old German word *buan* that means both *to build* and *to inhabit*. "To build, we mean to say, is not only a means toward dwelling; building already is, by itself, dwelling" (Heidegger, 1958, p. 172). A still more decisive suggestion of language is seen by the comparison between *to inhabit* and *to be*:

> "I am, you are" mean: I inhabit, you inhabit. The way you are and the way I am, the way we humans *are* on the earth is the *buan*, the dwelling. Being human means: being on earth as a mortal, that is, to dwell. (Heidegger, 1958, p. 173)

Thus, "the fact that in one language 'I dwell' and 'I am' may have been used indistinguishably is a sure indication of the extent to which dwelling is coexistensive with the essence of the human being" (Liiceanu, 1983, p. 105).

Liiceanu (1983) points to something similar in Greek, which is illustrated in the following passage:

> The Greek verbs designating dwelling: *oikein, naiein, demein,* etc. . . . communicate through the idea of *duration/stability*, the fact of existing, and it is interesting to see that in Greek they are the only verbs entirely interchange-

able with the verb "to be," with which they are genuinely synonymous. (p.
106)

Thus, in both languages, *dwelling* is to be understood not only on the
basis of the activities it shelters or generates but also on the basis of its
instrumentality. In Heidegger's terms, it gathers the "Fourfold," by
which he means that the dwelling must provide space for the experience
of the sacred. Similarly, the role played by the earth in Heidegger's
thought should not evoke a romantic or pastoral revery (Grange, 1977,
quoted by Seamon, 1982). Heidegger's point is rather a validation of the
earth as the fundamental shelter of humanity, that is, as soil for life's
roots and the shelter for the final act of dwelling, that is, the funeral
rites The Fourfold evokes nothing else but the multidimensionality of
the human dwelling and hence the multidimensionality of the being,
that is, the *openness* of both to the world.

When dwelling is conceived of as the fundamental characteristic of
the human condition, what other messages does language convey?
Through the study of the initial forms that designate *building* and *dwelling*, etymology again provides the grounds for showing that dwelling,
lived from the outset as "habitual" (Heidegger, 1958, p. 174), is associated with peace, residence, care, and integration in the Fourfold. Generated order is also preservation and consideration; that is to say something *positive*.

This experience of dwelling is also apparent in Liiceanu's examination of the meaning of Greek words. For the Greek, we read that the
oikos (house) did not refer to the dwelling as building but was a guarantee of stability:

> It was the order in which took place and unfolded the fundamental actions of
> life. *Oikos* meant birth, childhood, kinship, all possessions, their manage-
> ment, the conception of descendants, and the framework for their birth.
> (Liiceanu, 1983, p. 106)

Thus, any wandering, any exile was a rupture with oneself, and any
"going-home-again" amounted to a returning to oneself. Furthermore,
the word *ethos* used to mean "habitual residence," or "dwelling," including the notion of habitual activities. The home, therefore, is this
sum of immobility, of stability, and of continuity that every being needs
in order to weave the links between identity and essence constantly.
After wandering, it is the place where one experiences the return to
unity with oneself.

Levinas's work, and more particularly his essay on exteriority, *To-
tality and Infinity* (1961), widens the range of the meditation on dwelling
initiated by Heidegger's hermeneutics. It is in the chapter devoted to the

dwelling that we find the idea of self-communion (*recueillement*), that is, a necessary condition for nature to be represented and processed and that is actualized as dwelling. It is after having "dwelt" in himself or herself that a person dwells in a building. Self-communion also amounts to creating a distance from the outside world, arising from an intimacy that is dwelling itself: "Concretely, the dwelling is not situated in the objective world, but the objective world situates itself in relation to my dwelling" (Levinas, 1961, p. 126). However, any intimacy is *intimacy with someone*; that is to say, any solitude as well as any interiority is situated in a world that is already human. Self-communion always refers to a welcoming, an openness toward the Other. The hospitable welcome circumscribes the field of intimacy. Thus, Levinas brings in the theme of withdrawal, which is seen as a process of identity elaboration, as well as the theme of *secrecy*, which is a requirement for this process. This is why the separated being meanders between visibility and invisibility, between work—seen as an involvement in the world, as action that organizes it, and therefore relates us to others—and the movement toward the self through which the being secures interiority.

Finally, the dwelling enables the being to pause; it suspends the immediate exposure of the being to the exterior world, just as it is, by nature, "a perpetual postponement of the time when life is liable to come to an end" (Levinas, 1961, p. 139). The consciousness of death as the primary postponement that opens up the dimension of time is thus found in both Levinas's and Heidegger's work, thereby disclosing another field to our thoughts about dwelling. Does not the French language call the grave *the last abode*?

PHENOMENOLOGICAL DIMENSIONS OF DWELLING

On the basis of the preceding lines of thought, I propose to define the fundamental characteristics of dwelling as the following:

1. Setting up an inside/outside. Hence, the question of interiority will raise that of visibility.
2. Visibility is the gaze the inhabitant is exposed to: the gaze directed at oneself, the gaze of others upon oneself. Visible and concealed at the same time, the subject gives herself or himself to be seen through her or his practices, her or his mode of insertion in space. Thus, the third characteristic appears.
3. This is *appropriation*, by which is meant that home usage has consequences on one's experience of dwelling. One's inner self

is thus transformed and grows because of one's actions in space (or, in this case, in one's home).

THE INSIDE/OUTSIDE

The question of the shift from "space" to "place" is the question of boundaries, that is, the differentiation and qualification of space. The dwelling is a place in that it is an "inside" as opposed to an "outside," an inside whose boundaries are as many links with the outside. It also is a place in that it always means "generating order." Finally, it is a place because it makes room for being, for dwelling, through the events that constitute the gestures and the human relationships that develop in it. This is why one can say that the question of the shift from "space" to "home-as-place" is the question of "making place" and "taking place."

The home may be represented by the door and the window. Through the door, one gains access at will either to one's intimacy or to the indefinite outside (Simmel, 1976, p. 96). Furthermore, established as a *limit within* ourselves, the door makes us feel the impulse toward freedom. Its beneficial, formative function defines the door as a postulated limit on the level of freedom, or as the accepted limit.

In a different mode, the window continuously ensures the relationship between the inside and the outside. But its finality and its limitations originate in the fact that it is chiefly designed to allow the gaze from the inside toward the outside.

Thus, any "fixed residence" where one has "settled down" is, on the philosophical level, tantamount to an accepted existential situation (Eliade, 1983). In addition, any dwelling possesses or is likely to possess an "opening" making possible the passage into "another world"—that is, the ontological rupture. For Eliade, the symbolic value of the house openings observed in various kinds of habitations proves the "universality and the perenniality of the communication with the other world, the world above" (Eliade, 1983, p. 74), or the world of a personal transcendental experience. Therefore, it is the image value of the openings in the dwelling that is significant for our purposes.

By *house*, Eliade does not mean only the *house-as-temple* and the *house-as-cosmos* but also the *house-as-body*. This homology between the house and human body is indeed to be found in secular (Boughali, 1974; Choay, 1974) and sacred speech (Eliade, 1983) as well as in popular art (Lassus, 1974). It also derives from the polysemy in the French word *intérieur* that in its adjectival form, means *inside* and in its substantival form means either *home* or *the inside* (of something). Finally, this homology is also proposed on the basis of the common etymology between *interior* (i.e., inside) and *intestine*, both of which derive from the Latin adverb *intus* (i.e., "within"). This idea that, on the experiential level, bodily interiority and the inside of the dwelling are identical is reinforced by the complex idea, drawn from Freudian theory, that the self is the body (Freud, 1970), and by Anzieu's concept of the skin-self (*Moi-peau*) (Anzieu, 1974).

THE HIDDEN AND THE VISIBLE

Because any dwelling is closed and open, it conceals me and shows me; it designates me as a unique individual and as a member of a community. It obviously conceals me more or less, depending on my character and personal history, depending on my degree of acceptance of a cultural pattern (Bernard & Jambu, 1978). Nevertheless, the dwelling is essentially what ensures secrecy and visibility: secrecy in closing doors and windows, secrecy in chests and shut closets, secrecy in putting the outside world at a distance; visibility in hospitality and shared meals and in conflicts and contradictory claims. The question of the hidden and the visible in the dwelling, therefore, is the question of the relationship between secrecy and the relationships with others. Goffman's distinction (1973) between *stage* and *backstage* in the home partially sums up these relationships because it designates the home as being simultaneously a visage and a mask.

In a study devoted to the hidden spaces in the dwelling (Korosec-Serfaty, 1984), I have shown that secret knowledge is not a trivial knowledge among a person's other kinds of knowledge and have underscored the etymological kinship between the two words *secret* and *excrement* (Levy, 1976). This kinship is empirically translated in all the gestures that create and reinforce order and tidiness in the home. By these gestures one seeks to substitute a domesticated nature to a certain organic savagery, leading Médam (1977) to characterize the dwelling as "a set of interlocking secrets" (p. 72).

Research by historians (Evans, 1982) as well as by ethnologists (Zonabend, 1980) shows that changes in the physical shape of the dwelling and in material and social conditions affect the meaning of the dwelling and hence modify the dweller's relationship to his or her home. However, even if the historical and social dimensions of home use are taken into account, it is necessary to assume that, in any dwelling, there exists a particular way of establishing the relationship between the "hidden" and the "shown," *whatever the nature of this hidden may be*, for example, women (Bayazit, Yonder, & Öszoy, 1978; Boughali, 1974; Dun-

can, 1982), servants and their hall (Martin-Fugier, 1982), or the body
(Flandrin, 1976). Until recently, in several rural French regions, the main
room (*salle*) constituted the focus of family life, the place where daily
work was planned. Its uses were governed by rigid customs that maintained the distance between the "showable" and "the hidden." In Bour-
gogne, for instance, the uses of the main room followed several rules
concerning the crossing of thresholds, access to other rooms, precedence, generational relationships, and especially right of speech. These
rules also made it imperative to suppress any signs of women's private
lives and to diminish the frequency of the opening of the *salle* toward the
outside (Zonabend, 1980).

In this perspective, the housewife in the Western cultural context is
"the careful warden of a denial" that operates against the organic and
the sexual (Médam, 1977, p. 73). It should, however, be added that the
analysis of secrecy cannot be reduced to this one theme. The stakes
involved in secrecy are the preservation of *identity* (Smirnoff, 1976). To
demand "a full confession," that is, in the case of the home, total availability, openness, and transparency, amounts to demanding a complete
surrender from the dweller. Hidden things and places help to situate the
boundaries of the self and help to gain confidence in one's own capacity
to control one's "inner self" (Margolis, 1976; Korosec-Serfaty, 1984).

The social meaning of secrecy is strength. It is not incidental that, in
European societies for instance, the elite's rules of etiquette imposed a
far-reaching mastery of the body, the voice, the eyes, and facial expressions. As long as one retained one's composure, one retained, in a
way, control of the situation. Similarly, the house interiors had to be
kept fully under control. Domestic practices had to be ritualized, particularly with the help of numerous servants who ensured the status (i.e.,
the mastery of money) and the accessibility of the different territories in
the home (i.e., the mastery of the "inside").

However, by its order, its arrangement, its maintenance, the dwelling is also a facade that expresses hospitality and openness. These care-
taking gestures that we said had ontological value will now be examined.

APPROPRIATION

The concept of *appropriation*, which originates in Marxian thought
(Marx, 1894/1934, pp. 92–104), was used frequently in French urban
sociology research in the 1960s and 1970s (Lefebvre, 1968a,b). Indeed, it
was a concept that was used in general psychology before the notion of

space appropriation was defined (Korosec-Serfaty, 1973, 1975; Graumann, 1978).

Marx viewed work as the primary impulse. The individual reproduces himself or herself through the production of things, which thus constitute

> the actualization of powers or of potentialities which would otherwise remain implicit. . . . Work is reified through products and the producer finds himself faced with objects which are foreign to him unless he appropriates them by means of operations and activities. . . . These operations or activities always coincide with the appropriation of knowledge or know-how, whose real subject is not the individual but society. (Graumann, 1978, p. 121)

However, in all the phases of humanity,

> each man not only appropriates the heritage which has reached him, but experiences, through his own activities, a personal venture of appropriation, i.e., he produces and generates himself. (Leontiev, cited in Graumann, 1978)

Because it partakes of acting and making, appropriation necessarily takes place in a world of modification, alteration, and transformation. It implies that nothing is definitively "given"; on the contrary, the "given" always constitutes the basis for a necessary appropriation.

The Marxian origin of the appropriation concept has frequently led to incorporating in all circumstances, appropriation, ownership, and work. That it is indispensable to resist such generalization (Sansot, 1978) is manifest as soon as proper emphasis is placed on the fact that ownership can occur only where actions leading to appropriation have already taken place. On the other hand, it is true that "work attempts to endow things with a still more significant and more finished form," whereas "appropriation occurs through a progressive transformation of the being" (Sansot, 1978, p. 65). That is, it occurs *in its own way*, in places where reality has already been worked upon by others. Ornamentation, maintenance, and housework (in a home that has seldom been built by the dweller) evidence this drive to appropriate it. Appropriation, however, does not function only by modifying things. It is also at work in all the identification processes that I consent to. Numerous kinds of work do not give rise to appropriation because they are not willingly accepted. This acceptance amounts to investment and, more particularly, bodily involvement. For instance, the city that I cannot transform may be strolled in and appropriated through the fatigue of having walked through it or through the familiarity of routinely walking the same streets (Sansot, 1978, p. 69). Thus, appropriation never is a "by-product" of something else (Raymond, 1978, p. 75) but is always a process that has ontological value in that it coincides with a development and an actualization of the self. However, like the artist or craftsman, one must attain an "active unobtrusiveness" with regard to the things thus appropriated and remain aware that these things are not owned (Sansot, 1973, p. 69).

In this context, what is appropriated is not space or the home but their meaning and the modes of the relationships one establishes with them (Graumann, 1978). The dwelling is arranged, maintained, and modified only when the person has appropriated the significance of the shelter. Similarly, in order to be able to deal with the appropriation of the dwelling, it is necessary to comprehend the whole dwelling experience while keeping in mind that, in a way, things reveal themselves only partially, with much imprecision, trial, and error. The appropriation of the dwelling does not merely amount to what can be directly observed (personalization, maintenance, affective and financial investments), even though all these aspects may be part of it. Thus, personalization, which derives from the need to differentiate (Kron, 1983) and which varies as a function of the individual's financial, cultural, and/or intellectual capital (Bourdieu, 1979), shows that the alteration of the being has been accepted and that the openness of the home has been recognized.

All the gestures through which the home is transformed from *space* into *place* simultaneously introduce the risk that appropriation may break down. Indeed, home appropriation does not occur only through the gestures that modify the dwelling but also in the effects these actions have on the dwelling experience. Consequently, any praxis contains its risk of alienation when it is carried away by its own movement and loses touch with its finality or when the subject no longer wants to invest it with meaning. The tone used in contemporary analyses of domestic or "housewifely" chores is representative in this respect. For instance, after having been said to be satisfying for nearly two centuries, housework is now viewed as alienating (Aron, 1980; Friedan, 1964).

BEING BURGLARIZED

If some credibility is granted to the preceding discussion, there should be consequences when one's dwelling is violated by burglary. In this section, I shall use the phenomenological perspective to elucidate some of the psychological significance of burglary. That is, from the experiential view, how does the person react to this blatant negation of the experience of dwelling? We shall attempt to define, through its dramatization, what is vitally damaged when one is burglarized.

The following analysis is based on data collected during non-directed interviews centered on burglary. Twenty-six adults living with their families and belonging to the upper middleclass were interviewed. All of them had been burglarzied at least once, about a year prior to the interview. The respondents were randomly selected from the official list of burglarized homes, and interviews were then arranged by a subdivision of the city police in Strasbourg, France.

The interviews reveal more than anger, feelings of vulnerability, and grief for the lost things or an increased suspicion after being burglarized. They reveal, in addition, these points, on which we shall focus exclusively:

1. that being burglarized is experienced as being defiled; and
2. that being burglarized causes a specific psychological and affective impact on the person's relationships with others.

DESTRUCTION OF THE INSIDE/OUTSIDE BOUNDARIES

The words used by the respondents and designating burglary as a *rape,* a *violation of privacy,* a *violation of one's universe* underscore the brutality of the rupture of the boundary between the inside and the outside. The door is ultimately protected by its status of boundary, by collective respect for its symbolic value. The metal casing and the safety locks installed after a burglary aim at restating that the dwelling is not accessible to everyone. The dwellers are outspokenly reluctant about these locks, saying that they are ugly, expensive, and too-visible signs of the degradation in social trust. ("One has to be careful . . . that's bad," said one 35-year-old woman.) Yet they also symbolize a code indicating the private character of certain territories (Brown & Altman, 1983; Korosec-Serfaty, 1978; Rapoport, 1982), a code that the burglar appropriates in bypassing it, thus causing the dweller to retreat to two facts: the vulnerability of his or her house interior, and the fragility, or absence of a protecting community, or at least a community that sides with the resident.

THE CONFUSION BETWEEN THE VISIBLE AND THE HIDDEN

The word *rape* moreover emphasizes the articulations of the home experience and the body-as-self. This articulation appears, on the one hand, at the level of *sight* and, on the other hand, at the level of *touch.* Says a 40-year-old man:

They've violated our privacy, these people who broke in here. We tell our-

selves, well they *saw* things which belong to us, which are, well they're our
own little *secrets*, they're not anybody's business; we don't tell them to anyone. That's it, it's this aspect of the thing, rather than what they stole.
(emphasis mine)

This foreign gaze, imposed, loaded with deceit ("we've certainly been
watched"), ransacks what "is nobody's business" and which is generally closed: the boxes, chests, drawers, closets, and "the dressing table,
where you always keep a few things" (60-year-old woman); "letters, the
papers, the photographs, the addresses, the nooks and corners, really
the most private places" (35-year-old woman). This reification through
the gaze (Sartre, 1943) is the more difficult to bear because it goes together with disclosed secrets: "What they can *tell* to others about us after
they're gone [*laughter*]," secrets that they no longer have any hold on
but that may be reused at any time to reinforce the reification: "I mean,
they're people that you can pass in the street, they can recognize us, but
we can't [recognize them]" (35-year-old woman).

The fear of defilement, violation of self and reification, is revealed
by the way the respondents described the burglaries in which there was
neither breakage, soilage, or, sometimes, any disorder. In such cases,
burglary is called *work* and is said to have been "cleanly done" (28-year-
old man). The burglars then "did something which was almost logical . . . well planned, well done . . . it was tidy" (36-year-old man).
This "work" is said to be "clean" because the range of the gaze and of
contact has been mastered and limited to the "necessary": the dweller's
secrecy and identity have not been reached (Korosec-Serfaty, 1984).

APPROPRIATION OF ONE'S DWELLING BY OTHERS

The loss of mastery over the visible/hidden distinction goes together with a feeling of disgust due to a gross, arrogant, imposed contact, as pointed out by the respondents' expressions that describe
burglars as "these people" who "sniff in corners," "poke their nose into
every place," or "put their paws everywhere." The burglar's body is
repulsive because it imposes a shared appropriation of what, by nature,
it might be said, is appropriated individually or by a restricted group:
"Especially that, they rifle through your clothes, through everything
private. I think it hurts a great, great deal" (70-year-old woman). "Dis-
gusting, like for my daughter, they had touched her clothes" (60-year-
old man). This emphasizes one's complete vulnerability: "You tell your-
self, they went into the bedroom, they've been on the beds" (30-year-old
woman). The burglar eats your food that, when shared, symbolizes
hospitality and friendship: "They took ice cream from the freezer and

ate it on the sofa" (60-year-old man). And they use your home as an open, nearly public space: "They used the bathroom" (60-year-old woman). Thus, the burglar "touches" the dweller, by engaging in all the small gestures by which any person appropriates his or her home and his or her body: "The bathroom had been ransacked, that really *hurt* me; there was my makeup: it was open, it had been tried on, it really made me mad" (35-year-old woman).

In this context, the loss of things that in our society are viewed as extensions of personality (Simmel, 1976) and as symbols of self (Graumann, 1974; Korosec-Serfaty, 1984; Rochberg-Halton, 1984), is made more painful because it is associated with the disorder created by the burglar and which amounts to an appropriation of the home through destruction (Graumann & Kruse, 1978; Korosec-Serfaty, 1973, 1975). The disorder created by the dweller remains within the dweller's order because the things and their "order" form a configuration familiar to him or her, made by him or her. Things, thus, are perfect mirrors, reflecting the desired image rather than the real image (Baudrillard, 1968) of the *dweller's own coherence*. The disruption brought about by burglary actualizes the fear of inner fragmentation, this fear that is usually mastered by setting up an order or outer coherence around oneself, that is, in one's dwelling.

RESTORING BOUNDARIES

The interviews reveal extensive concerns about the burglar's personality, identity, and motivations, about the reason why he or she chose the victim personally, an anxiety that appeared the stronger because it sent the dweller back to questioning his or her own identity and his or her relationships with others. The French euphemism *visit* for burglary is one of the forms of denial and dedramatization that seems to enable the dweller to continue to live in the home. Someone who "visits" the home is not (or cannot be) hostile. Among the respondents, the one person who failed to undertake this work of self-reappropriation following a burglary, moved into another apartment on the very next day. This move can be seen as a confession of powerlessness when confronted with identity loss and the burglars' appropriation of the home through invasion. In order to go on living in the home, the dweller must go beyond the questions asked by the three bears in *Goldilocks*, that is, beyond "who sat in my chair?" and reappropriate the home and his or her own identity (Bettelheim, 1976).

In addition to denial, one of the means to this end is laughter, whose purposes and targets are numerous. The analysis of laughter during the interviews shows some of its well-known functions (Victoroff, 1952), among them the cathartic and tension-reducing ones. Thus, we are told about the "visit" made by burglars who did not soil anything but "only" stole money and jewelry: "They might at least have left some flowers for me [*laughter*]" (35-year-old woman). The respondents, thus, reintroduce, on the verbal level, an interaction ritual that civilizes the relationship and reinstates the burglarized dweller's dignity. Burglary was also described as a *relationship*: "It creates *bonds* [*laughter*], direct ones even, but you stay out" (35-year-old woman). Because these bonds exist, it is necessary to reintroduce distance, the separation between the *shown* and *concealed*, to tame the gaze of others so that this relationship may be lived with: "When my son refuses to clean his room, I tell him he ought to do it, if only for the burglars [*laughter*]."

Therefore, to the numerous questions that the dwellers asked themselves—"Who did it? Why pick on me? Why did they steal *and* destroy? What were they looking for?" and so forth—a single answer emerges. Just as rape is not a crime of lust but of violence and power (Brownmiller, 1975), burglary can be seen as not mere stealing but also power acquisition through defilement and identity theft.

IMPLICATIONS FOR FUTURE RESEARCH

In this essay, we have laid out a brief description of key aspects of the phenomenological perspective, defined some directions for the phenomenology of dwelling, and shown how this perspective can be used to elucidate the psychological experience of burglary. Response to burglary represents only one phenomenon that can be examined from a phenomenological orientation, and we shall turn to Bachelard's seminal work (1981) to guide us toward other potential areas. *The Poetics of Space* illustrates at the same time the importance of phenomenology's contribution to the study of dwelling, the problems it raises, and the directions of research that it opens.

Bachelard successfully tackled the themes of the home as a fortifying, enclosing, and secret shelter, as a place for centered intimacy and solitude. His specifically original contribution resides in his project to show that "the house is one of the greatest powers of integration for the thoughts, the memories, and dreams of mankind. The binding principle in this integration is the daydream" (Bachelard, 1981, p. 26). Reverie is the way of access to dwelling. It means experiencing a certain and immediate happiness, and it is triggered by images such as "the nest" that, according to Bachelard, like any image of rest and quiet, is associated with the image of the "simple house" and of the hut as the primal engraving (p. 46).

The first limitation observed in Bachelard's (1981) book derives from the direct transfer of ontological analyses in the realm of value judgments. Heidegger's term *preservation* (p. 175), the experience of dwelling viewed by Bachelard as "being well" (p. 26), Levinas's concept of "self-communion" (p. 125) originating in a "greater kindness to oneself," Liiceanu's analysis of the Greek words that designate dwelling as stability, all of this, understood in the ordinary sense of the words and outside of an ontological context, would give an exceedingly trivial and narrow image of the dwelling, imagined as a single-family house, limited to security, material comfort, and, above all, stability (Cooper, 1976; Marc, 1972). Phenomenology is not betrayed when due emphasis is placed on the cultural variations of the architecture of houses. Although these variations indeed introduce a reflection on the mode of actualization of cultural patterns, they in no way alter the exercise of being in dwelling or being through dwelling (Korosec-Serfaty, 1984).

Another opportunity is illustrated by the Bachelardian refusal to account for those aspects of dwelling that give rise to conflicts. Bachelard (1981) undertakes a topoanalysis based on what he called "topophilia" and that, consequently, is applied to "eulogized" spaces (1981, p. 17). Such an attitude has the potential to stifle any project designed to analyze the negative experiences or conflicts in dwelling. However, these negative experiences deserve great attention precisely because dwelling is neither produced nor experienced in a static way. The preceding analysis of reactions to burglary showed that after the event, subjects had to come to terms with this disruption of experienced mastery over their homes. As we said in the examination of appropriation, burglarized individuals had to be able to project their capacity to dwell elsewhere, so as to avoid being appropriated by the place they inhabited. That is, because any appropriation incurs the risk of its alienation, it is necessary to approach, at the level of subject dynamics, the conflict-provoking aspects inherent in the home experience.

Moreover, any dwelling is a social space and, here as well, phenomenology is not betrayed when the study of dwelling takes into account the fact that the dwelling also features social conflicts and, therefore, negative memories. Acknowledging the fact that conflicts occur permits us to examine the consequences of such conflicts. For example, it is likely that the dwelling is sometimes given up with relief when it is associated with anguish, unhappiness, and so forth.

Bachelard and numerous other authors following him seek to grasp the dwelling experience without bringing in the practices underlying it. Furthermore, several studies devoted to home practices evoked only briefly the effect of uses upon experience and never even raised the question of the ontological relationships between *being* and *doing*, that is, between *dwelling in* and *appropriating* the home.

However, a study that examined attics and cellars in homes (Korosec-Serfaty, 1984) indicated that the appropriation practices related to hidden, dark, and dirty places could result in changes in the designation and characterization of these places. After appropriation, these places were then perceived as capable of being mastered and better integrated into the home. Similarly, Barbey's research (Barbey, 1984; Barbey & Korosec-Serfaty, 1982–84) about writers' rooms shows the articulation of the writer's solitary work to the dwelling experience in these rooms. This points to a fundamental direction for research, which demands an understanding of the interactions between *being* and *doing* as well as of their integration of individual dynamics on the one hand and, on the other hand, to the collective history of a given society.

For things indeed contribute to creating a setting or theatrical universe only because they are produced toward this end by a given economic system. Because things "speak" as symbols, it is "through alienated things that alienation is expressed" (Adorno, 1983, p. 53), an alienation that is revealed by the refusal to admit that the "things" from one's "home interior" are themselves historical and social products of the outside world.

Thus another necessity for future studies on dwelling is illustrated, that is, that of a dialectical approach. This ought to emphasize the dynamic tensions on the one hand between the inside (of the home) and the outside (of the home and the outside world) and, on the other hand, between the subterritories (rooms, kitchens, cellars, garages) that the house is made of, for the dwelling experience is indeed a global one. The experience of the home is an experience of "inside" as well as an experience of the world in which it has its place.

Lastly, Bachelard's (1981) description of full and well-ordered cupboards, chests, and closets should not be understood as a celebration of conventional order in home but as an image that conveys his approach of "felicitous space" (p. 17) and that has complex links with his own culture. Conventional order is defined by social rules. It constitutes a basis and a reference for social communication as well as for expression of the self. But what is perceived as a "disorderly" house by a visitor is not necessarily perceived as such by the inhabitant. As we said earlier, *order* refers ultimately to our relations to the things surrounding us. Thus, this familiar configuration of objects and places deserves to be studied in relation to conventional or socially defined order (Sauer, 1982).

The preceding description of future directions of research for the phenomenology of dwelling encompasses the diverse intentions of the phenomenological endeavor. Therefore, it should help to achieve knowledge of the multiple facets of the home experience as introduced earlier and through this knowledge, to sustain the quest for the unity of meaning that animates the phenomenological activity as a whole.

REFERENCES

Adorno, T. W. Intérieur. *Urbi*, 1983, 7, 48–55. (Reprinted from T. W. Adorno, *Kierkegaard: Konstruktion des Aesthetischen* (Chapter 2). Frankfurt: Suhrkamp, 1962, pp. 75–86.)

Altman, I., & Gauvain, M. A cross-cultural and dialectic analysis of homes. In L. Liben, A. Patterson, & N. Newcombe (Eds.), *Spatial representations and behavior across the life span*. New York: Academic Press, 1982, pp. 283–320.

Anzieu, D. Le moi-peau. *Le dehors et le dedans, Nouvelle Revue de Psychanalyse*, Spring 1974, 9, 195–208.

Aron, J.-P. *Misérable et glorieuse, la femme au XIXe siècle*. Paris: Fayard, 1980.

Bachelard, G. *La poétique de l'espace*. Paris: Presses Universitaires de France, 1981.

Barbey, G. *L'habitation captive: Essai sur la spatialité du logement de masse*. St.-Saphorin, Switzerland: Editions Georgi, 1980.

Barbey, G. *Effets de sublimation dans l'architecture domestique*. Paper presented at the 8th International Association for the Study of People and their Physical Surroundings Conference (IAPS 8), Berlin, 1984.

Barbey, G., & Korosec-Serfaty, P. Une chambre. Etude de la spatialité intime. *Architecture and Behavior*, 1982–1984, 2, 171–182.

Baudrillard, J. *Le système des objets*. Paris: Gallimard, 1968.

Bayazit, N., Yönder, A., & Özsoy, A. B. Three levels of privacy behavior in the appropriation of dwelling spaces in Turkish homes. In P. Korosec-Serfaty (Ed.), *Appropriation of space*. Strasbourg, France: Louis Pasteur University, 1978, pp. 225–264.

Bernard, Y., & Jambu, M. Espace habité et modèles culturels. *Ethnologie Française*, 1978, 8(1), 7–20.

Bettelheim, B. *Psychanalyse des contes de fées*. Paris: Laffont, 1976.

Boudon, P. *Pessac de Le Corbusier*. Paris: Dunod, 1969.

Boughali, M. *La représentation de l'espace chez le Marocain illétré*. Paris: Anthropos, 1974.

Bourdieu, P. *La distinction. Critique social du jugement*. Paris: Editions de Minuit, 1979.

Brown, B., & Altman, I. Territoriality, defensible space, and residential burglary: An environmental analysis. *Journal of Environmental Psychology*, 1983, 3(3), 203–220.

Brownmiller, S. *Against our will: Men, women, and rape*. New York: Bantam Books, 1975.

Buttimer, A. *Values in geography* (Commission on College Geography, Resonance Paper No. 24). Washington, D.C.: Association of American Geographers.

de Certeau, M., Giard, L., & Mayol, P. *L'invention du quotidien: Arts de faire* (Vol. 1), *Habiter, cuisiner* (Vol. 2), Paris: Union Gederale d'Editions, Collection 10–18, 1980.

Choay, F. La ville et le domaine bâti comme corps dans les textes des architectes théoriciens de la Première Renaissance Italienne. *Le dehors et le dedans*, Spring 1974, 9, 239–251.

Chrétien, J. L. De l'espace au lieu. In C. Tacou (Ed.), *Les symboles du lieu. L'habitation de l'homme*. Paris: L'Herne, 1983, pp. 117–138.

Clerc, P. *Grand ensembles et banlieues nouvelles. Enquête démographique et psychologique*. Paris: Presses Universitaires de France, 1967.

Cocâtre, P., Desbons, F., Quan-Schneider, G., Villéla-Petit, M., & Vidal, H. *Problématique du rapport humain à l'espace*. Paris: Institut de l'Environnement et Ministère de l'Equipement, 1977. (Mimeographed)

Cooper, C. The house as symbol of self. In H. M. Proshansky, W. H. Ittelson, & L. G. Rivlin (Eds.), *Environmental psychology*. New York: Holt, Rinehart & Winston, 1976, pp. 435–448.

Csikszentmihalyi, M., & Rochberg-Halton, E. *The meaning of things: Domestic symbols and the self*. Cambridge: Cambridge University Press, 1981.

Duncan, J. S. From container of women to status symbol: The impact of social structure on the meaning of the house. In J. S. Duncan (Ed.), *Housing and identity*. New York: Holmes & Meier, 1982, pp. 36–54.

Ekambi-Schmitt, J. *La perception de l'habitat*. Paris: Editions Universitaires, 1972.

Eliade, M. Architecture sacrée et symbolisme. In C. Tacou (Ed.), *Les symboles du lieu. L'habitation de l'homme*. Paris: L'Herne, 1983, pp. 96–100.

Evans, R. Figures, portes et passage. *Urbi*, April 1982, *5*, 23–41.

Flandrin, J. L. *Familles, parenté, maison, sexualité dans l'ancienne société*. Paris: Hachette, 1976.

Freud, S. *Le moi et le ça: Essai de psychanalyse*. Paris: Payot, 1970.

Friedan, B. *La femme mystifiée*. Paris: Gonthier, 1964.

Gauldie, E. *Cruel habitations: A history of working class housing 1780–1918*. London: Allen & Unwin, 1974.

Gleichman, P. R. Des villes propres et sans odeur: La vidange du corps humain; ses équipements et sa domestication. *Urbi*, April 1982, *5*, 88–100.

Goffman, E. *La mise en scène de la vie quotidienne*. Paris: Editions de Minuit, 1973.

Grange, J. On the way towards foundational ecology. *Soundings*, 1977, *60*, 135–149.

Graumann, C. F. Psychology and the world of things. *Journal of Phenomenological Psychology*, 1974, *4*, 389–404.

Graumann, C. F. The concept of appropriation (Aneignung) and the modes of appropriation of space. In P. Korosec-Serfaty (Ed.), *Appropriation of space*. Strasbourg, France: Louis Pasteur University, 1978, pp. 113–125.

Graumann, C. F. *Phénoménologie, psychologie et la recherche écologique*. Lecture given at the Institute of Psychology, Louis Pasteur University, Strasbourg, 1979. (Mimeographed)

Hansen, W. B., & Altman, I. Decorating personal places: A descriptive analysis. *Environment and Behavior*, 1976, *8*, 491–504.

Haumont, N. *Les pavillonaires*. Paris: Centre de Recherche d'Urbanisme, 1975.

Haumont, N., & Raymond, H. *Habitat et pratique de l'espace: Etude des relations entre l'intérieur et l'exterieur du logement*. Paris: Institut de Sociologie Urbaine, 1975. (Mimeographed)

Hayward, G. D. Home as an environmental psychological concept. *Landscape*, 1975, *20*(1), 2–9.

Heidegger, M. *Essais et conférences*. Paris: Gallimard, 1958.

Heidegger, M. *Être et temps*. Paris: de Walhens, 1964.

Heller, G. *Propre en ordre. Habitation et vie domestique 1850–1930: l'exemple vaudois*. Lausanne: Editions d'En Bas, 1979.

Husserl, E. *Recherches logiques* (Vols. 1–4). Paris: Presses Universitaires de France, 1959–1963.

Ion, J. Détermination historique et sociale des pratiques d'habitat. *Annales de la Recherche Urbaine*. Special issue: *Vie quotidienne en milieu urbain*. Paris: Centre de Recherche d'Urbanisme, 1980, pp. 61–68.

Jacquier, C., & Jantet, A. *Transformanions de leurs logements par les habitants: Déterminants sociaux et processus de production*. Grenoble: Groupe d'Etudes Urbaines, 1976. (Mimeographed) (Available from GETUR, 3, Place aux Herbes, 38000 Grenoble, France).

Korosec-Serfaty, P. The case of newly constructed zones: Freedom, constraint and the appropriation of space. In R. Kuller (Ed.), *Architectural psychology*. Stroudsburg, Penn.: Dowden, Hutchinson, & Ross, 1973, pp. 389–396.

Korosec-Serfaty, P. Comment définir le concept d'appropriation de l'espace? *Bulletin de la Société Française de Sociologie*, 1975, 2(5), 24–26.

Korosec-Serfaty, P. Formes de l'accueil et du rejet dans l'habitat: Fonctions et statut de l'entrée d'immeuble. *Neuf. Revue Européenne d'Architecture*, September 1978, 76, 25–32.

Korosec-Serfaty, P. *Une maison a soi: Déterminants psychologiques et sociaux de l'habitat individuel*. Strasbourg: Department for Economic and Statistical Surveys of the French Ministry of the Environment, 1979.

Korosec-Serfaty, P. The home, from attic to cellar. *Journal of Environmental Psychology*, 1984, 4(4), 172–179.

Kron, J. *Home psych. The social psychology of home and decoration*. New York: C. N. Potter, 1983.

Kruse, L. *Privatheit*. Bern: Hans Huber, 1980.

Lassus, B. De plus à moins: Les habitants paysagistes. *Le dehors et le dedans, Nouvelle Revue de Psychanalyse*, Spring 1974, 9, 253–268.

Lefebvre, H. *Le droit à la ville* (suivi de) *Espace et politique*. Paris: Anthropos, 1968. (a)

Lefebvre, H. *La vie quotidienne dans le monde moderne*. Paris: Gallimard, 1968. (b)

Leontiev, A. M. Probleme der Entwicklung oles Psychischen, cited in C. F. Graumann. The concept of appropriation and the modes of appropriation of space. In P. Korosec-Serfaty (Ed.), *Appropriation of space*. Strasbourg: Louis Pasteur University, 1978.

Leroy, C., Bedos, F., & Berthelot, C. *Appropriation de l'espace par les objets*. Paris: Direction Générale de la Recherche Scientifique et Technique, 1971.

Levy, A. Evaluation étymologique et sémantique du mot "secret." *Du Secret, Nouvelle Revue de Psychanalyse*, Autumn 1976, 14, 117–129.

Liiceanu, G. Repères pour une herméneutique de l'habitation. In C. Tacou (Ed.), *Les symboles du lieu. L'habitation de l'homme*. Paris: L'Herne, 1983, pp. 105–116.

Lévinas, E. *Totalité et infini: Essai sur l'extériorité*. The Hague: Martinus Nijhoff, 1961.

Lugassy, F. The spatialization of identity supported by the body image and the dwelling. In P. Korosec-Serfaty (Ed.), *Appropriation of space*. Strasbourg: Louis Pasteur University, 1978, pp. 300–309.

Marc, O. *Psychanalyse de la maison*. Paris: Seuil, 1972.

Margolis, C. J. Identité et secret. *Du secret. Nouvelle Revue de Psychanalyse*, Special issue: Autumn 1976, 14, 131–140.

Martin-Fugier, A. *La place des bonnes: La domesticité féminine à Paris en 1900*. Paris: Fayard, 1982.

Marx, K. *Morceaux choisis*. Paris: Gallimard, 1934. (Originally, published, 1893.)

Mauss, M. *Sociologie et anthropologie*. Paris: Presses Universitaires de France, 1950.

Mazerat, B. Appropriation and social classes. In P. Korosec-Serfaty (Ed.), *Appropriation of space*. Strasbourg: Louis Pasteur University, 1978, pp. 247–254.

Médam, A. Habiter en famille. *De la construction de l'espace á l'espace de la creation. Cahiers de Psychologie de l'Art et de la Culture*, Autumn 1977, 2, 61–75. (Available from Ecole

Nationale Supérieure des Beaux Arts. Sections d'Arts Plastiques—17, Quai Mala-
     quais—75005 Paris, France).
Merleau-Ponty, M. *Phenomenology of perception.* London: Routledge & Kegan Paul, 1967.
Murard, L., & Zylberman, P. Le petit travailleur infatigable ou le prolétaire régénéré.
     [Villes-usines, habitat et intimités au XIXè siècle.] *Recherches,* 1976, *25.*
Norberg-Schulz, C. *Genius loci: Towards a phenomenology of architecture.* London: Academy
     Editions, 1980.
Palmade, J. *La dialectique du logement et de son environment.* Paris: French Ministry of the
     Environment, 1970. (Mimeographed.)
Perrot, P. L. *Le travail des apparences.* Paris: Seuil, 1984.
Pratt, G. The house as an expression of social worlds. In J. S. Duncan (Ed.), *Housing and
     identity: A cross-cultural perspective.* New York: Holmes & Meire, 1982, pp. 135–180.
Proshansky, H. M., Fabian, A. K., & Kaminoff, R. Place identity: Physical world and
     socialization of the self. *Journal of Environmental Psychology.* March 1983, *3,* 57–83.
Rapoport, A. *The meaning of the built environment.* London: Sage, 1982.
Raymond, H. Some practical and theoretical aspects of the appropriation of space. In P.
     Korosec-Serfaty (Ed.), *Appropriation of space.* Strasbourg: Louis Pasteur University,
     1978, pp. 70–77.
Rochberg-Halton, E. Object relations, role models, and cultivation of the self. *Environment
     and Behavior,* 1984, *16,* 355–368.
Sansot, P. *Poétique de la ville.* Paris: Klincksieck, 1973.
Sansot, P. Notes on the concept of appropriation. In P. Korosec-Serfaty (Ed.), *Appropriation
     of space.* Strasbourg: Louis Pasteur University, 1978, pp. 67–65.
Sartre, J. P. *L'être et le néant.* Paris: Gallimard, 1943.
Sauer, L. *Design and values.* Paper presented at the 2nd Environmental Psychology Sym-
     posium, University of California, Irvine, Social Ecology Program, 1982.
Seamon, D. The phenomenological contribution to environmental psychology. *Journal of
     Environmental Psychology,* June 1982, *2,* 119–194.
Servais, E., & Lienard, G. Inhabited space and class ethos. In P. Korosec-Serfaty (Ed.),
     Appropriation of space. Strasbourg: Louis Pasteur University, 1978, pp. 240–246.
Simmel, G. La société secrète. *Du Secret. Nouvelle Revue de Psychanalyse,* Autumn 1976, *16,*
     281–305.
Simmel, G. Pont et porte. In C. Tacou (Ed.), *Les symboles du lieu L'habitation de l'homme.*
     Paris: L'Herne, 1983, pp. 96–100.
Smirnoff, V. N. Le squelette dans le placard. *Du Secret. Nouvelle Revue de Psychanalyse,*
     Autumn, 1976, *14,* 27–53.
Spiegelberg, H. *The phenomenological movement* (Vols. 1, 2). The Hague: Martinus Nijhoff,
     1960.
Verret, M. *L'espace ouvrier.* Paris: Colin, 1979.
Victoroff, D. *Le rire et le risible.* Paris: Presses Universitaires de France, 1952.
Villéla-Petit, M. L'espace chez Heidegger: Quelques repères. *Les Etudes Philosophiques,*
     1981, *2,* 189–210.
Zonabend, F. *La mémoire longue.* Paris: Presses Universitires de France, 1980.

4

The Ritual Establishment of Home

DAVID G. SAILE

*Slowly it is becoming our house. With each new coat of paint,
each box unpacked, each tile set into place, we begin to feel our
presence in its past. . . . We treat the house, the house which is
slowly becoming ours, with some respect. We, after all, have
moved into it. It may be our new house, but we are its
newcomers. . . . Yes, other families have settled here, other lives
have been played out here. But now it is our time. We renovate,
renew this structure, make changes. Slowly it is becoming ours.*

—Goodman, 1982, p. 5

INTRODUCTION

The theme of this essay is centered upon ritual processes involved in the
transformation of inert physical and spatial fabric into living, participating, and richly experienced home places. Through such rituals not only
is the physical environment transformed but so too are the human participants and their relationships with the changed place. This theme

DAVID G. SAILE • School of Architecture and Urban Design, University of Kansas, Lawrence, Kansas 66045. This investigation was partially supported by an award from the
General Research Fund, University of Kansas, Summer 1983.

emerged from my studies of Pueblo house-building procedures and, although these studies focused upon the Pueblo world during the past 100 years, there appear to be lessons for learning about homes in other cultures and times (Saile, 1977, 1985).

This essay looks at studies that illuminate repeatable, cyclical, ritual activities that reinforce and support home environments. The more detailed Pueblo findings, the examples from other societies, and reflections on this ritual theme by other scholars allow a glimpse of fundamental processes in human habitation. In the Pueblo case, and perhaps in all cultures, these fundamental processes are integrated with and regulated by cycles of the seasons, of the regional biosystem, and of the human life span.

A whole series of procedures is prescribed to be performed in relation to the home. They may occur at ground breaking, topping out, or at house warming. They may occur at birthdays, weddings, or funerals. They may mark special community or religious occasions. They institute and mark rhythms of behavioral adjustment and recurrent religious significance. Humans are rhythmic animals (Rykwert, 1982), and their making of dwelling places both reflects and constitutes their rhythmic patterns.

The first section of the essay makes some initial comparisons of rites associated with homes. It uses available cross-cultural surveys and illustrates a range of ritual activities. House construction and dedication rites, home festivals, family rituals, and domestic routines are outlined here to indicate their possible contributions to the qualitative shift toward, or reaffirmation of, home place. The second section discusses aspects of ritual process and uses selected ethnographic, theological, and anthropological studies to outline the nature of rituals and the roles that they can assume.

The third section is a summary of two case studies. The first outlines the purpose and nature of rituals that accompanied house construction as described in the ethnographic literature about the Pueblo villages of the southwestern United States. The rituals were believed to help tie the lives of the residents to the healthy and strong life of the fabric of the houses. They also enabled houses and other buildings to become legitimate and participating members of the Pueblo world system. These processes of becoming echo the findings in many studies of home places in which all kinds of residences in many cultures come to possess a sense of home. The case of the dual reciprocating dwelling system of the Eskimo is used to discuss social rhythms, cycles of habitation and calendric reaffirmation of homes. Some suggestions for further study are made in a brief final section.

RITUALS OF THE HOME

This section of the essay looks at those aspects of ritual associated with the establishment of homes in different cultures. Notions of home are explored in detail in other essays of this volume and many of these explorations make distinctions between the experienced, valued and familiar home place and the less-embraced fabric of house, town or landscape. The focus of this essay, therefore, is upon procedures which accompany those qualitative shifts occuring when individuals, families and groups form especially meaningful ties with their places of habitation, their "existential footholds" in the world (Norberg-Schulz, 1980, p. 5). Making a home is equated here with this process. This brief survey of such procedures may appear to take descriptions of activities out of their cultural contexts. This is, of course, misleading. The activities can only be fully understood with reference to their contexts. The intention in this survey is to introduce the kinds and extent of home-related rituals and descriptions of cultural context are necessarily brief. In the third section of this essay activities involved in the making and re-making of homes in two cultures, Pueblo and Eskimo, are described in more detail and with fuller reference to the social, religious and environmental constructs of their respective worlds.

There are widespread descriptions of ritual behaviors involved in the choosing of "auspicious" house sites, with laying foundations and constructing roofs, and with house thresholds and first occupation (Eliade, 1958; Raglan, 1964; Rossbach, 1983; Rykwert, 1976, 1982; Trumbull, 1896).

In addition to rites such as these that are directed *toward* dwellings and that include house building, house warming, and spring cleaning, there are others that are prescribed to be, and whenever possible are, dwelling related or home based. In the contemporary United States these might include Thanksgiving meals, July 4th celebrations, birthdays, and some religious celebrations such as Christmas. There are still others that simply occur frequently in dwellings but that may occur in other habitations (such as hotels and campsites) and other situations. These might include greeting invited guests, personal hygiene and sleep routines, and the daily organization of food preparation and consumption (Browne, 1980).

The most obvious "making" of home occurs through construction, and we will see that in the Pueblo world this construction activity and its rituals are both practical and religious. Territory is also made safe, habitable, and ordered through similar prescribed procedures.

When the Scandinavian colonists took possession of Iceland and cleared it for settling, they looked upon this as the repetition of a primordial act—the transformation of chaos into a cosmos by the divine act of creation. (Eliade, 1960, p. 361)

The need to live in an ordered and consecrated microcosm is expressed by many peoples. Rituals at boundary markers, at gateways, at centers of territories and incorporated into the making or clearing of land fix and make known the order and extent of the habitable region. In some cases the act of clearing constitutes the ritual:

To ring something around is a persistent theme of Ndembu ritual; it is usually accompanied by the process of making a clearing by hoe. In this way a small realm of order is created in the formless milieu of the bush. (Turner, 1969, p. 23)

In other cases, rituals accompany the clearing and preparing of sites for human occupancy (Rykwert, 1976).

Lord Raglan also used the abundant evidence of rituals at the boundaries of territories and at the foundation of cities, villages, and houses to state that all these bounded areas were "islands of sanctity in a profane world. Temples, palaces and houses are inner sanctuaries within the outer sanctuaries, that is to say the towns and villages" (Raglan, 1964, p. 25). Rituals for Raglan were evidence of the sacred or of connections with the power of a cosmic order. He found that even in the mid-20th century houses were not purely secular in many parts of the world and that they appear to have been certainly more sacred in older times. As evidence he cited sacrifices, rituals, offerings, altars, fire and flames, ancestors' images and ancestor objects, spirits of the hearth, house shrines, spirits in the floor, four corners and threshold, and sometimes burials in houses (Raglan, 1964, pp. 9–13).

Ritual procedures connected the construction of Pueblo dwellings with the order and power of the Pueblo world. These ritual connections are not unique to the Pueblos. The Amarasi house of Indonesian Timor was ritually constructed and was a ritual center. The traditional house expressed social and political order through the names of parts of the house and their forms. Furthermore, Cunningham found that

the references extend beyond the social order: space and time, man and animals, man and plants, and man and supernatural are conceived to be ordered by principles related to those expressed in the house, and symbols involving all of these occur in the house. (1964, pp. 66–67)

Proper dwellings have these connections, and in many cases the house is not "real" or "right" unless these links are firmly made. A residence should provide suitable spaces for household activities and should be structurally and climatically sound, but it becomes a home, a "true house," through ritual links. For the Mehinaku of the Amazonian Basin of Brazil, the proper house had to be built according to a traditional pattern, and, as Thomas Gregor found, this "true house, *pai*, has a higher status than other buildings because it is built collectively, often in the name of a spirit or village chief" (1977, p. 56). Prescribed building procedures, written and spoken prayers, and offerings help make houses suitable for residents by associating house and residents with both cosmic and social powers (Eliade, 1969, p. 39; Hildburgh, 1908; Littlejohn, 1960; Raglan, 1964; Trumbull, 1896; van Gennep, 1908/1960).

Although in the modern Western world there are fewer explicit connections between home and religious organization, there are repeated procedures for bringing places of habitation into the realm of social order. In cementing relations with friends and in bringing a new residence into a social network, many North Americans hold some form of house warming. The greater the status involved the more likely are formal rituals for this "first" welcome of guests to the home. About 10 years ago I went to a wedding in rural Wisconsin. In one day prior to the ceremony, relatives and friends traveled from far and near and finished constructing the body and roof of the couple's house. Materials and labor were exchanged for meals and a night-time party. The first stage in the formation of this home was thereby made, and the house became a focus of social cohesion and a reiteration of proper house forms, craftsmanship, and family dealings and reciprocities.

Such procedures are explicitly connected with forming the home and play roles in changing ways in which it is regarded. Other rituals reaffirm and add to the significance of home because the home is the prescribed site or place of their enactment. Home place endows the ritual with meaning just as the ritual endows the home with meaning. For example, much home-based ritual, led by religious specialists, occurs in the Navajo family hogan in the southwestern United States. "The hogan is considered as the house or home given to the Navajos by the gods . . . the hogan also is linked to rites of passage, bad times, illness and death" (Crumrine, 1964, p. 44; C. Mindeleff, 1898). The hogan has orientations, spaces, materials, and details that are essential for certain ceremonies. The hogan also has distinct functional, social, and sexual spatial divisions for daily activities and social communication. There is evidence of a long history and widespread occurrence of an identical "sexual, honorific, and ceremonial subdivision of interior space" among traditional houses of Siberia and other Eurasian groups in addition to other North American Athapaskan groups (Jett & Spencer, 1981, p. 23). The hogan is considered properly built and beautiful insofar as it follows the traditional pattern. It becomes a proper and harmonious home through blessings at initial construction, but its importance as home is reinforced through recurrent ceremony (Haile, 1942; C. Mindeleff, 1898).

In some form this reinforcement has wide currency in many home environments. There are many festivals, anniversaries, and celebrations that are meant to be enacted in the home. These may be related to shared religious beliefs or social expectations or may be unique to a family or group. In the United States, many families prepare a Thanksgiving meal at home. Family members are expected to return at least for this meal if not for a longer holiday. Such is the case for Christmas celebrations and for July 4th. Meals, some parts prescribed, others by choice, or other food preparation and consumption rituals are frequently essential components of the events. A study of the social communicative aspects of meals is required as a part of a graduate course in the Built Form and Culture Studies Program in Architecture at the University of Kansas. In these studies, meals are found to be continuing markers of social relations and position, of status changes, of seasonal change, and of spiritual connections. Many are intimately related with the home and are meticulously prescribed. In all cases, aspects of the setting are also prescribed, and there are complex sequences and relationships among seating arrangements, displays, decorations, appropriate dress, and the use of particular rooms or furniture.

These patterns of setting and ritual are often the framework on which memories of home places are located. In a study of autobiographies from the first half of the 20th century in the United States, Bossard and Boll describe recollections of home in this way: "they seem to recall most easily, and remember as the basic reality of their home life, those things which were habitual to it, even though they may think of them as one certain occasion" (1950, p. 35).

The researchers studied family rituals in autobiographies and found at least one third of the descriptions dealt with religious activities, holidays and anniversaries, family recreation, and homecoming (Bossard & Boll, 1950). These celebratory rituals can reinforce the feeling of home by distinguishing home events from an outside range of activities for work or vacation. Buttimer describes home as a secure and familiar base from which people explore their world, physically and psychologically, and to which they return for rest, regeneration, and sense of self-identity. She suggests that our notions of place depend upon "a *home* and *horizons of reach* outward from that home. The lived reciprocity of rest and movement, territory and range, security and adventure, housekeeping and husbandry" (1980, p. 170). Celebrations can reinforce this home base by marking the occasions of return and departure. In our culture there are differences in the expected roles and time sequences of men and women away from the home, and this might mean differences in their notions of home and their homecoming rituals (Tognoli, 1979, pp. 604–606).

Bossard and Boll's study also described other home-based rituals in addition to celebrations. Their data were gathered from more than 400 families, and they indicated a range of categories of ritual. For many families the meal was highly ritualized, and there were many rules for serving, seating, and eating.

> In our own family, father and mother sat side by side behind the tea-tray at the top of the table; in theirs, grandfather sat at one end and grandmother with her tea-urn at the other end of a very long table. It was with astonishment that we saw how differently grandfather drank his tea or ate cake; we, in our manners lifted the cup from the saucer, and left the saucer on the table; but grandfather lifted both together. (Kendon, 1930, p. 100, in Bossard & Boll, 1950, p. 36)

In public, or with friends at home, such rules come under the general heading of etiquette. Rituals also regulated and demonstrated appropriate behavior of children in relation to parents, relatives, other nonkin adults, and in relation to appropriate spaces and objects. Patterns were also made for, and from, the routines of child care. In addition to celebrations like birthdays, other family changes and cycles were also ritualized (Bossard & Boll, 1950).

Do these social and family interaction rituals in a household contribute to the establishment of home? Certainly, they seem connected with the "rightness" of home life. Bossard and Boll spoke of "deep emotional coloring" (1950, p. 58) and of feelings of pride and attachment to ritual forms and settings. However, not all home rituals are remembered with warmth; the Hare family rituals included

> holiday—Christmas: inappropriate presents from family with necessary show of gratitude from child; usual pastimes cleared away; required to sit for hours reading Foxe's *Book of Martyrs*; two 8-mile walks to church. (Bossard & Boll, 1950, p. 47)

The atmosphere of sanctity of the family home is mentioned in this North American study and in examples from other cultures (Raglan, 1964; Rapoport, 1982). For example, the Mayo house of northwestern Mexico is considered a haven; it is a place where certain things are kept secret through behavioral and spatial rules; and it is a place sanctified by the cumulation of house-related rituals and ritual objects (Crumrine, 1977, pp. 110–120).

Adjustment to house environments also entails developing some smooth habits for everyday survival. These routines may be integrated with rituals of family and social interaction, like those of greeting and parting, but may also be individually prescribed "ways of doing things" in the kitchen, workshop, or other domestic spaces. In making a home in the United States many choices about house color, furniture, and domestic activity are made with reference to patterns experienced in childhood (Tognoli & Horwitz, 1982). The sense of home in descriptions in residential histories was frequently "compared and contrasted with their childhood home" (Horwitz & Tognoli, 1982). Sometimes this involved using elements "based on values diametrically opposed to their family of origin," but in other cases making home "might include actually keeping furniture which was originally in the parents' or grandparents' house, or it might simply involve repeating familiar household patterns and routines" (Tognoli & Horwitz, 1982, p. 322). In both cases familiar objects and routines were involved in definitions of home.

Celebrations that have some formality and that are more connected with social or religious power or behaviors that infringe social rules may focus attention on these everyday routines, but for the most part they are undertaken habitually and unconsciously. This relaxation of attention is also considered a component of the feeling of "at-homeness." In studying the habitual nature of everyday activities, Seamon suggests that some senses of being at home derive from familiar, taken-for-granted activities (1979). People at home do not have to think about what they are doing all the time; they can just do things and be "themselves." Once patterns of mutual adjustment with dwellings are established and unselfconscious, they are persistent. A conscious effort is needed to change them. In one of Seamon's study groups using phenomenological methods, one member described how he forgot to replace a clean dish towel and "when he washed dishes he found himself reaching for the towel, even though a few minutes before he had already looked and not found it there" (Seamon, 1980, p. 153). When smooth routines contribute to the feeling of being in control of the residential environment, they also seem to contribute to the feeling of being at home (Tognoli & Horwitz, 1982, p. 326).

At many levels, therefore, this range of prescribed and repeatable activities contributes to the making of homes. Ritual activities transform or reaffirm the nature of homes in cyclical or periodic ways. They make manifest and transmit ideas of family, society, and home through the generations. They relate the home and residents to broader notions of order, and the home is given power by more formal ritual association with the powers of the world. This introduction has touched upon a few examples of studies in which ritual has accompanied the qualitative change of residential environment into a more embraced home.

ASPECTS OF RITUAL PROCESS

If ritual is indeed contributing in some ways to the establishment of home, in what ways does it function? It will be valuable to briefly examine the nature of rituals in various situations and the roles that they can assume. In this essay it is not so important to define ritual as it is to point to important aspects of the process. Some kind of framework, however, is necessary to come to terms with the broad range of rituals that have been indicated in the foregoing pages. The following seven aspects have been selected from ethnographic, theological, and anthropological studies and appear to be important in understanding the nature of ritual process. They are my personal condensations of findings and ideas in many works, but they are particularly supported by evidence in the Pueblo and Eskimo case studies described later. Observations on these seven aspects are followed by suggestions for clarifying and mapping different classes of rituals and their roles.

1. Rituals refer to a wide range of *prescribed* behaviors including recitation, gestures, sequences of actions, and large dramatic ceremonials (Bossard & Boll, 1950; Douglas, 1973; Moore & Myerhoff, 1977). They may be prescribed explicitly and formally through rules and force of law or may be prescribed more informally by custom.

2. If they are prescribed, they are also therefore *repeatable,* and there are always rules for at least the performance of core actions and roles. The knowledge of rules is therefore shared from ritual event to ritual event at least by a small number of participants and often by a much wider group. Rituals are normally repeated but not in all cases (Colson, 1977), and they appear to be *intended to be performed cyclically,* but this is not always achieved.

3. Most, if not all, rituals have purposes related to *transformation and modification* or to *reaffirmation and renewal.* They are concerned with an individual person's or a group's joining, changing, becoming, marking, leaving, and rejoining in terms of state, status, or power (Duncan & Duncan, 1976; Firth, 1972; Turner, 1969, 1977; van Gennep, 1908/1960). This transformation or reaffirmation may affect a position in a family, in a broader social or political system, or in a cosmico-religious scheme. "Position" here is influenced by power regardless of whether it is religious or secular. Periodic reaffirmation and renewal echoes other

rhythms; for example, midwinter rituals for rebirth of the new year and renewal of living things, life–status ritual transitions reoccurring in family cycles from generation to generation, and toiletry rituals related to the cycles of day and night, workweek, and weekend.

4. Both the order and the actions of ritual are *related to a larger network of order*. They both refer to a framework of categories for dealing with each other as humans and with living in the world. There may be particular emphases, but all rituals nonetheless are concerned with relations among individual, group, culture, and world (Deal & Kennedy, 1982; Douglas, 1966; Eliade, 1954; Gluckman, 1962). The framework of categories to which they refer involves orders of meaning, of space, and of continuity. Rituals often refer to an historical framework or to a presumed history.

5. Rituals are media of communication for the groups and individuals who perform and witness them. They *make sense* or *seem right* and often throw other activities into significant perspective (Firth, 1970, 1973; Goffman, 1967). A useful analogy is with the organization of popular songs with verse and chorus. The structure of the song *and* the repeated chorus carry the important messages. The (ritual) chorus shows the verse in perspective; the verse indicates variations on, or enriches, the ideas of the chorus. This is also much like vacations and weekends providing a refreshing (at least different) perspective on the daily routine. Some rituals are more meaningful than others, and the ritual pattern, as opposed to content, appears to be important in this regard (see No. 6). Although rituals are normally repetitive, they are not exactly so. Those of social interaction especially are full nuances and not-quite-rightnesses so that when a full program of ritual is seen to be carefully enacted it all seems "right" (like returning to harmony in music).

6. Rituals make things, places, persons, and powers *manifest*. They act as markers and indicators of social position and change. They contribute to the constitution of the social system and reinforce the frameworks of order of a society and its ordering of the world (see No. 4). Ritual form makes things and ideas manifest as much as its content or explanation. As Douglas has pointed out in speaking of the ritual forms of the Dinka:

> It is form indeed, but inseparable from content, or rather there could be no content without it. It is appearance, but there is no other reality. Public rituals, by establishing visible external forms, bringing out of all the possible might-have-beens a firm social reality. (1982, p. 36)

Consumption rituals manifest social positions; status requires the learning of appropriate rituals. Position in space contributes to the nature of ritual; ritual makes space significant by "setting it apart" and contributing to its qualitative differentiation from surrounding space (Rapoport, 1982).

7. *The greater the manifest power,* secular or religious, *the greater the tendency for formality* and exact prescription. Such increase occurs especially during those states of rituals most directly and explicitly concerned with transformation and reaffirmation of that power. Ritual forms are less questionable the closer they are to the seat of power and order (Ferguson & Mills, 1978; Firth & Spillius, 1963). Conversely, the less the associated power or "spiritual capital" (Douglas, 1982) the more informal the ritual acts may be, the more like customary behavior and the more open they may become to popular question and variation. Apprehended power is equated here with the term *spiritual capital.* Douglas includes four kinds of capitals under this heading—cultural capital, social capital, symbolic capital, and honorific capital. "It is convenient to think of holdings in those four kinds of capital as spiritual resources; combined with economic resources they form a personal patrimony" (1982, p. 129).

Aspects 1, 2, and 7 are really characteristics of rituals, whereas aspects 3 and 6 are roles or purposes of rituals. Relationships between these characteristics and roles are diagrammed in Figure 1. As the foregoing paragraphs describe and the diagram illustrates, a major relationship between characteristics and roles is affected by power or *spiritual capital.* All these aspects of ritual have direct implications for this discussion of the making of home. They deal with changes in the qualitative nature of space and residents or participants. They are concerned with human attachments to places and groups and with the performance of appropriate roles in a broader society. No distinction is made here between the natures of *primitive* ritual and the rites of the corporate boardroom. Neither is there a clear division between prescribed religious behavior and other prescribed behaviors. There are, however, some differences in the scope of relations that those rituals possess and in their degree of formality.

Figure 2 is a map or chart that can clarify these differences in scope of relations and in formality. The vertical axis of the chart indicates association of a ritual with increasing social or supernatural power. It also indicates increasing formality and exactness in prescription (No. 7). Examples of house-related rituals are arranged in this order to the right-hand side of the chart. The body of the chart indicates the relationships and roles of house-related ritual (or any ritual). At higher degrees of formality, rituals possess a larger component dealing with greater power and with broader human roles in the world, but they also possess an

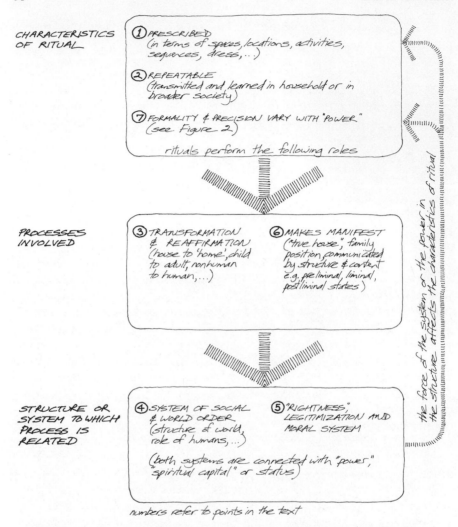

Figure 1. A diagram of relationships between characteristics and roles of rituals.

informal, implicit component; it is smaller perhaps but is always present. With less associated power and formality, rituals possess a more local focus, perhaps an individual behavioral adjustment to the dwelling, and are more connected with individual and social communication. Conversely, they are also related to sanctity and the broader cultural order but to a lesser degree.

It will now be valuable to look at the two case studies that illustrate this scheme and from which the theme of this essay was derived.

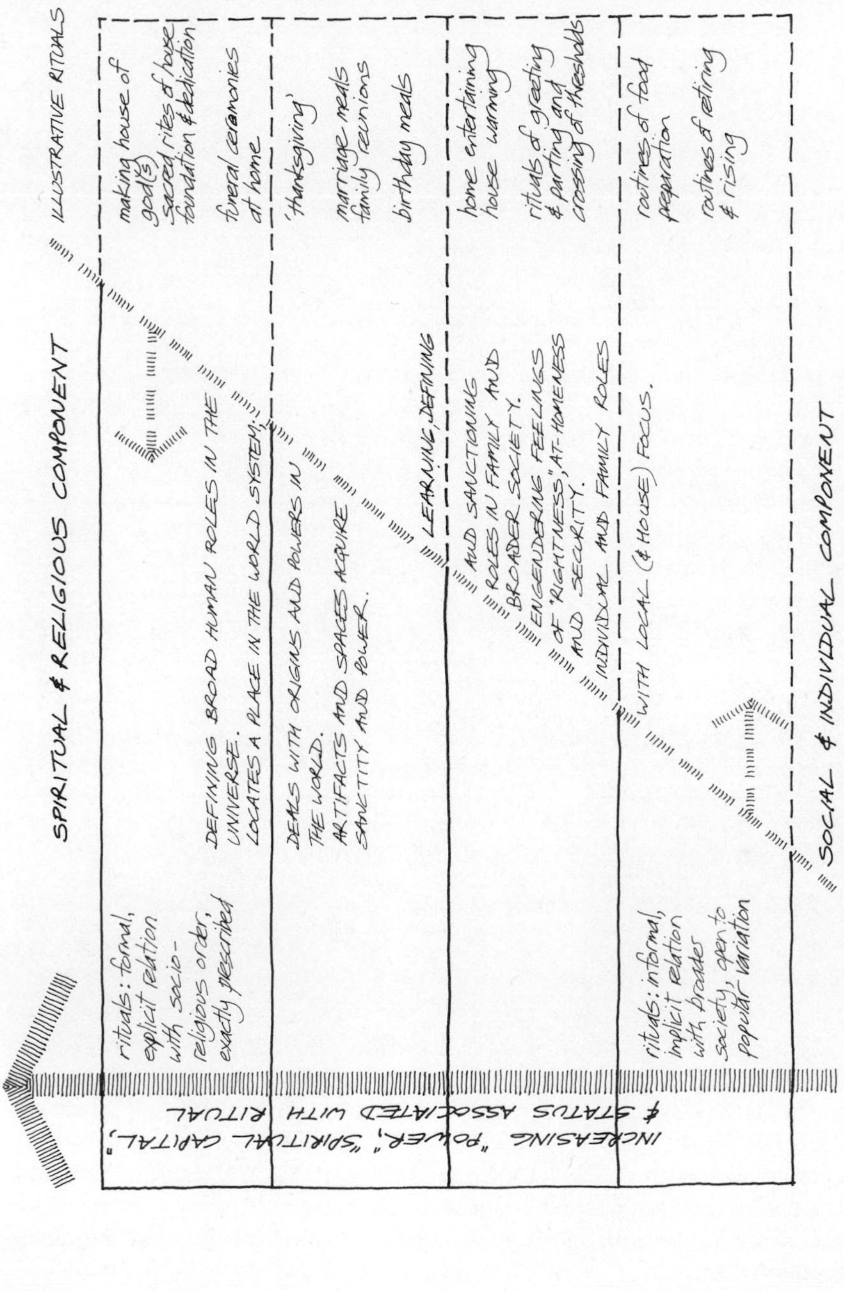

Figure 2. Variation of house-related rituals with power.

HOUSEBUILDING RITUALS IN THE PUEBLOS

All spaces in the Pueblo world had everyday, useful, and observable attributes and were suffused with spiritual and supernatural attributes and associations (Bunzel, 1932; Ortiz, 1969, 1972; Parsons, 1939; White, 1962). Certain places, however, were potentially much more powerful and dangerous than others. This power derived from supernaturals who resided in the spiritual strata of the world. These strata lay both above and below the semiarid earth's surface where the Pueblo people lived their mortal lives.

Places on the earth's surface that allowed access to the upper and lower levels were therefore potentially very powerful (Saile, 1977). Such places in the Pueblo environment included mountain peaks because they touched the spiritual upper stratum of the sky and were made of earthly rock and soil. Caves were often powerful because they were situated in hills and mountains and they opened into the spiritual underworld. Other connections between the mortal and spiritual levels occurred through lakes and springs that provided life-sustaining moisture from the underworld and also reflected the sky. Clouds and mist touched mountains, and the sacred rain and lightning connected sky and earth.

Excavations in the earth therefore made connections with the spiritual world and were often very dangerous places. They were made very carefully and with appropriate sequences, prayers, rituals, and thoughts. Small shrines on the outskirts of villages required this preparation and would be approached with care and in a prescribed manner. Visits to the mountains or expeditions to procure salt required prayers and ritual preparation before setting out. They similarly required ritual procedures at the destination and before rejoining the everyday world of the village upon their return (Beaglehole, 1937, pp. 52–56). Power in Pueblo environments, villages, fields, or landscapes was therefore related to the power of spirits and supernaturals in upper and lower cosmic levels. And this relationships influenced both building activity and the nature of village spatial organization.

When, for example, a stone was quarried to make a *piki* (waferbread) baking surface for a house in the Hopi villages of northeastern Arizona, many preparations were required. Quarrymen were only free to find the stone after their leader had planted prayer objects in a previously made shrine at the site (Titiev, 1944, p. 197). Cornmeal was also sprinkled on the spot where the stone lay. The men were careful not to wear stone ornaments with markings on them, or the baking stone would be "scored" or "split" as it was quarried (Beaglehole, 1937, p.

59). It was said that *piki* stones were best quarried in March, and if they were extracted out of season they were considered "cold" and would cause frost (Titiev, 1972, pp. 142–143).

When the stone was brought back to the house the women took over. Four longitudinal marks of moistened *piki* wafers were made on the stone "to feed the spirit of the stone" and to stop any damage during the finishing of the surface (Beaglehole, 1937, p. 59). There were prohibitions on speaking, crackling firewood, or any other noise to avoid cracking of the stone (Mindeleff, 1891, p. 175). (A comparable full sequence of quarrying, preparing, and installing *piki* stones at the village of Zuni in western New Mexico is described in detail in a report on Zuni domestic life at the turn of the 19th century by Cushing [1920, pp. 324–333].)

Ritual accompanied the construction of segments of the Pueblo environment at all levels: baking stone, shrine, house, communal ceremonial chamber (popularly termed *kiva*), plaza, and whole village. Not all villages exhibited similar ritual concerns and procedures, however. Construction of houses was attended by much ritual in the western Pueblo villages of the Hopi and Zuni. There appears to have been much less house-building ritual in the villages to the east, along the Rio Grande in New Mexico. Some did occur there, however, and there also there was a villagewide ritual focus on the building or renovation of ceremonial buildings, society houses, moiety houses, and kivas.

A large number of ritual procedures associated with construction and a smaller number of purposes and accompanying prayers expressed by Pueblo participants have been recorded during the past century. Published records were summarized and analyzed in my earlier studies (Saile, 1976, 1977). In spite of wide variety and the many gaps in the records, are there common patterns or ideas that may help us understand both ritual and the role of ritual in the making of home? Let us look at some repeated themes and orders. Cardinal directions are insistently reiterated in the poetic ritual prayers that accompany prescribed building activities and in the activities themselves. Phrases and actions are repeated four times, or six when the directions of the zenith and nadir are included. The cardinal directions are the places of residence of supernatural powers. When the first Pueblo peoples emerged in their crude and unfinished state in the lower cosmic stratum they were helped and reformed by these powers. Certain special Pueblo people were made responsible for looking after the various needs of the first villagers. Some were responsible for hunting, medicine, defense, or for the village and its fields.

Sequences of prayers and rituals reiterated the sequence of activities of the first beings and supernaturals. Each direction possessed an associated series of powers, colors, trees, animals, and other phenomena that were said to reside in the sacred mountain, lake, or cloud of that direction. This sequence was intricately connected with the subsistence and ritual calendars of the Pueblo year (Ford, 1972). Particular supernatural figures and their directions were concerned with specific seasonal activities (e.g., east and north with hunting, west and south with agriculture). Other figures were connected with all directions and played roles in all major activities of the seasonal cycle.

In another repeated theme, building fabric was considered to be alive. Houses were "fed," and they could have blossoms and roots (Voth, 1901, p. 76). During construction and dedication rituals, the house fabric became a participating element in village and world processes. Prayers requested the health and strength of occupants and the strength of walls. This strength was related to the power of the supernaturals and first beings and ultimately to the creators of the world.

To become a participating element in the world system, the element had to be connected with both the spatial framework of the powerful levels and directions and with the actions of first beings. Powers focused inward from the villages. "Home" or "mother" villages were the centers of these world frameworks. Farming villages without kivas, ceremonials, and dance plazas were not home villages (McIntire, 1968, pp. 192–199). Home villages were made by ritual at their beginnings, according to the myth of origin of each village, and they were ritually reaffirmed at important times in the ceremonial calendar (Parsons, 1939, p. 8). In the recent past, villages were virtually deserted during summer when crops needed tending and harvesting; only religious specialists made sacred retreats to the villages with infrequent public ceremony. Winter was, and still is, a time of intense ritual activity, and tribal members living long distances from the village returned to give and receive strength associated with the home center.

Communication with the powers was effected through ritually constructed places. In a way, a power or supernatural needed a ritually constructed home through which to act. Home as understood here was not just a place of residence or action; it was also a human device for controlling or "housing" otherwise chaotic, random, and dangerous power. Ritual helped form boundaries and channels for power so that benefit would accrue to the village and its residents.

In summary, Pueblo house-construction rituals enabled a domestic structure and its spaces to become located with respect to a world framework. Through such procedures, beneficial supernatural aid was brought to the residents. Structures or villages were not proper home places unless they were made with this ritual accompaniment, and they became more secure through ritual reaffirmation or periodic strengthening and purification during the ceremonial year. The home so constructed became a model of the universe and of the position of Pueblo society within it. It also became a model of family relations and social organization by reference to the mythical society of first beings. As well, it became a center, a source of benefit and nurturance, and a place from which family members went out to farm or work for wages and to which they returned for ceremonies important to the sense of Pueblo identity and power.

One last example will focus upon these calendric rhythms in the making of home. It also may serve as an example of a superb synthesis of detailed ethnographic material concerning the dwellings of a widespread cultural group. The synthesis, taken from the work of Marcel Mauss and Henri Beuchat, is centered upon the 19th-century settlement system of the Eskimos, and was first published in 1904–1905 (Mauss & Beuchat, 1904–1905/1979). The authors noted that most previous students of the Eskimos had recorded two settlement forms. Dispersed tents constituted summer dwellings, and more permanent coastal house groups were the winter dwellings. This dual settlement organization reflected a pervasive system: "In accordance with these two forms there are two corresponding systems of law, two moral codes, two kinds of domestic economy and two forms of religious life" (1904–1905/1979, p. 76). Details and particulars varied, but this basic binary pattern existed from western Alaska to Greenland.

The summer dwelling was transportable and built by stretching reindeer skins over a conical frame of poles. It had one raised sleeping bench and usually one oil lamp. The winter dwelling was a larger stone, log, and earth house, sometimes arranged with others in a group, and it had a long protected entrance tunnel. There was a raised bench for each of a number of families and a lamp for each bench. There were also benches near the entrance for unmarried youths and guests.

The summer tent usually housed only a man and wife with unmarried children. It was a patriarchal arrangement with the man, as hunter and provider, making the family decisions. Except for the tent, most property was individually owned; hunting equipment by men; cooking, other utensils, and the lamp by women. Summer-born children were called *ducks* and were associated with the sea. Their first meal was a soup made from a land animal. Summer life had a slackened pace and a more relaxed attitude toward religion and social responsibility. The winter houses were occupied by from 1 to 10 families, usually 3 or 4, and they were collectively owned. Provisions and equipment were collectively distributed through borrowing or giving. Winter-born children were called *ptarmigan*, a bird associated with the land. Their first meal was a salted soup of a sea animal. The transition between summer and winter was marked, often abruptly, by association with game animals. When announcement was made that the first walrus of winter was caught, all work on summer skins such as reindeer and caribou had to cease immediately. Winter was also characterized by intense social activity.

In summer, religious rites were restricted to private domestic rituals and those of birth, death, and common summer prohibitions. Winter, on the other hand, was a season of almost "continuous religious exaltation" (1904–1905/1979, p. 57). A third building type—the *kashim*—was used for communal ceremonies, dancing, and public confession. It had the form of a large winter house but without bench divisions and with the addition of a fireplace. Activity stressed the unity of the group. There was great sexual license, and wives and nubile girls were exchanged at certain festivals. At the feast of the dead, the children most recently born were named after the persons who had most recently died; this was a kind of rebirth of ancestors. At the winter solstice all the lamps in the community were extinguished and relit from a single new source. The sexual pairing associated with this festival was according to the names of male and female mythical pairs, again stressing a sharing with an ancestral community (1904–1905/1979, pp. 57–68).

Eskimo identity required and was refreshed by the reciprocity of these two modes of life. The Eskimo home was a combination of intense communal winter cohesion and the relaxed and freer separation of summer dispersal. The winter communal home was reinforced by rituals stressing togetherness. In contrast, the summer home was a necessary and reenlivening contact with wider horizons and domestic tranquility. This rhythmic alternation of individual and social needs finds expression in the ritual cycle, the seasonal subsistence pattern, and in the forms of the dwellings and settlement. Mauss and Beuchat remarked on the geographically widespread occurrence of these rhythms and noted: "Furthermore, though this major seasonal rhythm is the most apparent, it may not be the only one; there are probably lesser rhythms within each season, each month, each week, each day" (1904–1905/1979, pp. 77–80).

These observations support the basic notion discussed by Altman and Gauvain "that homes reflect the dialectic interplay of individuality and society," especially their temporal interplay (1981, p. 283). Similar periodic separation and aggregation of groups in other cultures was noted by Altman and Gauvain in their examination of the dialectic interplay of social "accessibility/inaccessibility" (1981, p. 314).

Such regular rhythms of social and domestic alternation occurred in most Northwest Coast American tribes and many in California (Mauss & Beuchat, 1904–1905/1979, p. 77). This alternation is also a characteristic of most nomadic and seminomadic groups. Movement for judicious utilization of natural resources for domestic life and pasturage is not random; it follows traditional and cyclical paths and is contrasted with intense, crowded gatherings for trade, political bargaining, marriages, and other examples of social cohesion. Even during recent adjustments to new ways of livelihood, for example in the Navajo Southwest and in Tuareg areas of southern Algeria (Bencherif & Bencherif, 1984), the patterns of alternation do not disappear.

Mauss and Beuchat also mentioned the summer migrations of pastoral mountain peoples in Europe that emptied the villages of their male populations. They also wished to point out that in their native France urban life entered "a period of sustained languor known as *vacances*" during late July and that rural life followed the reverse pattern (1904–1905/1979, p. 78).

This reciprocity seems much like the cycles of renewal of home villages and dwellings of the Pueblo world. It also echoes the urban American rhythms of work and leisure, of vacation and home, and of the dispersal and regathering of family members at significant times in the cycles associated with home places. Some of the power and significance of the home is initially made and then reinforced and reaffirmed through the ritual cycle. When rituals do not become established, the rightness of the home is lessened, and its order and security seem weaker. Research into the rhythms of social life and environment, which Mauss and Beuchat considered important, is rarely mentioned in environmental design research fields. The purposes of this essay have been to indicate the value of a focus on these ritual themes and to speculate on the important roles of ritual in the establishment of home.

IMPLICATIONS FOR FUTURE RESEARCH

The study of ritual (more accurately, the reexamination of ritual) promises to be a valuable focus in person–environment research. Most observations in this essay have been taken from the literature of disciplines like anthropology and cultural geography, in which there is much widely dispersed data on homes and rituals. The availability of this material, however, makes the cross-cultural study of home rituals more possible. Although the material varies in specificity, accuracy, and quantity in different places, it is possible to examine similarities and differences across cultures. Benefits of cross-cultural study are multiple.

Aspects of homes and home places that are experienced unself-con-
sciously by the insiders and by researchers in their own cultures may be
highlighted by cross-cultural investigation. A greater range and depth of
evidence may be utilized, and "foreign" activities and ideas may pro-
voke additional and valuable theoretical insights (Altman & Chemers,
1980; Rapoport, 1980).

Much work can focus upon the reexamination of detailed ethnographic information dealing with house architecture, economy and
subsistence, beliefs, domestic rituals, and everyday behavior of particular cultural groups (Altman & Chemers, 1980; Altman & Gauvain, 1981;
Rapoport, 1969). Such reexamination should aim to understand house
activities and domestic spatial categories in terms of the context of the
culture of the household. Within this material, of course, are observations of prescribed ritual procedures accompanying house construction.
My studies of Pueblo building ritual were possible because of the availability of ethnographic, geographic, photographic, and other documentation from the same time period (Saile, 1981). Similar study should be
possible, for example, for the Navajo and some other North American
cultures. Much can be done using folklore studies from North America,
Europe, and the Near and Far East. Each state is proud of its folklore,
and collections of local lore including house-building and homemaking
lore are published or are available through an official folklorist or local
historical society. The richness of such material is indicated, for example, by the farmstead and lore studies found by Stilgoe (1982, pp. 137–
170). There have been periodic wide surveys of this material since the
mid-19th century (Eliade, 1958, 1972; Raglan, 1964; van Gennep, 1960)
that are very useful in locating relevant studies.

Valuable work can be undertaken using residential histories and
autobiographies that describe residential environments. Journals kept
during the early settlement and westward expansion in the United
States often reveal feelings toward remembered homes in the east or in
the home country. They also describe ways in which home and community were made and maintained during the struggles of travel and upon
arrival at the new destination. Rules of Western societies for home rituals and homemaking are also recorded in studies of domestic manners
and etiquette. Homemaking material is largely ignored in environment–
behavior studies and may allow insights into popular notions of home
and the patterns of ritual required by domestic custom. In this vein,
there are also many novels that may be valuable in revealing experiences
of home in an author's culture. Not only may varieties of home etiquette
be revealed, but students' analyses of certain novels dealing with, or
focused upon, residences suggest that it may also be possible to gain

insights into the nature of homes and their establishment (e.g., studies at the University of Newcastle upon Tyne, 1973–1975).

Environment–behavior studies will benefit by integrating or comparing their approaches and findings with major speculations and theories in theological, anthropological, and phenomenological treatises. In particular, there are important works for understanding ritual processes in relation to domestic space and architecture. Studies by Eliade on the phenomenology of religions (1958), Turner on ritual process (1964, 1969), Douglas on symbolic and social anthropology (1973, 1982), Rykwert on ritual themes in architecture, (1972), Firth on ritual communication (1973), and Goffman on interaction ritual (1967) are especially fruitful in this regard.

In addition to research using these largely literary sources, of course, there is also need for more direct observation and recording of the making, use, and experience of home. There are few studies of change in home environments or of the mutual adaptation of residents and residences. Some exciting work is being done on temporal aspects of environments (Werner, Oxley, & Altman, 1983) in phenomenological approaches involving long-term participation and involvement in home environments (Relph, 1976; Rowles, 1978; Seamon, 1979) and in examination of individual, social, and cultural identities manifested in dwellings (Duncan, 1981). Studies in the making, structuring, and reaffirmation of homes are more likely to benefit from a rich mix of methods and approaches than from any one technique or focus. This is partly because both home and ritual are themselves complex human phenomena, and understanding of their multifaceted natures requires richly integrative concepts and approaches.

Acknowledgments

I thank James Mayo and Harris Stone for valuable discussion and comment on the ideas in this paper.

REFERENCES

Altman, I., & Chemers, M. M. *Culture and communication*, Monterey, Calif.: Brooks/Cole, 1980.

Altman, I., & Gauvain, M. A cross-cultural and dialectic analysis of homes. In L. S. Liben, A. H. Patterson & N. Newcombe (Eds.), *Spatial representation and behavior across the life span*. New York: Academic Press, 1981, pp. 283–320.

Beaglehole, E. *Notes on Hopi economic life* (Yale University Publications in Anthropology No. 15). New Haven: Yale University Press, 1937.

Bencherif, A., & Bencherif, S. Masters degree studies of dwelling and environmental change in Ahaggar, southern Algeria, School of Architecture and Urban Design, University of Kansas, 1984.

Bossard, J. H. S., & Boll, S. *Ritual in family living*. Philadelphia: University of Pennsylvania, 1950.

Browne, R. B. (Ed.). *Rituals and ceremonies in popular culture*. Bowling Green, KY: Bowling Green University Popular Press, 1980.

Bunzel, R. L. *Introduction to Zuni ceremonialism* (Bureau of American Ethnology 47th Annual Report 1929–1930) Washington, D.C.: Smithsonian Institution, 1932, pp. 467–544.

Buttimer, A. Home, reach and the sense of place. In A. Buttimer & D. Seamon (Eds.), *The human experience of space and place*. London: Croom Helm, 1980, pp. 166–187.

Colson, E. The least common denominator. In S. F. Moore & B. G. Myerhoff (Eds.), *Secular ritual*. Assen, The Netherlands: Van Gorcum, 1977, pp. 189–198.

Crumrine, N. *The house cross of the Mayo Indians of Sonora, Mexico. A symbol in ethnic identity* (Anthropological Papers of the University of Arizona No. 8). Tucson: University of Arizona Press, 1964.

Crumrine, N. R. *The Mayo Indians of Sonora*. Tucson: University of Arizona Press, 1977.

Cunningham, C. E. Order in the Atoni house. *Bijdr. Taal. -Land-Volkenk.*, 1964, *20*, 34–68.

Cushing, F. H. *Zuni breadstuff* (Indian Notes and Monographs 8). New York: Museum of the American Indian, Heye Foundation, 1920.

Deal, T. E., & Kennedy, A. A. *Corporate cultures. The rites and rituals of corporate life*. Reading, Mass.: Addison-Wesley, 1982.

Douglas, M. *Purity and danger. An analysis of concepts of pollution and taboo*. London: Routledge & Kegan Paul, 1966.

Douglas, M. *Rules and meanings. The anthropology of everyday knowledge*. Harmondsworth, England: Penguin, 1973.

Douglas, M. *In the active voice*. London: Routledge & Kegan Paul, 1982.

Duncan, J. S. (Ed.). *Housing and identity. Cross-cultural perspectives*. London: Croom Helm, 1981.

Duncan, J. S., & Duncan, N. G. Social worlds, status passage, and environmental perspectives. In G. Moore & R. Golledge (Eds.), *Environmental knowing*. Stroudsberg, Penn.: Dowden, Hutchinson and Ross, 1976, pp. 206–213.

Eliade, M. *The myth of the eternal return* (W. R. Trask, trans.). Princeton, N.J.: Bollingen Foundation, Princeton University, 1954. (Original work published 1947)

Eliade, M. *Patterns in comparative religion*. New York: Sheed and Ward, 1958.

Eliade, M. Structures and changes in the history of religion. In C. H. Kraeling & R. M. Adams (Eds.), *City invincible*. Chicago: University of Chicago Press, 1960, pp. 351–366.

Eliade, M. *Images and symbols* (Philip Mairet, trans.). New York: Sheed and Ward, 1969.

Eliade, M. *Zalmoxis the vanishing god. Comparative studies in the religions and folklore of Dacia and eastern Europe* (W. R. Trask, trans.). Chicago: University of Chicago Press, 1972.

Ferguson, T. J., & Mills, B. J. *The built environment of Zuni Pueblo: The bounding, use and classification of space*. Paper presented at the 77th Annual Meeting of the American Anthropological Association, Los Angeles, 1978.

Firth, R. Postures and gestures of respect. In J. Pouillon & P. Maranda (Eds.), *Échanges et communications. Mélanges offerts a Claude Lévi-Strauss à l'occasion de son 60ème anniversaire* (Vol. 1). The Hague: Mouton, 1970, pp. 188–209.

Firth, R. Verbal and bodily rituals of greeting and parting. In J. S. LaFontaine (Ed.), *The interpretation of ritual*. London: Tavistock, 1972, pp. 1–38.

Firth, R. *Symbols: Public and private*. Ithaca, N. Y.: Cornell University Press, 1973.

Firth, R., & Spillius, J. *A Study in ritual modification* (Royal Anthropological Institute Occasional Paper No. 19). London: Royal Anthropological Institute, 1963.

Ford, R. I. An ecological perspective on the eastern Pueblos. In A. Ortiz (Ed.), *New perspectives on the Pueblos*. Albuquerque: School of American Research, University of New Mexico, 1972, pp. 1–17.

Gluckman, M. (Ed.). *Essays on the ritual of social relations*. Manchester: Manchester University Press, 1962.

Goffman, E. *Interaction ritual. Essays on face-to-face behaviour*. Harmondsworth, England: Penguin, 1967.

Goodman, E. On "second time" marriages and houses. *Lawrence Daily Journal World* November 23, 1982, p. 5.

Gregor, T. *Mehinaku. The drama of daily Life in a Brazilian indian village*. Chicago: University of Chicago Press, 1977.

Haile, B. Why the Navaho hogan? *Primitive Man*, 1942, 15(3–4), 39–56.

Haywood, D. G. Home as an environmental and psychological concept. *Landscape*, 1975, 20(1), 2–9.

Hildburgh, W. L. Notes on Sinhalese magic. *Journal of the Royal Anthropological Institute*, 1908, 38, 148–205.

Horwitz, J., & Tognoli, J. Role of home in adult development: Women and men living alone describe their residential histories. *Family Relations*, 1982, 31, 335–341.

Jett, S. C., & Spencer, V. E. *Navajo architecture: Forms, history, distribution*. Tucson: University of Arizona Press, 1981.

Kendon, F. *The small years*. Cambridge: Cambridge University Press, 1930.

Littlejohn, J. The Temne house. *Sierra Leone Studies*, 1960, 14, 63–79.

Mauss, M., & Beuchat, H. *Seasonal variations of the Eskimo. A study in social morphology* (J. J. Fox, trans.). London: Routledge & Kegan Paul, 1979. (Originally published 1904–1905.)

McIntire, E. G. *The impact of cultural change on the land use patterns of the Hopi Indians*. Unpublished doctoral dissertation, University of Oregon, 1968.

Mindeleff, C. *Navaho houses* (Bureau of American Ethnology 17th Annual Report, Part 2). Washington, D.C.: Smithsonian Institution, 1898, pp. 469–517.

Mindeleff, V. *A study of Pueblo architecture: Tusayan and Cibola* (Bureau of American Ethnology 8th Annual Report). Washington, D.C.: Smithsonian Institution, 1891, pp. 3–228.

Moore, S. F., & Myerhoff, B. G. Secular ritual: Forms and meanings. In S. F. Moore & B. G. Myerhoff (Eds.), *Secular ritual*. Assen, The Netherlands: Van Gorcum, 1977, pp. 3–24.

Norberg-Schulz, C. *Genius loci. Towards a phenomenology of architecture*. New York: Rizzoli, 1980.

Ortiz, A. *The Tewa world. Space, time, being, and becoming in a Pueblo society*. Chicago: University of Chicago Press, 1969.

Ortiz, A. Ritual drama and the Pueblo world view. In A. Ortiz, (Ed.), *New perspectives on the Pueblos*. Albuquerque: School of American Research, University of New Mexico, 1972, pp. 135–161.

Parsons, E. C. *Pueblo Indian religion* (2 vols.). Chicago: University of Chicago Press, 1939.

Raglan, Lord. *The temple and the house*. New York: Norton, 1964.

Rapoport, A. *House form and culture*. Englewood Cliffs, N.J.: Prentice-Hall, 1969.

Rapoport, A. Cross-cultural aspects of environmental design. In I. Altman, A. Rapoport, & J. Wohlhill (Eds.), *Human behavior and environment, advances in theory and research* (Vol. 4) New York: Plenum Press, 1980, pp. 7–46.

Rapoport, A. Sacred places, sacred occasions and sacred environments. *Architectural Design*, 1982, 9(10), 75–82.

Relph, E. *Place and placelessness*. London: Pion, 1976.

Rossbach, S. *Feng shui. The Chinese art of placement*. New York: E. P. Dutton, 1983.

Rowles, G. Reflections on experiential fieldwork. In D. Ley & M. Samuels (Eds.), *Humanistic geography*. Chicago: Maaroufa, 1978, pp. 173–193.

Rykwert, J. *On Adam's house in paradise*. New York: Museum of Modern Art Papers on Architecture, 1972.

Rykwert, J. *The idea of a town*. London: Faber and Faber, 1976.

Rykwert, J. (Ed.). *The necessity of artifice*. New York: Rizzoli, 1982, pp. 131–133.

Saile, D. G. *Pueblo building rituals. Religious aspects of a productive activity*. Unpublished manuscript, Arizona State Museum Library, Tucson, 1976.

Saile, D. G. Making a house: Building rituals and spatial concepts in the Pueblo Indian world. *Architectural Association Quarterly*, 1977, 9, 72–81.

Saile, D. G. *Architecture in the Pueblo world. The architectural contexts of Pueblo culture in the late nineteenth century*. Unpublished doctoral dissertation, University of Newcastle upon Tyne, 1981.

Saile, D. G. Many dwellings: Views of a Pueblo world. In R. Mugerauer & D. Seamon (Eds.), *Dwelling, place and environment*, The Hague: Martinus Nijhoff, 1985.

Seamon, D. *A geography of the lifeworld*. London: Croom Helm, 1979.

Seamon, D. Body–subject, Time–space routines, and place ballets. In A. Buttimer & D. Seamon (Eds.), *The Human experience of space and place*. London: Croom Helm, 1980, pp. 148–165.

Stilgoe, J. R. *Common landscape of America, 1580 to 1845*. New Haven: Yale University Press, 1982.

Stirling, M. W. *Origin myth of Acoma and other records* (Bureau of American Ethnology Bulletin 135). Washington, D.C.: Smithsonian Institution, 1942.

Titiev, M. Old Oraibi: A study of the Hopi Indians of Third Mesa (Papers of the Peabody Museum of American Archaeology and Ethnology 22). Cambridge, Mass.: Harvard University Press, 1944, pp. 1–277.

Titiev, M. *The Hopi Indians of the Old Oraibi. Change and continuity*. Ann Arbor: University of Michigan Press, 1972.

Tognoli, J. The flight from domestic space: Men's roles in the household. *The Family Coordinator*, October 1979, pp. 599–607.

Tognoli, J., & Horwitz, J. From childhood home to adult home: Environmental transformations. In P. Bart, A. Chen, & G. Francescato (Eds.), *Knowledge for design* (Proceedings of the Annual Meeting of the Environmental Design Research Association). Washington, D.C., 1982, pp. 321–328.

Trumbull, H. C. *The threshold covenant: Or the beginning of religious rites*. Edinburgh: T. and T. Clark, 1896.

Turner, V. W. *Betwixt and between: The Liminal period in rites de passage* (Proceedings of the American Ethnological Society, Spring Meeting). Seattle: University of Washington Press, 1964, pp. 4–20.

Turner, V. W. *The ritual process. Structure and anti-structure*. Chicago: Aldine, 1969.

Turner, V. W. Variations on a theme of liminality. In S. F. Moore & B. G. Myerhoff (Eds.), *Secular ritual*. Assen, The Netherlands: Van Gorcum, 1977, pp. 36–52.

van Gennep, A. *The rites of passage* (M. Vizedom & G. Caffee, trans.). Chicago: University of Chicago Press, 1960. (Originally published, 1908.)

Voth, H. R. *Oraibi Powamu ceremony* (Field Columbian Museum Publication 51), Anthropological Series 3:2. Chicago, 1901.

Werner, C., Oxley, D., & Altman, I. *Temporal Aspects of Environments. Christmas Street, Salt Lake City.* Workshop presented at the Annual Meeting of the Environmental Design Research Association, University of Nebraska, Lincoln, 1983.

White, L. A. *The Pueblo of Sia, New Mexico* (Bureau of American Ethnology Bulletin 184). Washington, D.C.: Smithsonian Institution, 1962.

5

A More Humane History of Homes

RESEARCH METHOD AND APPLICATION

RODERICK J. LAWRENCE

> *The organization of thought and of social relations is imprinted on the landscape. But, if only the physical aspect is susceptible of study, how to interpret this pattern would seem to pose an insoluble problem.*
>
> —Douglas, 1972, p. 513.

INTRODUCTION

This chapter discusses theoretical and methodological principles with respect to the analysis of home environments. It defines and illustrates those principles that form the nucleus of an analytical method that employs an historical or temporal perspective. I believe that this approach can enrich our comprehension of domestic environments.

This essay illustrates that the fundamental difference between historical, ethnographical, and architectural studies of home environments is not one of subject matter nor of goals: each shares the same subject,

RODERICK J. LAWRENCE • Université de Genève, 1211 Genève 4, Switzerland.

which is the spatial surroundings of domestic life, and the same goal, which is a better understanding of home environments. Nonetheless, they traditionally have differed in their choice of perspectives and methods. In this chapter, however, these perspectives and methods are considered as complementary rather than competitive. Such a reorientation and diversification of the analysis of home environments presents a new method that other architects, ethnographers, historians, and environmental psychologists can employ.

This chapter contends that even the most penetrating analysis of home environments and household life can attain full significance only if the historical processes underlying contemporary patterns are analyzed. Our present-day experience of home environments includes a warehouse of material culture and social customs, routines, and rituals handed down from previous generations. In both material and affective terms, these products of parentage influence the design, meaning, and use of domestic environments in tacit and sometimes unconscious ways (Csikszentmihalyi & Rochberg-Halton, 1981). Thus, it is important to analyze the spatial and behavioral ordering of home environments through the passage of time. This orientation evokes certain problems: past residential experiences exist in the mind of the resident; they cannot be measured, yet they clearly manifest themselves in contemporary life (Lawrence, 1983b). In sum, past and present rejoin. One objective in writing this chapter is to illustrate the transactions between the material order and the mental constructs of home environments. To achieve this goal, both these attributes ought to be analyzed together, to reveal the underlying properties of home environments that exist operationally in diverse cultural, social, and historical contexts.

The following section of this chapter discusses those theoretical and methodological frameworks that can support the redefinition and diversification of current housing history. Here it is necessary to emphasize that historical research methods are considered in a very broad sense: on the one hand, the historical analysis of extant dwellings is achieved by fieldwork and the study of documents pertaining to the construction and use of buildings; on the other hand, the study of spoken and written narratives of homes and household life illustrates that the interaction between people and houses acquires its form and meaning from many sources—the social history of domestic architecture, technology, the use of household space and facilities, and the biography of an individual's residential experience during his or her life cycle. The interaction between the social and personal histories of residential environments are illustrated in the third section of this chapter by referring to the morphogenesis of domestic architecture in South Australia from 1836, the year of British colonial settlement, and by an analysis of the personal archives of a pioneer family. The fourth and final section will discuss the implications of this essay for future research on home environments.

HOUSING HISTORY: THEORY, METHOD, AND APPLICATION

Housing history has commonly considered exceptional rather than typical kinds of dwellings. However, during the last two decades the growth of interest in urban and housing history has produced a large volume of research about many building structures not previously included in the field. According to Daunton (1983), issues or themes, such as public health and sanitation, housing policies, and building legislation, have been employed to provide the framework for these studies. Furthermore, there have also been numerous studies of houses built for different socioeconomic classes in diverse societies, some limited to specific towns and others to specific periods (Daunton, 1983). It has been common practice, however, for many architectural and social historians to examine domestic buildings in terms of their construction and the development of domestic technology while overlooking the interaction between human values and the design and use of dwellings (e.g., Burnett, 1978). Other recent studies of housing and urban history have described either the layout of residential areas or the housing policies implicated in their construction: Swenarton (1981) maintains, for example, that social historians have dealt with economics, politics, and society while ignoring design, whereas architects and architectural historians have overlooked everything but the design of buildings. Both these approaches imply "that design and society are not involved in a single process but are separate and distinct" (Swenarton, 1981, p. 3). This obvious shortcoming ought to be corrected.

In his monograph, however, Swenarton only considers the design of government-subsidized houses as a central issue of politics and government policy, while treating the organization of domestic space in a cursory fashion. In this respect, although his contribution diversifies predominant interpretations of housing history, it does not include an analysis of the interaction between room layouts and household life and the economic and political factors he examined in detail. On the contrary, studies such as Le Roy Ladurie's (1980) illustrate the interaction between social ideas and values associated with the design and use of dwellings in medieval French society. The author's analysis of the published edition of the Inquisition Register of the Bishop of Pamiers enables the sociospatial relations of a peasant society to be reconstructed.

Whereas the majority of current knowledge of vernacular housing and folk life during the Middle Ages has come from archaeological fieldwork or from paintings of that epoch, Le Roy Ladurie's research reveals how the peasants described their daily lives. Throughout this fascinating study, the author is concerned with domestic life, especially with ideas about space and time. This precedent has not been widely followed by architectural or social historians, but it will be utilized in this chapter to explore those social ideas and values about the design and use of residential environments in terms of wider developments in society.

Beyond the back cloth of sociohistorical ideas and values about buildings, it is important to account for personal attitudes and values concerning the experience of home environments. Despite the growing volume of research on the history of the family (e.g., Hareven, 1978), there are few biographical accounts of the interaction between people and their homes during the life cycle; the historical study of the life course is, in general, devoid of spatial location. Whereas attention has focused upon individual development, the family cycle, kinship groups, the temporal structure of life events, and time budgets (Hareven, 1978), there has been no systematic consideration of how the biography of individuals and household groups interacts with the spatial context of dwellings. This shortcoming has only recently been addressed, for example, by oral history and environmental autobiographies (Ladd, 1977). By the explicit recollection of the past, this approach makes past residential experience explicit.

In an analysis of household objects, to cite but one study, Csikszentmihalyi and Rochberg-Halton (1981) have shown how domestic possessions are endowed with meanings that vary between people of different generations. This study indicates that a temporal perspective is crucial to understand the affective ties between a resident and his or her domestic wares; although this analysis does not include the design of homes, it presents certain cues for research on this subject. Nonetheless, such research ought to relate the personal, idiosyncratic meanings of domestic space and objects to their wider social value, as Douglas and Isherwood (1979) and Pratt (1981) have shown.

With this qualification in mind, I intend to illustrate the pertinence of a dual historical perspective for the analysis of home environments. Unlike the two predominant kinds of housing histories briefly outlined, it considers the macrosocial and the micropersonal residential histories in a complementary way. Thus, the social history of domestic architecture in South Australia will be complemented by an analysis of written documents that provide first-hand accounts of the residential biography of a pioneer family in 1860. This example of the reorientation and diversification of the history of housing stems from specific ontological and methodological principles which will now be discussed briefly.

HOUSES ARE SOCIOCULTURAL ARTIFACTS

The home environment is a sociocultural artifact; several scholars in diverse branches of the social sciences have shown that its meaning and use can be understood only with respect to its sociogeographical context (Bourdieu, 1977; Douglas, 1966). The house and household life are ordered by the customs, habits, and classification categories of the residents. Furthermore, within cultures, there are subcultures, social groups, and individuals. The ordering and use of domestic space and objects reflects this diversity (Lawrence, 1983b; Pratt, 1981). Bourdieu (1977) employed the concept of *habitus* to define the cultural predispositions of residents in their dwelling environments: *habitus* relates to the house in that domestic space is appropriated by the resident and can be interpreted as a system of predispositions or customs that are generated by past residential experience. This concept illustrates that dwelling environments are a matrix of past and present, which provides a framework for daily household experiences. Both the setting, the daily activities, and their associated customs and conventions are commonly taken for granted. Yet, as Leach (1982, p. 126) has noted,

> These distinctive features of our own way of life are not of our own making. We do not live exactly as our parents lived but whatever we do now is only a modification of what was done before.

This citation shows that the meaning of domestic space and household life transcends the historical dimension of a specific social and geographical context. Moreover, these contextual conditions do not determine the meaning and use of dwellings but provide a framework in which human groups and individuals live.

Nonetheless, this essay maintains, as Lévi-Strauss (1967) wrote:

> Scorning the historical dimension on the pretext that we have insufficient means to evaluate it except approximately will result in our being satisfied with an impoverished sociology, in which phenomena are set loose, as it were from their foundations. Rules and institutions, states and processes seem to float in a void in which one strains to spread a tenuous network of functional relations. One becomes wholly absorbed in this task and forgets the men in whose thought these relationships are established, one neglects their material culture, one no longer knows whence they came and what they are. (p. 23)

Bearing this quotation in mind, it is suggested that the subjective interpretation of architectural history is pertinent for studies of buildings

(Lynch, 1972). Owing to the fundamental enduring quality of architecture, buildings of all kinds are handed down as a legacy from one generation to the next; they illustrate the permanence and elasticity of the spatial organization of societies; they are one vehicle for the embodiment of social ideas (Douglas, 1966; Pratt, 1981). Yet if there is a spatial and social order of dwelling environments, then that order, however it interacts with social irregularities and personal attitudes, is an agent of both stability and change. In architecture, the relationship between building form, its use, meaning, and time is a transactional process between physical and affective factors. Thus, apart from the enduring quality of building structures, both the sociocultural and the psychological processes implicated in their construction and use cannot be ignored.

Given this perspective, it is clear that information embodied in the design and use of domestic architecture cannot be understood solely by a synchronic investigation, such as observation and documentation by fieldwork. When such an investigation is not extended beyond its traditional level of analysis and interpretation, the scholar is only informed about what the building is and has little knowledge about how it was constructed and had been used. A comprehensive methodology is urgently required.

HOUSES ARE WAREHOUSES OF PERSONAL EXPERIENCE

The reinterpretation of domestic architecture and household life requires an analysis of sociohistorical processes. Yet, beyond the social, cultural, and historical back cloth of domestic culture, it is important not to ignore those personal, affective ties that each individual has with houses during his or her life. It is necessary, therefore, to explore how specific spaces acquire differential values for members of the same household and how these spaces are appropriated in diverse ways through the passage of time. To explore these themes, it is necessary to cross what Cobb (1978) described as "the tempting threshold"; to go inside the dwelling (rather than discuss its external form), and consider each resident's viewpoint about the layout and use of interior spaces.

Although this intention is an admirable and necessary one if the current comprehension of housing history is to be broadened and enriched, it is rare to find information based on first-hand records of the inhabitants prior to the 20th century. Moreover, it has been suggested that these records are selective and elitist because the majority of the population was illiterate. Although this criticism may be valid with respect to many societies during the 19th century, this is not so in the context of the Australian colonies; there are several collections of written documents of pioneers who were eager to correspond with their kin about daily life "in the new world." The third section of this chapter shows how an analysis of these personal narratives can enrich our understanding of the history of housing. Moreover, it stresses that the interaction between people and their homes takes its form and meaning from a private, residential history that is the personal experience of past residential experience and the history of domestic buildings that are artifacts with a context-dependent and a temporal connotation.

This perspective evokes a set of important theoretical and methodological principles. First, the enduring quality of buildings enables people to experience their physical and affective qualities during a relatively long period of time; second, during the passage of time buildings not only undergo certain physical transformations; their meanings and uses change as well. Given this fundamental principle, the following theorem is crucial for research on domestic space: the relationship between habitat and inhabitant is dynamic or changeable, and it includes factors that may remain unresolved over a relatively long period of time. This theorem is derived from recent research by scholars in social psychology, including Altman, Vinsel, and Brown (1981) and Harré (1979), which has shown that "all the evidence we have, slender though it is, suggests that social forms and individual cognitions of these forms are highly unstable and in rapid flux" (Harré, 1979, p. 183). This state of continual change has not only been recognized as a fundamental property of social institutions but also of the built environment. Having established this set of principles, the historical analysis of home environments is founded upon the following:

1. fieldwork or observational studies of the design, the construction, and the furnishing of dwellings built at various dates in the same society; and
2. analysis of diverse documentary sources, which not only consider the design and construction of houses but also record how they were used by inhabitants in bygone years.

These sets of theoretical and methodological principles will now be illustrated in the following section of this essay.

NARRATIVES OF HOMES AND HOUSEHOLD LIFE IN SOUTH AUSTRALIA

Given the orientations briefly outlined in the preceding sections, it is clear that no single concept or method can be employed to deepen our current understanding of home environments. This section discusses how both the material and the affective characteristics of dwellings can be studied using diverse sources in a complementary way. In the first instance, the development of colonial houses following the foundation of South Australia in 1836 will be discussed. This subject has been chosen to illustrate the principle that ethnographic research of domestic architecture dating from the recent past is instructive.

THE MORPHOGENESIS OF HOUSES

The development of domestic architecture in South Australia is particularly interesting owing to the cultural diversity of the pioneers and the conscious emphasis given to town planning. The contribution of these two factors is still evident today from the scant numbers of vernacular buildings constructed about 1850 in diverse regions of South Australia. These buildings illustrate a variety of construction techniques, including simple masonry walling (employing random rubble, limestone, and sun-dried bricks), timber construction (using post-and-beam construction, half-timber framed walling, and split-gum framing), and diverse roofing materials, including bark, thatch, slate, and corrugated iron sheeting (Berry & Gilbert, 1981).

At first sight, it becomes clear that these materials were used according to their availability; yet the fact that a range of materials and construction methods were employed concurrently suggests that such a simple explanation, tied to physical factors alone, is not as pregnant or pertinent as are interpretations of diffusionism and cultural or social factors. As fieldwork alone can reveal, in the same settlement either English, Scottish, or German customs were practiced (or modified), according to the availability of building materials and local topographical and climatic conditions. Thus, in the German settlements in the Mount Lofty ranges, both the *construction techniques* and the *house plans* were borrowed by the settlers from their native country: even the layout of the rural town was reused. To these Lutherans it was vernacular architecture reemployed in South Australia, whereas to a Scottish or English settler it was foreign.

During the last half of the 19th century "hybrid" architectural forms were built to adapt to local conditions; the addition of verandahs ably illustrates an attempt to respond to a local climate quite different from that in Europe (Sumner, 1978). Moreover, fieldwork has revealed that, irrespective of the kinds of building materials used, by the end of the 19th century construction techniques that had been borrowed from Europe were modified (Berry & Gilbert, 1981). In sum, people with diverse cultural origins borrowed (or exchanged) "rules of thumb" about house building. This was an internal indigenous development that was due to social interaction between the pioneers and to the merits and demerits of their building customs when used in a different context. On the other hand, by the beginning of this century, the influx of external influences had also been well established. On the one hand, there was a continual stream of immigrants who commonly transplanted their own habits and material cultures; on the other hand, beginning in 1837, there was a proliferation of publications about domestic architecture in the colony (Hodder, 1893). Thus, apart from isolated examples of colonial houses that still exist, there is a series of official and private manuscripts that have not only recorded the design but also the furnishing and use of houses in Australia from the earliest years of settlement. It is invaluable to consult all of these sources, no matter how few they may be because, used in connection with fieldwork studies of extant vernacular houses, such documents provide complementary information about their morphogenesis.

SPATIAL ANALYSIS OF DWELLINGS

Although the dwellings constructed soon after the settlement of South Australia were tents or one-room huts, within a decade many more substantial structures with at least two rooms existed. In general, fieldwork has indicated that it was most likely that the earliest houses developed from one- or two-room timber or stone structures; then verandahs were added and, sometimes, they were enclosed to create additional rooms (Berry & Gilbert, 1981).

From these meager beginnings the standard of domestic construction and facilities improved rapidly. By 1850 houses had four or six main rooms, and it was common for the bathroom and toilet to be set apart at the rear. As Twopenny (1883, pp. 34–35) noted in his travel diary:

> The favourite type of Australian house is laid out in an oblong block bisected by a three to eight foot passage. The first door on one side as you go in is the drawing room, on the other [side] the dining room. Then follow the bedrooms, etc., with the kitchen and scullery at the end of the passage, or sometimes in a lean-to at right angles to the hinder part of the house proper. Happily every house has a bathroom though it is often only a mere shed of wood or galvanized iron put up in the back yard. . . . This kind of cottage is almost universal in Adelaide amongst the middle and upper middle classes and invariable in the working-class throughout Australia.

The descriptions of houses that authors have recorded throughout the 19th century indicate that the development of domestic architecture did not follow preestablished house types in Europe, especially Britain, from where the majority of settlers emigrated. Furthermore, indigenous house forms developed despite the explicit models evoked by building regulations that were introduced in London from 1667 and were then diffused to English provincial towns and the colonial states of Australia. These building regulations prescribed building plans and construction materials; the standard plan form was copied or modified when built in Australia; it is commonly known as the *single-fronted cottage* or *terrace house*. Nonetheless, the fact that the attached dwelling, including the noble terrace house of many Georgian towns in Britain, was not built in large numbers suggests that the organization of domestic space followed a different pattern in Australia from that in Britain. Indeed this divergence is still evident today, and reasons for this have been analyzed elsewhere and will not be repeated here (Lawrence, 1983a).

Domestic architecture in South Australia followed a pattern that led to the generation of a limited number of *house types* during the 19th century. The first type was a *single-fronted dwelling* which was often a semidetached or terraced house with each room aligned one behind the other, usually including a passage along one side. The second type was a *double-fronted house*, which consisted usually of four (sometimes six) main rooms with the front door opening into a passage that bisected either the front two rooms or the whole of the floor plan. These two house types are illustrated in Figure 1. Both these house types initially were built without sanitary and cooking facilities incorporated in the main structure of the house (Freeland, 1972). Subsequently, they included additions at the rear, in the form of a lean-to, which became the location for a bathroom, wash house, and toilet, with the kitchen being an internal, main room. Analysis of numerous house plans reveals that by the 1850s the kitchen was often integrated into the main structure of the dwelling, whereas the other services were accessible only from under the lean-to roof (Lawrence, 1983a).

Research by some authors, including Lawrence (1982), suggests that the concept of *architectural type* can be employed to analyze dwellings that share the same or similar spatial characteristics. The concept of architectural type is employed here not in a functionalist sense but in terms of the morphology and meaning of house forms. This formal interpretation stems from the work of Quatremère de Quincy (1823), and it ought to be contrasted with a more prevalent interpretation that is employed by architectural historians such as Pevsner (1976). Pevsner has classified buildings according to their social function (e.g., public offices, museums, hotels, or mansions), their architectural style, and their date of construction. Moreover, the buildings included in this approach are often "architectural celebrities" rather than characteristic ex-

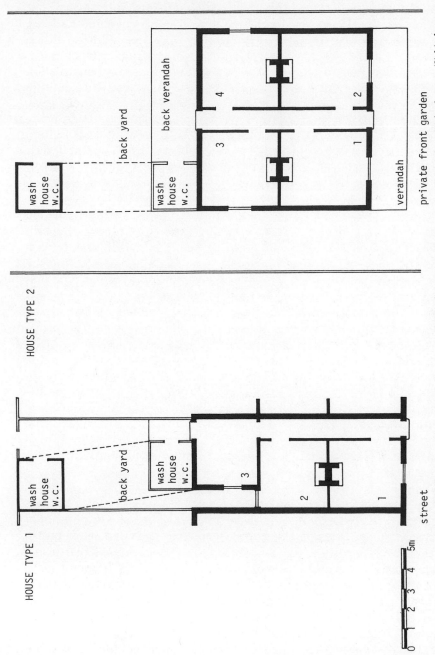

Figure 1. The two predominant house types built in South Australia during the 19th century: (1) parlor, (2) bedroom, (3) kitchen, (4) sitting room.

amples, and there is no explanation of *why* built forms housing such functions have changed. Yet, as the typical houses evolved in South Australia (for example, by the inclusion of sanitary facilities and domestic appliances), certain important changes occurred in their design. These innovations raise the problem of accounting for the historical development of houses and household life; this problem is ably illustrated by the development of the Australian domestic kitchen during the 19th century (Lawrence, 1983a). This example serves to illustrate that diverse factors engendered the morphogenesis of house forms in Australia during the 19th century and that this development did not occur in a fixed chronological manner. This finding highlights the need for a structural analysis of all those factors implicated in the design and use of dwellings.

DECIPHERING THE MEANING AND USE OF ROOMS

The preceding section suggested that the analysis of house types was a systematic way of studying the morphology of extant buildings, whatever their date of construction. Nonetheless, such an analysis is only informative about their characteristics when they were initially constructed. In this respect they are interpreted only as fixed objects by a static abstraction that overlooks their life history: What if internal changes or external extensions were made to these houses by different residents? How were the rooms furnished and intended to be used every day of the week, month, and year? Was there a distinction between common use and the usage on special occasions, such as birthdays and other festivities?

Such questions relate to the design and use of dwellings; they cannot be answered by a typological analysis alone. Therefore, to limit the analysis of domestic architecture to a study of configuration would be quite misleading because the meaning and use of domestic space is not solely dependent on its form. Thus, the preceding analysis must be enlarged to include those transactions between the physical, the affective, and the temporal qualities of homes. One means of achieving this goal is by studying how dwellings have been appropriated and used by residents since the mid-19th century.

There are numerous public and private documents that describe the furnishing and use of Australian houses built in the 19th century. In his monograph, for example, Twopenny (1883) recorded the range of furniture and equipment that he commonly saw in houses he visited in the main towns during his sojourn. Therefore, apart from localizing the names of the rooms in the typical houses of that era, it is possible to develop an understanding of the social customs used to furnish these spaces. In this respect Twopenny (1883, p. 45) noted:

> The real living-room of the house is the dining room, which is therefore the best furnished, and on a tapestry carpet are a leather couch, six balloon-back carved chairs, two easy chairs, a chiffonier, a side-table and a cheap chimney glass. . . . The kitchen is summarily disposed of; Biddy has to content herself with a table, dresser, safe, paste board and rolling-pin and a couple of chairs.

In smaller cottages, Twopenny observed that there was no drawing room "but the parlour aspires to comfort quite undreamt of by an English tradesman." Some Australian novelists have recorded the incidence of the parlor during the 19th century. The meaning and use of "this sanctuary" was recreated from a remembrance of the coding for that room commonly found adjacent to the front door of English houses. Apparently, many households in the colony adopted customs and conventions like the traditional parlor during the Victorian era in England. Moreover, with respect to the temporal perspective advocated in this essay, a series of autobiographies and private papers indicate that these kinds of customs were passed on to later generations of Australians. For example, when Porter (1963, p. 13) wrote his autobiography, he described the parlor, or "the front room on the left," in the house he remembered from his childhood prior to World War I:

> I am a child of an era and a class in which adults are one tribe and children another, each with its separate rights and duties, freedoms and restrictions, expected gentleness and condoned barbarities, each with its special reticences and sacred areas. One area taboo to children is the front room.

Porter has recalled the furnishings of "the front room," which he was permitted to enter only on special days, when his parents would use that room for entertaining. Analysis of narratives like those of Twopenny and Porter reveal many characteristics of home environments of bygone years and whether these characteristics have changed from one generation to the next. Apart from localizing domestic activities and what furniture was commonly associated with them, these narratives illustrate how social norms and rules were employed to regulate the use of space in homes. It is important to develop an understanding of these norms and rules because they are more informative about the use of rooms than the nomenclature or furniture layout suggests.

It is noteworthy that this regulation of the use of space cannot be considered in a direct, linear sense: on the one hand, the age and social status of members of households provide clues about the incidence of domestic roles, rules, and conventions and how these are associated with the appropriation and use of homes (Lawrence, 1983a); on the other hand, some authors, including Boyd (1968), have observed, with respect to Australian domestic architecture, that the parlor was commonly superseded by the living room about the time of World War II and that, unlike the parlor, this room was freely accessible to all members of the household each day of the week.

ANALYSIS OF DOMESTIC ACTIVITIES AND THE LIFE CYCLE

The preceding study of the design, the furnishing, and the use of dwellings can be enriched further by an analysis of household life, either by examining how it was recorded in diverse manuscripts or by contemporary ethnographic research. In this section, the use of both kinds of sources will be discussed and illustrated.

When Mr. Joseph Elliott of Jeffcott Street, North Adelaide, wrote to his mother in Britain in August 1860, he not only sketched the design of his house and all the furniture therein but also described each item of furniture and the use of rooms (Elliott, 1860/1984). There are several manuscripts of this kind written by the pioneers, which are available for consultation and which warrant analysis.

The Elliott family lived in a double-fronted cottage, of the type illustrated in Figure 1, built in 1856. On either side of the passage, after entering the front door, was the parlor (on the left) and the main bedroom (on the right): behind the parlor was the kitchen and behind the main bedroom was the sitting room.

Joseph Elliott drew all the furniture in these rooms. Although this is informative, his description is more so, given that it accounts for past and present uses of specific items, for example, the baby's cradle or cot in the main bedroom:

> Now the next thing we jump into is the Cradle or as we call it the cot, but I beg your pardon it is too small to jump into—so we'll look at it only—& while looking at it may please remember that our poor Joseph was ill & died in that same cot! And we know he has got a richer cot in Heaven—would to Heaven we were all as sure! All the babies have slept & *cried* in it & Master Joseph has lately slept very well in it. And Miss Beppy contrives some mornings to cram herself into it when she is tired of her own. It is covered with a patchwork quilt—octagon—commenced by Elizabeth and finished by Becky. (p. 35)

This description reveals that for Elliott the cradle or cot evokes both previous and contemporary experiences of child rearing. He associates a matrix of events with it, including the birth of several children and the death of one. In this sense, this item of furniture has unique associations and meaning for him. However, it is inadequate not to extend this text analysis further to include the social or cultural characteristics of this furniture. In general, beds are archetypal domestic objects with social values related to family unity and continuity and to stages of the life cycle, including birth, procreation, and death. Thus, in the context of the Australian pioneers, beds, including the baby's cot (which were commonly manufactured items, not handmade), evoke positive associations with one's heritage. Therefore, the meaning of the cradle described in this context can be fully grasped only by the superposition of the social values and conventions and the unique personal values accumulated through an individual's experience. Analysis of written narratives prompts an understanding of the interaction between cultural, social, and personal values and meanings invested in the home, household objects, and household life in a bygone era.

Beyond the development of this understanding, it is also instructive to decipher narratives of homes and household life in terms of the occurrence of domestic activities and events. In this respect, Elliott's letter (1860) to his mother explicitly describes the weekly round of domestic chores and other commitments. Between each Sunday, when church attendance and mealtimes followed a set timetable, there is clearly a recurrent pattern as the following extracts show:

> *Monday.* We rise generally between six and seven—& I get to town between 8 & 9, taking some lunch with me for 1 o'clock. Leave town at about 5 & dine on cold *mutton* & warm potatoes with mint sauce—of which I am very fond. Monday evenings is one of my holiday evenings—so we pass it in music or some way or other very agreeable to us—Monday, also, with my dear Rebecca is her holiday—so she generally calculates on some sewing that day—& takes out the children for a stroll to their grandmamas—about 5 or 10 minutes walk away. If we are asked to any music party . . it is generally on Monday—that being about my only evening.

> *Tuesday*—the day passes the same. We generally dine on either mutton or beef; beef or mutton—not much change here. This night is the first of my school nights—So, soon after dinner I am pretty busy— & after School I am pretty tired so we retire.

> *Wednesday* is ditto—excepting the evening—and every other Wednesday I have to attend my Lodge, of which I have been Secretary for the last 4 years—for which I get £15 per year. When it is not Lodge night we generally pass the evening in music or reading. This is Becky's worst day in the week—Washing day—I need not trouble you with any account of this—She is generally very tired after it—but yet sometimes (Lodge night) she gets her ironing done in the evening!

> *Thursday*—as usual—this evening is my School night and so I have not much time to spare for anything else.

> *Saturday* winds up the week—& I get home about 4 o'clock. Whatever can be

> done in the shape of cookery for Sunday is done this evening—& the chil-
> dren get their Saturday nights washing—& if I have any tinsmith or carpen-
> try work I generally have plenty of time this evening for the purpose—and
> after all is over—we retire having as usual thanked God for his mercies
> during the day & also during the week—& glad that the next day is Sunday.
>
> And so the days pass—oh how quickly too—from Sunday to Sunday only
> seems like a day—What is the passing of time so quickly bringing us to? (pp.
> 39–40)

This quotation serves to emphasize certain characteristics of domestic life. First, domestic activities are associated with regularity and routine. Although the Elliott family, like any other, have the ability to live an unstructured home life, a growing body of research indicates how a space–time continuum is dissected into specific, repetitive elements (Leach, 1976).

The essence of domestic life is expressed through its temporal characteristics. The daily repetition of domestic chores, the weekly and several rituals and annual celebrations (such as birthdays or cultural festivals) all express the *cyclical qualities* of family life, in sharp contrast to the explicit, divisible nature of educational and commercial enterprises. Nonetheless, this cyclical quality of family life can be contrasted with a temporal dimension that is composed of a series of sequential stages in the life cycle: the first months of marriage, the early years of parenthood, the adolescence of children, and then their departure from the parental home. In this sense, domestic life has an explicit *linear quality* in which there is no turning back, at least in a biological sense.

Furthermore, Elliott's narrative illustrates the clear distinction between male–female roles and parent–child roles in the home: housework is women's work, whereas it is common for men to be involved in diverse activities outside the house. Within the house, those rooms located at the front overlooking the street were less frequently used than those behind them. This was still the custom when Porter (1963) wrote his residential biography, as the preceding citation shows. In both cases, the parlor was used only for entertaining visitors and for other exceptional cases; Elliott's letter indicates that the fireplace in that room was never used. Whereas the parlor was "the showpiece" of the home, the kitchen was not entered by visitors; it was the most secular room, not only being used for cooking and household chores but also for eating daily meals.

This analysis of first-hand personal records of how a pioneer family furnished and used domestic spaces and facilities enables the neutral, static nature of a common colonial house to be understood as the most significant place in the daily lives of this household. In this respect, the macrosocial history of the morphogenesis of a predominant house type has been complemented and enriched by the microhistorical analysis of the meaning and use of the home and the household objects of a pioneer family.

IMPLICATIONS FOR FUTURE RESEARCH

The preceding sections of this chapter have illustrated a dual historical perspective for the analysis of homes. On the one hand, a macrosocial analysis of those processes leading to the development of predominant house types in South Australia during the earliest decades after British settlement; on the other hand, a micropersonal history of the residential biography of a pioneer family living in one of these types of houses.

The dual historical perspective presented and illustrated here can be reapplied in any context. Indeed, it ought to be so that an analysis of the morphogenesis of house plans (and how this process is related to economic, political, and technological factors) can be enriched by an analysis of personal diaries and reports of daily household life. Yet, this approach has rarely been proposed and illustrated. Nonetheless, it is essential to pursue research of this kind for two fundamental reasons:

- *The sociospatial characteristics of houses are endowed with personal values and meaning.* When the analysis of home environments does not account for the interaction between the spatial and the affective qualities of dwellings, then at best, the study deals with a narrative of house form and/or a study of its use at a specific point in time, whereas at worst the dwelling ceases to be space for human purposes and is reduced to a petrified object.
- *Domestic space and household life have inherent temporal qualities.* The analysis of homes should include a study of continuous processes rather than isolated actions, so that the qualitative nature of home environments is understood.

These guidelines for future research contradict a current trend in architectural history and practice that interprets the form of buildings as if space has an objective meaning that communicates itself to the building user. This notion of meaning in architecture has been ably criticized by Coloquhoun (1978). A more general refutation of this interpretation of material culture has been presented by Leach (1976) who cleverly demonstrated that the organization of forms, whether two dimensional (paintings) or three dimensional (objects or spaces) must be attributed to a set of conventional meanings not inherent in the forms themselves. This principle has been illustrated in this chapter by the differential meaning attributed to those rooms at the front and the back of colonial houses built in South Australia. In contrast to current architectural practice, this example serves to emphasize that dwellings are endowed with meaning and values that ought to be understood prior to the design of residential areas.

The catalyst for this task is a reinterpretation of the history of domestic architecture and household life. In contrast to contemporary historical interpretations described at the beginning of this chapter, future analyses of home environments can be enriched by exploring the interaction of cultural and social models and of personal residential experience if the dual historical perspective presented here is used.

This study has illustrated some important findings for architects and planners. First, it is apparent that houses or any other types of buildings ought to be designed with an awareness of those symbolic and secular images that specific persons associate with the built form of domestic space and objects. Second, it has become apparent that to answer user requirements that are only considered as functional or pragmatic is insufficient, if those representations and images associated with the built form of man-made space are ignored. It is evident that architects and planners should accept that the physical forms of man-made spaces and objects and the social systems in which they occur are interwoven and inseparable. The key to an understanding of the meaning of building form stems from acknowledgment of the principle that a fundamental aspect of the relationship of a person to his or her home is residential history. In other words, in any specific context the historical value of personal representations of domestic space provide the way to understand and accommodate a meaningful relationship between people and their homes. Therefore, if architectural design and research methods can be redefined to incorporate sociohistorical and psychological information of the kinds discussed here, then they would enrich and diversify the design of home environments.

CONCLUSION

This chapter has illustrated how home environments can be analyzed by employing ethnographical and historical research methods. This collaboration has indicated that if domestic space and objects are to be considered as a reflection of the ideas of the residents, one cannot assume that there is a one-to-one correspondence between the physical and affective characteristics of home environments. Furthermore, the multiple associations between these characteristics can be understood only in terms of an historical or temporal perspective. By history, one does not mean only the passage of time but also the past experience of residents.

In essence, the organization of domestic space, objects, and activities is the reflection of ideas; these ideas are the generators of spatial layouts, objects, and actions in the home. This implies that research should not merely focus upon manifest empirical things but on implicit tactic structures of household life. Given this interpretation, this chapter concludes with a request for further research of this kind: that is, studies of the transactions between the material world of domestic space, objects, and activities *and* the nonphysical world of ideas, symbols, and images, *and* how these transactions are modified through the passage of time.

REFERENCES

Altman, I., Vinsel, A., & Brown, B. Dialectical conceptions in social psychology: An application to social penetration and privacy regulation. In L. Berkowitz (Ed.), *Advances in experimental social psychology* (Vol. 14). New York: Academic Press, 1981, pp. 107–160.

Berry, D., & Gilbert, S. *Pioneer building techniques in South Australia.* Adelaide: Gilbert Partners, 1981.

Bourdieu, P. *Outline of a theory of practice.* Cambridge: Cambridge University Press, 1977.

Boyd, R. *Australia's home: Its origins, its builders and occupiers.* Ringwood, Victoria: Penguin Press, 1968.

Burnett, J. *A social history of housing 1815–1970.* Newton Abbot, England: David and Charles, 1978.

Cobb, R. The tempting threshold. *The Listener,* 6 April 1978, pp. 438–439.

Coloquhoun, A. Sign and substance: Reflections on complexity, Las Vegas and Oberlin. *Oppositions,* Fall 1978, *14* 26–37.

Csikszentmihalyi, M., & Rochberg-Halton, E. *The meaning of things: Domestic symbols and the self.* New York: Cambridge University Press, 1981.

Daunton, M. Experts and the environment: Approaches to planning history. *Journal of Urban History,* 1983, *9*(2), 233–250.

Douglas, M. (Ed.). *Rules and meanings.* Harmondsworth: Penguin Press, 1966.

Douglas, M., & Isherwood, Baron *The world of goods* New York: Basic Books, 1979.

Elliott, J. Manuscript catalogue number D2759L held in the State Archives of South Australia. Adelaide: 1860. S. Pikusa (Ed.), *Joseph Elliott's cottage of 1860 with architectural commentary.* Sydney: The Flannel Flower Press, 1984.

Freeland, J. *Architecture in Australia: a history.* Ringwood, Victoria: Penguin Press, 1972.

Hareven, J. (Ed.). *Transitions: The family and the life course in historical perspective.* New York: Academic Press, 1978.

Harré, R. *Social being: A theory of social psychology.* Oxford: Blackwell, 1979.

Hodder, E. *The history of South Australia.* London: Sampson, Low and Marston, 1893.

Ladd, F. Residential history: You can go home again. *Landscape,* 1977, 22(3), 15–20.

Lawrence, R. L'espace domestique: typologie et vécu. *Cahiers Internationaux de Sociologie* 1982, 22(1), 55–75.

Lawrence, R. The comparative analyses of homes: Research method and application. *Social Science Information,* 1983, 22(3), 461–485. (a)

Lawrence, R. Understanding the home environment: Spatial and temporal perspectives. *International Journal for Housing Science and its Applications,* 1983, 7(1), 13–25. (b)

Leach, E. *Culture and communication: The logic by which symbols are connected.* Cambridge: Cambridge University Press, 1976.

Leach, E. *Social anthropology.* London: Fontana, 1982.

Le Roy Ladurie, E. *Montaillou: Cathars and Catholics in a French village 1294–1324.* Harmondsworth: Pergamon Books, 1980.

Lévi-Strauss, C. *The scope of anthropology.* London: Allen Lane, 1967.

Lynch, K. *What time is this place?* Cambridge, Mass.: M.I.T. Press, 1972.

Pevsner, N. *A history of building types.* London: Thames and Hudson, 1976.

Porter, H. *The watcher on the cast iron balcony: An Australian autobiography.* London: Faber and Faber, 1963.

Pratt, G. The house as an expression of social worlds. In J. Duncan (Ed.), *Housing and identity: Cross-cultural perspectives.* London: Croom Helm, 1981, pp. 181–197.

Quatremère de Quincy, A. *De l'imitation.* Paris: Editions de Paris, 1823.

Sumner, R. The tropical bungalow: The search for an indigenous Australian architecture. *Australian Journal of Art,* 1978, 1, 27–30.

Swenarton, M. *Homes fit for heroes.* London: Heinemann Educational Books, 1981.

Twopenny, R. *Town life in Australia.* London: Elliot Stock, 1883.

6

The House as Symbol of Social Structure

NOTES ON THE LANGUAGE OF OBJECTS AMONG COLLECTIVISTIC GROUPS

JAMES S. DUNCAN

INTRODUCTION

There is a relatively small group of scholars who have conducted field-work specifically on the meaning of housing in Third World societies. Richardson (1974) in Latin America, Bourdieu (1973) in Africa, Austin (1976) in the Pacific, and King (1976) and the Duncans (1976, 1980) in South Asia are some of the names that come to mind. And yet there exists a vast amount of primary material available on this topic that has been collected by anthropologists whose principal interests lie not in housing *per se*, but whose broad ethnographic nets have yielded a rich catch of housing data nevertheless (see Guerry, 1975; Hogbin, 1939; Jackson, 1977; Lessa, 1966; Lewis, 1965). Similarly, the small and yet burgeoning field of women's studies also yields, as a by-product, per-haps the most interesting and detailed research on the use of the house conducted by researchers whose principal focus again is not on housing

JAMES S. DUNCAN • Department of Geography, Syracuse University, Syracuse, New York 13210. Research for this chapter was funded by the Social Sciences and Humanities Research Council of Canada.

(see Giele & Smock, 1977; Jeffrey, 1979; Matthiasson, 1974; Patai, 1967; Reiter, 1975).

One of the urgent research tasks that faces those of us interested in this topic is to assemble and make some sense of these housing data that are scattered throughout these literatures. Rapoport (1969, 1982), whose research on housing literally spans the globe and whose stimulating monographs serve both as generators of research questions and extensive bibliographies for researchers, has, of course, engaged this task for the past 15 years. More recently he has been joined by others such as Altman (Altman & Gauvain, 1981; Gauvain, Altman, & Fahim, 1983), Ardener (1981), Oliver (1975), and Lawrence (1980) who have also attempted to order some of these data.

Several years ago in an attempt to grapple with these data, I put forward the view that at least two distinct cross-cultural patterns in attitudes toward the house can be identified and that the explanation for these regularities lies in a broader set of cross-cultural patterns—the varying forms of social structures by which societies can be classified (Duncan, 1981). For my purposes, I have found it most useful to classify societies on the basis of two major forms of social structure, collectivistic and individualistic. These must be understood as ideal types, intellectual constructs designed to characterize polar types of relations. Neither whole societies nor even social groups within a society should be viewed as neatly slotting into either of these ideal types. Rather they should be seen as heuristic *pure types* with empirical cases arrayed along a continuum between them. The ideal typical nature of these categories is illustrated by the fact that Third World societies that traditionally were highly collectivistic have been moving along the continuum toward individualism, thus producing some of the structural and psychological dilemmas of what is termed *modernization* or *Westernization*. Societies that approach the collectivistic pole of the continuum (rural segments of South Asian societies, for example) tend to be characterized by relatively impermeable social groups composed of known others. Kinship is the most important organizing principle of the group with the society typically being organized along the lines of such collectivistic groupings as caste, tribe, clan, or lineage. The identity of individuals is intimately tied up with membership in the group. Material surplus is normally consumed by members of the group through various rituals of redistribution. This kind of consumption pattern is much more common than the individualistic consumption or display so typically found in North America. In societies characterized by these types of social relations, the private house is rarely an object of status display. People gain status more often through contribution to the group, and therefore the communal, group house is more likely to be the object of elaboration. The private house under collectivism becomes a functional dwelling, a place of the family, that, because it is like the houses of others in the group, has the effect of reinforcing one's identity within the group.

Individualism, on the other hand, as an ideal type stands at the opposite pole of the continuum. It represents a kind of reversed mirror image of collectivism. Within individualistic groups people see themselves first and foremost as individuals rather than as members of a caste, tribe, lineage, or extended family. Status seeking is manifested through a dependence upon private objects to affirm identity because collective markers of identity such as caste and extended family are either very weak or nonexistent. The house, for most people, is the largest and costliest private object whereby individuals can assert their identity. It is used to display to others who one is, what one's class, lifestyle, and tastes are, in other words to help others situate the potentially free-floating individual within the social structure.

These ideal types provide a key to understanding the distinct patterns of attitudes toward housing found in different cultures. Under individualism, the house is an important object of status for the individual (both male and female), whereas under collectivism the house is not a status object at all, as prestige is sought through community-oriented activities in community places such as the communal house, the dance ground, or the café.

By focusing upon individual status display as I did in my article (1981), the house in individualistic societies appears to take on a rich set of meanings, whereas its counterpart in collectivistic societies seems relatively meaningless. In both cases the house mirrors the social structure, but in the case of collectivism it appears as a nonstatus object. It would be unfortunate if readers were left with the impression that the house under collectivism is relatively meaningless, for nothing could be farther from the truth. If, for example, we consider corporate identity (how individuals mark their incorporation into the group) rather than individual status display (how they mark their apartness from their fellows), then the house under collectivism takes on rich meaning, and it is the house under individualism that begins to appear vacant. The house, therefore, contains not one set of symbols, but many; it is *multivocal*, to use Turner's (1969) term. It speaks in the language of objects and only answers those questions that it is asked.

In this paper I would like to begin where I ended my earlier paper (1981) and discuss the role played by the built environment in incorporating individuals into a collectivistic social structure. This incorporation is achieved in two principal ways, the first of which is cosmological.

Through myth both the group and the landscape are symbolically converted into a divine creation that exerts a powerful effect over the individual's life and provides him or her with a fixed place both socially and spatially within the cosmos. After considering this subtle dialectic of group, deity, and place, I will turn to a consideration of the second type of incorporation, how particular types of social organizations in collectivistic societies become crystallized in the built environment and how this crystallization in turn aids in legitimation of the social order by reaffirming the close links between the individual's lived experience and the dominant social structures of the society. The built environment has a powerful role to play in the social process. As a concretized, objectified part of the social structure it is a human construct, a product of culture; however, its very concreteness makes it appear as an object of nature, as natural and through myth as god given. The power of landscape lies precisely in its dual role as a creation of culture and of nature. The culturally assigned themes of hierarchy, belonging, and so forth communicate silently but insistently in the language of everyday experience that the cultural order in which the individual is embedded is a natural one and that the world is indeed in order, and as it should be.

THE ENVIRONMENT AS SYMBOL

The notion that attitudes toward the house both flow from and reinforce the central structuring relations of a society presupposes that the environment has affective meaning for people, although clearly this varies across cultures, as does the specific content of that meaning. It also presupposes that the environment mirrors social structure, although again, in some cultures, the image is clear, whereas in others it is clouded at best. These presuppositions, in turn, are logically underpinned, or so it seems to me, by a particular model of human beings. Humans in this view are seen as *au fond* symbolizing creatures who strive to seek and create meaning out of a world of objects (Geertz, 1973, pp. 126–141).

The environment serves as a vast repository out of which symbols of order and social relationships can be fashioned. It serves, of course, not only to represent meaning to the individual creator but also to others who share a common perspective or who at least can understand the meaning that is encoded, even if they do not accept that meaning as the only truth or even as one of many truths. Symbols, in other words, are social; they arise and are sustained within the public arena. They are used to communicate what is believed to be the nature of the world and humans' place in that world (see Firth, 1973; Geertz, 1973). The environment thus can be viewed as a text that can be read by those who know the language of built form. Interpretation of the environment may be a conscious and articulated activity; to use Giddens's (1979) term, it may constitute *discursive knowledge*, or it may more commonly be a form of *practical knowledge*, a kind of tacit understanding among participants in a cultural system.

Various approaches to cultural objects as texts are to be found in the works of Geertz (1973, 1983); Boon (1982), and Barthes (1977), and because choosing among divergent theoretical positions always entails a risk, I would, to adapt a phrase from Cicero, *prefer to err with Geertz*. A growing number of scholars approach the environment as a text. For writers such as Clay (1973), Lindsey (1985), and Preziosi (1979), the text is in prose, whereas for Bachelard (1969) it is poetry. I prefer Geertz's analogy of the text as a play, richly peopled with actors among highly symbolic stage sets. Although each culture's play is composed of a dizzying swirl of subplots, some tragedy and some farce, at one level it is always a morality play, a statement reflecting the culture's own particular vision of how the world should be. It is, as Geertz (1973) would say, a story they tell themselves about themselves.

As a geographer, my interest is focused upon the role that the environment plays in this story that members of a society tell themselves. What, to return to the analogy of the play, is the role of the stage sets in this morality play? The answer is that the stage sets are crystallized social relations. They are statements intentionally and unintentionally built into the environment about how people should behave toward each other. The stage sets speak to this issue of the moral order, of how the world should be ordered, in the language of objects, a language that largely operates at a practical rather than discursive level. It is a language that communicates values concerning the worth of individuals and community membership and, as such, helps place the individual, for better or for worse, within the matrix of their culture.

MYTHS OF INCORPORATION: COSMOS, ENVIRONMENT, AND GROUP

Foundation myths play an important role in incorporating individuals into groups. Myths linking the group to some divine force remove much of the potential arbitrariness of the group structure by making it appear as if it were a divine rather than a human creation. In myth, the group is made to appear important not only to the individuals that compose it but to the very gods themselves. Through myth then, the group becomes naturalized, an integral part of the fabric of the cosmos. It articulates for individuals the relationship between themselves, the group, and the cosmos. It tells them that their identity is inextricably woven into these larger entities and that apart from the group that serves as their link to the cosmos they are utterly lost.

But those mythic relationships also have a spatial component, for, according to foundation myths, the group occupies a special place within the cosmos assigned to it by the divine. The individual, then, is divinely rooted not only to a specific group but to a specific place as well (Sopher, 1979). It is through his or her location in this sociospatial matrix that a person knows his or her position in the cosmos. Through myths, the place of the group becomes loaded with symbolic significance. The contours of the land, the hills, the trees tell the person who he or she is, as does the form of the village, the house, and the shrine. The environment through the medium of symbols concretizes individuals' identities. They are able to see the truth of the group's myths etched in the landscape, and this truth binds them more tightly to the group. Although one could point to myriad examples of such beliefs, we will examine only three, each of which represents a slightly different variant on the common theme.

OUR HOME IS THE WHOLE OF THE WORLD

Perhaps one of the strongest expressions of the belief that a group's relationship to its land is divinely sanctioned is found among the Tiwi of Bathurst Island off the coast of northern Australia (Hart & Pilling, 1960). For the Tiwi, their island alone was the land of the living. The coast of Australia, which could be faintly discerned on the horizon and by extension all other lands, represented the land of the dead. Sailors who had the misfortune to be shipwrecked on Bathurst Island were quickly dispatched with clubs and spears, for to the Tiwi they were dead spirits whose presence could not be tolerated in the land of the living. To the Tiwi, then, their land represented not only the most favored place but the whole of the habitable world. This perhaps is the most powerful type of myth of incorporation into the group and place that is conceivable, for according to it only members of this group who are in this place are alive. All else is the realm of the dead.

OUR HOME IS THE WHOLE OF THE ORDERED WORLD

Other groups, such as central Australian aboriginal bands, distinguish between their own ordered world and the "chaos" that lies beyond. This transformation of their tribal world from a "chaos" to a "cosmos" is accomplished through ritual. They ritualize their territory through the medium of ancestor myths, landmarks associated with the sacred ancestors, and *churinga*, which are sacred ritual objects that represent the tribal territory. These nomadic bands follow routes within their territory that were laid out by their sacred ancestors during the "dream time." The band's claim to land is sanctioned through myth that establishes not only a connection to the place through time but also the inherent orderliness of the place in contradistinction to the implied physical and social chaos that exists beyond (Rapoport, 1975; Sopher, 1967). To these bands, then, the socially ordered world is defined by the group. For the individual the landscape is heavy with symbols of the group and its ancestors. In fact, given the structure of aborigine myths, individuals are only able to understand the nature of the landscape within which they live as a manifestation of the group to which they belong. The group defines not only the social reality but the physical one as well.

OUR HOME IS THE CENTER OF THE WORLD

In the territory of the Samake, a tribe of the Bambara group of farmers of the Upper Niger in Mali, there lies a rise in terrain near the Plain of Kurula that is thought of alternatively as the cosmic mountain, the first stone, or the star of fire that gave origin to the whole cosmos (Guidoni, 1978). The entire territory of the Samake and beyond it the rest of the world is believed to revolve around this mountain. Not only do the Samake see their place as the center of the cosmos, but they also feel that they have a central role to play in their place in order to preserve life on earth. Annual sacrifices are performed on the plain and at the base of the mountain, and every seventh year they perform a rite in order to renew the world. This territorial centrality with all its symbolism of sacredness (Eliade, 1959; Sopher, 1967; Tuan, 1974) is replicated at the smaller scale as well. Within every village there is a cosmic image (the mountain) represented by a stone placed in the center of a small pool (the plain). The stone and the pool are symbols of the unity of the cosmos, the territory, and the village, and they symbolize to the Samake the touch of the divine that has fallen on them alone in their place.

Throughout the whole of the Sudanese culture realm that includes the Samake, the Dogon, about whose architecture so much has been written (see Griaule & Dieterlen, 1954; Guidoni, 1978), and the Fali there exists the notion of cosmic centrality and a kind of nested hierarchy of the divine, whereby the cosmos is symbolically reproduced over and over from the scale of the tribal lands down to that of the individual house. The Fali exemplify this nesting quite clearly. Their interpretation of the environment rests upon a myth of the creation of the universe based upon the balanced correspondence of the two cosmic eggs—the tortoise and the toad. This subdivision is reflected in human society by the division of people into two groups—male and female—the organization of their territory—inhabited and wilderness—and the layout of the dwelling whose design was learned from the tortoise and which is composed of male and female parts. Proceeding in a manner not unlike the Hegelian dialectic, all life is based upon a series of alternate movements of these opposites. Every social group, every element of the built environment embodies this divine plan in that it either moves clockwise or counterclockwise or acts as a pivot for the surrounding parts. The house, for example, is composed of a feminine, cylindrical shell of masonry, surmounted by a masculine covering of rafters and straw, each of which circles in inverse direction to the other. Not only is the built environment seen as an extension of the divine order of things, but it also symbolizes in the male covering the female the naturalness of procreation, the fertility of the individual, the group, and the land. The built environment expresses for the Fali the logical proof of the unity of all things; the link between the people, their objects, and the infinite (Guidoni, 1978).

Among the collectivistic groups considered here, it is not enough merely to live in a place; one must link that place to the divine order of the world. (For other examples see Durkheim & Mauss, 1970; Jung, 1964; Rapoport, 1969). The attempt to convert the home place into a kind of sacred space serves both as a powerful legitimator of the group itself as well as of a group's occupance of a territory, for in this way the settlement at large and the home within it form a part of a divinely ordered nature rather than being a creation of mere human interest and desire. Individuals in their homes are tied not only to the social group but to the gods; the layout of the environment—the rock in the pool, the male roof on the female base, the hills and copses that represent the dead ancestors—all tell them this in the language of the concrete.

STRUCTURES OF INCORPORATION: INDIVIDUAL, ENVIRONMENT, AND SOCIAL STRUCTURE

The first act of the morality play that serves as an analogy for a culture concerns cosmology. It stresses unity: the oneness of the individual, the group, the home place, and the cosmos. The naturalness and goodness of the individual's incorporation in the group are reaffirmed through myths of belonging and through the symbolic reproduction of the sacred within the secular, the periphery within the center, the universe within the home plan. People can see the moral order writ large in the environment, and they know it is true because it is objective, tangible, and prescribed by myth. Who can doubt the truth of such a seamless web; of a oneness that encompasses both the ethereal nature of a foundation myth and the solid reality of the stone and clay that surrounds them?

But the play continues, for there are other stories to be told. The second act, though more mundane, is no less meaningful, for it concerns the socially ordered world. Here the story is one not of the unity of the whole group but of partition within the group and of how individuals find their rightful place within this well-ordered system. It speaks of commoners and nobles, clans and lineages, and of castes. It speaks of hierarchy as well as of belonging. And the play has its different stage sets, its spatial relations and buildings, which mirror symbolically in frozen form the moral order. A person's identity as a male, a Bororo, a member of the crocodile clan, or of the dhobi caste is not something passive that he or she possesses. It is, as Mead (1934) argues, active, something that one has to act out, to continually reaffirm through one's thoughts, one's actions, and the objects one surrounds oneself with. This reconfirmation of social identity, although active, is largely unconscious.

SYMBOLS OF COMMONERS AND CHIEFS

The status differences between commoners and chiefs are reaffirmed both behaviorally and artifactually in the environment. Among the Trobriand Islanders, hereditary chiefs had absolute rights over their people. This dominance was encoded in the environment in a set of sumptuary laws. There existed a status gradient whereby the chiefs' houses were in the center and those of the commoners were at the periphery. In the center there were also the sacred, elaborately decorated yam storage houses that only the chiefs could possess (Fraser, 1968; Malinowski, 1929). The political power of the chiefs was symbolized by their location in the sacred center and by their possession of the decorated storehouses. Their proximity to the sources of cosmic power clearly articulated and validated their claims to secular power.

Among the Konyak Nagas of Assam there is an aristocracy as well, but some villages are more aristocratic than others. In Thendu villages, where the chiefs are very strong, the chiefs' houses are huge, often larger than the communal bachelor halls that are found in each village. The chiefs' houses, unlike those of the commoners, also have elaborately carved posts and lintels depicting mythic scenes and symbols of fertility. That the environment mirrors social structure is also clearly seen in villages such as Wakching where the institution of chieftainship has been in decay for quite some time. In this village the chief has little power, and his house is no larger than that of any commoner. It still occupies the highest point of land in the village, but this is simply a holdover (Von Furer Haimendorf, 1969). The power had decayed, and the symbols of that power slowly decayed as well. Environments have an inertia that makes them lag behind the ideas that create, support, and ultimately destroy them.

SYMBOLS OF MOIETIES, CLANS, AND LINEAGES

The secondary groupings within collectivistic societies commonly take the form of moieties (a division of the group into halves that people are associated with from birth), clans (groups that have a common ancestor that is thought of as nonhuman), and lineages (groups who have a common human ancestor). The Omaha tribe of the Sioux Indians, for example, is divided into two moieties each of which contains five clans. The social identity of the Omaha individual is centrally tied to membership in both a moiety and clan, and this identity is encoded in the spatial structure of the environment. When the tribe camps, it forms a circle, and each particular group has a fixed place within it. First, the two moieties position themselves to the right and left of the route followed by the tribe. Then, within the semicircle occupied by each moiety, every clan has a location with respect to every other. The places assigned to them symbolize their social functions in the tribe and the nature of the things that they are thought to have influence over. Thus each moiety has a clan that stands in a special relationship to thunder and war, and they are placed facing each other at the entrance of the camp. The other clans are arranged in relation to them, according to the same principle. Because the Omaha moved so often, their houses were relatively simple affairs, and therefore their identities as members of subgroups were inscribed more in the language of spatial arrangement than of objects. But again, as Durkheim and Mauss (1963, p. 165) remind us, the environmental code speaks of more than simply moieties and clans, important as those things are:

> From the moment that the wolf people, for example, belong to a particular quarter of the camp, the same necessarily applies to the things of all sorts

which are classified under this same totem. Consequently, the camp has only to be oriented in a fixed way and all its parts are immediately oriented, together with everything, things and people, that they comprise. In other words, all things in nature are henceforth thought of as standing in fixed relationships to equally fixed regions in space. Certainly, it is only tribal space which is divided and shared in this way. But just as for the primitive the tribe constitutes all humanity, and as the founding ancestor of the tribe is the father and creator of men, so also the idea of the camp is identified with that of the world. The camp is the center of the universe, and the whole universe is concentrated within it. Cosmic space and tribal space are thus only very imperfectly distinguished, and the mind passes from one to the other without difficulty, almost without being aware of doing so.

A similar relationship between social structure and use of space has been noted among such geographically diverse groups as the Bororo and Sherente of Amazonia (Lévi-Strauss, 1967, 1972), the Trobriand Islanders in Melanesia (Malinowski, 1929), and the Nagas of Assam (Von Furer Haimendorf, 1969), suggesting a shared human response to communicating identity to oneself and others. Among the Nagas, social structure is encoded not only spatially but artifactually as well. Naga settlements are composed of wards, each of which is centered around a *Morung* (bachelor house). The residents of the wards form clans, and each ward acts as an exogamous unit in that sexual relations between members of a ward are seen as incestuous. Of all the Naga groups, the Konyaks have the largest and most imposing Morungs and, correspondingly, Morungs as an institution have the most important function among the Konyaks (Von Furer Haimendorf, 1969). Once again, built form follows social structure.

Among the Talensi of East Africa the house is the symbol par excellence of the lineage. In fact the same word is used for the house as for the family itself. A man's house is built and repaired by his kin out of material that they have collected. The condition of the house, then, is used by the Talensi as a marker of a man's ties to his kin. If he has a fine house in good repair, his ties are strong, whereas, if his house is in disrepair, it is a statement for all to see that here is a man whose relations with his lineage are unsatisfactory. Furthermore, the house is thought to belong not to the individual living in it but to the head of the family who built it, a dead father or grandfather, and as such serves as a mythic link connecting the present generation to the ancestors. This acts as a further inducement to maintain one's social obligations, for a deteriorating house brings shame upon one's ancestors, and woe be unto him who causes the ancestors to be dishonored (Fortes, 1949).

Symbols of Caste

Traditionally in India there has existed a rigid spatial and social separation of castes. In the typical village, each of the so-called *clean* castes lives on a street of its own, and the untouchables live beyond the pale in a hamlet, perhaps separated from the village by a stream or a piece of scrubland. This general pattern of spatial separation of residence is reproduced at different scales. Hazlehurst (1970) notes that in the typical north Indian town of Puranpur the central, ritually pure residential space of the Brahmans and Vaisyas is separated from the peripheral polluted space of the low castes. The brick houses of the pure castes also represent their high status. Within this pure space there is a further spatial differentiation as the various high castes occupy different neighborhoods. This differentiation is mirrored within the realm of ritual pollution as the *unclean* castes—sweepers, leatherworkers, barbers, and washermen—living in their poor mud houses separate themselves from each other on the basis of the different ritual services that they perform for the higher castes (Hasan, 1976). In Sri Lanka, although caste practices are less strictly observed than in India, residential segregation is still the rule (Obeyesekere, 1974). Most interaction is among neighbors who are castemates and often kin as well. Although people of different castes interact in public spaces such as in the fields, the home realm is not for such mixing. On the rare occasions when people of different castes come together in the home, these are stiff, formal affairs, heavy with an etiquette symbolizing hierarchy. Caste inequality is symbolized in the home by the restriction of the lowest castes to the veranda or outer courtyard and those slightly above them to a special low-caste bench just inside the house. Only the higher castes would be offered a chair (Ryan, 1953). The result of this is that in these times of increasing sensitivity about caste inequality, members of low-caste groups avoid going to the homes of high-caste people for fear of being treated in what is now seen as an insulting manner. While in Sri Lanka, I lived for 10 months in the house of a well-to-do Muslim family in a predominantly low-caste Batgama village. The Batgama were continually coming to ask small favors of my Muslim landlord, a glass of water, a bandage for a cut foot, or a telephone call in an emergency, but they would not have dreamed of asking the same of affluent fellow Buddhists because of the difference in caste. The home is a place of ritual honor, of the etiquette of hierarchy that constitutes the heart of a caste system whose guiding principle is, of course, inequality. It is here in the home where caste identity is strongest and therefore where one cannot afford to lower the barriers as one does in the less socially meaningful public places, such as fields and roads.

COMBATTING SYMBOLS OF NONINCORPORATION:
THE SOCIAL FUNCTION OF A BELIEF

The various environmental symbols of incorporation discussed previously do not guarantee incorporation. They suggest it to individuals but can in no way compel them to feel as one with their fellows. And yet, although not deterministic, these environmental symbols are important for they encode the dominant collective values of the culture in such a way as to make them a tangible part of everyday life. But increasingly in collectivistic societies, there are other competing values being symbolized in the environment—those of individualism, of separation from one's fellows. The private access to more material goods than one's kin, immediate neighbors, or other villagers is often the major symbol of differentiation within an otherwise homogeneous community. These material goods are typically associated with the home, and, as such, housing can operate as a major symbol of nonincorporation. How is this symbolism that contradicts the dominant ideology, discouraged? For one answer to this question, let us return to the Sri Lankan villagers whom I studied.

In Sri Lanka, the unity of an individual with his kin, caste, and village is held as an ideal. This is reinforced by the Buddhist doctrine of brotherhood, nonacquisitiveness, and the sharing of one's possessions. In reality, although there is much solidarity in the village, it is preeminently a world of strained relationships that always threaten to fragment the village. As one informant said: "In our village everyone sees what the other person has, so of course there is a lot of jealousy." Visible differences in wealth are a prime cause of tensions within families, among neighbors, and within castes, for these differences, if symbolized in the environment through the acquisition of objects, threaten the ideal of equality within these groups. They deny the ideal of incorporation. There exists an intense ambivalence in regard to materialism because, on the one hand, the average villager wants consumer goods and yet, on the other, this desire for material things causes tension within the group. One can see this ambivalence clearly within the home realm. Many villagers would like a larger house, new furniture, a television set, or an automobile—all clear symbols of prestige—but would be reluctant to spend money on such items of conspicuous consumption, on such flagrant symbols of separation from their less-affluent fellow villagers.

This ambivalence is expressed by the individual as jealousy or guilt associated with possessions, and these feelings are in turn transformed from individual psychological states into a powerful form of social control through the medium of the evil eye. Belief in the evil eye is found in many cultures (Maloney, 1976) and serves, as I have argued in more detail elsewhere, as a powerful force for incorporation (Duncan, 1984).

In Sri Lanka, if someone is thought to give one the evil eye because he or she envies some valuable thing that one has, misfortune is sure to result. Perhaps the new thing will break, or a member of one's family will fall ill and possibly even die. The evil eye is a powerful force that works against conspicuous consumption, for it strikes fear in the heart of anyone who has more possessions than his or her fellows. People who buy new things, therefore, either try and hide them from the view of others or protect themselves through magical charms. For example, virtually without exception, if a new house is built or major exterior renovations are undertaken, a *Cadjan* (palm leaf) screen is built to hide the construction from the evil eye. Upon completion of the house, during the dead of night when no one can see, the screen is removed, and an ash pumpkin is hung on an exterior rafter because it has the power to draw all of the evil eye to itself. Even so, this is no guarantee of protection, and many informants stated that they would spend money on the interior of their houses but not on the exterior for fear of the eye. Another informant confided that he had made a serious mistake recently by buying a television set (a rarity in the village). Since he bought the set his wife and children had been constantly ill, and he was sure that it was caused by the evil eye. I asked him what he intended to do about it, and he said that he would have someone perform a ceremony in order to remove the evil eye and henceforth would only turn on the television after he had shut his windows and doors and was assured that the neighbors had gone to sleep.

Even the acquisition of new furniture involves a risk as jealous neighbors or kin who come into the house can give the evil eye. As a result, a common practice is to completely cover a new piece of furniture, such as an *almirah*, with a white cloth for a period of 6 months so that although visitors will see that there is a new piece of furniture they will not see its quality. After people have become used to seeing the shape over a long period of time, the cover is finally removed. Doing it this way, I was told, reduces the shock of seeing something nice and lessens the danger. If such precautions are taken over a piece of furniture, what if someone bought an automobile? I asked a young man of 30 who came from a lower middle-class background in the village what would happen to him if he bought a car. He replied "I would be finished, I could not survive it." Had he come from a more well-to-do background, he could have bought the car but, given his background, it would have created too much discordance between who he was and who the car symbolized that he claimed to be. It would have placed too great a distance between himself and his kin and neighbors. When I asked him if it would be safe to have a car if he left his village, he replied: "Of course—no one would know me then."

Goods that others do not have, whether they be almirahs or automobiles, are symbols of nonincorporation. A new house is not simply a better shelter; the owner is seen as "putting on airs." "He thinks he is above us now," one woman remarked of her cousin who had just completed a new house in the village. Private objects serve to redefine social relationships, and, as such, they are threatening to the social order. When I asked my informants who was most likely to give them the evil eye, they overwhelmingly replied that it was their own kin and neighbors (usually of the same caste). In other words, it is from those closest to one that the greatest threat of the evil eye comes, and surely this is logical, for the purpose of the eye is to fight against the threats to group solidarity that private material display symbolizes.

Just as we have earlier seen that incorporation is symbolized in the environment of collectivistic societies, so nonincorporation, the separation of an individual from other members of the group, is also symbolized through objects. Private objects stand as dramatic testimony to the fact that there is individualism within the group and that the social ideal of collectivism is at odds with the social reality. Societies have belief systems that act as social mechanisms to support their central ideologies and suppress contradictory ones. The evil eye is one such belief whose social purpose in collectivistic societies appears to be to discourage the creation of symbols of individualism in the environment and therefore to produce social incorporation. The stage sets must support the central theme of the play; they are too important to be allowed to contradict it.

CONCLUSION

This essay examines the central role played by the built environment in incorporating individuals into collectivistic social systems. Two principal means of incorporation have been elucidated. First, it was shown how myths serve to reinforce the links between the individual, the group, the home place, and the cosmos. The act of symbolically transforming the landscape through myth gives divine sanction not only to the group of which the individual is a part but the home place as well. Second, it was demonstrated that the meaningful social categories within collectivistic societies are also powerfully articulated in the landscape. The environment, by incorporating a set of concrete symbols of group identity, provides a visual context within which individuals act out their daily lives; thus it constantly reinforces the incorporation of the individual into the group in a natural, one could argue, almost subliminal and highly effective way. The built environment, in addition to providing shelter, serves as a medium of communication because encoded within it are elements of the social structure. It speaks in the language of objects about the moral order of the culture. It serves as the stage set for the morality play, the backdrop for that collection of stories that a people tell themselves about themselves, in order that they may better know who they are, how to behave, and what to cherish. These stories are overwhelmingly stories of incorporation, of individual subservience to the group. For this reason, the built environment serves as one of the most powerful legitimators of the social structure in these societies.

IMPLICATIONS FOR FUTURE RESEARCH

The ideal types of collectivism and individualism were posited with some trepidation in order to simplify reality. In point of fact, there are few societies indeed at either end of the individualist-collectivist continuum. The categories are useful, I believe, because they provide a conceptual lever to prize apart the complex interrelations between housing and the other elements in the system. But both the schema that I have outlined and the relationships that I hope to have shed some light upon represent only a first attempt to solve the puzzle. What are now needed to help elucidate these relationships more completely than I have done here are detailed case studies of the meaning of housing in contemporary Third World societies. These societies are undergoing rapid cultural change that is increasingly moving them toward the individualistic pole of the continuum and consequently, if my thesis has merit, is generating changing meanings of the home. We must find answers to such questions as the following: Are some of the collectivistic symbols encoded in housing disappearing, and if so, how are they being replaced? Under conditions of rapid culture change, to what extent does the environment lag behind other elements in the system? Is the population of these changing cultures differentially affected by these changes? And, are there rural-urban differences, and what is the impact of change upon different age groups, social classes, genders, and other corporate groups?

In addition to undertaking detailed field studies of changing attitudes toward housing in Third World societies, it would be profitable for scholars to continue to search for analytical frameworks with which to analyze the data already collected by anthropologists and others. One would hope eventually to see a variety of different perspectives brought to bear upon the relationship between housing and other elements of social systems; for example, structural and interactionist perspectives, idealist and materialist ones, liberal and Marxist interpretations, and hopefully a dialogue among them all. This kind of dialogue, however, in part depends upon a good accessible body of data on housing. It would be of great value to have a compilation across a whole range of societies of rich and detailed data on housing and the important social characteristics of each society. This body of data, a kind of Human Relations Area File devoted exclusively to housing, would at least provide a common base upon which to build our analytical frameworks. Only after we begin to collect these data in a systematic fashion can we truly begin to explore the symbolic richness of the built environment and the integral role that it plays in the ongoing social process.

Acknowledgments

I am grateful to Gerald Pieris, head of the Department of Geography, University of Peradeniya, who invited me to be a visiting research fellow at the University of Peradeniya during 1983. I am indebted to Shanta Hennayake and Nalini Meulilatha who were superb field assistants and to Majid who served as key informant and friend.

REFERENCES

Altman, I., & Gauvain, M. A cross-cultural and dialectic analysis of homes. In L. Liben, A. Patterson, & N. Newcombe (Eds.), *Spatial representation and behavior across the life span.* New York: Academic Press, 1981, pp. 283–320.

Ardener, S. *Women and space: Ground rules and social maps.* London: Croom Helm, 1981.

Austin, M. R. A description of the Maori marae. In A. Rapoport (Ed.), *The mutual interaction of people and their built environment.* The Hague: Mouton, 1976, pp. 229–241.

Bachelard, G. *The poetics of space.* Boston: Beacon Press, 1969.

Barthes, R. *Image-music-text.* New York: Hill and Wang, 1977.

Boon, J. A. *Other tribes, other scribes: Symbolic anthropology in the comparative study of cultures, histories, religions, and texts.* Cambridge: Cambridge University Press, 1982.

Bourdieu, P. The Berber house. In M. Douglas (Ed.), *Rules and meanings.* Harmondsworth: Penguin, 1973, pp. 98–110.

Clay, G. *Close up: How to read the American city*. New York: Praeger, 1973.

Duncan, J. S. From container of women to status symbol: The impact of social structure on the meaning of the house. In J. S. Duncan (Ed.), *Housing and identity: Cross-cultural perspectives*. London: Croom Helm, 1981, pp. 36–59.

Duncan, J. S. *On evil eye and the fine house: An essay on the dangers of individualistic consumption in Sri Lanka*. Paper presented at the Annual Meeting of the Association of American Geographers, Washington, 1984.

Duncan, J. S., & Duncan, N. G. Residential landscapes and social worlds: A case study in Hyderabad, Andhra Pradesh. In D. E. Sopher (Ed.), *An exploration of India: Geographical perspectives on society and culture*. Ithaca: Cornell University Press, 1980, pp. 271–288.

Durkheim, E., & Mauss, M. *Primitive classification*. London: Cohen and West, 1963.

Eliade, M. *The sacred and the profane*. New York: Harcourt Brace, 1959.

Firth, R. *Symbols: Public and private*. Ithaca: Cornell University Press, 1973.

Fortes, M. *The web of kinship among the Talensi*. Oxford: Oxford University Press, 1949.

Fraser, D. *Village planning in the primitive world*. New York: Braziller, 1968.

Gauvain, M., Altman, M., & Fahim, H. Homes and social change: A cross-cultural analysis. In N. R. Feimer & E. S. Geller (Eds.), *Environmental psychology: Directions and perspectives*. New York: Praeger, 1983, pp. 180–218.

Geertz, C. *The interpretation of cultures*. New York: Basic Books, 1973.

Geertz, C. *Local knowledge*. New York: Basic Books, 1983.

Giddens, A. *Central problems in social theory: Action, structure and contradiction in social analysis*. Berkeley: University of California Press, 1979.

Giele, J. Z., & Smock, A. C. (Eds.). *Women: Roles and statuses in eight countries*. New York: Wiley, 1977.

Griaule, M., & Dieterlen, G. The Dogon. In D. Forde (Ed.), *African worlds: Studies in the cosmological ideas and social values of African peoples*. Oxford: Oxford University Press, 1954, pp. 83–110.

Guerry, V. *Life with the Baoule*. Washington: Three Continents Press, 1975.

Guidoni, E. *Primitive architecture*. New York: Abrams, 1978.

Hart, C. W. M., & Pilling, A. R. *The Tiwi of North Australia*. New York: Holt, Rinehart & Winston, 1960.

Hasan, M. *The social organization of residence in urban India* (Department of Geography Discussion Paper 17). Unpublished manuscript, Syracuse University, 1976.

Hazlehurst, L. Urban space and activities. In R. G. Fox (Ed.), *Urban India: Society, space and image*. Duke University Press, 1970, pp. 186–188.

Hogbin, H. I. *Experiments in civilization: The effects of European culture on a native community of the Solomon Islands*. London: Routledge, 1939.

Jackson, M. *The Kuranko: Dimensions of social reality in a West African society*. New York: St. Martin's Press, 1977.

Jeffrey, P. *Frogs in a well: Indian women in purdah*. London: Zed, 1979.

Jung, C. *Man and his symbols*. New York: Doubleday, 1964.

King, A. *Colonial urban development: Culture, social power, and environment*. London: Routledge & Kegan Paul, 1976.

Lawrence, R. J. Houses and people: A cross-cultural perspective. *Cultures*, 1980, 7, 150–169.

Lessa, W. A. *Ulithi: A Micronesian design for living*. New York: Holt, Rinehart & Winston, 1966.

Lévi-Strauss, C. *Structural anthropology*. New York: Doubleday, 1967.

Lévi-Strauss, C. *Tristes tropiques*. New York: Atheneum, 1972.

Lewis, O. *Village life in northern India*. New York: Vintage, 1965.
Lindsey, S. The semiosis of urban behavior. *Semiotica*, 1985, *6*, 17–25.
Malinowski, B. *The sexual life of savages in northwest Melanesia*. London: Routledge, 1929.
Maloney, C. (Ed.). *The evil eye*. New York: Columbia University Press, 1976.
Matthiasson, C. J. (Ed.). *Many sisters: Women in cross-cultural perspective*. New York: Free Press, 1974.
Mead, G. H. *Mind, self, and society*. Chicago: University of Chicago Press, 1934.
Obeyesekere, G. A village in Sri Lanka: Madagama. In C. Maloney (Ed.), *South Asia: Seven community profiles*. New York: Holt, Rinehart & Winston, 1974, pp. 42–80.
Oliver, P. (Ed.). *Shelter, sign and symbol*. London: Barrie and Jenkins, 1975.
Patai, R. *Women in the modern world*. New York: Free Press, 1967.
Preziosi, D. *The semiotics of the built environment*. Bloomington: Indiana University Press, 1979.
Rapoport, A. *House form and culture*. Englewood Cliffs, N.J.: Prentice-Hall, 1969.
Rapoport, A. Australian aborigines and the definition of place. In P. Oliver (Ed.), *Shelter, sign, and symbol*. London: Barrie and Jenkins, 1975, pp. 38–51.
Rapoport, A. *The meaning of the built environment*. Beverly Hills: Sage Publications, 1982.
Reiter, R. *Toward an anthropology of women*. New York: Monthly Review Press, 1975.
Richardson, M. The Spanish American (Colombian) settlement pattern as a societal expression and a behavioral cause. In H. J. Walker & W. G. Haag (Eds.), *Man and cultural heritage: Papers in honor of Fred B. Kniffen. Geoscience and Man* (Vol. 5). Baton Rouge: Louisiana State University, 1974, pp. 35–51.
Ryan, B. *Caste in modern Ceylon*. New Brunswick: N.J.: Rutgers University Press, 1953.
Sopher, D. E. *The geography of religions*. Englewood Cliffs, N.J.: Prentice-Hall, 1967.
Sopher, D. E. The landscape of home: Myth, experience, social meaning. In D. W. Meinig (Ed.), *The interpretation of ordinary landscapes*. New York: Oxford University Press, 1979, pp. 129–152.
Tuan, Y-F. *Topophilia*. Englewood Cliffs, N.J.: Prentice-Hall, 1974.
Turner, V. *The ritual process: Structure and anti-structure*. Ithaca: Cornell University Press, 1969.
Von Furer Haimendorf, C. *The Konyak Nagas: An Indian frontier tribe*. New York: Holt, Rinehart & Winston, 1969.

7

A Conceptual Framework for Residential Satisfaction

SUE WEIDEMANN AND JAMES R. ANDERSON

INTRODUCTION

There is little doubt that in contemporary industrial societies housing is multifaceted in character. It is viewed as an investment, a commodity, an element of the federal tax system, a design problem, a building, a set of buildings, a community asset, and so on. However, all housing is ultimately viewed by someone as a place for *home*. As a "place" for home, it represents the core of the physical portion of the social-physical environment that is home.

The multifaceted character of housing complicates its evaluation. Approaches that focus on a single dimension of housing are sufficient only if interest is limited to the perspective of that evaluation. Further, a single-facet approach to evaluation is unable to provide information about the relative importance of other areas of housing to housing quality.

Traditionally, some aspects of housing have been the object of evaluation more than others, in particular, the economic, structural, health, and community-planning facets. And, although the quality and appro-

SUE WEIDEMANN • Department of Landscape Architecture and Housing Research and Development Program, University of Illinois, Urbana-Champaign, Illinois 61801.
JAMES R. ANDERSON • School of Architecture and Housing Research and Development Program, University of Illinois, Urbana-Champaign, Illinois 61801.

priateness of these evaluations has sometimes been questioned (e.g., Hartman, 1963; Hempel & Tucker, 1979; Marcuse, 1971), a number of these areas have been the focus of evaluation for some time (e.g., economic issues of housing since the 1930s; community-health aspects of housing go back even further, to the social reformers of the late 19th century).

Interest in the evaluation of housing in its role as *home* has been fairly recent. The reason for this may be, as indicated by Rapaport (1969), that because every person lives in a dwelling, every person feels that he or she knows what dwellings are. Or, the reason may be, as indicated by Anderson and Weidemann (1984), that the focus of concern has been elsewhere; it has been on the impact of poor housing on society. Or, it may be related to the emphasis in our culture on other issues, for example the emphasis on the free enterprise system. This market view leads to the view of housing as a product. As with any product in a market society, there is the view of caveat emptor.

Whatever the reason for the tardiness in the development of interest in the evaluation of housing as *home*, it is clear that such interest is now a reality. The existence of a considerable literature in the postoccupancy evaluation of housing was demonstrated by the Environmental Research and Development Foundation (1977). Tognoli (1984) has described a variety of issues and viewpoints found in the literature examining the social-psychological environment in which people live. From these reviews, it is clear that much of the literature is disjointed and merely descriptive in nature. There is little underlying theory to organize studies of the evaluation of the home.

In this chapter, it is our intent to focus on the evaluation of the home in terms of the satisfaction of the occupant. First, existing theoretical models will be briefly reviewed, and a synthesizing framework for the concept of *satisfaction* will be proposed. This will be followed by a demonstration of the "fit" of existing research literature within the framework. Finally, directions for future research and theory development suggested by the synthesizing model will be presented.

THE EVALUATION OF HOME

The evaluation of *home* occurs naturally for its occupants. It is the researcher's task to elicit and interpret the naturally occurring evaluation of the home by its occupants.

There are a number of methodological issues related to eliciting the residents' evaluation, or perception, of the quality of their home environments. For example, it can be seen in the literature that there is a disparity between various *operational measures* of the same theoretical construct. Also, researchers have used different *methods* of gathering information (e.g., self-reports and behavioral observations), with differing levels of sophistication. And, it can be seen that researchers in this area have demonstrated differential familiarity with, and use of, various *analytic procedures* for dealing with that information. (Certainly, analytic procedures are not only a methodological concern, for their selection, use, and interpretation also reflect theoretical orientations.)

All of these issues can affect the quality and nature of empirical results. However, because Desbarats (1983), Marans (1976), and Wilcox (1981a,b) review many of these and because there is ample literature dealing with methodological issues in general, we will not continue with a detailed review of the problems of eliciting from the residents their evaluations of the qualities of their homes. It should be sufficient to point out the extreme importance of methodological rigor and its necessity in allowing one to have confidence in the attainment of dependable knowledge.

The focus will instead be directed more toward the theoretical and substantive issues related to the interpretation of people's responses to their homes.

Interpreting the Occupant's Evaluation: Theoretical Issues

There are some general conceptual issues to consider when thinking about interpreting the occupant's evaluation of his or her home. What must be examined first is the question, How do individuals respond to their housing environment? Ajzen and Fishbein (1981) refer to the "age-old trilogy" and point out that people display three general categories of responses to any social object: affective, cognitive, and behavioral. In fact, these three categories also describe the potential ways in which an individual can respond to all physical and social-physical objects. Thus, these are the ways that people respond to their home, and these are the dimensions available for understanding the evaluation of house as home. It will be seen that keeping this trilogy in mind can provide a useful perspective both for organizing past research examining residents' evaluations of their homes as well as for the development and testing of specific theoretical frameworks.

Of the responses in the trilogy, *affect* is the emotional, the feeling response. In addition, it is an evaluative response because it has *valence* (Fiske, 1981), a positive or negative value. In reality, affect is not represented by a single response but by a category of responses. These categories can be distinguished in terms of different levels or scales (Horley, 1984; Marans, 1976). Thus, for example, we can conceive of affect with respect to specific aspects of the home, that is, particular rooms, household members, furnishings, events. We can also conceive of affect at a more general level, that is, with respect to the dwelling itself, the structure and exterior space, or a whole community. Furthermore, we can conceive of affect not only with the physical environment, the dwelling or house, but with the total social-physical environment.

It is in this way that we conceive of residents' satisfaction with where they live. It is the emotional response to the dwelling, the positive or negative feeling that the occupants have for where they live. As such, it is a global representation of the affective response of people to the social-physical environment in which they live. At the same time, it must be remembered that satisfaction, that is, affect, is but one of three ways in which individuals respond to their dwellings.

An Early Model of Residents' Satisfaction

Francescato, Weidemann, Anderson, and Chenoweth (1974, 1979) proposed that people's satisfaction with where they lived was sufficiently important in itself to merit examination. Understanding the determinants of satisfaction became the focus of their study of 37 multifamily housing developments. They initially proposed a model that can be interpreted as focusing on the affective response of residents to their housing environment. They conceived of satisfaction, or affect for the home, as being a function of different categories of variables: the objective characteristics of the residents (e.g., age, sex, previous housing experience), the objective characteristics of the housing environments, and the occupants' perceptions or beliefs about three aspects of their housing environment (e.g., the physical environment, the housing management, and the other residents). These beliefs represent a second part of the triology—cognition.

In conducting their study of the 37 sites, Francescato et al. set about to empirically determine, for sets of variables composing each of these aspects, which sets were, in fact, predictors of residents' satisfaction.

A More Inclusive Conceptual Model of Residents' Satisfaction

Whereas Francescato et al. focused on the use of residents' satisfaction as a criterion, Campbell, Converse, and Rodgers (1976) were interested in examining residents' satisfaction as a determinant of perceived quality of life, which is perhaps the broadest affective concept. In addition, Marans (1975) and his colleagues indicated the importance of including objective measures of the physical environment in a model of satisfaction.

As a result, Marans and Sprecklemeyer (1981) presented a conceptual model for use in the understanding of, and guiding research on, relationships between objective conditions, subjective experiences, and residential satisfaction. This model has also been used in conjunction with research on recreational environments and institutional settings. More extensive versions of this model are also in Marans and Rodgers (1975) and Marans (1976). The basic conceptual framework is presented in Figure 1. This framework explicitly recognizes the physical environment by indicating that *objective attributes* of the particular environment have an influence upon a persons's *satisfaction* through the person's *perceptions and assessments* of those environmental attributes. In addition, this model recognizes another element of the triology—behavior. It states that a person's *behavior* is influenced by satisfaction, the perceptions and assessments of the objective environmental attributes, and the objective attributes of the environment itself.

Satisfaction can be seen to serve either as a *criterion* for evaluating the quality of the residential environment (by measuring the effect of perceptions and assessments of the objective environment upon satisfaction) or as a *predictor* of behavior.

Including Affect, Cognition, and Behavior in a Single Model

The model of Marans and Sprecklemeyer (1981) contains, at least implicitly, all of the elements of the response trilogy, and it also includes the physical environment as a response object. There have always been difficulties with models such as this in social psychology, however. One of the best-documented and most discussed issues in the literature dealing with attitudes is the finding that attitudes often do *not* directly predict behavior. Fishbein and Ajzen (1975) use an intervening variable, which they refer to as *behavioral intentions*, to diminish this attitude–behavior discrepancy. For example, although one may have negative feelings about an object (his or her current home, for example), he or she may still have no intentions of moving away from it; therefore he or she does *not* move. Behavioral intentions are seen as mediating between one's affective response and one's actual behavior.

In addition, for affect to be a determinant of behavior, that behavior must be possible. It must be volitional behavior, that is, a behavior that can be chosen by the individual. It is further necessary that the indi-

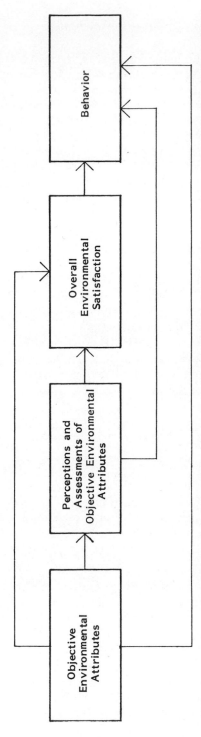

Figure 1. Basic conceptual model of resident satisfaction. From *Evaluating Built Environments: A Behavioral Approach* (p. 122) by R. Marans and K. F. Spreckelmeyer, 1981, Ann Arbor: University of Michigan Institute for Social Research. Copyright 1981 by R. Marans and K. F. Spreckelmeyer. Reprinted by permission.

vidual is able to perform the behavior, that is, there is a requirement for competency, physical, financial, demographic, or whatever.

The Fishbein–Ajzen concept of behavioral intention is very useful in conceptualizing relationships between people's beliefs, affective attitudes, and their behavioral responses. We feel, after carefully considering our own research on residents' satisfaction and the work of others, that integrating this into the previously discussed models can be useful. By *useful*, we mean that such an integrated model can be used both to better characterize the existing research as well as to suggest particular relationships that have received little empirical attention. Major portions of the particular integrated model presented later have been conceptually proposed previously by Cutter (1982) and tested for a sample of suburban homeowners. In this case, the model was seen as an improvement in terms of percentage of variance in residential satisfaction accounted for by the predictor variables.

An Integrated Model

The models of Francescato *et al.*, and Marans seem to be quite compatible in that they share major conceptual relationships. An affective component (satisfaction) is found in both. Beliefs, the cognitive component, are seen as determinants of the affective component in Francescato *et al.*; equivalently, "perceptions and assessments" of attributes of the objective environment are determinants of affect in Marans's model. The models differ in the extent to which they include elements of the trilogy: beliefs, affect, and behavior. They also differ in the extent of their inclusion of characteristics of the objective environment. Yet neither view explicitly considers behavioral intentions, which Fishbein and Ajzen (1975) have proposed and for which extensive support exists. Therefore, the integrated model shown in Figure 2 contains all these elements.

One characteristic of the previous models is that they directly indicate causal linkages between different components in the models. In fact, most theoretical and empirical explorations postulate such causal relationships. More recently, however, various authors have been suggesting that these relationships may indeed be more complex and reciprocal than it was previously thought. For example, in considering the relationship between cognition and affect, cognition is generally treated as a determinant of affect. Yet this view of primacy has been recently debated, and empirical evidence supporting the view that either can "cause" the other has been presented (Lazarus, 1984; Zajonc, 1984). Of more direct relevance for residential environments is the approach taken

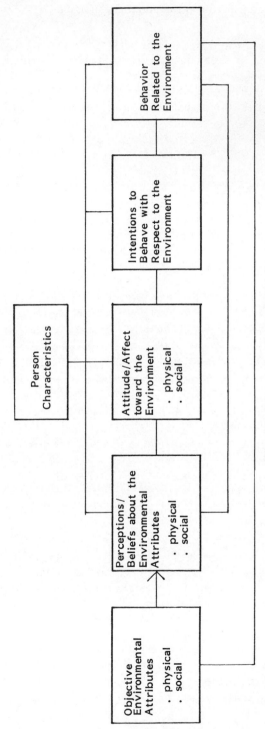

Figure 2. Integrated conceptual model.

by Altman and others (e.g., Altman & Gauvain, 1981; Brown, 1984; Gauvain, Altman, & Fahim, 1983). This is much more representative of a true "systems" perspective in that it is thought to be likely that any variable can influence any other variable. Therefore, the conceptual model in Figure 2 is shown with lines (rather than arrows) linking the various components. This suggests that the relationships can be theoretically multidirectional. It is important to note, however, that the bulk of current empirical and theoretical approaches still reflects a general sense of causality when moving from left to right in this diagram. Obviously, this issue is one of the more intriguing directions for future work.

Another important aspect of this model is the explicit inclusion of information about objective environmental attributes. Although those directly involved with the planning, design, and management of the physical environment do not neglect this aspect, those more traditionally associated with the social and behavioral sciences often begin their empirical research with the perceptions of (or beliefs about) the environment and thereby neglect objective measures of the environment. Exceptions to this generalization, however, are increasing. For example, work at the Institute for Social Research, cited in Marans (1976), has been directed toward the degree of agreement between perceptions of the neighborhood and objective physical measures of the actual conditions around them. Similarly, Weidemann, Anderson, Butterfield, and O'Donnell (1982) and Anderson and Weidemann (research in progress) have examined the relationship between objective measures of attributes of homes, residents' perceptions and beliefs about those attributes, and residents' satisfaction with their home environments. As Rodgers and Converse (1975), Craik and Zube (1975), Hempel and Tucker (1979), and Snider (1980) point out, both subjective and objective inputs are important, and neither can be properly interpreted in the absence of the other.

Yet another important component of this model is the explicit linking of affective attitudes (satisfaction, in this case) to behavior via behavioral intentions. The usefulness, in predicting behavior, of measuring behavioral intentions has been widely recognized in the marketing and social science literature. Consideration of this link between attitude and behavior in future environment–behavior research should be correspondingly useful.

Characteristics of the individual must also be considered as another component of this integrated conceptual model. These can be conceived of as including both personality and sociodemographic characteristics. For example, Francescato et al. (1975) examined measurements of internal-external control in relationship to residents' satisfaction, and Marans and Rodgers (1975) postulated that a person's satisfaction with his or her residential environment depends partially on the person's own characteristics, such as social class and life-cycle stage. Marans and Spreckelmeyer's (1982) conceptual model for evaluating work environments depicts "person characteristics" as directly influencing both environmental satisfaction and performance and indirectly influencing perceptions of environmental characteristics. Hourihan (1984) reviews other literature that considers "person" characteristics in relation to residential satisfaction. There certainly seems to be sufficient interest in characteristics of the individual in relation to satisfaction to warrant inclusion in this conceptual model. However, we feel that this issue needs much greater empirical and theoretical exploration in terms of where the strongest links with other components occur.

An Extension of the Model

Finally, when satisfaction has been used as a criterion of residential quality, it has varied widely in scale. That is, satisfaction with the county of residence, the community, the neighborhood as well as the housing development or dwelling unit have all been operationally measured. However, these various levels have been clearly differentiated less frequently when authors have been reviewing the literature and considering consistencies or inconsistencies of results. We feel that the more elaborate version of Marans's model (1976) would be quite useful in assisting this distinction. In that conceptual model, the residential milieu of an individual is seen to consist of the community, the macroneighborhood, the microneighborhood, and the dwelling and lot. There would be objective environmental attributes, perceptions and assessments (beliefs), and levels of satisfaction associated with *each* of these. In fact, the studies that measure objectively and subjectively perceived attributes of the "residential environment" often include variables representative of these different levels of scale, although they are seldom explicitly considered in this way.

In addition to differing levels of scale for satisfaction criteria, there have also been differences in the emphasis placed upon physical versus social components of the home environment. If we think of satisfaction with home (or the residential setting), it is reasonable to expect that our beliefs about and relationships with the other people in that setting should also influence our affective response. In fact, for example, research by Anderson and Weidemann (1980) has shown that beliefs that neighbors are similar to oneself in terms of various characteristics are directly related to one's satisfaction with the residential environment. Thus, the integrated theoretical model shown in Figure 2 should really be expanded to explicitly include social as well as physical components of home environments as well as levels of scale. Figure 3 demonstrates this expansion.

Within each of the levels of the physical environment (room, unit, development, neighborhood, community), there are also social and/or organizational relationships. The research that has been conducted has often included variables intended to measure these social characteristics, although they are not commonly examined in conjunction with physical variables in efforts to assess their relative contribution to satisfaction. As Altman (1975) has suggested, further theoretical and empirical work needs to consider the integration of people and environments into the same conceptual system.

The extended conceptual model offers a way of integrating the current research about residential environments. We will now characterize various research efforts and present substantive results concerning the relationship between the residential environment, beliefs about the residential environment, satisfaction, and behavior.

EMPIRICAL ISSUES

Literature representative of various segments of the integrated model will now be considered. We found that research efforts rarely empirically examined variables representative of the whole range of the integrated model. They instead tended to focus upon a subset of the components. Although the lack of broad focus could easily have been a result of the generally greater effort and resources that would be required of such an approach, it also seemed that various researchers simply did not feel that some of these components were relevant. This broader conceptual model suggests that these need to be more carefully examined.

We will consider the issue of *levels* of satisfaction and *analytic approaches* first. Then examples from the literature will utilize this conceptual framework to integrate satisfaction as it relates to behavior as well as satisfaction as an *affective criterion* of the quality of the home.

Levels of Satisfaction

Marans (1976) and Prak (1982) are among those who report extensive evidence that the majority of residents are either moderately or totally satisfied with the place in which they live. Also, Michelson (1977)

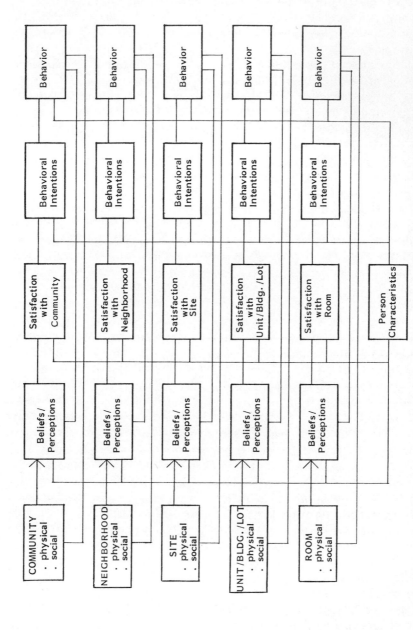

Figure 3. Conceptual model of satisfaction: Extended to include levels of scale, and social components of the residential environment.

and Suttles (1968) found overall high levels of satisfaction even though a number of the respondents' needs and desires were not completely met. However, we would suggest that at least three critical variables in this issue are ones that concern the age and income level of the user and the type of residence that is being evaluated. For example, residents of planned communities report high levels of satisfaction (e.g., Weiss, Burley, Kaiser, Donnelly, & Zehner, 1973; Zehner, 1977). Yet these are generally new facilities, for other than low-income people, and they have generally been the recipient of positive publicity (Nathanson et al., 1976). Homes that have been built by owners are also highly evaluated by those owners (Floro, 1983; Vischer, 1984). Dissonance theory can certainly suggest possible explanations for this. Furthermore, there is relatively consistent evidence, from research examining responses of elderly persons to their residential environment, that the elderly generally provide highly positive evaluations of their housing.

In contrast, it has been our experience, with low- and moderate-income residents of multifamily housing (Anderson & Weidemann, 1980; Francescato et al., 1979; Weidemann et al., 1982) as well as with elderly residents in moderate high-rise housing (Turnbull, Thorne, Anderson, Weidemann, & Butterfield, 1983) that levels of satisfaction are not uniformly high. Hourihan's (1984) more recent work also supports this finding for people living in different types of residential environments. And although the distribution of responses generally has means more positive than the midpoint of the satisfaction scale, there is still substantial variation both within and across sites. Although much of this research that considers level of satisfaction often compares different types of housing, there is recent evidence (Thorne & Turnbull, 1984) that satisfaction levels for equivalent high-rise buildings for the elderly differ significantly. Thus, there certainly appear to be other characteristics of the residential environment in action.

Furthermore, although the level of satisfaction with a particular site may be quite important to its residents and to other people dealing with that particular housing (e.g., developers, owners, managers, etc.), it is more useful from the viewpoint of theory and research to examine the variation associated with the responses to the measure of satisfaction. One of the useful ways of focusing on variation is by treating satisfaction as a criterion variable in a conceptual and operational model, where variables measuring various physical, social, and contextural attributes of the residential environment as well as individual characteristics are used as predictors of satisfaction. It then becomes possible to test various hypothesized models (e.g., by the use of regression and path analyses), to empirically examine which of the attributes of the residential environment and of the individual have either direct, indirect, or no relationship with satisfaction (e.g., Anderson, Weidemann, & Butterfield, 1983). Thus, it is the extent of covariation of satisfaction with other variables rather than the level of satisfaction that should be the focus of those who wish to learn what attributes are predictors of, or are related to, residents' satisfaction with their homes. Furthermore, this covariation can be examined by a number of different analytic techniques.

Analytic Techniques

Without dealing with specific statistical procedures, other than as examples, we wish to note that there is great variability in approach, in terms of developing and testing theories, and certain approaches are more useful and powerful than others.

One of the least useful, in our view, is that of simply reporting descriptive information (e.g., frequency distributions, percentages, measures of central tendency). Although descriptive information *can* be quite useful (if the question being asked is a descriptive one), it is limited. Anderson, Weidemann, Chenoweth, and Francescato (1974) discussed this issue in terms of levels of satisfaction with various attributes of residential environments. For example, measured attributes of the residential environment could be ranked according to the relative level of satisfaction expressed with each. One approach would be to say that the most important are those attributes found to be least satisfactory. (The implication would be that those lowest in satisfaction should be the ones to attempt to improve.) But simply because a particular attribute in itself is found to be unsatisfactory, it does *not* follow that the attribute is important for, or related to, a measure of *overall* satisfaction with the residence. In order to determine this, *multivariate* analyses need to be used. That is, at least two variables, and preferably more, need to be examined in terms of their relationships to each other. Fortunately, there are multivariate techniques (e.g., regression and path analyses) that examine the relative importance of two or more variables in terms of their contribution to a criterion variable.

And if one is attempting to measure *many* attributes of the residential environment, there are other multivariate procedures (e.g., factor, component, or cluster analysis) that result in *sets* of highly correlated variables that represent a similar concept.

Furthermore, these techniques can be used in combination (e.g., Anderson *et al.*, 1983; Francescato *et al.*, 1979; Weidemann *et al.*, 1982). For example, factor analysis can reduce a large number of variables, intended to measure various attributes of the residential environment, to a smaller number of sets of highly related items. These sets can in turn be used to test hypothetical models by way of path analysis. Figure 4 represents one such partial model to test both direct and indirect predictors of the affective criterion of *residents' satisfaction*.

By evaluating statistically the degree of these hypothesized relationships, information can be gained that can be used to revise existing theoretical views and to suggest potentially important areas that need further study.

Although there are always advantages and disadvantages associated with the usage and interpretation of results from any specific statistical technique, a more comprehensive multivariate approach to the analysis of data can aid in both theoretical and substantive advances in knowledge about the residential environment.

The next section will briefly illustrate both theoretical and substantive information about satisfaction as a predictor of behavior. Satisfaction as a criterion of the residential environment will be considered subsequently.

Affective Components as Predictors of Behavior

Both *satisfaction* and *preference*, operationalized in a variety of ways, have often been considered to be predictive of behavior. Marans (1976) and Tognoli (1985) refer to numerous studies of behaviors associated with the residential environment. And when satisfaction levels (or preferences) are measured, they are often used as predictors of migratory, or moving, behavior. In terms of the effect of satisfaction upon moving behavior, Marans (1976) summarizes research comparing the relative importance of satisfaction with the dwelling versus satisfaction with attributes of the neighborhood. Although both have been found to be predictive of moving behavior, their relative importance has been found to vary with age of resident, the nature of the neighborhood in terms of high versus low stress, and the nature of the neighborhood in terms of new town versus other types of residences. Speare and others (1974, 1975) developed a model of residential mobility in which satisfaction was the major predictive variable. Rossi (1980) considers, in addition to satisfaction, the effects of the family composition, life-style changes, and housing characteristics upon mobility. Studies such as these indicate the importance of considering characteristics of the environment and the individual as well as social and economic aspects.

Nathanson, Newman, Moen, and Hiltabiddle (1976) viewed residential mobility as a behavioral index of satisfaction. They found that satisfaction with the dwelling unit was the second most important vari-

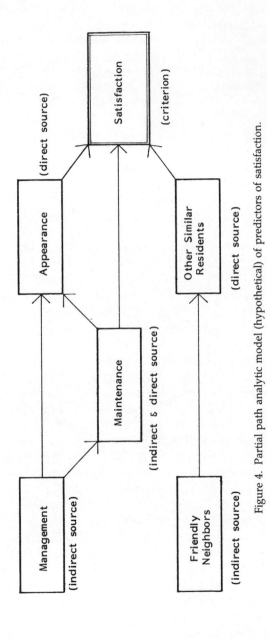

Figure 4. Partial path analytic model (hypothetical) of predictors of satisfaction.

able in explaining moving plans for owners and the third most important for renters. In terms of the integrated model, characteristics of the individual demographic valuables, beliefs about neighbors, behavior (frequency of participation in community activities), and an affective component (satisfaction) were all predictors of a behavioral intention (plans to move). It should be noted, however, that the percentage of variance in the criterion (moving plans) that was explained in their set of data was relatively small; R^2 was less than 25%. This certainly suggests, conceptually, that other variables need to be considered.

As an example of another relatively elaborate study (in terms of conceptual model and analytic techniques), Newman and Duncan (1979) examined demographic variables, characteristics of the housing context (in terms of city size), respondent reports about attributes of the housing, beliefs about problems of the neighborhood, an affective response (housing satisfaction), behavioral intentions (to move), and actual behavior (mobility). They found that there were both direct and indirect effects on actual mobility. Satisfaction with housing and mobility intentions were direct predictors of mobility behavior. Indirect effects on mobility, operating through housing satisfaction, were perceptions of the neighborhood's being crowded, age of household head, and whether the home was owned or not. Again, however, although statistical relationships were significant, the percentage of variance accounted for by the various sets of predictor variables still tended to be small ($R^2 < .25$).

Although satisfaction with the current dwelling unit, neighborhood, or community has been a key variable used to explain migratory intentions and behaviors, McHugh (1984a) feels that additional social psychological determinants of migration intentions and behaviors must also be considered. Those that he used were adapted from Fishbein and Ajzen's (1975, 1981) attitude-based model and included "attitude toward moving" and "subjective norms." Both of these were found to discriminate among different types of intended movers and stayers. His satisfaction measure also distinguished among types, although less strongly. Those less satisfied were more likely to be movers than stayers.

McHugh (1983) also used path analysis to test a model based on Fishbein and Ajzen's framework by measuring subjective norms, beliefs, anticipated constraints, intentions to move, and moving behavior. Unlike other studies, which often predict only a modest portion of the variance in migratory behavior, McHugh's path model explains a substantial proportion of variance ($R^2 = .65$ for intention to move and $R^2 = .62$ for moving behavior). This study offers considerable support for the usefulness of a more comprehensive model such as that suggested here. McHugh also found that attitude (+ or −) toward moving, subjective norms, and anticipated constraints were more strongly related to migra-tion intention and behavior than either the desire to move or the level of residential satisfaction. It should be noted, however, that his satisfaction variable, in both papers, consisted of a single item measuring the re-spondents' satisfaction with their *county*, rather than with their home. It would be interesting to test the relative strength of an index of items focused on the more immediate residential environment in this model.

Much of the work on migration behavior, which often includes residential satisfaction as a predictor, exhibits many of the theoretical and methodological issues previously mentioned. An article by Des-barats (1983) and a reply by McHugh (1984b) examine these, and, in particular, they focus on the use and interpretation of Fishbein and Ajzen's model. Although they differ in their interpretation of the model, they both emphasize its usefulness, in terms of theoretical understand-ing and predictive power. Their position and results support our conten-tion that a more comprehensive theoretical framework should be consid-ered and tested.

In general, it seems as if the theory base for this portion of the integrated model that examines predictors of behavior is somewhat better developed and tested, at least for mobility and migration behav-ior, than is the portion where an affective component is utilized as a criterion of the quality of the residential environment. That is not to say that a relatively large amount of research has not occurred; it just seems to be less integrated in terms of a common theoretical model.

The next section will address studies using some measure of resi-dential satisfaction as an affective criterion of the quality of residential environments. Their respective position in the integrated theoretical model discussed previously as well as general results will be considered.

Satisfaction as an Affective Criterion

It should be noted, however, that other affective criteria of environ-mental quality have been examined, the most common of which is that of preference. Preferences are often asked about environments that the respondent is not directly experiencing (e.g., Tremblay, 1979). Satisfac-tion, in contrast, usually concerns a response to an experienced environ-ment. Although the predominant view of preference is that it is consid-ered to be evaluative or affective in nature, (e.g., Fiske, 1981; Wohlwill, 1976), operational definitions do not always reflect this. Leven and Mark (1977) use "price paid to move from one neighborhood to another." Tognoli (1984) refers to both *preference* and *satisfaction* in a section on cognitive and behavioral aspects of housing, although many of the studies considered therein treated various objective and cognitive attributes (beliefs) of the environment as *determinants* of affective measures of preference or satisfaction. Thus, one of the difficulties in dealing with the literature evaluating the quality of residential environments is the looseness with which the terms *preference* and *satisfaction* have been used. Although there is extreme diversity in operational definitions, the concepts themselves have occasionally been used interchangeably on a conceptual level, or at least they were not explicitly differentiated (e.g., Kaplan, 1983). This fact also illustrates the need for a more unified general framework in which the concepts and their hypothesized relationships are made explicit, and thus become more easily testable.

Preference has been viewed as a social indicator of the quality of a community (Hempel & Tucker, 1979), as reflecting perceptions of the physical condition of the building and yard (Borukhov, Ginsberg, & Werczberger, 1978) and as a result of evaluations of neighborhood attributes (Cadwallader, 1979). More recently, Nasar (1983) found that four visual attributes of residential environments (upkeep, ornateness, openness, and clarity) accounted for a large proportion of the variance ($R^2 = .64$) in a four-item composite preference score. With respect to the integrated model, Nasar's composite preference score could be considered to consist of both *beliefs* (e.g., high versus low rate of robbery) as well as an *affective component* (e.g., pleasant/unpleasant).

These studies certainly reflect the existence of work relating the perceptions of attributes/beliefs about the environment to a criterion that is often thought of as being evaluative or affective in nature. Yet there is little common theoretical ground that they share, other than at this very general level.

The expanded model (Figure 3) suggests that both physical and social variables should be related to one's satisfaction with home. In addition, the issue of level, or scale, of the type of environment being studied should be considered. Table 1 allows an overview of various studies that have considered the relative effectiveness of physical and/or social variables (as measured by objective, subjective, or behavioral means) in predicting people's satisfaction with their home. These are further characterized by whether the variables have been concerned with the unit or house scale, the development scale, or the neighborhood or community scale. Also in Table 1 are the various satisfaction criteria that have been used as well as (where reported) the total percentage of variance in the criterion accounted for by significant predictors.

Snider (1980) also has emphasized the importance of studying objective, subjective, and behavioral data sets in his research on indicators related to the satisfaction of occupants with their accommodations. In

TABLE 1: Components of the Residential Environment as Predictors of Satisfaction[a]

Criterion	Physical		Social			Physical and social	R²	Studies
			Development					
	Unit/house	Development	Unit/house occupants	Other residents	Management	Neighborhood community		
Satisfaction with accommodations	O,S	O,S	O,S,B		O,S		Not reported	Snider (1980)
Satisfaction with present accommodations	O,S	O,S	O	S		S	$R^2 = .50$	Davis & Fine-Davis (1981)
Satisfaction with dwelling	O,S	S	O,B		S		$R^2 \geq .13^b$	Johnson & Abernathy (1983)
Satisfaction with development	O,S	S	O,B		S		$R^2 \geq .13^a$	Johnson & Abernathy (1983)
Satisfaction Index	O,S	O,S	O,S,B	S	S	S	$R^2 = .50–.60$	Francescato et al. (1975)
Satisfaction Index	O,S	S	O,S,B	S	S	S	$R^2 = .59$	Anderson & Weidemann (1980)
Satisfaction Index	O,S	S	O,S,B	S	S	S	$R^2 = .49$	Weidemann et al. (1983)
Satisfaction Index	O		O,B			S	$R^2 = .19$	Cutter et al. (1982)

[a]Types of data: (O) Objective, (S) subjective, (B) behavior intentions or behavior.
[b]Apparent bivariate R^2.

his study of 1,253 low-income families living in 88 multifamily housing projects in Alberta, Canada, he finds that subjective data (e.g., relations with management, satisfaction on arrival) from the tenants rank highest in accounting for satisfaction, although behavioral (e.g., plans to move) and objective measures (e.g., type of unit design, number of shared barriers) were also related to satisfaction. For example, the behavioral intention of the tenant regarding plans to move was negatively correlated with satisfaction. When variables were categorized as being related either to design, tenants, or management, the design-related measures were found to be more strongly related (zero order correlations) to satisfaction with accommodations.

Davis and Fine-Davis (1981) examined various objective attributes and subjective beliefs about which housing and neighborhood conditions were most related to residents' satisfaction with their present accommodations, satisfaction with their neighborhood, and life satisfaction. Thus, they were dealing with different scales of both environmental predictors and satisfaction levels. Their analyses were based upon a nationwide survey of over 1,600 owners and renters in the Republic of Ireland, although the sample was not partitioned in terms of type of residence (e.g., single versus multifamily). Although those who were older and those who had higher incomes expressed more satisfaction with their housing than those who were younger and poorer, these variables were not found to be predictors of satisfaction. The major predictors were subjective and objective measures of physical aspects of the accommodation, although a subjective evaluation of neighbors was also among the variables explaining 50% of the variances in "satisfaction with accommodations." This reasonably large amount of explained variance supports the view presented in the integrated model that satisfaction with home is a result of complex interrelationships, operating at different levels.

Johnson and Abernathy (1983) provide us with an example of a study focusing primarily on the relationship between affective responses to specific aspects of the housing environment and more general affective satisfaction responses. They obtained objective and subjective measures of residents and subjective measures (in the form of satisfaction scales) of the dwelling, development, and development relationship with community (e.g., transportation, nearness to schools). These were used as bivariate predictors of "satisfaction with dwelling" and "satisfaction with development." In addition, the sample of interviews from 755 residents of multifamily housing in the Greater Vancouver area of British Columbia was partitioned into those residing in highrise, three-story buildings, or townhouses for these analyses. Significant predictors of dwelling satisfaction came from all types of information; however, the subjective measures relating to physical features and management were the strongest. Furthermore, predictors of satisfaction with the dwelling *differed* for residents of high-rise versus three-story buildings versus townhouses. As Francescato, Weidemann, Anderson, and Chenoweth (1977) also found, in their comparison of responses from residents of high- versus low-rise multifamily housing, management was a stronger predictor of satisfaction for residents of high-rise than for low-rise buildings; however, privacy from neighbors was a significant predictor only for the high-rise sample. Johnson and Abernathy (1983) also found that satisfaction with various physical attributes of the home (layout, space, room size) were predictors of dwelling satisfaction, but the bivariate R^2s were generally not large. Because their analyses apparently did not test the potential predictors in a multivariate regression analysis and because we have no information about the degree of multicollinearity among those predictors, it is not possible to know what the total R^2 would be for this set of variables.

The work begun by Francescato *et al.* (1974), using a sample of over 1,800 respondents from 37 multifamily housing developments in the United States, was extended to site-specific research for site improvement purposes by Anderson and Weidemann (1980), Weidemann and Anderson (1980), and Weidemann *et al.* (1982). All of these studies focused upon the use of a variety of subjective measures as predictors of satisfaction wih the home. However, there are several differences between this research and the previously mentioned research examples. One of these, in terms of the integrated theoretical framework, has to do with the depth (or wide variety) of beliefs about the residential environment's being examined with respect to satisfaction with one's home.

In this series of studies, the number of variables being considered has varied between 100 and more than 300. These have primarily consisted of subjective measures of beliefs about many aspects of the physical, organizational, and social components of the residential environment (e.g., appearance of unit, buildings, and development; amount and demarcation of spatial arrangements; maintenance of and personalization of unit, building, and grounds; perceptions of safety, privacy, degree of control of own space; trustworthiness, behaviors and similarities of other residents; rules, responsiveness, and strictness of management; access to friends and relatives and to facilities within the community; and beliefs about characteristics of the surrounding neighborhood, etc.). However, only a few objective measures of the physical environment (e.g., density) and a few objective measures of the respondents (demographics, e.g., age, sex, level of education, etc.) were obtained. Analytically, these variables were reduced to a smaller number of sets of highly related variables by factor (or component) analysis. These components were then used as predictors of an index of four highly correlated items used as the measure of residents' satisfaction. The R^2s obtained in this set of studies have varied from .49 to .68. So, in contrast to many studies, this work has examined a more varied set of beliefs. Yet it has not examined objective measures as extensively as other studies have. Work in progress by Anderson and Weidemann, as well as a joint research effort (Weidemann & Anderson, 1980) by the University of Illinois, University of Saskatchewan, and the I. B. Fell Research Centre in Sydney, Australia (Weidemann & Anderson, 1984), evaluating housing for the elderly has utilized more subjective measures of beliefs about the physical environment and more objective measures of the physical environment.

Another difference is that an index of four highly correlated items has been used as the measure of residents' satisfaction by the authors and their colleagues, instead of a single-item measure that many others have used. (A somewhat extreme exception to this is the 74-item index of satisfaction used by Onibokun [1976]). An index generally gives somewhat more consistent reliability than a single item, and this particular 4-item index has been used for a variety of different respondents, in a variety of types of residential settings.

However, the 4-item index actually represents both an *affective* component ("How satisfied are you with living here?") and *behavioral intention* (e.g., "Would you recommend this place to friends?"). The integrated model (Figures 2 and 3) would suggest that these elements be considered and examined empirically separately. This separation of affective and behavioral elements would also encourage the examination of a whole range of behavioral intentions and behaviors related to the residential environment. In addition to focusing on mobility intentions and behaviors, it would be quite useful to consider intentions and behaviors related to, for example, personalization, control, maintenance of home, social interactions, and so forth. This model proposes that a clear conceptual and operational distinction be made between affective and behavioral components of the criterion of interest (e.g., between satisfaction as affect and recommendations to friends as behavioral intention).

A final example of research examining residents' satisfaction with their homes is that done by Cutter (1982), who presents a refinement of the Marans and Rodgers's (1975) model by using Fishbein's theory of reasoned action (Ajzen & Fishbein, 1980). In this study, approximately 1,000 home buyers were surveyed by telephone interviews to obtain measures to test the refined model. The primary criterion of residential satisfaction was, however, a one-item question, "How would you rate this community as a place to live?" Satisfaction with the housing unit was used as one of the potential predictors of this criterion. In terms of the integrated model, satisfaction at one level of scale (home) would be expected to be related to satisfaction at a more complex level (community). In testing the refined model, Cutter was disappointed with the degree of correlation between the one-item community satisfaction score and the calculated satisfaction score (consisting of measures of importance and evaluation of various community attributes); the R^2 was .36. She suggests that other variables need to be included in the model. In determining residential satisfaction with the community, social influence variables and satisfaction with the housing unit were found to be more important than were the assessments of the community attributes.

In other analyses, Cutter used demographic variables and measures of the house and community to predict satisfaction with the house. Although the variance accounted for was low ($R^2 = .19$), the importance of the house over the community (subjective measure), the house size (objective measure), the expected increase in house value over time (subjective), and perceived low percentage of blacks in the community (subjective) were the strongest predictors.

Although this study is of interest both because it does test a version of the integrated model and because it examines single-family homes, it also represents work that could be enhanced by the use of a wider range of variables (as suggested by the expanded model in Figure 3). In many cases, where a low percentage of variance has been accounted for, it seems to be primarily those studies that do not examine many variables, either in depth (within a component of the integrated model) or in breadth (across components in the model).

IMPLICATIONS FOR FUTURE RESEARCH

The integrated model (Figure 2) and its expanded version (Figure 3) can certainly be useful in organizing the existing literature and thereby assisting in the comprehension of the many varied relationships between examined variables. However, when this is done, we feel that the model also serves an additional important function: that of explicit indication of needed future empirical research and theoretical development.

First, *within* the various components of the model (e.g., sets of objective attributes, beliefs, etc.), there has generally been too little emphasis upon the examination of a greater variety and number of variables. There is little reason to expect that only a few types of objective attributes or beliefs will sufficiently explain a complex human response of, for example, satisfaction with the home. Indeed, those studies that have tried to expand the number and variety of variables generally are able to account for a greater percentage of the variance in the criterion. In particular, we feel that the incorporation of an increased number of objective measurements of both the physical environments and characteristics of people would be useful. Furthermore, greater consideration should be given to the examination of a variety of behavioral components, which may also be able to serve as criteria for the success of a home or residential environment.

Second, within the various components of the model, there may be unstudied alternatives. For example, the current model conceives of the cognitive aspect as a set of beliefs about the physical environment. There is at least one other possible conceptualization for this part of the model. Within the theory of reasoned action (Ajzen & Fishbein, 1980), this aspect is seen as a value expectancy interaction. From this perspective, it would not be sufficient to know only the set of beliefs about an environment. It would also be necessary to know the relative importance, or value, associated with each of the beliefs. Unimportant or unvalued beliefs should not contribute to affect, whereas important ones should.

Third, relationships *between* components need to be empirically expanded. Relatively little research can serve as an example of a test of major portions of the whole model. One example is the work of Newman and Duncan (1979) who related beliefs about structural features of the house, satisfaction with the house and neighborhood, intentions to move, and actual moving behavior. Research examining more components at one time can provide a better test of the explanatory power of this model.

Fourth, the *links* or relationships between the components need further examination. Although some have been studied extensively in the existing literature, for example, the link between beliefs or assessment of the residential environment and the affective response of satisfaction, others have received less attention. For example, the link between satisfaction and behavioral intentions and behaviors has been rarely examined for any behaviors other than migration. It should be quite useful, both in terms of theory and application, to learn if satisfaction with one's home is related to increased level of maintenance, or greater personalization (or, for example, decreased vandalism and vacancy rates in multifamily housing). Also, to what extent are behaviors that occur in the home setting able to change or influence our beliefs about the home? This link is suggested by the integrated model, but we know of no research relating to the home that could be considered to be a direct test of this particular link.

Fifth, the model in this chapter, which integrates objective attributes of the residential environment with subjective beliefs and attitudes and behavioral responses, is just one of a variety of perspectives that have been put forth about the relationship between the physical environment and human behavior. It does incorporate both the "objectivist" and "subjectivist" approaches, as reviewed by Gauvain *et al.* (1983). And it is possible for it to be expanded, even to the cultural level. However, we are not at all certain how it would compare to another recently developing view of the relationship between people and their homes, for example, that of the transactional perspective as proposed by Altman and others (e.g., Altman & Gauvain, 1981; Gauvain *et al.*, 1983). This approach synthesizes the objectivist and subjectivist orientations by proposing a different unit of analysis: a process/place unit. How these differing views can be compared in terms of their use of theory development and suggestions for research remains to be seen.

Finally, within this chapter, the concept of satisfaction with one's home has been treated both as an affective *criterion* of the quality of the residential environment and as a *predictor* of behaviors related to the home. Yet there are other variables that may be equal or greater in terms of their explanatory power. Questions concerning the effectiveness, validity, or reliability of the concept of satisfaction (Andrews, 1981; e.g., Wilcox, 1981a,b) as compared to other concepts need to be resolved by methodologically careful empirical examinations of more explicit theoretical networks.

REFERENCES

Ajzen, I., & Fishbein, M. *Understanding attitudes and predicting social behavior.* Englewood Cliffs, N. J.: Prentice-Hall, 1981.

Altman, I. *The environment and social behavior: Privacy, personal space, territory, crowding.* Monterey, Calif.: Brooks/Cole Publishing Company, 1975.

Altman, I. Crowding: Historical and contemporary trends in crowding research. In A. Baum & Y. Epstein (Eds.), *Human responses to crowding.* Hillsdale, N. J.: Erlbaum 1978.

Altman, I., & Gauvain, M. A cross-cultural and dialectic analysis of homes. In L. Liben, A. Patterson, & N. Newcombe (Eds.), *Spatial representation and behavior across the life span: Theory and application.* New York: Academic Press, 1981, pp. 283–320.

Anderson, J. R., & Weidemann, S. Planning and monitoring change in multifamily housing. In R. Thorne (Ed.), *People and the man-made environment.* Sydney, Australia: University of Sydney, 1980, pp. 116–135.

Anderson, J. R., & Weidemann, S. The user's perspective on government housing: The United States. In W. van Vliet, E. Hutton, & S. Fava (Eds.), *Housing needs and policy approaches: Trends in thirteen countries.* Durham, N. C.: Duke University Press, 1985.

Anderson, J. R., Weidemann, S., Chenoweth, R., & Francescato, G. Residents' satisfaction: Criteria for the evaluation of housing for low and moderate income families. In

Papers of the National Conference of the American Institute of Planners. Washington, D. C.: American Institute of Planners, 1974, pp. 1–24.

Anderson, J. R., Weidemann, S., & Butterfield, D. I. Using residents' satisfaction to obtain priorities for housing rehabilitation. In *Renewal, rehabilitation and maintenance* (Vol. 1). Gavle, Sweden: The National Swedish Institute for Building Research, 1983.

Andrews, F. M. Comments. In D. F. Johnston (Ed.), *Measurement of subjective phenomena.* Washington, D. C.: U.S. Government Printing Office, 1981, pp. 21–30.

Andrews, F. M., & McKennell, A. C. Measures of self-reported well being: Their affective, cognitive, and other components. *Social Indicators Research*, 1980, *8*, 127–155.

Borukhov, E., Ginsberg, Y., & Werczberger, E. Housing prices and housing preferences in Israel. *Urban Studies*, 1978, *15*, 187–200.

Brown, C. R. *The dialectics of senior citizens' transactions with their residential environment.* Unpublished doctoral dissertation, Department of Psychology, University of Saskatchewan, Canada, 1984.

Cadwallader, M. T. Neighborhood evaluation in residential mobility. *Environment and Planning*, 1979, *11*, 393–401.

Campbell, A., Converse, P. E., & Rodgers, W. L. *The quality of American life.* New York: Russell Sage Foundation, 1976.

Craik, K. H., & Zube, E. H. *Issues in perceived environmental quality research.* Amherst: Institute for Man and Environment, University of Massachusetts, 1975.

Cutter, S. Residential satisfaction and the suburban homeowner. *Urban Geography*, October-December 1982, pp. 315–327.

Davis, E. E., & Fine-Davis, M. Predictors of satisfaction with housing and neighborhood: A nationwide study in the Republic of Ireland. *Social Indicators Research*, 1981, *9*, 477–494.

Desbarats, J. Spatial choice and constraints on behavior. *Annals of the Association of American Geographics*, 73 (3), September 1983, pp. 340–357.

Environmental Research and Development Foundation. *Post occupancy evaluations of residential environments.* Washington, D. C.: U.S. Department of Housing and Urban Development, 1977.

Fishbein, M., & Ajzen, I. *Belief, attitude, intention and behavior.* Reading, Mass.: Addison-Wesley, 1975.

Fiske, S. T. Social cognition and affect. In J. H. Harvey (Ed.), *Cognition, social behavior and the environment.* Hillsdale, N. J.: Erlbaum, 1981, pp. 227–264.

Floro, S. *Potential user's and homeowner's perceptions of earth sheltered homes.* Unpublished manuscript, University of Illinois, 1983.

Francescato, G., Weidemann, S., Anderson, J. R., & Chenoweth, R. Evaluating residents' satisfaction in housing for low and moderate income families: A multi-method approach. In D. H. Carson (Ed.), *Man–environment interactions: Evaluation and applications* (Vol. 5). Washington, D. C.: Environmental Design Research Association, 1974, pp. 285–296.

Francescato, G., Weidemann, S., Anderson, J. R., & Chenoweth, R. Predictors of residents' satisfaction in high-rise and low-rise housing. In D. Conway (Ed.), *Human response to tall buildings.* Stroudsburg, Penn.: Dowden, Hutchinson and Ross, 1977, pp. 160–167.

Francescato, G., Weidemann, S., Anderson, J. R., & Chenoweth, R. *Residents' satisfaction in HUD-assisted housing: Design and management factors.* Washington, D. C.: U.S. Department of Housing and Urban Development, 1979.

Fried, M., & Gleicher, P. Some sources of residential satisfaction in an urban slum. *Journal of American Institute of Planners*, 1961, *27*, 305–315.

Gauvain, M., Altman, I., & Fahim, H. Homes and social change: A cross-cultural analysis.

In N. Feimer & S. Geller (Eds.), *Environmental psychology: Directions and perspectives*. New York: Praeger, 1983, pp. 24–62.

Hartman, C. W. Social values and housing orientations. *Journal of Social Issues*, 1963, 113–131.

Hempel, D. J., & Tucker, L. R., Jr. Citizen preferences for housing as community social indicators. *Environment and Behavior*, 1979, *11*(3), 399–428.

Horley, J. Life satisfaction, happiness, and morale: Two problems with the use of subjective well-being indicators. *The Gerontologist*, 1984, *24*(2), 124–127.

Hourihan, K. Context-dependent models of residential satisfaction. *Environment and Behavior*, 1984, *16*(3), 369–393.

Johnson, P. J., & Abernathy, T. J. A research note on: Sources of urban multifamily housing satisfaction. *Housing and Society*, 1983, *10*(1), 36–42.

Jones, R. C., & Zannaras, G. The role of awareness space in urban residential preferences: A case study of Venezuelan youth. *Annals of Regional Science*, 1978, 12(1), 36–52.

Kaplan, R. The role of nature in the urban context. In I. Altman & J. F. Wohlwill (Eds.), *Behavior and the natural environment*. New York: Plenum Press, 1983, pp. 127–162.

Lazarus, R. S. On the primacy of cognition. *American Psychologist*, February 1984, 124–129.

Leven, C. L., & Mark, J. H. Revealed preferences for neighborhood characteristics, *Urban Studies*, 1977, *14*, 147–159.

Marans, R. Perceived quality of residential environments: Some methodological issues. In K. H. Craiks & E. H. Zube (Eds.), *Perceiving environmental quality: Research and applications*. New York: Plenum Press, 1976, pp. 123–147.

Marans, R., & Rodgers, W. Toward an understanding of community satisfaction. In A. Hawley & V. Rock (Eds.), *Metropolitan America in contemporary perspectives*. New York: Halsted Press, 1975, pp. 299–352.

Marans, R., & Spreckelmeyer, K. F. *Evaluating built environments: A behavioral approach*. Ann Arbor: University of Michigan, Institute for Social Research and the Architectural Research Laboratory, 1981.

Marcuse, P. Social indicators and housing policy. *Urban Affairs Quarterly*, 1971, 7, 193–217.

McHugh, K. E. *Incorporating constraints into an attitude-based model of migration-intentions*. Paper presented at the *Population Association of America* Annual Meeting, Pittsburgh, April 1983.

McHugh, K. E. Explaining migration intentions and destination selection. *The Professional Geographer*, 1984, *36*(3), 315–325 (a)

McHugh, K. E. Commenting on: Spatial choice and constraints on behavior. *Annals of the Association of American Geographers*, 1984, *74*(2), 326–328. (b)

Michelson, W. *Environmental choice, human behavior, and residential satisfaction*. New York: Oxford University Press, 1977.

Michelson, W., & Reed, P. The time budget. In W. Michelson (Ed.), *Behavioral research methods in environmental design*. Stroudsburg, Penn.: Dowden, Hutchinson & Ross, 1975, pp. 180–234.

Nasar, J. Adult viewers' preferences in residential scenes: A study of the relationship of environmental attributes to preference. *Environment and Behavior*, 1983, *15*(5), 589–614.

Nathanson, C. A., Newman, J. S., Moen, E., & Hiltabiddle, H. Moving plans among residents of a new town. *Journal of the American Institute of Planners*, 1976, 295–302.

Newman, S., & Duncan, G. J. Residential problems, dissatisfaction, and mobility. *Journal of the American Institute of Planners*, April 1979, pp. 154–166.

Onibokun, A. G. Social system correlates of residential satisfaction. *Environment and Behavior*, 1976, *8*(3), 323–343.

Rapoport, A. *House, form and culture*. Englewood Cliffs, N. J.: Prentice-Hall, 1969.

Rapoport, A. *Human aspects of urban form.* New York: Pergamon Press, 1977.

Rodgers, W. L., & Converse, P. E. Measures of the perceived overall quality of life. *Social Indicators Research,* 1975, 2, 127–152.

Rossi, P. H. *Why families move* (2d ed.). Beverly Hills, Calif.: Sage Publications, 1980.

Russell, J. A., & Mehrabian, A. Some behavioral effects of the physical environment. In S. Wapner, S. B. Cohen, & B. Kaplan (Eds.), *Experiencing the environment.* New York: Plenum Press, 1976, pp. 5–18.

Russell, J. A., Ward, L. M., & Pratt G. Affective quality attributed to environments: A factor analytic study. *Environment and Behavior,* 1981, 13(3), 259–288.

Saegart, S. Crowding and cognitive limits. In J. H. Harvey (Ed.), *Cognition, social behavior, and the environment.* Hillsdale, N. J.: Erlbaum, 1981, pp. 373–391.

Snider, E. L. Some social indicators for multiple family housing. *Social Indicators Research,* 1980, 8, 157–173.

Speare, A., Jr. Residential satisfaction as an intervening variable in residential mobility. *Demographics,* 1974, 11, 173–188.

Speare, A., Goldstein, S., & Frey, W. *Residential mobility, migration, and metropolitan change.* Cambridge Mass.: Ballinger Publishing, 1975.

Stokals, D. On the distinction between density and crowding. *Psychological Review,* 1972, 79, 275–277.

Suttles, G. D. *The social order of the slums: Ethnicity and territory in the inner city.* Chicago: University of Chicago Press, 1968.

Thorne, R., & Turnbull, J. A. B. *High-rise living for low-income elderly: Satisfaction and design.* Paper presented at the International Association for the Study of People and their Physical Surroundings, Berlin, 1984.

Tognoli, J. Residential environments. In D. Stokols & I. Altman (Eds.), *Handbook of Environmental Psychology.* New York: Wiley, 1985, pp. 65–84.

Tremblay, K. R., Jr. *Empirical research on housing preferences: An annotated bibliography.* Monticello, Ill.: Vance Bibliographies, 1979.

Turnbull, J., Thorne, R., Anderson, J. R., Weidemann, S., & Butterfield, D. An evaluation of the interaction between elderly residents and high-rise flat accommodation in Sydney, Australia. In D. Joiner *et al.* (Eds.), *People and physical environment research.* Wellington, New Zealand: New Zealand Ministry of Works and Development, 1983, pp. 367–380.

Ulrich, R. S. Aesthetic and affective response to natural environment. In I. Altman, & J. F. Wohlwill (Eds.), *Behavior and the natural environment,* New York: Plenum Press, 1983, pp. 85–126.

Vischer, J. C. *Changing models of user needs research in housing: A Canadian perspective.* Manuscript submitted for publication, 1984.

Weidemann, S., & Anderson, J. R. *Using a multi-site evaluation of housing as the basis of post-occupancy evaluation.* Paper presented at the American Psychological Association Annual Conference, Montreal, 1980.

Weidemann, S., & Anderson, J. R. *Satisfaction with residential environments for the elderly: A cross-cultural comparison.* A symposium presented at the annual conference of the Environmental Design Research Association, California Polytechnic State University, San Luis Obispo, June 1984.

Weidemann, S., Anderson, J. R., Butterfield, D. I., & O'Donnell, P. Residents' perceptions of satisfaction and safety: A basis for change in multifamily housing. *Environment and Behavior,* 1982, 14(6), 695–724.

Weiss, S., Burley, R., Kaiser, E., Donnelly, T., & Zehner, R. *New community development: A national study for environmental preferences and the quality of life.* Chapel Hill, N. C.: Institute for Research in Social Science, 1973.

Wilcox, A. R. Dissatisfaction with satisfaction: Subjective social indicators and the quality of life. In D. F. Johnston (Ed.), *Measurement of subjective phenomena.* Washington, D. C.: U.S. Government Printing Office, 1981, pp. 1–20. (a)

Wilcox, A. R. Response to comments. In D. F. Johnston (Ed.), *Measurement of subjective phenomena.* Washington, D. C.: U.S. Government Printing Office, 1981, pp. 31–35. (b)

Wohlwill, J. F. Environmental aesthetics: The environment as a source of affect. In I. Altman, & J. F. Wohlwill (Eds.), *Human behavior and the environment* (Vol. 1). New York: Plenum Press, 1976, pp. 37–86.

Zajonc, R. B. On the primacy of affect. *American Psychologist,* February 1984, pp. 117–123.

Zehner, R. B. *Indicators of the quality of life in new communities.* Cambridge, Mass: Ballinger, 1977.

8

Home and Near-Home Territories

RALPH B. TAYLOR AND SIDNEY BROWER

ORIENTATION

Home does not end at the front door but rather extends beyond. This chapter is about that region beyond, those exterior spaces adjoining the home: porches, steps, front yards, back yards, driveways, sidewalks, and alleys. These spaces are of crucial interest for two reasons. First, they immediately adjoin the home; consequently, what happens in these outside spaces strongly influences the quality of life in the home. Second, they represent spaces where the two major types of settings in residential life—the private, personal, and owned versus the public, shared, and open to the community—interpenetrate. Consequently, these settings are of considerable interest for understanding the dialetic between individuals and local society.

To expand on this point for a moment we would encourage the reader to recall a time when he or she dropped two stones, simultaneously, and fairly close together, into a still pond. As ripples went

RALPH B. TAYLOR • Department of Criminal Justice, Temple University, Philadelphia, Pennsylvania 19122. SIDNEY BROWER • School of Social Work and Community Planning, University of Maryland at Baltimore, Baltimore, Maryland 21201. Portions of the research described here were supported by a grant from the National Institute of Justice to Ralph B. Taylor. Opinions stated here do not reflect the opinions of the Department of Justice or the National Institute of Justice.

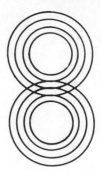

Figure 1. Interpenetration of home and near-home territorial functioning.

out from each point of entry, the two ripple patterns reached a point when they began to intersect (Figure 1). Imagine that with a very high-speed camera, one could "freeze" the action at the previously mentioned moment, when two patterns of ripples have begun to interpenetrate. The points of origin are the public–community versus the private–personal domains of everyday life. Surrounding each domain are expectations and norms, which decrease in strength as we move away from the point source, that tell us how to regard that space and how to act when we are in it. Where these two spheres of influence overlap, in the residential environment, is in the home and near-home outside territories that surround and buffer the home. This interpenetration is well expressed in Thomas Hardy's (1886/1962) *The Mayor of Casterbridge* (pp. 66–67). Elizabeth, newly come to the city, is walking down the street on market day, on her way to see Henchard.

> The front doors of the private houses were mostly left open at this warm autumn time, no thought of umbrella stealers disturbing the minds of the placid burgesses. Hence, through the long straight entrance passages thus unclosed could be seen, as through tunnels, the mossy gardens at the back. . . . The old fashioned fronts, rose sheer from the pavement, into which the bow-windows protruded like bastions . . . every shop pitched out half its contents upon trestles and boxes at the kerb, extending the display each week a little further into the roadway, despite the expostulations of the two feeble old constables. . . . And any inviting recess in front of a house that had been modestly kept back from the general line was utilized by pig dealers as a pen for their stock.

This quote suggests in several ways how public and private domains flow into one another. Vistas into private houses and yards become part of the public scene, and private entrepreneurs encroach onto the street.

The mingled public and private nature of home and near-home territories is one of the themes that we hope to illuminate through the concept of *territorial functioning*. Territorial functioning refers to a system of interlocked attitudes, sentiments, and behaviors concerned with who has access to what particular spaces and what activities go on in those spaces (Sundstrom, 1977). Thus, cognitions and expectations regarding who has how much control in a space, or over others in a space, who has how much responsibility for what goes on in a particular location, and whether one will see strange or familiar faces in a location, all refer to territorial functioning. Relevant behaviors include maintenance and beautification efforts as well as actions that indicate proprietorship, defense, or assertions of control. The locations in question are usually limited and often delimited. Thus, in the present analysis, the concept will be applied to houses, yards, sidewalks, and even property that stretches further, but will not be applied to larger scale domains such as neighborhoods, cities, and countries.

In this view, public and private areas are mutually influencing, and the influence can be more or less beneficial, depending upon a complex set of factors. Public spaces like the sidewalk benefit from oversight by the adjacent private individual; private spaces, like yards or steps, are commonly infringed upon by the public, but they can also contribute to the deterioration of the private area. One theme that we will explore is that these territorial zones, when they function smoothly, benefit from and contribute to the individual and collective residential quality of life.

A second theme we wish to illustrate is concerned with the topography or spatial distribution of territorial attitudes and behaviors. We suggest that, as one moves away from the home, feelings of territorial control and responsibility diminish, as do actual attempts to exert control. Further, we will suggest that the shape of this spatial distribution—its gradient or steepness if you will—is a reflection of the degree of order and harmony prevailing on a particular block, and in the surrounding neighborhood.

Implicit in this notion is our third theme: the *open system* nature of territorial functioning in these home and near-home territories. More specifically, we will suggest that the strength and distribution of territorial functioning is a reflection of the composition of the local population and the nature of the social links between neighbors.

Finally, we will suggest that territorial functioning can be integrated with ecological psychology. We will propose that territorial functioning is a multichannel system serving to ensure a fairly regular standing pattern of behavior and that street blocks can be viewed as behavior settings. A street block consists of the space between houses on the two sides of a street, extending between two cross streets. This unit, and individuals within such units, will be the scale at which we focus our inquiry.

In the following section, we articulate and join these themes into a loose general framework of territorial functioning in the residential context, drawing on other studies of territorial functioning in outdoor spaces as appropriate. We then develop in a more systematic way a framework that integrates the territorial and behavior setting material. This heuristic allows us to recast issues of territorial functioning into a more explicitly spatial frame. We close with some directions for future research.

PRELIMINARY STATEMENT OF HOW TERRITORIALITY FUNCTIONS IN THE RESIDENTIAL ENVIRONMENT

The house called home is nested in a larger context. It is situated on a street, with other houses nearby. The street is a public amenity and arena. And, there are other facilities in the neighborhood such as playgrounds, schools, corner stores, laundromats, and so on, which are also "open to the public." The "bridge" between the private home and these public settings is the exterior territories immediately adjacent to the home. These are territories because individuals either own or have legitimized access to them (Edney, 1976b), as in the case of porches and yards and steps, or because they are areas that are used on a regular basis by individuals (Edney, 1976a), such as alleys and sidewalks. On the daily round, when leaving home and returning, these zones must be traversed. Further, occupants or proprietors expect to have some degree of control over who has access to these territories, and what activities go on in them (Sundstrom, 1977). Although we will later take a more fine-grained look at this zone surrounding the house, for present purposes we can treat it as an undifferentiated area, linking the home to the larger neighborhood and beyond. Altman (1975), using a sociological classification most clearly stated by Landis (1949), has suggested that territories fall mainly into three types: primary, where one encounters members of one's primary reference group such as family, kin, or very close friends; secondary, where one encounters members of a secondary reference group such as well-known neighbors, fellow members of a club or organization, or work mates; and public territories, where one encounters mostly strangers or minimal acquaintances. According to this typology, the outside territories we are discussing here would probably qualify as secondary, or hybrid secondary/public territories.

Evidence suggesting such a zone distinct from but linking the public and private areas has been quite scarce. This is because investigators have been content to ask only about the general neighborhood context and have not distinguished such from the near-home arena. Only very recently have researchers begun a more differentiated examination, and the results have been quite striking. Taylor and Stough (1978) found that expectations of control and of meeting friends decreased as one went from nearby outside to more distant and public locations. Greenberg, Rohe, and Williams (1981), in an Atlanta study, found that fear and worry about potential street hassles or crime were lower in the two-block area right around the home, as compared to the rest of the neighborhood. A Minneapolis study (McPherson, Silloway, & Frey, 1983) came up with a similar finding. Thus, there does appear to be support for positing the distinct zones we are calling *home* and *near-home* territories.

Furthermore, the way territoriality functions in these arenas is influenced not only by individual traits and achieved characteristics of the occupant (whether or not he or she is sociable; whether he or she is an owner or a renter) but is also influenced by the larger, enclosing context. In short, territorial functioning is not a closed, solipsistic system, but rather is an "open" system that responds to exogenous input. (It also contributes to the local context, but that is a point we will discuss later.) It is shaped by the overarching social and cultural context. Evidence supportive of this notion can be marshaled from several studies. A Baltimore study comparing the territorial cognitions of inner-city and suburban residents found that in the latter case secondary territories were quite similar to primary territories, whereas in the former case the secondary territories were much more like public territories (Taylor & Stough, 1978). It appeared, based on knowledge of the areas and information supplied by the respondents, that the difference was a function of radically different social climates. In the suburban case, residents constituted a homogeneous group and were similar to their neighbors on many background factors as well as attitudes and interests. In the inner-city case the residents were in a heterogeneous context, surrounded by persons of different class, ethnic, and value backgrounds. To use Rosenberg's (1972, 1975) terminology, the suburban setting was a *consonant* social context for respondents, whereas the inner-city setting was a *dissonant* social context.

The same link between social context and territorial functioning, using a more behavioral criterion, was suggested in a Kansas City study by Greenbaum and Greenbaum (1981). They examined the presence of territorial markers and levels of upkeep and found that residents of houses where yards and sidewalks were better maintained had more local friendships, thus emphasizing how territorial functioning was bound up with local social dynamics. Such linkages have previously been observed for indoor territorial functioning (Taylor & Ferguson, 1980).

The same Kansas City study also examined impacts of another contextual factor: ethnicity. Ethnic and nonethnic households in a predominantly Slavic area were compared. Ethnic, as compared to nonethnic households, displayed more territorial markers on and around their properties, suggesting that the markers in part symbolized group membership. Ethnicity has previously been determined to have a strong impact on indoor territorial functioning (Scheflen, 1971; McMillan, 1974).

Consideration of ethnicity leads us to the broader context of cultural differences. Altman (1975) and Altman and Chemers (1980) have provided many examples of how cultural background shapes territorial functioning. A pertinent example comes from a study of responses to territorial contamination (Worchel & Lollis, 1982). The researchers expected that because culture determines, in part, how various territories around the home are classified, members would react differently to bags of litter. At households in Greece and in the United States, bags of litter were left either in the front yard, on the sidewalk in front of the residence, or in the street next to the curb. Households in the United States, as compared to Greek households, removed litter faster from the sidewalks and the curb, suggesting that in the United States these areas are viewed as semiprivate, whereas in Greece they are not. Thus, culture, too, influences territorial functioning in the near-home arena.

We have been suggesting up to now that territorial functioning is a coherent system. This implies that, for maximum efficacy, the constituent parts of the system covary closely. Three broad elements of the system include attitudes (responsibility, perceptions of control), behaviors (responding to intrusions or potential intrusions, exercising control over activities in the territory), and markers (signs, embellishments, and so on). If territoriality functions as a system individuals or blocks that are "high" on one of these components should be "high" on another. This is because each component responds to, supports, and stimulates the other components. Very little evidence, however, is available to support this contention. One early study by Edney (1972) found that an intruder ringing a bell at houses with "keep out" or "no trespassing" signs was responded to more speedily than at houses with no such signs. Indirect evidence comes from a study by Brown (1979; Brown & Altman, 1983) in which burglarized and nonburglarized households were compared on territorial cues. Nonburglarized homes had more extensive markers indicating privacy and personal expression (e.g., signs with name or address). The strongest differences were between burglarized houses and nonburglarized houses on nonburglarized blocks. Such results suggest that residents with more territorial cues had stronger territorial attitudes and that burglars inferred this and avoided these sites.

Now we come to a more difficult but nonetheless unavoidable question: What does territorial functioning do? What is it good for? Much previous attention has been given to the benefits that accrue to individuals or isolated groups from territorial functioning (for reviews see Altman, 1975; Edney, 1974, 1976a; Taylor, 1978). In this instance, however, we will be concentrating, in keeping with our contextual perspective (Stokols, 1983), on individual households considered in the context of, or in relation to, the immediate local society. And, we propose that in the same way near-home territories are physically interposed between the home and the larger neighborhood settings, territorial functioning is sociodynamically interposed between the individual household and local, on-block society. Furthermore, we suggest that the linkage is bidirectional. Not only does territorial functioning "serve" or benefit the individual household, it also "serves" the immediate society; not only do social factors influence the functioning of individual households' territoriality, but the characteristics of particular households influence the life of the street (see Figure 2).

Before detailing how we expect that this process works, we should admit straightaway that our view of this process suggests a paradox regarding the territorial system. Since the system distances or buffers the household from the local society, it also facilitates the joining and integration of that household with and into that society. Home and near-home territories help give each household "its own space"; at the same time, they provide an arena where "tentative social feelers" (Cooper, 1975) can be put out, or an individual can keep close watch on

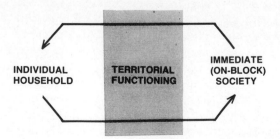

Figure 2. Links between individuals and immediate society via territorial functioning.

street life (Jacobs, 1961). This paradox is resolved, however, if we differentiate, in terms of functions, between those that serve the individual household and those that serve the immediate society. Such a distinction allows us to overcome the dichotomy between self-interest and the public interest, and suggests that the system can be both egocentric *and* assist in the production of public goods such as local safety and orderliness.

To be more specific regarding this bidirectional process, consider first the impact of territorial functioning on the individual household. The zone of immediately adjacent outdoor territories is a locale over which the householder can have some degree of control, and can, to some degree, regulate activities. As we shall see later, the extent to which such control can be exercised is strongly influenced by contextual as well as household factors. Noisy or rambunctious children can be "shooed" off the lawn, loiterers can be threatened with police action if they do not get off the steps, and so on. By reducing noise, unwanted intrusions, and unregulated activity in these outdoor spaces, the sense of security, orderliness, and the quality of life inside the house is enhanced. "Quiet" activities—reading or sleeping—are less likely to be disturbed. Attention need not be constantly diverted to what is going on outside. Worry is reduced. To put it very simply: life inside the home is better and less intruded upon. Thus, territoriality does for households what it does for individuals: it enhances both perceived and actual control (Edney, 1976a) and privacy (Altman, 1975).

To consider the other end of the loop—how territorial functioning benefits the immediate society—we must first make some assumptions about the nature of street blocks and how they function. We propose that the street block is a behavior setting (Barker, 1968; Wicker, 1979); that like accepted behavior settings, such as a drugstore or a high school basketball game or a Sunday service, it contains a standing pattern of behavior and circumjacent physical milieu.

Focusing first on physical features, the block is bounded by two cross streets and the physical fronts of houses. Barring extreme cases, what occurs beyond the boundaries is of much less import to the setting and its occupants than what happens on the street. The boundaries are not, of course, completely impermeable, as shown by our selection from *The Mayor of Casterbridge*. Information and activities (e.g., children roller-skating) can pass across these boundaries. Nonetheless, the focus of most resident activity is within the boundaries. Stated differently, the circumjacent physical milieu acts as a loose container for important co-resident interactions.

Nested within the overall setting are smaller *synomorphs* that are also, to some extent, physically delineated. A synomorph, in ecological psychology, is a portion of a behavior setting which is influenced by other subsections (or synomorphs) within the behavior setting. For example, a drug store, as a behavior setting, might have nested within it synomorphs such as a soda fountain and prescription counter. In this case, the steps, porches, driveways, and yards of each individual structure are considered synomorphs. Less delineated but nonetheless important are the stretches of sidewalk in front of people's houses or apartments, or stretches of off-street parking spaces. Sidewalks or corners in front of corner stores, albeit not delineated, can also be important synomorphs within the setting.

Other aspects of synomorphs, in addition to simple location, include the relevant people and activities. The activities that contribute to the standing pattern of behavior are routine, and they recur regularly on a daily, weekly, monthly, or seasonal basis. On a daily basis the following events may routinely take place: paper carriers make early morning rounds, particular people walk dogs, children and parents leave for work and school, certain groups of men and women may sit out and chat, postal carriers arrive, children and parents return in the afternoon and evening, and dogs are walked again at night. On a weekly basis trash is set out, or in the summer people cut lawns and garden. On a monthly basis certain residents may sit out on the porch waiting for the postal carriers to deliver unemployment, disability, or other checks. And seasonal factors determine outside house repairs, gardening, and other activities. Life on the block is a complex pattern of overlapping, largely routine rhythms. They recur regularly and are largely predictable; thus these routines qualify as a standing pattern of behavior. They are also supported by the physical environment. In streets running north–south in lower income neighborhoods, groups of men sitting out in summer routinely switch sides of the street in order to stay in the shade as the sun swings around. (Of course, in spring and fall they may switch to stay in the sun.)

Not only are the behavioral patterns routinized, but participants in those patterns can be distinguished according to levels of participation as in traditional ecological psychology. At the lower level are audience members—strangers and other passersby en route elsewhere. More involved are street regulars who routinely hang out on the street and residents who use the space on a routine basis. Suttles (1968) and Whyte (1943) both describe such regular corner groups. Their roles may be minimal most of the time but may become more central when they disrupt the setting (e.g., make late-night noise, try to start a fight) or when they actively assist in maintaining or restoring order to the setting.

Persons playing a major role may include a block leader (official or unofficial), gang leader, mail carrier, owner of a corner store (like Mr. Hooper on "Sesame Street"), or persons who manage a large building on the block. In times gone by the beat policeman also played a major role in the setting. Levels of penetration in the setting can be distinguished.

Another aspect of the standing pattern of behavior is that there is agreement on which behaviors are acceptable in the setting and which are not. Kids shooting craps may be acceptable in the alley, outside the setting, but not out front, in the setting. Working on cars may be acceptable in the alley but not on the street. Furthermore, we would suggest that street blocks, as behavior settings, have deviation-countering and vetoing mechanisms, such as informal social control (Janowitz, 1975; Meier, 1982) and territorial functioning.

At this juncture and to further amplify the preceding point, we must introduce a caveat. The "rules" regarding which behaviors are acceptable out on the street and which are not are defined with varying levels of clarity and are adhered to by varying portions of the population, across different street blocks. Thus, definition and acceptance vary depending upon neighborhood compositional factors (e.g., social class, heterogeneity) and on-block factors (objective and perceived similarity, block size, proportion of youth population, and so on). So, in comparing blocks, one may find some where bounds of acceptable behavior seem much broader or more diffuse, or where there are more conflicts regarding rule following. A person doing engine work out in front of his or her house may threaten a next-door neighbor who suggests that the work be carried out, instead, in the backyard. Nonetheless, even on such blocks there will be some agreement regarding acceptable behaviors as well as agreement regarding who is deviating, even though the standing pattern of behavior is itself very broad. In short, although the amount of behavioral structure and the degree to which it is accepted may vary, the pattern is always there.

Focusing for a moment on an even more microscopic level, we would suggest that there are also behavioral regularities associated with particular synomorphs within the larger setting. Teens learn that they may play cards on Mrs. X.'s steps but not Mrs. Y.'s; residents may learn to avoid going by Mrs. L.'s front porch when she is sitting out because she is always ready to complain and oblige others to listen, and so on. New residents moving onto a block must learn these regularities.

Finally, we return to the unanswered previously mentioned question: How does territorial functioning contribute to the functioning of the immediate society? It does so in several ways. First and perhaps most obviously, attempts to exert territorial control are part and parcel of the deviation-countering and vetoing mechanisms of a block behavior setting. Telling rowdy teens to turn down their tunes or young children retrieving a baseball not to step in the petunias or kids to stop cutting across one's backyard are all instances of deviation countering and the exercise of territorial control. Vetoing includes reprimands where the offending person (e.g., a street bum sitting on the curb) is asked to leave. In all of these instances the individual resident involved is contributing to the maintenance of the overall standing pattern of behavior.

The second and third ways territoriality contributes to the overall regularity of the setting center around territorial markers. We are using the term *marker* quite broadly here to include behavioral traces, levels of upkeep and maintenance, signs of beautification, and signs of identification and barriers. These contribute to the standing pattern of behavior in two ways. First, such markers "send messages" to outsiders. Markers such as ornaments as well as barriers and signs tell the passerby: "We care about where we live and we're watching out, so stay where you belong." To use Rapoport's (1982) perspective, these markers are channels of nonverbal communication. They convey what is expected. Wicker (1979, Chapter 4) has discussed how physical cues can contribute, through conditioning and social-learning processes, to an understanding of what behaviors are appropriate where.

Second, markers such as beautification and upkeep "send a message" to other residents. By (to use a middle-class, suburban example) keeping the house freshly painted and in good repair, the lawn and shrubs neatly trimmed, and the flowerbed brightly planted, one is telling one's neighbors: "I've invested in where I live, I like my neighborhood, and I can be counted on to help out if there is any local emergency." These signs contribute to the establishment of mutual trust and respect and thereby facilitate the effective functioning of local social control. If there are some teens setting off firecrackers down the alley and one needs assistance, it is much easier to call up and enlist a partially trusted neighbor who also cares about local events than to call a neighbor about which one knows nothing. In short, these markers and their impacts facilitate collective action when it is needed or at least reinforce the feeling that one will be backed up by neighbors if solitary action is required. Either way, the standing pattern of behavior is reinforced and clarified, and the deviance is countered. This explains how territorial functioning contributes to the equilibrium of the immediate, local society.

TERRITORIAL DYNAMICS

At this juncture we would like to illustrate some points about the dynamics of residential territorial functioning by referring in general terms to some results of a recent Baltimore study. More detail on this study and its findings can be found in Brower, Dockett, and Taylor (1983), Taylor, Gottfredson, and Brower (1981, 1984), and Taylor, Gottfredson, Brower, Drain, and Dockett (1980). The general dynamics discussed are displayed in Figure 3.

Figure 3 suggests that territorial functioning works as a system; that is, that attitudes and behaviors may work together to reinforce each other. Some individual-level analyses that we carried out illustrated this point. For example, responses to a household survey and analyses of house and yard photos indicated that, controlling for neighborhood context, respondents whose territorial attitudes indicated a better ability to discriminate between insiders and outsiders in spaces immediately adjacent to the home were more likely to be engaged in high-demand gardening, and were more likely to have units that were better kept up. Thus, how people felt about home and near-home territories was reflected in what they actually did there; this, in turn, influenced their social cognitions.

Figure 3 also suggests that on-block and off-block neighborhood factors can influence territorial functioning. These points were illuminated by an analysis of territorial cognitions of individuals. For example, residents who perceived other residents as more like-minded and homogeneous reported more territorial control and fewer problems in near-home territories (sidewalk in front of house, alley behind house). The larger, less immediate context was also important. For example, in less stable neighborhoods (lower income levels, higher proportion of renters), respondents reported feeling less responsible for what went on in outdoor territories. The contextual instability was associated with a shrinking of the sphere of territorial functioning.

On the outcome side, Figure 3 suggests that territorial functioning can underpin the local social order. In an analysis of 63 street blocks, we observed that territorial cognitions were associated with levels of disorder. More specifically, on blocks were residents felt more responsible for what went on in near-home territories, calls to the police for crimes of violence (e.g., muggings) and fear levels were lower. The unique contribution of territorial functioning (i.e., independent of resident characteristics and block social climate) suggests that strong territorial functioning was intimately linked with feelings of safety and the maintenance of public order.

Perhaps more intriguing in our results was the variation in attitudes across different types of territories. As respondents' attention was directed from home territories (front yard, backyard) to near-home territories (sidewalk in front, alley behind) to off-block territories (nearby

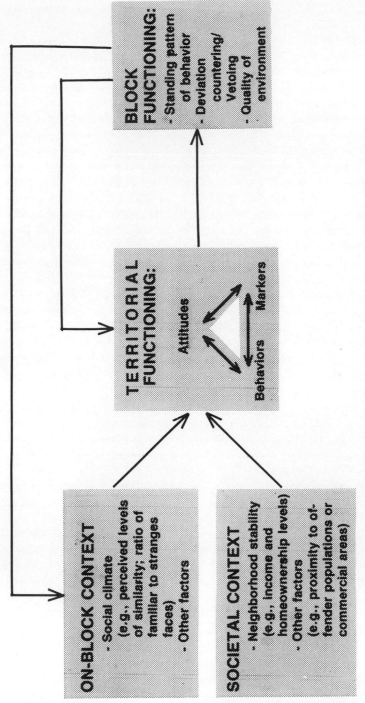

Figure 3. General outline of determinants and consequences of local territorial functioning.

store, playground), we found that their territorial cognitions changed considerably. Perceived control, as reflected in increased perceived problems, waned, as did feelings of responsibility and recognition of others. These findings are in keeping with the fact that as we move across the territorial gradient from territories that are proximal to the home to territories that are more distal, we are moving from more to less central territories in the life space (Altman, 1975; Taylor & Stough, 1978). What is surprising is that changes in territorial functioning were so marked, especially inasmuch as near-home territories directly abut home territories, and off-block territories are literally "just around the corner." Moving very short distances results in a major shift in how occupants view their relationship to the territory in question, and the kind of events and persons they expect to encounter.

Our results, then, basically have illustrated three points. First, territorial functioning is an open system, influenced by block and neighborhood contextual factors. The nature of this contextual impact is to influence not only overall levels of territorial functioning but also the gradient of territorial functioning across different types of territories on the block. Second, different elements of territoriality work in a systemlike, complementary fashion. And finally, territorial functioning contributes to the maintenance of the local order, and feelings of security.

THE STEP FRAMEWORK

At this point we wish to recast the discussion in a much more explicitly spatial and wholistic framework by drawing on a model. This model, or "step framework," concerns itself with the psychological significance of spaces near to and far from the home, and the points in this psychological continuum at which there are distinct changes, or "steps" that demarcate a shift in psychological significance. The step framework is concerned with the "contour" of territorial attitudes across various spaces. How differentiated are those spaces, how strong or weak are the attitudes in particular spaces, and how similar or dissimilar are the cognitions across spaces?

Our step structure starts with three major propositions. First, we assume that a territorial continuum exists, ranging from the outdoor spaces that are most proximal to and actually part of the home, such as the porch, to those public spaces that are most distal from the home, such as a downtown street. Second, in addition to being closer to or further from the home, these spaces are also more or less important in terms of the roles they play in family or individual functioning. More proximal spaces play more central roles. These more central roles are also important for the functioning of the immediate society—the block. Thus, the spaces differ in their centrality and vary along a centrality-of-setting continuum.

Finally, our third assumption is that the most central spaces are the most sensitive to threat, the most easily disrupted by unusual, unpredictable behavior, the most stoutly defended, and the ones in which occupants are most demanding in their need for territorial control and the most insistent on regulating access and use.

Our use of the concept of *centrality* harks back to Lewin (1936), who suggested that some people and places played more pivotal roles in the life of the individual and thus were of higher centrality. More recently, Altman (1975, pp. 110–111) has resurrected this term. But his definition of centrality focused mostly on the type of people encountered, whereas our use focuses on the importance of the setting as a supportive context for daily functioning. Spaces whose loss or whose disruption is more upsetting or stressful for daily routine are the spaces that are more central. Our centrality continuum is multifaceted. Obviously, the type of people encountered will vary at different points on the continuum, as Altman has suggested. In addition, feelings of responsibility and control will vary as well. And, behaviors, such as deviation countering, will vary across the continuum.

Related to the centrality continuum are two perceived attributes. One attribute is *potential* or *appraised threat*. Each space along the territorial continuum contains some quantity of potential harm or danger to the perceiver. The quantity may vary somewhat, depending on time of day (after dark) or day of week (weekend), but the amount is by and large stable. The level of appraised threat is based on a judgment regarding the likelihood that something harmful, fear arousing, unexpected, or just plain annoying and problematic will transpire in that space. Our use of appraised threat is quite similar to Lazarus's (1966) use of the concept of *threat profile*, albeit somewhat broader, inasmuch as we include lesser stressors, which do not entail bodily harm, such as "daily hassles" (Lazarus & Cohen, 1977).

A second attribute is *desired control*. In a particular space, to what extent does a person feel that he or she should control who comes and goes, what activities go on there, and the maintained qualities of the space? To what extent should his or her personal agency, or in the case of a group, their collective agency, determine the life of that space?

One important aspect of both perceived threat and desired control deserves clarification. In the case of both of them there may be substantial slippage between the actual and perceived situations. In the case of threat, the most common discrepancy is that people, due to past history, personal characteristics, foibles, and so on, perceive a threat greater than what actually exists. In the case of control, the most likely situation is that the person will experience less actual control than is desired. And, as we shall consider later the location of this discrepancy on the centrality continuum strongly determines the consequences of slippage for the individual. Before we consider such complexities we will articulate our three major concepts–centrality, threat, and control—in an "ideal" setting, one where reality accords with the desired levels.

RELATIONS BETWEEN THE MAJOR CONCEPTS: THE IDEAL CONTINUUM

The integration of the three major concepts is displayed graphically in Figure 4; it represents the ideal distribution of territorial claims, how things might operate in a context where expectations and reality are in a state of stability and balance, or mutual determination.

The territorial centrality continuum is arrayed along the bottom. More central, proximal territories appear on the left, with increasingly distal, less central territories appearing as we move to the right along the continuum until we finally reach the most distal, least central territory.

The potential threat dimension appears along the right-hand axis, with potential threat increasing as we move up the axis. And, as we move from more central to less central territories the potential threat inherent in the territory increases. This is demonstrated by the amount of the shaded area underneath each "step," with each step representing a territory on the continuum.

The desired control dimension appears along the left-hand axis with desired control increasing as we move down the axis. Thus the unshaded space between each step and the top of the diagram represents the amount of control desired in that territory.

Represented in this "ideal" situation are the following propositions:

1. As we move from more central to less central spaces, desired control progressively decreases, and perceived threat progressively increases.
2. Decreases in desired control and the increases in potential threat are perfectly coupled, such that the two dimensions, although conceptually distinct, in essence mirror one another. The balance between these two forces is represented by the height of the step, with one step for each territory in the diagram.
3. The height or "riser" between adjacent steps represents a differential between adjoining spaces in threat and control. This differ-

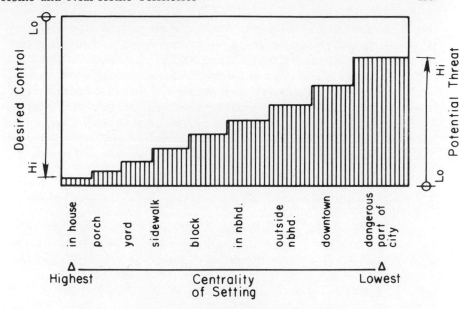

Figure 4. Step heuristic: an ideal distribution of territorial claims.

ential is represented cognitively as a boundary and may also be represented physically as a boundary, such as a wall or a back-yard gate.

4. As we move from more central to less central spaces, the differential between adjacent territories on the continuum, in terms of threat and control, increases. Thus, the "riser" between adjacent steps increases in height. The rate at which threat and control change increases as one moves further from the home: out of the house and yard, out onto the street, and off of the block.

5. Consequently, given the slight differentials between adjacent, highly central outdoor spaces, symbolic markers are likely to be perfectly capable of maintaining the distinction between the two locations. In many instances changes in surface treatment, low fences or rails, planting beds, display of personal objects, and other evidence of occupancy, use, and caring would be adequate for this purpose.

6. In less central spaces, however, the differential between adjacent territories is considerably greater, as is represented by the taller "riser" between adjacent steps. Consider for example, a housing project situated adjacent to a working-class or middle-class neighborhood. With the large increase in threat one experiences as one crosses such a boundary, the impacts of possible spill-

overs from the less central to the more central space become much more alarming. The more central space is exposed to a far wider range of unacceptable and highly aversive behaviors from the adjacent space than is the case at the left end of continuum. It is not surprising, therefore, that to maintain such a boundary or differential, stronger defensive measures are needed, like physical barriers or active surveillance. The "privatizing" of streets in St. Louis, via blocked or narrowed entranceways, discussed by Newman (1979), would be an example.

The parameters of the framework can also be altered, however, to describe particular settings. That is, if we vary certain parameters of the model it then describes a different type of residential setting. Thus the model can capture the particular relationships between territories that exist in different kinds of blocks and neighborhoods. Furthermore, we can use this depiction of the distribution of territorial claims to consider how exogenous threats, resulting in perturbations, may influence the territorial system, and the types of responses that can be made.

Describing Responses to Change Using the Model

What happens when a person or group suddenly experiences a change in their territorial continuum and the status quo is perturbed by a specific change somewhere along the continuum, usually in the form of an increase in threat level? The following might all be examples of such an event: a planned public housing project on a plot of land adjoining a neighborhood; the opening of a bar or carry-out pizza establishment around the corner from a particular block; a string of street attacks on a block; or the moving-in of a problem family next door. All of these events constitute an increase in potential threat at a particular point along the territorial continuum.

One guiding assumption that we are making here is that when perturbations occur, when there is an increase in threat somewhere due to physical or social conditions, such that previously held cognitions regarding control and threat are no longer accurate, then the parties involved seek to return to a balanced state; there is a striving for matters to come into line. A mismatch or lack of congruence between the cognized continuum and extant conditions is a source of stress that seeks resolution or alleviation.

In fact, such processes of accomodation are probably constantly going on. The local ecology, particularly in urban areas, may be in a fairly constant state of flux, to which people are responding. Thus, even though we discuss fairly dramatic changes and very noticeable responses, the same processes may be going on in a more subtle fashion over a longer period of time.

We envision basically three generic types of responses: *expansion* or *reassertion, bulwarking,* or *retreat*.

Expansion or Reassertion

In this response residents seek to restore control and reduce threat in a disputed location along the territorial continuum. Actual control is enhanced so as to come in line with desired control. The disputed location is reclaimed, and there is a restoration of the amount of desired control; actual threat is reduced to the expected level. This response has the effect of displacing the threat from a more central location to a less central one. A couple of examples help clarify how this might work.

The senior author has had recounted to him a situation where, in a fairly mixed neighborhood, a particular block experienced a sizable increase in the number of loitering teens. The teens were creating problems; some purse snatches occurred. This situation had gone on for some time when a new resident finally decided to do something about it. He and his wife began talking with various residents about the problem and about what could be done. Almost to a household those contacted expressed relief that the situation had been brought up. They had experienced considerable stress due to the situation and its unresolved nature. (One resident, a former serviceman, had taken to hiding in the bushes, in blackface, in unsuccessful attempts to catch the troublemakers.) The residents agreed that they should form a block organization and they did. The organization made contact with the police and was successful in getting the kids moved off the block. The block organization persisted for another 2 years, with regular block parties.

On a somewhat more homogeneous block, only a few blocks from the one described in the first example, the following occurred. A string of two or three burglaries took place in a fairly short period of time. (The block had previously been crime-free.) Residents at one end of the block knew one another and were fairly similar in that many of them were blue-collar workers employed at one or two plants. Very soon after the burglaries occurred residents formed into patrol groups. Due to extant levels of acquaintanceship an actual organization was not needed; rather, arrangements for protection were worked out informally, albeit systematically. Groups took responsibility for patrolling the alleys at particular times. Subsequent to these arrangements the burglaries stopped, and after a few more weeks the patrol operations were stopped.

An expansionist approach to disruptions carries with it several implications. First, such an approach is inherently a collective response. Thus, its success depends upon the quality of the interpersonal relations among the affected residents. On blocks where residents share common concerns, backgrounds, values, and ties, the collective approach is likely to emerge more quickly and succeed. On heterogeneous blocks where residents are or perceive themselves to be dissimilar to each other, the approach would be less likely to succeed. Homogeneity facilitates the development of consensus, and thus the emergence of the group itself. It facilitates success in that with homogeneity and more widespread adherence to particular norms, more "leverage" against miscreants is available.

Second, the expansionist approach requires considerable effort from those involved. At the collective level, it is very energy intensive. Success is only within reach if there is widespread commitment and cooperation. It is quite possible that although residents may insist on a higher level of control, they may not be able to achieve it. Considerable distress would then ensue. If they do achieve their goal, however, or at least feel that they are making progress toward their goal, they will probably experience feelings of mastery, control, or lessened fear (Cohn, Kidder, & Harvey, 1978).

Third, inherent in the expansionist approach is the possibility of a tyranny of the majority. In seeking to make their street or park or neighborhood safer, residents may resort to discrimination and attempts at segregation. They may seek to deter or bar those who do not pose a threat, but who are just different. They may seek to exercise too much control. This is exactly the problem with neighborhood covenants, and is one of the factors that led to the demise of the neighborhood concept in the late 1940s (Isaacs, 1948).

In sum: the expansionist approach requires a congenial social climate; is effortful and may result in distress, or mastery; and may go awry in that too much resident-based control may be desired.

Bulwarking

A second approach is to establish strong defensive barriers between the area where desired control is less than actual, and the adjacent, more proximal area. This approach relies primarily on surveillance and use of mechanical or physical devices to protect a setting against a large differential in potential threat in the adjacent less central setting. This approach does not eliminate the "high riser" in the staircase, but instead it is a form of accommodation to it. Thus, a resident whose yard abuts a busy sidewalk can erect a wall or fence with gates, install an alarm system, a warning or surveillance device, or use a guard dog. The bulwark approach can also be used by a group, and it can be used in combination with an expansionist approach. For example, an association of residents, where each resident has a part in the collective appropriation of the street, can respond to a large step-up in threat at the entrance to the street by creating a cul-de-sac at one end and by installing a gate and gatehouse with guard at the other. Medieval cities with their walls and gates serve as historical examples of the use of this approach.

Several features of a bulwarking approach are notable. First, in the standard residential environment such an approach may be costly. It takes money to build fences or install alarms. Thus, such an approach is not likely to be popular among persons or groups with slim financial resources. Second, the establishment of strong defensive barriers is most likely to occur on boundaries of private property. Establishment of control over public areas like pocket parks may occur, but rarely. The collective agreements necessary to establish such boundaries around collective areas constitute a sizable impediment to such bulwarking. Thus, this barrier-oriented approach is tantamount to giving up on control over public places. Third, the barrier-oriented approach, because it can be an individual-level response, is not necessarily dependent upon social climate for its success. But at the same time, it is not likely to lead to improvements in social climate either. It is potentially atomistic, at some level. Fourth, this approach does not eliminate heightened threat but is a form of accommodation to it. More central spaces are protected against potential damage or contamination from the less central space. In sum, then, the establishment of defensive barriers is a predominantly individual-level approach that is expensive, but that may lead to less regulation of behaviors in some settings, and to a deterioration of local social ties.

Retreat

In this approach, a resident, who is faced with an unacceptable level of threat in a particular setting does not attempt to shift the threat away (as in the case of expansion) or to build defenses against it (as in the case of bulwarking) but instead reduces territorial claims to the troublesome space, or even abandons it entirely, and retreats to the adjacent, more central setting. In recognition of low levels of actual control, amounts of desired control are reduced. In the place to which the resident retreats he or she may use a bulwarking approach. Thus, a resident faced with continuing trespass and vandalism in the front yard may cognitively and behaviorally redefine the yard as an extension of the sidewalk rather than of the house. In such a setting, lower levels of resident control, care, and maintenance are justified; and the same outsider behavior is seen as far less threatening. In the same way, a group of residents, faced with a sudden influx of through traffic, may redefine their street as a public thoroughfare and resort to closing their windows, or to erecting walls and fences around their individual yards.

One of the beneficial results of such withdrawal is that, although there is no change in the level or type of outsider behavior, this behavior is no longer labeled as a problem. The situation is cognitively redefined. Levels of desired control are reduced. In the long run, however, this approach may be more stressful because in actuality a higher level of potential threat has moved closer to more central spaces. This may well result in higher fear levels. Furthermore, such an approach, in contrast (respectively) to the first and second approach, requires little effort and little cost. And, in contrast to the first approach, there is no continuing ambiguity about who has how much control over particular spaces; the discrepancy between actual and desired control can be eliminated almost immediately.

Which Approach?

Naturally, the question arises: Which response will be used in which situation? This is probably a function of several factors: resources potentially available to the residents involved, social climate, location, and perceived nature of the threat.

As available resources increase, residents may look to other solutions beside social action to put a cap on the menace. In higher income neighborhoods a wave of burglaries might merit some discussion in the meetings of the local association, and perhaps even some calls to the relevant city councilperson. But the more efficacious response may simply be the installation of sophisticated house protection devices. Residents in such a locale are likely to have the dollars needed to purchase such protection and thus guarantee security. Thus, the problem can be effectively solved without reliance upon one's neighbors (cf. Rich, 1980). Furthermore, in high-income areas, the type of on-the-street problems that may be an expected feature of the lower-class or working-class areas and that would require collective action are simply less likely to occur due to the nature of residential patterns. Thus, given the resources, boundary reinforcement and bulwarking seem more likely.

In an upper income area, resources may be applied to a more distal threat, also resulting in bulwarking, but in a somewhat different way. Individuals or organizations may use ties to people or groups outside of the neighborhood in order to take care of a distal threat; they may draw on their political capital (cf. Rainwater, 1966). For example, the residents of a fairly affluent neighborhood in northeast Baltimore, surrounded largely by middle-, working-, and lower-class neighborhoods, had lived for some time with a heavily traveled shortcut going through the middle of their district. On this route a child was apparently injured one day, following which the local organization went to their city councilperson who collaborated with them in getting the Department of Planning to completely change the traffic pattern, so that the through route was cut off a block into the neighborhood. This is an instance where available resources, in the form of political ties, obviated the need of the neighborhood residents to organize and voice their concerns on a wide scale.

Social climate facilitates the collective action that is necessary if a group is to reclaim an area that has experienced an increase in threat. Block patrols, citizens on patrol (COP), or neighborhood watch all require some measure of organization and co-resident communication. As a block or neighborhood becomes more cohesive, more homogeneous, or its residents better acquainted, this increases the ability to respond quickly to a situation of increasing actual threat, and to attempt to reduce actual threat to its previous level. Efforts to "regain" an area require considerable effort that can only be mounted and sustained by a group. Granted, a leader or cadre of leaders may also be a necessary catalyst, but without a group commitment there is no hope of mounting a successful reclamation effort.

Persistence of the threat and its location on the centrality continuum also influence responses to it. More severe or apparently uninexcludable threats would appear to preclude expansion efforts, and to some extent bulwarking, making an ostrichlike response more likely. More proximally located threats are more likely to engender expansionist attempts to cast out the menace, simply because a threat in a more proximal space is more disruptive to everyday functioning and therefore is more stressful.

Given the foregoing, let us consider residents living on a typical low-income, heterogeneous, high-crime block. Available resources are low. Residents have little material or political or other capital to use as leverage against possible threats. Given the nature of the high-threat environment, co-resident distrust is likely (Rainwater, 1966), thereby precluding widely supported and thus effective social action. Further, the threat itself (serious crime) occurs so frequently that to residents it appears to be a very persistent, overdetermined, and unimpeachable threat. This perception will probably reduce the residents' willingness to "take on" the problem. In other words, the prerequisites for either an expansionist or bulwarking response are lacking, leaving only the option of retreat.

A Different Focus on Responses to Threat

We can also consider the problem of high threat, and how blocks and individuals respond to it from a slightly different angle, one that uncouples levels of desired and actual control: in these situations actual control is less than expected. Graphically focusing only on outdoor spaces, the situation could be portrayed as is shown in Figure 5. In high-centrality near-home spaces, such as a sidewalk directly in front of a residence, actual control no longer matches expected levels of control. The three modes of adaptation we have been discussing can be viewed as ways to resolve this discrepancy. The modes are displayed in Figure 6. In the case of expansion there is not a decrement in desired levels of control; efforts are made to increase actual control, and return matters to the earlier state of congruence all along the centrality continuum. In the case of bulwarking, there is some diminution in levels of expected control in threatened spaces but not in the most proximate outdoor spaces. And, more importantly, the more central spaces are at the same time supported and defended, in an effort to reduce the discrepancy between achieved and expected control in the most vital outdoor spaces. And finally, in the retreat case, expectation levels are lowered to resolve the discrepancy. Thus, only in the expansion mode is the formerly accepted situation, or "comparison level" (Thibaut & Kelly, 1959), retained. In the retreat mode there is an across-the-board lowering of the comparison level; in the bulwarking mode there is a partial revision of the comparison level or standard along a particular range of the centrality continuum.

If we view losses in control as accompanied by losses in privacy,

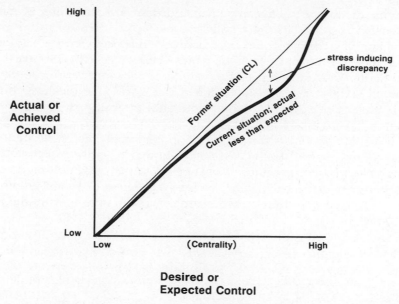

Figure 5. Understanding stresses on territorial system: Desired versus actual control.

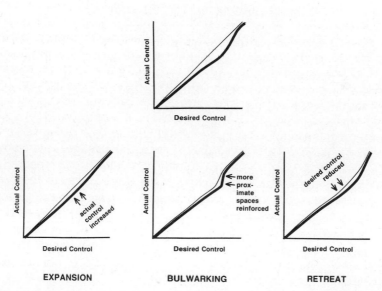

Figure 6. Resolving stresses on territorial system: Desired versus actual control.

then our distinctions between actual and desired control can be but-
tressed by pointing out the parallels between our concepts here and
Altman's (1975) distinction between *desired* and *achieved privacy*. He suggested that when people experienced less privacy than desired, at that
point in time they probably felt crowded, and took steps to return to an
optimum state of privacy. A person might leave the situation, tune
others out, or block others out with physical means, such as closing a
door.

The situation we are describing here, when people experience less
actual control than is desired, is similar in many respects to the state
Altman describes when achieved privacy is less than desired privacy. In
both frameworks the discrepancy is viewed as stressful. In both models
individuals take steps to restore the situation to an optimum condition,
where what is desired and what is experienced are more closely in line.
Our approach to this discrepancy is different, however, in that (a) our
framework is more explicitly spatial, placing greater emphasis on where
the discrepancy occurs; and (b) our model focuses on both individual
and group responses. Nonetheless, the very strong parallels between
the situations described by the two frameworks provide an added dimension of understanding.

IMPLICATIONS FOR FUTURE RESEARCH

We see several ways that the step framework can be used as a
vehicle for and shaper of future research on territorial functioning in the
near-home environment. First, our discussion of the heuristic has concentrated mainly upon territorial attitudes, and to a lesser extent on
actual behavior and markers. This imbalance should be redressed in
future multimethod research, complementing attitudinal surveys with
behavior observation and physical assessment. Stream-of-behavior recording may even be appropriate in order to monitor levels and types of
territorial behaviors at different distances from the home. Gillis's (1983)
finding that people expect they will be more helpful to others when they
are closer to home is an excellent first step in such a direction, and this
lead needs to be pursued with more rigorous methods. Only with multifaceted studies will we be able to clearly define the systemlike properties
of territorial functioning.

Second, the gradient can be used as a guide in the design of investigations to shed more light on how territorial functioning contributes to

the standing patterns of behavior of the synomorphs on a street block. The synomorphs can be arrayed along a particular territorial gradient, and these differences in the standing pattern of behavior across synomorphs can be constructed using individual households as the focus, with a concentration on idiographic behavior patterns. Or they can be constructed using a street block as the focus, with a concentration on nomothetic behavior patterns. The flexibility of the gradient allows it to be applied at either level. But the main point is that the gradient can help us interpret differences in standing patterns of behavior across synomorphs within the same setting.

Third, if we keep the notion of the spatial gradient clearly before us, it forces us to consider at what scale, or what level of segmentation, we wish to couch our investigations. It is simply not practical, nor will it yield us much insight, to return to a more macrolevel focus, asking about territorial feelings within the neighborhood, or within a two-block area around the home. Such a level of resolution is so low that resulting answers have little validity. We must continue to focus at a smaller scale, a higher level of resolution. The functioning of the territorial system is quite differentiated; it is important to capture this differentiation if we want to understand what impacts territoriality, how it functions, and how it influences other matters. The step framework forces us to continue at this appropriate, higher level of resolution, and not to fall back to less focused investigations. Insight will not be provided by the latter approach.

Finally, the step heuristic forces us to include explicitly spatial and explicitly physical dimensions because adjoining territories are often separated by physical structures. This raises important issues for subsequent researchers. With regard to the spatial component, what are the links between societal, cultural, and physical factors and the "slope" of the gradient? So far we have only made some preliminary guesses at these links. With regard to the physical, at various points along the centrality continuum what range of physical structure or symbols suffice to indicate a "break" between territories? How much redundancy is needed, depending upon position along the continuum and exogenous factors such as threat or sociocultural parameters? A fuller understanding of person–environment–society links requires such investigations.

CLOSING COMMENTS

We have applied a (hopefully) reasoned and empirical territorial perspective to understanding the social dynamics and person–environment transactions occurring in the buffer spaces surrounding the home and further away. Home is not dislocated but is grounded in a community context. Linking home to the community, and at the same time buffering home from the community, are home and near-home territories. The control exercised over these outdoor locations, the responsibility for management of activities, and upkeep, contribute to the immediate society by helping to define and stabilize the standing pattern of behavior on the street block. Investigation of residential functioning in outside spaces moves us toward a more complete understanding of this most central setting—the home.

REFERENCES

Altman, I. *The environment and social behavior*. Monterey, Calif.: Brooks/Cole, 1975.

Altman, I., & Chemers, M. M. *Culture and environment*. Monterey, Calif.: Brooks/Cole, 1980.

Barker, R. *Ecological psychology*. Stanford, Calif.: Stanford University Press, 1968.

Bechtel, R. B. *Enclosing behavior*. Stroudsburgh, Penn.: Dowden, Hutchinson & Ross, 1977.

Brower, S., Dockett, D., & Taylor, R. B. Residents' perceptions of site-level features. *Environment and Behavior*, 1983 *15*, 419–437.

Brown, B. B. *Territoriality and residential burglary*. Paper presented at the annual meeting of the American Psychological Association, New York, 1979.

Brown, B. B., & Altman, I. Territoriality and residential crime: A conceptual framework. In P. J. Brantingham & P. C. Brantingham (Eds.), *Environmental criminology*, Beverly Hills, Calif.: Sage, 1981, pp. 55–76.

Brown, B. B., & Altman, I. Territoriality, defensible space and residential burglary; An environmental analysis. *Journal of Environmental Psychology*, 1983, *3*, 203–220.

Cohn, E. S., Kidder, L. H., & Harvey, J. Crime prevention vs. victimization. *Victimology*, 1978, *3*, 285–296.

Cooper, C. *Easter Hill village*. New York: Free Press, 1975.

Edney, J. J. Property, possession and permanence. *Journal of Applied Social Psychology, 2*, 275–282.

Edney, J. J. Human territoriality. *Psychological Bulletin*, 1974, *81*, 959–975.

Edney, J. J. Human territoriality: Comment on functional properties. *Environment and Behavior*, 1976, *8*, 31–47. (a)

Edney, J. J. The psychological role of property rights in human behavior. *Environment and Planning A*, 1976, *8*, 811–822. (b)

Gillis, A. R. Bystander apathy and the territorial imperative. *Sociological Inquiry*, 1983, *53*, 449–460.

Greenbaum, P. E., & Greenbaum, S. D. Territorial personalization: Group identity and social interaction in a Slavic-American neighborhood. *Environment and Behavior*, 1981, *5*, 574–589.

Greenberg, S., Rohe, W., & Williams, J. R. *Safe and secure neighborhoods* (Final report). Research Triangle Park, N.C.: Research Triangle Institute, 1981.

Greenberg, S. W., Rohe, W. M., & Williams, J. R. Safety in urban neighborhoods. *Population and Environment*, 1982, *85*, 117–134.

Hardy, T. *The Mayor of Casterbridge*. New York: Signet, 1962. (Originally published 1886.)

Isaacs, R. R. The neighborhood theory: An analysis of its adequacy. *Journal of the American Institute of Planners*, 1948, *14*, 15–23.

Jacobs, J. *The death and life of great American cities*. New York: Vintage, 1961.

Janowitz, M. Sociological theory and social control. *American Journal of Sociology*, 1975, *81*, 82–108.

Landis, P. H. *Man in environment*. New York: Crowell, 1949.

Lazarus, R. S. *Psychological stress and the coping process*. New York: McGraw-Hill, 1966.

Lazarus, R. J., & Cohen, J. B. Environmental stress. In I. Altman & J. F. Wohlwill (Eds.), *Human behavior and environment, advances in theory and research* (Vol. 2). New York: Plenum, pp. 89–127.

Lewin, K. *Principles of topological psychology*. New York: McGraw-Hill, 1936.

McMillan, R. *Analysis of multiple events in a ghetto household*. Unpublished doctoral dissertation, Columbia University Teachers College, New York City.

McPherson, M., Silloway, G., & Frey, D. L. *Crime, fear and control in neighborhood commercial center*. Minneapolis: Minnesota Crime Prevention Center, 1983.

Meier, T. Informal social control. *Annual Review of Sociology*, 1982, *8*, 35–55.

Newman, O. *Community of interest*. New York: Doubleday, 1979.

Rainwater, L. Fear and house-as-haven in the lower class. *Journal of the American Institute of Planners*, 1966, *32*, 23–31.

Rapoport, A. *The meaning of the built environment*. Beverly Hills, Calif.: Sage, 1982.

Rich, R. C. A political-economy approach to the study of neighborhood organizations. *American Journal of Political Science*, 1980, *24*, 559–592.

Rosenberg, M. *Society and the adolescent self-image*. Princeton, N.J.: Princeton University Press, 1972.

Rosenberg, M. The dissonant context and the adolescent self-image concept. In S. E. Dragastin & G. H. Elder (Eds.), *Adolescence in the life cycle: Psychological change and the social context*. New York: Halsted, 1975.

Scheflen, A. E. Living space in an urban ghetto. *Family Process*, 1971, *10*, 429–450.

Shumaker, S. A., & Taylor, R. B. Toward a clarification of people–place relationships: A model of attachment to place. In N. Feimer & E. S. Geller (Eds.), *Environmental psychology: Directions and perspectives*. New York: Praeger, 1983, pp. 219–225.

Stokols, D. *Scientific and policy challenges of a contextually oriented psychology*. Presidential address presented at the meeting of Division 34, American Psychological Association, Anaheim, California.

Sundstrom, E. Interpersonal behavior and the physical environment. In L. Wrightsman (Ed.), *Social psychology*. Monterey, Calif.: Brooks/Cole, pp. 511–549.

Suttles, G. D. *The social order of the slum*. Chicago, Ill.: University of Chicago Press, 1968.

Suttles, G. D. *The social construction of communities*. Chicago, Ill.: University of Chicago Press, 1972.

Taylor, R. B. Human territoriality: A review and a model for future research. *Cornell Journal of Social Relations*, 1978, *13*, 125–151.

Taylor, R. B., & Ferguson, G. Solitude and itimacy: Linking territoriality and privacy experiences. *Journal of Nonverbal Behavior*, 1980, *4*, 227–145.

Taylor, R. B., & Stough, R. R. Territorial cognitions: Assessing Altman's typology. *Journal of Personality and Social Psychology*, 1978, *36*, 418–423.

Taylor, R. B., Gottfredson, S. D., & Brower, S. The defensibility of defensible space. In T. Hirschi & M. Gottfredson (Eds.), *Understanding crime*. Beverly Hills, Calif.: Sage, 1980, pp. 53–71.

Taylor, R. B., Gottfredson, S. D., Brower, S., Drain, W., & Dockett, K. Toward a resident-based model of community crime prevention: Urban territoriality, social networks, and design. *JSAS Catalog of Selected Documents in Psychology, 10,* ms. 2044, 1980.

Taylor, R. B., Gottfredson, S. D., & Brower, S. Territorial cognitions and social climate in urban neighborhoods. *Basic and Applied Social Psychology,* 1981, *2,* 289–303.

Taylor, R. B., Gottfredson, S. D., & Brower, S. Understanding block crime and fear. *Journal of Research in Crime and Delinquency,* 1984, *21,* 303–331.

Thibaut, J., & Kelley, H. H. *The social psychology of groups.* New York: Wiley, 1958.

Whyte, W. F. *Street corner society.* New York: Norton, 1943.

Wicker, A. W. *Introduction to ecological psychology.* Monterey, Calif.: Brooks/Cole, 1979.

Worchel, S., & Lollis, M. Reactions to territorial contamination as a function of culture. *Personality and Social Psychology Bulletin,* 1982, *8,* 370–375.

9

Continuity and Change in the Tswana's House and Settlement Form

GRAEME J. HARDIE

INTRODUCTION

Planners and designers are not, on the whole, fully aware of the influence of beliefs and values on the manipulation of space. In this chapter I consider the concept of *expressive space* and try to show how it can aid planners in producing culturally acceptable designs.

More generally, cultural conceptions include those shared meanings and values that are explicitly or implicitly stated or that are publicly acted out and are thus observable in people's behavior. These culturally determined behaviors control, among other things, the conceptual and practical organization of space because most behavioral acts presuppose a specific area for their performance. Indeed, all things real or imagined occur in a conceptually and often physically delimited space and give it its peculiar character. "Space," as we know it, is thus a product and expression of a specific culture. For this culturally controlled organization of space, I use the phrase *expressive space*.

GRAEME J. HARDIE • National Institute for Personnel Research, P.O. Box 32410, Braamfontein, Republic of South Africa 2017. The author wishes to acknowledge receipt of a Fulbright-Hays Research Abroad Fellowship, from the United States Government, which enabled the research to be undertaken.

The expressive space of the Tswana of Botswana, South Africa, offers an excellent opportunity for investigating this idea, for a number of their organizing concepts are spatially expressed, especially those related to their cosmology, social status, and political organization. As detailed historical records exist, the continuity and change of each of these concepts and their subsequent spatial expression whether physical or behavioral can be noted. In this way an assessment can be made of those aspects of expressive space that have been most susceptible to change and those that have resisted alteration.

From the earliest records, Tswana settlements are characterized by two unique features that differentiate them from other expressions of the Southern Bantu cultural complex. First, the Tswana lived in large settlements with populations ranging from 5,000 to 10,000. This contrasted dramatically with the dispersed pattern of settlement usually found in southern Africa. Secondly, the settlements were often relocated. Lekatoo for instance, was observed in 1801 (Daniell, 1804) and in 1821 (Burchell, 1822–1824/1953). Between these dates the town moved three times and suffered a major split that removed half the population.

Some writers ascribe these unique features of Tswana settlements to their ecological context. The hot, dry climate and limited water resources are seen as major reasons for their spatial concentration and movement. However, this is perhaps an oversimplification because a number of reasons appear to have led the Tswana to adopt their particular settlement form.

This chapter has five major sections: (1) an explanation of expressive space and how it has been defined and observed in a variety of cultures; (2) a description of Tswana cosmology and how it has been manifested spatially; (3) a review of the social and political influences on the settlement and house form; (4) a discussion of continuity and change against the background of the Tswana example; and (5) the implications of this work for future research.

EXPRESSIVE SPACE

Many researchers have focused on particular spatial expressions of social and cultural concepts. For instance, Morgan in his pioneering study *Houses and House Life of the American Aborigines* (1881) showed that domestic architecture is an expression of social organization and its relation to the system of production. Douglas (1972) confirmed this, focusing her research on the ordering of domestic space according to symbolic principles signifying the social organization.

Rapoport in his numerous books and articles has documented many examples of the expressive space aspects of domestic architecture. In one article (1969a), he investigated reasons for the difference in the house forms of the Pueblo and Navajo Indians. The Pueblo Indians live in collective inwardly focused settlements, whereas the Navajo live dispersed on the plains in individual hogans. He argued that the contrast in settlement and house form is due to differences in world view expressing what is regarded as important in the social organization, religion, and ritual.

In his classic book *House Form and Culture* (1969b), Rapoport stated that from his extensive overview of domestic and vernacular architecture, sociocultural forces primarily shape the house form:

> What finally decides the form of the dwelling and moulds the space and the relationships is the vision the people have of the ideal life. The [built] environment sought reflects many socio-cultural forces, including religious beliefs, family and the clan structure, social organization, ways of gaining a livelihood, and social relations between individuals. . . . Buildings and settlements are the visible expression of the relative importance attached to different aspects of life and the varying ways of perceiving reality. . . . The forms of primitive and vernacular buildings are less the result of individual desires than of the aims and desires of the unified group for an ideal environment. (p. 47)

In *Human Aspects of the Built Form*, Rapoport (1977) referred to the built environment as a "reflection of people's value systems, environmental attitudes and preferences: it is congealed information." This aspect of architecture viewed as information communicating meaning is further developed in his book, *Meaning and the Built Form* (1982). This chapter will attempt to unravel the meaning and information expressed in the Tswana settlement and house form.

Eliade gave useful insight and background to the "expressive space" of the Tswana. In his book *The Sacred and the Profane: The Nature of Religion* (1959), he proposed that one communicational aspect of the built form is in establishing the concepts of the cosmos concretely on earth. He described how for many preliterate societies, space was not homogeneous; inhabited spaces were seen as sacred whereas all other space around was a formless, foreign expanse. Further Eliade (1959, p. 43) maintained that the religious man of fixed settlements, although he knew that his country, village, and temple all constituted the navel of the universe

> also wanted his own house to be at the center and to be an "imago mundi". . . . [He] could only live in a space opening upward, where the break in the plane was symbolically assured and hence communication with the

"other world," the transcendental world, was ritually possible. Of course the
sanctuary—the Center par excellence—was there, close to him . . . but he
felt the need to live at the center always.

Eliade holds that the house, like the temple and city, became a
symbol of the universe with manlike God at its center and in charge of
its creation. The house, like the temple or shrine was sanctified by ritual,
with emphasis on the threshold, for just as the entrance was, and still is
regarded as the dividing line between the sacred and the profane worlds
and is suitably embellished to ward off evil spirits that might attempt to
enter the inner sanctum, so the threshold of the house is regarded as
one of the most important dividing lines between the inner private space
and the outer public world.

A description of the Tswana's house and settlement reveals much of
what Eliade has presented, especially in the consecration of a new settlement site, the protection of the boundaries of the town, and the importance placed on the threshold of the house as a depository of charms to
protect the house from evil influences.

Other researchers have also emphasized the influence of a society's
cosmological view on the way in which cities, towns, and houses are
designed. For instance, Wheatley (1971) has discussed the Chinese conception of the cosmos and the way in which this influences a variety of
aspects of their house and settlement design. Reichel-Dolmatoff (1976)
wrote about the Tukano Indians of Columbia, whereas Goosen (1974)
described the Chamulas of Mexico, who appear to use the landscape to
express their concepts of time and space. Nitschke (1974) described how
the Japanese use a method of binding, called *shime,* as a symbolic action
in which "through an act of building, Heaven is brought back onto Earth
as a festival of renewal."

Rapoport (1969b), Griaule (1965), and Griaule and Dieterlen (1954)
have shown how the Dogon lay out their towns as a model of the
universe. Bordieu (1973), in his analytical essay *The Berber House,* suggested that to the Berber the house "is a microcosm organized according
to the same principles which govern all the universe."

In comparing the way traditional and modern societies perceive
their house in relation to themselves and the universe, Cooper (1976)
wrote:

It seems that consciously or unconsciously . . . many men in many parts of
the world have built their cities, temples, and houses as images of the universe. . . . Our house is seen, however unconsciously as the center of our
universe and symbolic of the universe. . . . Primitive man sees his dwelling
as symbolic of the universe with himself, like God, at its center. Modern man
apparently sees his dwelling as symbolic of the self but has lost touch with
this archaic connection between house-self-universe. (p. 446)

In describing the house as an expression of self, Cooper emphasized the notion of house as *fortress-to-be-defended*, but where defense is no longer regarded as important, the house becomes an individual expression of self-and-family. She claimed that by this change "the self-and-environment are seen in a state of mutual regard instead of in a state of combat." It will be noted that the Tswana house form is undergoing this change, becoming an expression of self-and-family although it is still regarded by some as a fortress-to-be-defended. Whereas Cooper emphasized the identification of the self with the house, Altman and Gauvain (1981) looked at the relationship between identity and communality and the effect on the house form. These are viewed dialectically as transactional dimensions of the built expression. The Tswana's house form traditionally emphasized community cohesion. As will be noted, the houses were of similar material with contiguous walls. Individualization was limited to such aspects as the decoration of the threshold or to trees grown within the lot. More recently, the emphasis has been placed on the individualization of the house, but yet it is still controlled by what is acceptable to the community.

From the foregoing it will be noted that expressive space has received attention from a number of researchers focusing on a variety of aspects. Let us now return to the expressive space of the Tswana, investigating the cosmological, social, and political influences on settlement and house form with each aspect being viewed in a context of continuity and change.

THE COSMOLOGY OF THE TSWANA
AND ITS SPATIAL IMPLICATIONS

The concepts that underlie the Tswana's expressive space are apparently entwined in their cosmological perspective, particularly in relation to their belief in the influence of the ancestors on their lives on earth. It is therefore necessary that these aspects should be investigated to understand the emphasis placed on maintaining "order" and "coolness" both between the living and the dead and within the community itself, and the physical expression of these values in the settlement and house form.

In a book on the Tswana entitled *Mind in the Heart of Darkness*, Alverson (1978) suggested that the Tswana believe that there was a creation—a beginning of the cosmos—but that the beginning continues throughout cosmologic time and hence one's origins are always present. He proposed that the Tswana view time in the following manner:

World time is orthogonal to cosmologic time and is finite. Moreover existing time has two aspects, both of which are given in the origins—world time and ancestral time. World time and ancestral time while in complementary position vis-à-vis the individual, parallel one another, each participating continuously in the origins of the cosmos. . . . Life in the world of the living is an aspect of life as a whole, not a period of time. The social order includes essentially the existence of the not living who by virtue of being ancestors are closest to the origins of the society and the people. (1978, pp. 168–170)

From Alverson's description, the importance of the ancestors is established. It is believed that the ancestors take an active interest in the fortunes of their living descendants over whom they are seen to exercise powerful control, rewarding with good health and prosperity those who treat them with respect and obedience, but punishing with sickness, economic loss, or some other misfortune those who neglect them or who offend the social values of which the ancestors are custodians. Belief in the power of the ancestors has incurred a host of ritual obligations and observances for securing their favor and support.

The social ordering found in earth time is believed to be a mirror image of that found in ancestral time and space. Those of highest status in the one world therefore have greatest influence in the other. Without going into a detailed description of the traditional Tswana civil state, it should be noted that Tswana society was hierarchically organized with the head of state, the *kgosi*, controlling the civil, military, and bureaucratic business of the state. The kgosi appointed trusted counselors to head the various offices of the judiciary and the army and to undertake tax collection and land distribution, and so forth, powers that now rest with the national government. These appointments were seldom to members of the royal household, for the kgosi's male relatives are a direct threat to his power.

It is perhaps in his relationship to the ancestors that the kgosi played his most important role. A leading Tswana authority, Sekgoma Khama, has written:

The traditional outlook is that . . . this superior human being [referring to Modimo, the great ancestor] has personal interests in the affairs of man but the interaction of such a being manifests itself through the chief—as the father of the community—it makes no difference whether this father of the community is dead or alive. (1977, p. 57)

The kgosi therefore has the important role of mediating between the people and the royal ancestors, which reinforces his powers.

Historically, the strength of the state depended on how it dealt with the vicissitudes of a hostile natural environment as well as hostile neighboring states. The kgosi, because of his position in the cosmos through his relationship with the ancestors, was responsible for handling these issues. If he was seen to be successful, his standing with the people was greatly enhanced and was seen as a practical expression of his wisdom and godlike qualities. However, good fortune within the state also depended on how its citizens dealt with potential malevolent influences and ensured order in social relations, in the settlement, and in the *lolwapa* (yard). This reflected the order within the cosmos that it was believed must be respected. This order was needed to keep the world, both physically and metaphysically "cool," and devoid of elements such as disputes that are seen as "hot events," which through their potential disorder could pollute one's well-being.

A number of rituals and observances were developed that manifested the desired order. These rituals often had a spatial dimension either in terms of a behavioral expression or in the way they physically organized space. For instance, there were rituals that were related to the inception of a new capital, the protection of state and house boundaries, burials, and the handling of disputes.

In the establishment of a new town, the kgosi as head of the state selected the site for the town. It is believed that he was guided in his selection by Modimo—the great ancestor. Choice of a site with a good water supply and fertile lands, with the resulting good fortune it brings the people, would in turn greatly enhance the kgosi's status and power.

At the time of the inception of a new town the kgosi and his wife were the first to sleep in the new settlement, signifying the normal relations that should exist in the life of the settlement. His son and heir cut the first branch to clear the site, signifying the future order recognized in the present. Then the fire in the central *kgotla* (meeting place) was started with embers brought from the central kgotla in the old town, and signified continuity with the past. From this fire all the fires in the various kgotlas, and eventually the fires in every household, were lighted.

Here is an element, fire—"hot," and potentially one that in disorder can be highly destructive—yet that when ordered, contained, and controlled, exemplifies the continuity of the life of the state as it was reestablished in the new location.

The ritual of establishing a town has obviously not been used for a long time, but there are other rituals, such as those carried out at the time of death, by which the order of the cosmos is concretized in the present. During the mourning period, the house of the deceased becomes the focus of events. If the deceased has not built a permanent home in the town of his birth, the mourning procedures are delayed until a member of the family agrees to hold the ceremony. This is not viewed positively by the community, as it means that the individual has not prepared for the accommodation of his ancestral spirit. When a death is announced, members of the community, and particularly kin, immediately congregate at the house of the deceased, which is never left empty until after the burial. The windows of the house are blackened, and at night a fire burns continuously, with singing and prayers in the lolwapa to keep away possible malevolent influences in this disordered time.

On the day of the burial the men gather outside the lolwapa. The coffin is placed with the head to the west. The women are then seated to the east, at the foot end of the coffin, and the men take up their superior position at the west end, on symbolically high ground. This displays the order of status that exists between men and women. After the burial, which now takes place in a cemetery and not in the cattle kraal as in the past, the people return to the house of the deceased. Before entering the lolwapa they wash their hands, symbolically cleansing and "cooling" themselves of the impurity of death with which they have been touched. On the following day, the kin of the deceased wash down the whole house, cleaning the windows and washing all the clothes of the deceased, in this way literally "cooling down" the house from the disorders that have struck it, and attempting to deal with the widower or widow whose blood has been excited by losing part of its blood now departed.

The form of this ritual is still maintained regardless of the religious denomination of the individual, and it graphically recalls and reestablishes for all the order of the cosmos that has been disturbed in the lolwapa.

Disorder, or a state of being "hot," can be generated in a number of ways for everybody is likely to have "hot" blood for short periods. For instance, this applies to anyone who has had sexual intercourse the previous night or who has just traveled a long distance or who has been at a funeral or visiting a sick person. It also applies to a woman smearing a floor or mixing earth. Longer periods of "hot" blood occur during menstruation, pregnancy, miscarriage, or widowhood. People with "hot" blood are considered dangerous to others and occasionally to themselves as well. They could bring sickness, or adversely affect the rainfall, the crops, and the cattle; so various restrictions are imposed on them to prevent their state of disorder from harming others. Some potentially "hot" events are removed from the town, so as not to disturb the necessary "cool" and order of the settlement. For instance, when the men in the kgotla disagreed in a potentially violent way, a *lekgotla* or full assembly of the men under arms was called. This is held in a place outside the town where differences can be settled without polluting the town. Likewise, initiation of the men and women is held outside the town. These events all mark a stage when no rules apply, a state of transition or liminality, for instance when a boy becomes a man, or a widow is purified by miscellaneous intercourse, or a dispute of a hostile nature can only be resolved by abnormal means such as fighting. By removing these events from the town, the established order within the center is maintained. However, outside the town it is possible for what is disordered to be "cooled," reordered, and returned to the center.

There are other ways in which the cosmological order is expressed spatially. These involve the protection of the state and house boundaries. Each year, potions were placed at the boundaries of the state, a practice no longer maintained. This ceremony was directed by elderly nonmenstruating members of the community, with girls and boys of prepuberty age acting as their messengers.

The houses were also protected. The anthropologist Schapera has described house protection procedures practiced when he was in Botswana in the 1930s (personal communication). At that time, mixtures of herbs and roots were ground together with sticks and pieces of leather that it was believed would turn into venomous snakes, bringing sickness and even death, if a sorcerer tried to enter the plot. Each traditional doctor had his own prescription for these procedures, which varied according to the client. Some doctors only dealt with the foundation, whereas others placed items in the walls as well. If the house was rectangular, it was customary for the doctor to place items at the entrance and in each corner before the foundation was laid. If the house was round, material was placed at the entrance and in two or three places on the circumference of the dwelling. The ritual was usually performed at night to avoid being observed by outsiders and may have involved the participation of the household. On placing their potions, doctors are reported to have made such exhortations as "Whoever bewitches these children, may his charms turn back on him" and "I establish this village; let them see whatever spoils it and so too a thief."

My own investigations carried out recently confirm that house protection procedures are still undertaken. Although traditional doctors still perform these rituals, they are increasingly being replaced by ministers of the African independent churches. Christian symbols such as water are used by these practitioners. For instance, a bottle of "blessed" water may be placed at each corner of a house, or water may be sprinkled over the whole plot; sometimes even the newly made bricks are sprinkled with the specially prepared water. In the rituals undertaken by the doctors, small leather strips are not often used now, but small wooden pegs are driven into the ground and serve the same purpose.

White is believed to be an auspicious color and symbolizes the protection of the ancestors. Decorations on the house gates are often of white clay, and the pillars of the gate to the central cattle kraal in Mochudi are painted white. An extension of this is the use of a plant that has a white flower and that, when cut, gives off copious amounts of white sap. This is placed at the entrance to a yard or cattle kraal.

The thresholds to the living units in the lolwapa are on the whole restricted to household members, with visitors being entertained in the lolwapa. When a woman is recovering from childbirth a stick is placed at the threshold to her house, and only her mother is allowed to see her. This seclusion of the woman is to prevent her from polluting other household members, because her blood is considered to be "hot," excited, and therefore in a state of disorder. On the other hand, other people whose blood might be "hot" could adversely affect the mother and child should they enter her house. This custom was noted 50 years ago by Schapera (1971, p. 210) and the practice continues today.

It is also believed that potions can be placed on one's path and if touched will adversely affect one. Obviously a crossroad is a most propitious place for carrying out this kind of sorcery, as it increases the chances of reaching the intended victim. The nature of the settlement pattern made it possible for a person to use many routes. This explains why in the new areas in the town a dead-end street with only one exit is not seen positively, and why many footpaths and routes of access to one's home are preferred.

In the informal settlement of Naledi on the edge of the capital, Gaborone, one man spoke of the "wild dogs" in the area, against which he required all the protection possible. He saw these dogs as posing a real threat, perhaps someone coming to steal, and figuratively in the form of jealousies. These jealousies could be roused by whatever one had that the neighbor lacked, for example, food, a job, or money, or means of self-employment. Another man gave this as a reason for not building a larger house, even though he could well afford to do so, because his neighbors might be jealous and adversely affect his fortunes and that of his family (Hardie, 1980).

One consequence of this attitude is that it is not desirable to share fences. The old adage *good fences make good neighbors* remains true, except that here the fences are designed to keep one separate, so that one cannot be polluted by the neighbors' feelings and hostilities. It would appear, therefore, that sharing walls, especially internal walls, would not be desirable. As long as the plots are large, as in Mochudi, there is no need for shared fences, even if these are only separated by a small space. Of course, in the past lolwapa walls were shared, but then neighbors belonged to the same social and administrative unit, and disputes could be formally resolved, but this would not apply to those living next to foreigners with no such connections.

The desire for order expressed in the organization of the settlement is further demonstrated in the maintenance and neatness of the lolwapa, the plastering of the floor, the bounding of the household space, and the clearing away of all vegetation from the plot. This custom of clearing the plot completely before occupation continues to be practiced and all that is allowed to remain are the trees. The reason given for the neatness is that it is customary to do so to avoid snakes. This reason for not planting near a house was recently given by a Black resident in urban Johannesburg, where snakes are seldom seen. The snake is symbolically potent, just as snakes are in reality, as highly poisonous ones are found in Mochudi, being referred to as "our conscience," and the "protector of the kgosi." Snakes are seen in this way because they travel between the world of the living and the underground world of the ancestors and are therefore liminal animals, at home in both worlds. If they should bite it is seen as a message from the ancestors—a rather grim one at that.

Figure 1. The *lolwapa* (yard) was noted for its neatness by the early European visitors to the Tswana. This is a practice that is maintained today.

A further factor that encourages the neatness of the lolwapa is the belief that if it falls into a state of disrepair or is left unoccupied for a long time the ancestors of that lolwapa will feel neglected and may possibly disturb their descendants. As a result, it is customary for an unoccupied lolwapa to be cleared at least once a year and the fire rekindled, so that the ancestors might know that they have not been forgotten, thus maintaining normal relations with them and keeping the yard "cool."

By clearing the lolwapa and smearing its floor with plaster, the world of the household is controlled by its inhabitants in a very explicit and highly defined manner. By contrast, the land beyond the wall is no-man's-land and is left untouched. Only the area around the ward kgotla is cleared, with all the households facing into the open space participating in this endeavor. It becomes obvious that the roads, pathways, and leftover spaces in a traditional capital like Mochudi are under no one's control. Similarly, in cities like Gaborone where open spaces have been left on the assumption that they will serve as play areas for children, they have been left untouched, becoming covered with litter and treated as a no-man's-land.

The threshold between the controlled lolwapa and the uncontrolled outside was, and still is, an important point of transition in space. In the past, with the high walls, the opening was small and thus could be secured easily in time of attack. Now the walls are low, but the threshold in the mud wall is clearly marked. On festive occasions such as weddings it is specially decorated. Even when the fence is made of thorn bushes, the opening is still marked and that is the only point of entry used, even though other breaks in the fence may occur. By limiting the points of entry, they can be treated by traditional doctors to ensure that those who enter will not act malevolently.

The organization of space has been shown to be a vital means of expressing the cosmological views of the Tswana and the values implied of maintaining order and "coolness" in the world of the living. What is of significance is the way in which this spatial expression has been maintained particularly for life cycle rituals such as at the time of birth, initiation into adulthood, and death. Further, the neatness of the yard and the practice of protecting the houses from malevolent influences has been continued. Except for the initiation, all these rituals are under individual control and are therefore not threatened by changing political structures and the like. Perhaps the diminishing role of the traditional authorities and their influence in the daily lives of the people to secure the relationship between the living and the dead has encouraged the adherence to traditional beliefs over which the people themselves exercise direct control.

SOCIAL AND POLITICAL INFLUENCES ON THE SETTLEMENT AND HOUSE FORM

The cosmological perspective of the Tswana also influenced their social and political organizations, particularly such aspects as status, which placed a person in either a higher or lower position in the real world, depending on one's accepted position in the world of the ancestors. These social and political patterns were also expressed in the organization of space, especially in the layout of the settlement. For instance, a Tswana town was not traditionally organized geometrically according to physical elements. Its form was generated from the conceptual model of the existing social order, following traditional rules and precedence. In describing the basis on which a town was laid out, the Rev. John Mackenzie wrote in 1871:

> In laying out a Bechuana town, the first thing is to ascertain where the chief's courtyard with the public cattle-pen is to be placed. As soon as this is settled the remainder is simple . . . as soon as the chief's position is ascertained, one says "my place is always next to the Chief on this side." Another adds, "And mine is always next on that side," and so on till the whole town is laid out. (1871/1971, p. 367)

Schapera confirmed this pattern of organization when he wrote:

> The disposition of ward settlements in a tribal capital or other large village is determined not by chance, numbers, or personal inclination, but by the status of each ward and by geographical division or tribal section to which one belongs. The village may move from one place to another, but its general plan remains the same throughout. This means that the members of a ward seldom choose a site themselves; they should always have the same neighbours, and lie in the same direction from the Chief's *kgotla*, no matter where the village happens to be. (1943, p. 72)

As has already been described, the Tswana had a central concept of government focused on the central office of the kgosi. This concept of government found its particular spatial expression in the large, dense urban settlements that the Tswana occupied. These settlements were organized into a number of territorially based clusters of citizens (*kgoro*, or wards), each controlled and directed by its own head and leader, consisting of people with kin and nonkin affiliation to the leader.

This description might give the impression that the organization was fixed. This was not so, for within these strictures movement was possible. In fact, the continual movement of the capital allowed the settlement pattern to be dynamic, accommodating changes in internal organization as they became necessary (Hardie, 1982, p. 205). Some of these aspects will be considered presently.

Figure 2. A view of Mochudi, the capital of Kgatla, showing the main meeting place called the *kgotla*. The traditional method of thatching is evident in this photograph, taken around 1907.

Mochudi, the capital of the Kgatla settled in 1871, differed from previous settlements in that Kgosi Kgamanyane kept all his followers together because there was a threat of attack from the Boers in South Africa and another Tswana state. Formerly, all "sectional" divisions of the kgotla and sometimes even a single ward, had its own village several miles apart from its neighbors. Neither did Mochudi follow the more usual threefold layout, where a division was located on either side of the kgosi's kgotla, and was referred to as the *ntlha ya godimo*, the "upper side" (or right-hand side) usually to the west and the *ntlha ya tlase*, the "lower side" (or left-hand side) to the east. Instead the wards were grouped in five main sections: Kgosing, Morema, Tshukudu, Mabodisa, and Manamakgote.

Schapera described the settlement this way:

> Kgosing [embracing all the royal wards] is in the center and west; Morema is north-west of the *kgotla*, and Tshukudu south and south-west; Mabodisa is in the east, Manamakgote in the north-west beyond Morema. The sections are ranked in the order that they have been named. The effect of their location, accordingly, is that the outskirts of the town are inhabited by the wards least in order of seniority, mostly people of alien origin. The royal wards, on the other hand, are situated around the chief and his *kgotla*. (1943, pp. 70–71)

Figure 3. A photograph of Mochudi taken in 1978; zinc roofs dominate the town.

Similarly, the individual ward was arranged in a way that was considered cosmologically valid, corresponding to the greater world order. Kuper confirmed that this is also true for the Kgalagadi of western Botswana:

> The east is associated with the rising sun and with life, the west with the setting sun and with death. The senior man should live in the east. To the west of him is his younger brother or father's younger brother, to the west of him the next senior man and so on. (1982, p. 261)

Paul Devitt in an unpublished manuscript (see Kuper, 1982) further supports this notion:

> The headman should be placed in front of the junior people. He will be just like a sun. He goes to the eastern part of the village and the people who come to ask for residence in his village . . . belong to him and they go behind him. (p. 261)

Kuper continues:

> Ideologically, then, the settlement is conceived of as a natural order, which maps out according to cosmological criteria the genealogical given group of people. The principles are worked out in detail. For example, south and north are also important—the south being feminine and the source of rain, the north masculine and the source of harsh winds. (p. 261)

Willoughby, writing in 1928, explored the disposition of people in terms of cosmological patterning where the term *godimo* may be used for "west" but also for "high" and "above":

> The houses of the chief's sons are located according to their standing in the family, that of the heir being on his father's right hand, west of the Chief's dwelling and consequently described by this word *godimo*, though it may not be on higher land. Nowadays . . . a chief's dwelling . . . does not always look south, and the house of his great son, though on his right hand, is not always on the west; the same term, *godimo*, is nevertheless used to indicate its location. (p. 67)

Within the ward of the kgosi the same patterning takes place, with the other royals circling counterclockwise from the west in order of their status. However, around the kgosi and separating him from the other royals are the residences of his trusted counselors and household staff who are placed to protect him.

When the young men go for initiation, a practice still continued today, the camp is set up like a town, according to the same principles of status and cosmological order, with the men of each ward siting their camp according to their prescribed position. When the men assemble, they line up according to status, usually with a member of the royal household at the head. This clearly establishes the status of the initiates. When the men return to town they are publicly welcomed, and they assemble in the same rank order, which declares the social status of each individual vis-à-vis the rest of the initiates.

The movement of the capital as a way of marking the installation of a new kgosi had practical implications because it allowed the settlement to be reorganized with the new kgosi locating himself centrally. If, for instance, the previous head of state had many wives, they would have been domiciled around the central kgotla. By moving the capital the new kgosi would then be able to place himself and his wives in the center of the settlement, displacing the wives of the former head. If, on the other hand, he maintained the settlement in the same place, he would continue to live alongside his father's many wives, all of whom were ambitious for their children to become head of state, and who would therefore be potential competitors of the new leader. Or he would be forced to establish his residence away from the appropriate central position of the town. In fact in Mochudi, which has been stationary for over 100 years, the latter course has been followed, with each new kgosi locating his royal house in a different part of the town.

Another example of forces leading to internal reorganization of the settlement may be seen in the ramifications caused by the death of the senior male of a lineage segment. It is the eldest son who takes up the position of status, yet it is the youngest son who inherits the lolwapa of the father. This means that the eldest son cannot locate his lolwapa according to his newly inherited status. This, of course, may be rectified when the settlement moves, allowing the eldest son to place his lolwapa correctly, in the most important position in relation to the lineage's kgotla.

A further dynamic was the incorporation of immigrants into the state. The historian Tlou (1974) proposed that at first the immigrant communities were placed on the outskirts of the settlement to serve as the town's front line of defense against outside invaders. But such a new community would probably not remain on the edge of the town, for with time it would more than likely prove its loyalty to the kgosi and, if he were well disposed toward it, he could make it an independent political and social unit within the settlement. To accomplish this the kgosi would physically relocate the community, with the geographical location signifying its newly achieved status within the state. The regular movement of the capital therefore facilitated this type of incorporation and rearrangement, allowing the expression of the social order to be spatially maintained.

The geographical location of a ward was particularly important when it consisted of commoners because this geographical position in relation to the center confirmed their status. In contrast, the status of wards headed by men of royal blood was confirmed by birth. This presents a problem now that the settlements have become stationary and are unable to accommodate the natural population increase.

For instance, Gardner (1974) has found that in Serowe when the wards of commoners became too congested and no land was available for their expansion, rather than the whole ward's moving together to the outskirts of the town, a portion of the ward remained at the center. In this way their presence at the center was maintained as was their position of status. On the other hand, royal wards when congested moved as an entire unit to new land that could accommodate all their members, for their royal blood permanently secured their social status.

Maintaining ward solidarity was confirmed elsewhere. For instance, investigations into the movement of one ward in Mochudi showed that its members had divided into separate sections but always maintained a base at the center of the settlement (Hardie, 1980). This ward consisted of 99 households, 90 of which were in Mochudi, with all but 2 being contiguous to a ward member. The last portion of land given to the ward was in 1955. The way in which this last allocation was divided is particularly significant in that instead of the yards forming a traditional circular pattern, the properties were arranged in rectangular blocks. The ward had been directed to establish this new area on a "modern" basis by the kgosi. In this way, the ward maintained its cohesion on the basis of occupying contiguous blocks, rather than around a central open space and kgotla. Thus, the adjustment to living in a modern rectangular town plan did not result in the ward's sacrificing its solidarity.

The British protectorate over Botswana accepted by the major Tswana states in 1885 eventually led to the fixing of boundaries. This had the effect of stabilizing most of the traditional capitals, and the settlement organization had to adapt to being stationary, while maintaining its overall pattern. The kgosi moved to a new location in the town, and wards broke into smaller parcels. However, the greatest outside pressure on the organization has come about since independence in 1966. Since 1970 all residential plots in the traditional capitals have been allocated by government land boards rather than by the kgosi and the ward head, as in the past. Land is also freely available to males and females, married or unmarried. This is a major change from the past when only married males were eligible for land. This approach represents the democratic principles adopted by the national government. The concepts of democracy have therefore become a major dynamic influencing the internal organization of the present settlement, replacing tribal land control with government procedures that are not sensitive to cultural conceptions and values.

In Mochudi, for instance, the land board since its inception has allocated 2,618 residential plots, of which 30% were made to women. This almost doubled the number of plots in the town from 2,816 enumerated in the 1971 census to 5,434 in 1978 (Hardie, 1980). In part, the change in allocation procedures was based on the belief that traditional ward patterns were no longer valued, but ultimately it established the national government's authority. In the face of this it is amazing that the ward described retained such a high degree of solidarity, and it demonstrates that the traditional pattern of contiguous settlements is still desirable and will survive.

However, new social patterns support the change in land allocations. Women, for example, had limited rights; now they have access to land, an option they have taken up with alacrity as it means they are no longer, if unmarried, under the control of their father or elder brother. My own investigations into attitudes toward living next to ward mates showed that 74% of the men favored this, whereas 55% of the women interviewed were against it (Hardie, 1980). This is perhaps not surprising as the women move to the ward of their husband and live surrounded by his family and ward mates. Women today prefer to live without these ties and social obligations.

As has been shown, the change in political control since independence is reflected in changes in the form of settlement. Land allocations having previously been under the jurisdiction of the traditional authority and as a result tightly controlled are now disbursed by the central government, which has made land more freely available, rapidly doubling the size of the town. Further, this change has discouraged long-established social propinquity that was deemed important in the past. However, as one ward has shown, the people have themselves attempted to maintain this cohesion. For some, and single women with dependents in particular, the new land allocation has been to their advantage and has allowed their desire for independence to be expressed spatially.

The house has undergone a number of physical changes. However, what is of interest is the way in which concepts of technology have been perpetuated while allowing for the incorporation of new building materials.

All the physical changes to the house form have for the most part

Figure 4. A typical house in Mochudi. To the left is a modern house, whereas in the background is a house following the traditional design.

Figure 5. *Boosh-wannah Hut* drawn by Samuel Daniell while visiting Leetakoo, the capital of the Thlaping, in 1801.

come about because they improve the quality of the house, reduce maintenance, accommodate furniture, or increase status. These changes are apparently not in conflict with social and cultural traditions and are acceptable although, as in the case of the cement block, they are made to conform to existing concepts of technology (see Hardie, 1980, for a discussion of the continuity of technological concepts).

An investigation of those features of the house form noted in the early descriptions that have not changed gives greater insight into the continuity of Tswana "expressive space." In a survey of 88 houses in a ward of Mochudi (Hardie, 1980), it was found that only three consolidated all their rooms under one roof. Although the physical form had changed from round to rectangular, the custom of separating members of the household by age and sex in different living units within the same plot had been maintained. The head of one of the consolidated houses complained that the house felt congested and tight.

CONTINUITY AND CHANGE

The built form does not stand in isolation from its context. As an expression of cultural and social values it physically reflects the continuity and change of these values. The example presented here of the Tswana settlement and house form demonstrates the way in which a number of particular values are expressed spatially and also shows that when values change so too does the physical expression.

In dealing with change, Gauvain, Altman, and Fahim (1983) suggested that "central values are often preserved under conditions of social change that are internally initiated and controlled." (p. 196) The case of the Tswana supports this argument, particularly exemplifying self-initiated change, although disruptive, externally induced change does exist. Those values under individual control have been maintained. For instance, it has been shown that values binding individuals to outside spiritual influences expressed in house protection procedures have been maintained, even though the form of such procedures has altered, reflecting changing religious patterns. Physical changes in the house form have focused on improvements of quality by adopting new building methods, but without changing the social organization of the household. In taking on new building procedures, these new technologies have been incorporated in ways that conform to traditional technological concepts.

On the other hand, externally induced change, such as political reorganization of the country that has displaced the power of the kgosi and his control over the land, has radically altered the settlement pattern. Nonetheless, ward members still seek adjacent locations. Where this has not been possible homeowners have taken their own precautions in dealing with foreign neighbors and do not share fences. However, the women have endorsed the move away from tribal land allocations because it gives them direct access to land. To some, then, the change is seen as a disadvantage, breaking down traditional social groupings that they have attempted to maintain. They have taken precautions to alleviate the potential dangers of the change. On the other hand, the change is embraced by those who see it to their advantage, such as single women who as a result of change gain greater independence.

IMPLICATIONS FOR FUTURE RESEARCH

This study would suggest that the home environment, encapsulating as it does the beliefs and values of the household and community, is resistant to change and is conservative by nature. Yet it could be hypothesized that the home environment in almost any context is continually undergoing change. This example has shown the change taking place in a setting that is dominated by a foreign, in this case, Western culture. Further descriptive and long-term investigations could be undertaken cross-culturally in order to make it possible to generalize from this study. Situations investigated could include both exotic and nonexotic home environments. Self-initiated changes by homeowners living in situations not threatened by dominating and different cultural values, such as the American middle-class home would be important in this research.

If further cross-cultural research were to be undertaken investigating the continuity and change of expressive space in different cultures it might be possible to generalize on those values that are more resistant to change and those susceptible to change. For instance are those concepts relating to political concepts more likely to change than those affecting social concepts? Further, are those concepts relating to issues of world view and cosmology and under individual control least likely to change?

In my own research I found it useful to develop a matrix that looked at a number of conceptual rules that had existed in the past and that related to specific social, political, and cosmological aspects of the lives of the Tswana. The behavioral and/or constructed expressions that arose from these concepts in the past were noted. Then the conceptual rules were investigated for their efficacy in the present and again behavioral and/or constructed expression was noted. By comparing the past and present conceptual rules and the resulting expression of each, it was possible to rate the degree of continuity and change that had been experienced. In this way the expressive space and the dimension of time could be heuristically combined and could be analyzed accordingly.

This procedure could well be followed elsewhere and would allow for useful cross-cultural comparison. Obviously, it would require an investigation of both the past and the present conceptual rules affecting specific areas of a culture and the attendant behavioral and/or constructed expression of each. This matrix would force the researcher to view the built form as an expressive instrument rather than simply documenting the continuity and change on a physical level alone.

By comparing this material, it may be possible to determine which changing or nonchanging aspects of expressive space are artifacts of a particular setting and which are shown to exist cross-culturally generally. The results could then be tested in other cultural settings to see if the assertions are maintained. The intention would be the development of a body of knowledge that would enable architects and planners undertaking assignments in different cultural situations to know what aspects of the expressive space they are working in must be more particularly investigated. Further, it might enable them to predict which aspects are most likely to alter or be maintained. In this way they could adapt their proposals accordingly.

Acknowledgments

The author wishes to thank A. Leeds of Boston University for his assistance and support.

REFERENCES

Altman, I., & Gauvain, M. A cross-cultural and dialectic analysis of homes. In L. Liben, A. Patterson, & N. Newcombe (Eds.), *Spatial representation and behaviour across the life span*. London: Academic Press, 1981, pp. 283–319.

Alverson, H. *Mind in the heart of darkness*. New Haven: Yale University Press, 1978.

Bourdieu, P. The Berber house. In M. Douglas (Ed.), *Rules and meanings*. Harmondsworth, England: Penguin, 1971, pp. 98–110.

Burchell, W. J. *Travels in the interior of southern Africa*. I. Schapera (Ed.). London: Batchworth, 1953. (Originally published 1822–1824.)

Cooper, C. The house as symbol of the self. In H. M. Proshanzky, W. H. Imelson, & L. G. Rivlin (Eds.), *Environmental psychology: People and their physical settings*. New York: Holt, Rhinehart & Winston, 1976, pp. 435–448.

Daniell, S. *African scenery and animals*. London, 1806.

Douglas, M. Symbolic order in the use of domestic space. In P. J. Ucko, R. Tringham, & G. W. Dimbleby (Eds.), *Man, settlement and urbanism*. Cambridge: Schenkman, 1972, pp. 508–519.

Eliade, M. *The sacred and the profane: The nature of religion*. Chicago: Harcourt Brace and World, 1959.

Gardner, R. Some sociological and physiological factors affecting the growth of Serowe. *Botswana Notes and Records*, 1974, 6, 77–88.

Gauvain, M., Altman, I., & Fahim, H. Homes and social change: A cross-cultural analysis. In N. Feimer & S. Geller (Eds.), *Environmental psychology: Directions and perspectives*. New York: Praeger, 1983, pp. 180–218.

Goosen, G. *Chamulas in the world of the sun: Time and space in Maya oral tradition*. Cambridge: Harvard University Press, 1974.

Griaule, M. *Conversation with Ogotemmeli*. London: Oxford University Press, 1965.

Griaule, M., & Dieterlen, G. The Dogon of the French Sudan. In D. Forde (Ed.), *African worlds*. London: Oxford University Press, 1954, pp. 83–110.

Hardie, G. J. *Tswana design of house and settlement—Continuity and change in expressive space*. Unpublished doctoral thesis, Boston University, 1980.

Hardie, G. J. The dynamics of the internal organization of the traditional tribal capital, Mochudi. In R. R. Hitchcock & M. R. Smith (Eds.), *Settlement in Botswana*. Johannesburg: Heinemann Educational Books in collaboration with the Botswana Society, 1982, pp. 205–219.

Khama, S. *Traditional attitudes to land and management of property with special reference to cattle.* Paper read at the Tribal Raising Policy conference, September, 1977.

Kuper, A. Social aspects of Kgalagari settlement. In R. R. Hitchcock & M. R. Smith (Eds.), *Settlement in Botswana.* Johannesburg: Heinemann Educational Books in collaboration with the Botswana Society, 1982, pp. 258–263.

Mackenzie, J. *Ten years north of the Orange River.* London: Frank Cass, 1971. (Originally published 1871.)

Morgan, L. H. *Houses and house life of American aborigines.* Chicago: University of Chicago Press, 1881.

Nitschke, G. Shime–binding/unbinding. *Architectural Design,* 1974, *12,* 747–791.

Rapoport, A. The Pueblo and the hogan. A cross-cultural comparison of two responses to the environment. In P. Olivier (Ed.), *Shelter and society.* New York: Praeger, 1969, pp. 66–79. (a)

Rapoport, A. *House form and society.* Englewood Cliffs, N.J.: Prentice-Hall, 1969. (b)

Rapoport, A. *Human aspects of the urban form.* Oxford: Pergamon Press, 1977.

Rapoport, A. *The meaning of the built environment.* Beverly Hills, Calif.: Sage Publications, 1982.

Reichel-Dolmatoff, G. Cosmology as ecological analysis: A view from the rain forest. *Man,* 1976, *11*(3), 307–315.

Schapera, I. *Native land tenure in the Bechuanaland Protectorate.* Lovedale: The Lovedale Press, 1943.

Schapera, I. *Married life in an African tribe.* Hammondsworth, England: Penguin, 1971.

Tlou, T. The nature of Batswana states: Towards a theory of Batswana traditional government—the Batswana case. *Botswana Notes and Records,* 1974, *6,* 57–75.

Wheatley, P. *The pivot of the four quarters.* Chicago: Aldine, 1971.

Willoughby, W. C. *The soul of the Bantu.* New York: Doubleday, 1928.

10

Understanding Mobility in America

CONFLICTS BETWEEN STABILITY AND CHANGE

SALLY A. SHUMAKER AND GERALD J. CONTI

INTRODUCTION

Throughout history, the United States has been characterized as a nation of wanderers. From the period of early colonizing and populating of the continent (1602–1900), to the Industrial Revolution with its concommitant rural to urban migrations (1890–1917), large portions of the population have appeared to change residences easily. Even today approximately 20%, or about 40 million individuals, move from one residence to another each year; and, within a 5-year period, almost half of the United States population relocates *at least once* (Kroger, 1980; Long & Boertlein, 1976). It is estimated that, on the average, an American will move *14 times* during his or her life (Heller, 1982; Kroger, 1980). In comparison, the Irish relocate about 3 times in their lives, the Japanese about 7 times, and the British about 8 times (Long & Boertlein, 1976).

Given this country's history of mobility, its image as a nation of wanderers is not surprising. What is surprising is that attitudes about this image have changed from predominantly positive ones in the early

SALLY A. SHUMAKER • Behavioral Medicine Branch, DECA/NHLBI, The National Institutes of Health, Bethesda, Maryland 20205. GERALD J. CONTI • MSE Library, The Johns Hopkins University, Baltimore, Maryland 21218.

years of this nation to the negative associations that exist today. Initially, the image embodied the concepts of "personal liberty and opportunity" (Kopf, 1977), and relocation was unambiguously reinforced by the government with measures like the Homestead Act (passed in 1862), which gave any citizen 160 acres of land west of the Mississippi River for nothing more than filing fees and the promise to work and improve it (Morris, 1953).

Once the country was settled, the positive feelings associated with relocation were replaced with concerns that mobility might be linked to social instability and fragmentation (Kopf, 1977; Kroger, 1980). Thus, the free spirit side of the wanderer image became overshadowed by the negative assumption that, as wanderers, Americans were unwilling to invest in community. As early as 1860 the Superintendent of the Census argued that mobility represented "an unfavorable trait in [the] American character" (Long & Boertlein, 1976, p. 26), and fears over mobility prompted ineffective government policy interventions designed to reduce mobility rates in America (Clark & Moore, 1982; Rossi & Shlay, 1982). Today, social commentators continue to argue that easy relocation has made the United States a nation without roots (cf. Packard, 1972; Toffler, 1970).

As with most characterizations, the image of Americans as wanderers is oversimplified. It ignores the large number of people who rarely move and the many stable communities that exist in this country (cf. Shumaker & Taylor, 1983). Moreover, such a characterization dismisses the complex factors that underlie people's decisions to move. In this chapter we draw on both historical and contemporary data to explore mobility in America. By considering the context within which relocation decisions are made, we examine the conflicting pressures toward stability and change that have always co-existed in this country, and we suggest ways in which people resolve these opposing pressures. Finally, we explore research agendas that emerge from a contextual perspective of mobility.

Understanding Mobility in America

Pressures Favoring Relocation

Pull Factors: Achieving the American Dream.   In describing why people move, contemporary researchers consider aspects of the new setting (*pull*) and the current setting (*push*) that might enter into a relocation decision (cf. Brazzell & Gillespie, 1981; Cebula, 1980; Speare, 1974; Speare, Goldstein, & Frey, 1975). Most pull factors are captured in the concept of the *American Dream*. Moving is often associated with achieving success for self and family. Although the specific ingredients may vary from generation to generation, the promise of attaining the American Dream has always been a component in people's decisions to relocate.

During the early colonization and settlement of this country, the dream was tied to the promise of new land with unlimited opportunities and the hope of a better life.

> We go westward as into the future, with a spirit of enterprise and adventure. (Thoreau, 1913, p. 169)

The British colonies of North America were founded by European peasants who had been landless farmers, made transient of necessity after the decay and dissolution of the British feudal system. They ventured to America in the hope of owning their own farms (Beard & Beard, 1930). Accustomed to movement, these early settlers were both capable of reestablishing themselves readily and were willing to move to other areas when better prospects presented themselves.

Whether it was a British yeoman crossing the Atlantic, a New England farmer deserting the mountains for the valleys of the Old Northwest, or a southern black migrating to a factory town, all believed that they were entitled to a better and more prosperous life if they had the "grit" to win it.

> They agreed in the one general object—that of bettering their condition; but the particular means by which each proposed to attain this end, were as various as can be imagined (Jessy Quinn Thornton of the 1846 Wagon Train). (Unruh, 1979, p. 91)

Private enterprise and the government played important roles in associating the promise of enriched opportunities with willing relocation. The selling of frontiers (and later industrial and suburban areas) was often the prelude to migration (Billington, 1974; Manchester, 1974; Unruh, 1979). From the earliest days of missionaries, trappers, and frontier surveyors, the promised lands in the written works of soldiers and travelers sparked interest in new areas.

> In the winter of 18 and 46 our neighbors got hold of Fremont's *History of California* and began talking of moving to the New Country & brought the book to my husband to read & he was carried away with the idea. (Schlissel, 1982, p. 28)

Coupled with the excitement of a new life was the patriotism and nationalism that was associated with settling the continent. Although the publicity promised settlers that they would fulfill their personal desires, patriotism stirred their spirits and made them feel a part of a great and mystical movement (DeVoto, 1943). Miriam Thompson Tuller wrote that her husband was "fired by patriotism" into beginning their 1844 journey to Oregon (Schlissel, 1982). As surely as one generation moved to Kentucky to play out its own destinies after leaving Virginia, the next ventured to Texas, Oregon, and California (DeVoto, 1943).

In addition to the Americans migrating west, the American Dream has been a factor in people's decisions to migrate to this country. For example:

> Agents working in Drammen, Norway, advertised Dakota Territory as Uto-
> pia. My father was impressed with the tales of gold and the beauties of the
> far off land. In April of 1881, I found myself on a combination sail and
> steamship. (Berg, 1982, p. 136)

The hope of achieving the American Dream still exists among people in this country and among the migrants coming to America. Many people continue to believe that anyone can succeed in America with the right amount of work and effort (Potter, 1954). Throughout history, social mobility has been translated literally into geographic relocation. In addition to representing opportunities for advancement, some settings embody the attainment of success. In America visible wealth is a key component in maintaining class distinctions (Potter, 1954), and place of residence (both in terms of home and community) is a clear signal of status.

Of course, the American Dream represents a very general and largely intangible motive for relocation. Embodied within it are several very specific and pragmatic pull factors that influence mobility decisions. When we compare these enticements to previous eras in American history, however, we find that the basic ingredients have not changed: job opportunities, nicer homes, and attractive neighborhoods all draw people to new places.

Push Factors. Juxtaposed against the exciting promise of a new place are the negative aspects of the current locale—or what social scientists refer to as the *push* factors in relocation decisions. For some portion of the people who move (estimated by Michelson, 1979, to be as high as 40%), the major "push" to move is forced relocation. For example, disasters (both natural and human caused) may necessitate relocation when people lose their homes. Forced relocation also occurs as a by-product of industrialization: the construction of dams for electricity and irrigation, urban renewal, the development of new road systems, the worker needs of new and expanding industries, and the shutdown of nonprofitable businesses. Also, the poor and powerless are sometimes relocated when their homes or lands become valuable to others.

Beyond forced relocation, there are a number of specific aspects of an environment that can create dissatisfaction and cause individuals to *choose* relocation. For early settlers moving from the colonized East to the Woodlands, the East began to represent a transplanted British culture, and these pioneers chose to escape (again), rather than timidly accept class distinctions, overcrowding, economic failures, and other uncongenial aspects of life in the established portions of the nation. For European migrants, political and religious oppression as well as depressed economic conditions in their homelands encouraged people to uproot their families and move to America (Berg, 1977).

The push factors associated with contemporary relocation decisions remain basically the same as they were in the past. People continue to leave their homelands because of ideological oppression and severely depressed conditions. In addition, within this country inadequate housing and environmental disamenities (e.g., crime, crowding, noise) cause some people to seek new residences (cf. Speare, 1974).

Pressures Favoring Staying

Attachment to Place.   Just as there are both push-and-pull factors that function in consort to reinforce relocation decisions, there are aspects of settings that encourage people to remain in the same locale. The major component favoring a decision to stay can best be summarized by the concept of attachment to place, or the "positive affective bond that develops between individuals (or groups) and their residential environment" (Shumaker & Taylor, 1983, p. 233). The rewards individuals receive from the people in their proximal social networks and the comfort they derive from familiar homes and communities can be important in their lives; and, relocation often entails a painful severing of these ties (cf. Fried, 1963).

Shumaker and Taylor (1983) suggest some factors that may influence the development of residential attachment. First, the *physical amenities* of a setting are probably important. The more resources available in homes and communities, the more likely people's needs will be met there, and they will be satisfied with the setting. *Choice* in setting is also important. It implies that people have had an opportunity to consider the resources of more than one place and select the setting they perceive will best fit their needs.

Aspects of the *individual* will influence his or her development of attachment. For example, there are people who are more adventurous and who actively seek out new and different environments. These individuals are unlikely to form lasting bonds with any particular place—

though one could argue that such a personality style leads to multiple attachments (Stokols & Shumaker, 1982). In contrast, there are people who prefer consistency, who travel through a relatively small sphere of the environment and who are content with the predictability of the same place over time (cf. Golant, 1982). Also, the *social networks* people develop that are tied to a particular locale may be important to the development of place attachment (cf. Fried, 1982).

Finally, the ways in which the present residence *compares* with past homes and other places that are currently available will influence the degree to which attachment develops (Stokols & Shumaker, 1981). For example, if a place represents the best possible environment for an individual at a particular stage in his or her life, than attachment to that place may be more likely to occur.

Although the general concept of attachment or bonding has existed for several centuries, it is applied to relationships among people; its application to a person's attachment to a physical environment is fairly recent, and it is rarely considered in models of mobility. Yet, there is ample evidence throughout American history of the strong attachment people have to their homes.

It is impossible to read the diaries and letters of migrants from any age without sensing the bittersweet emotions that accompanied every move. Women frequently expressed their regrets at selling their homes and leaving their friends forever (Schlissel, 1982). In addition, strong feelings of attachment to new homesteads are eloquently expressed in the writings of settled migrants. Voicing not only an active affection for home with its familiar objects and responsibilities, settlers also expressed an attachment to the larger frontier community (Billington, 1974; Ford, 1976; Stewart, 1961).

More recently, Harriette Arnow (1972) has provided a poignant description of the slow decline of a woman forced to leave her home in Kentucky to follow her husband to the factories in Michigan during World War II. Thousands of people relocated during this period in American history, leaving lands that had been in their families for decades. The yearning for home captured in Arnow's characterization of the *Dollmaker* (1972) provides a strong image of how disruptive and emotionally wrenching this type of change was for some families.

As other indications of attachment to place, there are examples of people choosing to stay in relatively adverse environments. It is not uncommon for people in this and other countries to rebuild their homes after they have been destroyed by fire, floods, earthquakes, and other disasters (Burton, Kates, & White, 1978). Also, in a study of relocation decisions among residents living near the Three Mile Island (TMI) Nuclear Plant, Goldhaber, Hauts, and Disabella (1983) found that concern over TMI did not add to the validity of predicting residential relocation. Similarly, Kiecolt and Nigg (1982) interviewed 1,450 randomly selected Los Angeles residents to determine if living in an earthquake-prone community influenced the intensity of their desire to relocate and found that the people with strong community ties were least likely to relocate regardless of the real or perceived hazards existing in the area.

The strength of attachment to place is also evidenced from research on forced relocations. For example, Fried (1963) found that moving was most negative for residents who were strongly committed to their pre-relocation setting. When respondents in Fried's research learned their homes had been torn down, some reported strong feelings of personal loss. "It was like a piece being taken from me" (Fried, 1963, p. 170).

Blocked Mobility. Just as there are many people who are forced to relocate, there are others who are forced to remain in the same place. Lack of financial resources has always been a major component in blocked relocation.

Except for moves to factory towns during the Great Depression of the 1930s and similar moves from homesteads during the 1890s, very few of the people who relocated in *any* historic period were poor. The frontier as safety valve for an economically depressed East was an illusion. Migration was and is an expensive proposition, from the cost of securing passage on the Maryland settlement ships the *Ark* and *Dove* in 1634, to the transportation to and financing of a tract home in the Sunbelt. Eastern textile workers of the 19th century may have comforted themselves with the potential prosperity of a new life in Kansas or Dakota, but few managed to finance the dream into a reality (Billington, 1974). The costs of traveling to the West Coast from the East in the 1840s, for example, ranged from $500 to $1,000 for a full outfit of wagon, oxen, and preserved and nonperishable food. This price was the equivalent of several years' profits to most farmers, and simply an unimaginable sum for most workers to contemplate.

Today, the people with limited residential options continue to be the poor. In their research on San Francisco's Chinatown, Loo and Mar (1982) found that the people "left behind" in a nondesirable physical environment were primarily the poor and elderly. In addition, minorities of all social classes are often blocked in their relocation options as segregated housing persists in America (Fairchild & Tucker, 1982).

The Context of Relocation Decisions

Aside from situations of forced relocation and blocked mobility, push and pull factors coupled with feelings of attachment influence relocation decisions, and most likely a complex comparative process between existing and possible future residences, embedded within the total context of a person's life, prevails (cf. Stokols & Shumaker, 1981).

A life-cycle model of mobility (cf. Michelson, 1977, 1979) focuses on some aspects of an individual's life situation that might be critical to relocation decisions. The basic argument in this model is that people's housing needs change at different life stages. For example, the majority of migrant men and women in the 19th and early 20th centuries were of marrying age (Billington, 1974; Schlissel, 1982; Unruh, 1979). Despite a few older travelers, those who sought lives in a new locale were establishing their own homes for the first time, many embarking in the days immediately following their weddings (Schlissel, 1982). Today, the typical mover in the United States is still a young adult. In fact, age is one of the best predictors of mobility (cf. Long & Boertlein, 1976; Speare, 1974).

When viewing mobility from a life-cycle perspective, the actual criteria used to evaluate an optimal setting varies at different stages. Michelson (1979) refers to these changing family needs as the *family mobility cycle*. Thus, mobility is seen as a normative way in which to meet the naturally occurring alterations in family needs. For example, as families grow they will seek housing that can accommodate the growth. However, a life-cycle model does not adequately explain why some people choose relocation, whereas others choose to remain, even when the life stages of the two groups appear to be the same. For example, although some people may move to a larger home as their families grow, others may choose to build on to their existing homes (Speare, 1974).

Attempts to place relocation decisions into a more integrative framework are represented by contextual models of mobility (cf. Stokols & Shumaker, 1982; Stokols, Shumaker, & Martinez, 1983). According to these models, people have multiple needs, some of which are satisfied within their home and community environments. When salient needs are not satisfied by the environment, people feel uncomfortable and are motivated to alter the situation in ways that reduce the incongruity. If the needs are specific to the immediate residential environment, then relocation is one way to promote a better fit. Determinants of congruence, however, are both multidimensional and cross-situational. Thus, "the level of congruence associated with one's current residential period depends on several circumstances both within and outside the residence" (Stokols & Shumaker, 1982, p. 155). Basically, an individual's home represents one among several places in which his or her needs are met. A person's work setting, recreational areas and school, for example, may also meet some of his or her needs. Therefore, to fully understand mobility, the individual's entire life space and the relative importance of each life domain must be considered.

Though complex, a contextual model provides important insights on mobility that are lacking in earlier models. By going beyond a single life domain, the *competing* demands that impinge on people's lives become clearer. Relocation represents one among several options, available to *some* people, to gain greater fit between salient needs and environmental resources. These needs, moreover, may derive from *any* life domain. For example, work demands may include relocation for career advancement (cf. Brett, 1982), and even when attachment to home and community are strong, people may choose to leave.

For the people who *can choose* between staying or moving, there are most likely multiple factors that feed into their ultimate decision that simultaneously favor and oppose relocation. The final decision is often a difficult compromise. This view of mobility seriously weakens the wanderer characterization of Americans. There remains, however, some question as to whether or not mobility, regardless of its causes, undermines the social fabric of this country (cf. Conger, 1981).

The Impact of Mobility

The People and Places Left Behind.   People who reside in undersirable communities and are unable to relocate may suffer. The impact of blocked mobility on individuals has received little empirical attention. Because the people with limited residential options are often more vulnerable to the stressors associated with an adverse environment (i.e., the poor, the elderly, children), however, it is reasonable to hypothesize that the consequences of such environments could pose emotional and physical health risks.

There may be important consequences for a community if its residents are nonattached and either choose or are forced to stay. If the neighborhood is one in which people can purchase the benefits derived from commitment (e.g., individuals to maintain physical appearances, security to protect against crime) then lack of attachment is, for the most part, inconsequential. In middle-income and working-class neighborhoods, however, a low proportion of people–place bonds can mean the slow deterioration of the community, creating a feedback loop that further reduces people's attachment to place (Taylor & Shumaker, 1982). On an individual level the nonattached person may react against his or her environment. Vandalism, for example, may result in part from noncommitment to place coupled with blocked mobility (cf. Baron, 1984).

The People on the Move

A large number of Americans are able to exercise the option of relocation, and, as we have seen, many people take advantage of this option. Is there a price associated with this choice? Two possible consequences of mobility have been discussed in the literature: poor mental and physical health and diminished social ties.

Mobility and Social Ties.   Some social scientists contend that mobile individuals suffer from the loss of a stable social network (Conger, 1981). The argument is intuitively appealing: individuals cannot establish and maintain social relationships when they are constantly changing physical environments. Given the growing literature on linking social relations to physical and emotional health (see Brownell & Shumaker, 1984; Cohen & Syme, 1985, for recent reviews), the potentially negative effects of mobility on relationships are important.

There are several weaknesses, however, in the argument that mobility disrupts friendships. Most moves (61.9% each year) are within short distances. Beyond the informal ties some people develop with neighbors, it is unlikely that these types of relocations have more than minimal impact on friendship networks. Furthermore, long-distance moves do not necessarily mean the end of persistent social ties (cf. Fried, 1984). Janowitz (1967) and Webber (1970) argue that rather than disrupting networks, advanced technology allows relationships to be maintained across distances. Proximity is no longer a prerequisite to friendship.

It is unlikely that distant relationships are able to provide all of the benefits (and costs) derived from friends living nearby. There are times in peoples' lives when face-to-face contact is probably preferable to a supportive voice on the telephone (Shumaker & Brownell, 1984). There is little question that at least for long-distance moves, social networks are altered. Whether they are enhanced and broadened or diminished as a result of mobility is not clear from the available research. There are studies, however, that assess the direct impact of moving on health.

The Impact of Mobility on Health.   In most research linking mobility with health outcomes, relocation is conceptualized as a major life event (cf. Holmes & Rahe, 1967). The underlying assumption in this perspective is that moving is stressful and requires adjustments that may exceed the adaptive capability of the individual, thereby impairing his or her physical and emotional health. Early studies on *forced* relocation support this proposed relationship. In his study of displaced working-class families, for example, Fried (1963) found that 46% of the women and 38% of the men experienced severe postrelocation grief. Similarly, research on forced relocation among the elderly is associated with poor physical and mental health (Heller, 1982; Rowland, 1977). Also, Brett (1980) found that many wives of frequently transferred corporation employees were depressed, and Syme, Hyman, and Enterline (1965) found a relationship between job transfers and coronary heart disease.

In circumstances where the move is desired and the new locale is comparatively better than the previous one, it is unlikely that poor health is always an outcome (Fischer & Steuve, 1977). Choice and prior familiarity with the new locale mediate the relationship between relocation and poor health (cf. Heller, 1982; Stokols, Shumaker, & Martinez, 1983).

Just as it is simplistic to consider why people move without also taking into account the context of their total life situation, it is too narrow to view relocation as always being a major life stressor; to understand its impact *on the mover*, one must consider the multiple forces that impinge on the decision and how moving fits into the individual's life. Given the opposing forces that exist in many relocation decisions, it may be that the less clear-cut the decision, the more likely a negative health outcome will occur, *whether the person stays or relocates*. For example, if a person chooses to move for career advancement even though he or she will be leaving an area in which there are strong attachments, this individual is more likely to suffer from the relocation than one who leaves a place where he or she feels little attachment. Conversely, the person who forgoes a major career opportunity to remain in a community may also suffer. The critical variable may be the amount of ambivalence surrounding the decision.

We are all forced to make decisions in our lives in which compromises are involved. Furthermore, most Americans will move during their lifetimes, probably more than once, and often leaving familiar and comfortable settings behind. The question is: How can we hold on to the past without having it dominate the present, and simultaneously go forward to new experiences and opportunities?

CONTINUITY WITHIN CHANGE: THE RE-CREATION HOME

Throughout history, people have brought a part of their previous homes and environments to each new location. The moving and storage industry has thrived from people's need to move their "homes" as well as themselves (Hess, 1973). What was established and constructed once the frontiers were reached was never a new society but rather a transplantation of the institutions, traditions, and structures of the parent communities (Abernethy, 1964). Travelers constructed the same types of buildings they had in their home territories, using the same tools, skills, and materials. In much the same way they established their laws, societies, and educational facilities. The pioneers did not abandon their homes as much as they took them with them, as they had their possessions, families, and talents.

From Ohio to California communities with children had schools with curricula to rival any Eastern academy (Billington, 1974). In building construction, although cabins, shanties, and soddies may have been the order of the day at first, hewn post and beam, clapboard, brick, and even stone residences soon replaced them as the immigrants sought to reestablish their solid and permanent homes (Andrews, 1974). In similar fashion, the frontier community sought, accumulated, and devoured books and periodicals, sponsored lectures, theater, and opera, held elections, established courts, levied taxes and fines, and generally copied their communities of origin (Billington, 1974).

Historically, one of the most concrete examples of continuity within change comes from military life. Often, as soon as military families became established at any one post, they were ordered to relocate again. In the post-Civil War, "Indian fighting" army families were frequently relocated, being sent to a different far-flung post each year. In spite of the hardships imposed on them, army wives such as Elizabeth Bacon Custer and Frances Boyd strived to maintain a sense of continuity. Precious possessions, frequent visits from friends and relatives, and carefully orchestrated theatricals, musical evenings, poetry readings, and other social gatherings made the lonely forts of the Plains more homey (Nevin, 1974). Items such as paintings, harps, libraries, fine crystal, silver, and European furniture were moved from post to post to make the "glittering misery" of army life more like home (Custer, 1961).

Army wives were not the only frontier travelers to bring their bits of home with them. There are many accounts of pioneers carrying their household furnishings and personal items across the plains, over the mountains, and around the Horn to provide them with familiar surroundings (Billington, 1974; Schlissel, 1982; Unruh, 1979).

The objects people choose to move from one home to another may provide them with a sense of continuity and allow them to establish each new setting as unique and personally theirs. As noted by Czikszentmihalyi and Rochberg-Halton (1981, p. 17),

> The home contains the most special objects: Those that [are] selected by the person to attend to regularly or to have close at hand, that create permanence in the intimate life of a person, and therefore are most involved in making up his or her identity.

By transporting a few selected and valued objects from place to place, people are able to re-create home in each new setting. Jacobi and Stokols (1983) further argue that certain physical objects within families "evoke a sense of history and symbolize the enduring values" of groups. Thus,

> as people encounter new homes, neighborhoods, and workplaces, the pres-
> ervation and display of traditional artifacts may provide the basis for main-
> taining one's sense of continuity and identity within relatively unfamiliar
> surroundings. (Jacobi & Stokols, 1983, p. 168)

Historically, mobile Americans carried with them objects that symbolized home. In addition, they frequently re-created in each new setting structures and life-styles that mimicked the places left behind.
These are not the behaviors of wanderers; rather, they represent the
responses of a people torn between two conflicting needs: the need for a
stable history and sense of home and the need to take advantage of
apparent opportunities for a better life. Thus, for mobile Americans,
home may be critical to identity and well-being; yet, it may also be a
constantly evolving part of people's aspirations.

IMPLICATIONS FOR FUTURE RESEARCH

Once relocation decisions are placed into the total context of individuals' lives, it is clear that the research emphasis on *why people move so
frequently* that has dominated this field has left many important aspects
of American mobility underinvestigated or ignored. Some of these areas
are next briefly discussed.

The People Left Behind

Blocked Mobility. If mobility represents a normative way to enhance one's opportunities within this society (cf. Harris, 1981), then
what are the effects of limited, or no relocation options? The impact of
blocked mobility has received almost no research attention. If home
represents an important source of self-identity or esteem, then many
people may be locked into situations in which their physical surroundings are a continual reminder of their apparent lack of worth within this
society.

The Stable American. Just as there are some Americans who are
forced to remain in poor housing or who move among comparably poor
housing environments, there are people who *choose* to remain in the

same place for most of their lives. Who are these stable Americans? How are they affected by mobile others? The long-term residents of American communities have traditionally been ignored by researchers. Are these the Americans who enable continuity to exist in spite of mobility? How much do they influence the values and traditions of individual communities across the United States?

Mobility

Much of the research on mobility has been limited to a few areas; for example, predicting who will move. Exploration of other important issues would broaden our understanding of relocation within this society.

Benefits of Mobility. Because mobility is often viewed as a stressful life event, researchers rarely examine the benefits derived from relocating. Harris (1981) argues that mobility may be a major method for mitigating social inequality. Other benefits may accrue from moving. For example, people may become more facile at developing social networks; rather than signaling the end of social ties, the mobile Americans may have a broader and more diverse social network than nonmobile individuals.

Mobility and Continuity. We have argued that continuity is important to adapting to the changes brought about by relocation. How do people make new places familiar? Do they simply transport valued objects, or do some mobile people select comparable housing and communities across locales, making the housing structure evoke a sense of home, rather than, or in addition to, personal objects.

Continuity may not be desired by all people. For some individuals, relocation may represent an opportunity to begin a new life in a new setting; to disassociate with one's past. For others a single historical place in their lives (e.g., birthplace) could serve the symbolic function of "home," whereas all other houses merely represent places to live. In both cases, the importance of personal objects and comparable housing stock may be minimal. In addition, the meaning of home may be very different for the person seeking a new self versus an individual whose home is established away from where he or she actually lives.

SUMMARY AND CONCLUSIONS

From America's earliest development there has been a large, mobile segment of the population. In the past 40 years, the mobility rate in the United States has remained fairly constant, at about 20%. This is clearly a nation in which relocation is seen as a natural way to adjust to one's changing needs or to advance oneself within the society. To assume, however, that mobility means that America is a nation of wanderers is to ignore many central aspects of American life. People continue to develop ties to their communities, and many neighborhoods thrive in this country. People who are forced to leave their homes often grieve for the places lost. Although mobility may provide *some* Americans with a way to improve their life-styles, it is not necessarily at the cost of social and geographic bonds. The historic emphasis on the image of Americans as wanderers has obfuscated many important implications of mobility and limited our view of how mobility relates to the meaning of home and fits into the total life situations of Americans.

Acknowledgments

The authors would like to thank Arlene Brownell and Gary Evans for their helpful comments on an earlier draft of the chapter.

REFERENCES

Abernethy, T. P. *Three Virginia frontiers.* Goucester, Mass.: Peter Smith Press, 1964.

Arnow, H. *The dollmaker.* New York: Avon Books, 1972.

Baron, R. *Preliminary findings on the equity-control model of vandalism.* Paper presented at a meeting of the American Psychological Association, Toronto, Canada, 1984.

Berg, F. M. *South Dakota: Land of shining gold.* Heltinger, N. Dak.: Northern Plains Press, 1982.

Billington, R. A. *America's frontier heritage.* Alburquerque: University of New Mexico Press.

Brazzell, J. F., & Gillespie, M. K. Comparative demography. *International Journal of Comparative Sociology,* 1981, *22,* 141–168.

Brett, J. M. The effect of job transfer on employees and their families. In C. L. Cooper & R. Payne (Eds.), *Current concerns in occupational stress.* New York: Wiley, 1980, pp. 99–136.

Brett, J. M. Job transfer and well-being. *Journal of Applied Psychology,* 1982, *67*(4), 450–463.

Brownell, A., & Shumaker, S. A. Social support: New perspectives in theory, research, and interventions. *Journal of Social Issues,* 1984, *40*(4), 1–9.

Burton, I., Kates, R. W., & White, G. F. *The environment as hazard.* New York: Oxford University Press, 1978.

Cebula, R. J. Geographic mobility and the cost of living: An exploratory note. *Urban Studies,* 1980, *20,* 353–355.

Clark, W. A. V., & Moore, E. G. Residential mobility and public programs: Current gaps between theory and practice. *Journal of Social Issues,* 1982, *38*(3), 35–50.

Cohen, S., & Syme, S. L. (Eds.). *Social support and health.* San Diego: Academic Press, 1985.

Conger, J. Freedom and commitment: Families, youth, and social change. *American Psychologist,* 1981, *36*(12), 1475–1484.

Custer, E. B. *Boots and saddles.* Lincoln: University of Nebraska Press, 1961.

Czikszentmihalyi, M., & Rochberg-Halton, E. *The meaning of things: Domestic symbols and the self*. New York: Cambridge University Press, 1981.

DeVoto, B. *The year of decision: 1846*. Boston: Little, Brown, 1943.

Fairchild, H., & Tucker, M. B. Black residential mobility: Trends and characteristics. *Journal of Social Issues*, 1982, *38*(3), 51–74.

Fischer, C. S., & Steuve, C. A. Authentic community?: The role of place in modern life. In C. S. Fischer, R. M. Jackson, C. A. Stueve *et al.* (Eds.), *Networks and places: Social relations in the urban setting*. New York: Free Press, 1977, pp. 163–186.

Ford, M. P. (Ed.). *Cynthia: The diaries of Cynthia Brown Carlton*. Burton, Ohio: Privately printed.

Fried, M. Grieving for a lost home. In L. J. Duhl (Ed.), *The urban condition*. New York: Basic Books, 1963, pp. 151–171.

Fried, M. Residential attachment: Sources of residential and community satisfaction. *Journal of Social Issues*, 1982, *38*(3), 107–119.

Fried, M. The structure and significance of community satisfaction. *Population and Environment*, 1984, *7*, 61–86.

Gerson, K., Stueve, C. A., & Fischer, C. S. Attachment to place. In C. S. Fischer, R. M. Jackson, C. A. Stueve *et al.* (Eds.), *Network and places: Social relations in the urban setting*. New York, Free Press, pp. 139–161.

Golant, S. Individual differences underlying the dwelling satisfaction of the elderly. *Journal of Social Issues*, 1982, *38*(3), 121–133.

Goldhaber, M. K., Hauts, P. S., & Disabella, R. Moving after the crisis: A prospective study of Three Mile Island area population mobility. *Environment and Behavior*, 1983, *15*(1), 93–120.

Harris, R. J. Rewards of migration for income change and income attainment, 1968–1973. *Social Science Quarterly*, 1981, *62*(2), 275–293.

Heller, T. The effects of involuntary residential relocation: A review. *American Journal of Community Psychology*, 1982, *10*(4), 471–492.

Hess, J. *The mobile society: A history of the moving and storage industry*. New York: McGraw-Hill, 1973.

Holmes, T. H., & Rahe, R. H. The social readjustment rating scale. *Journal of Psychosomatic Research*, 1967, *11*, 213–218.

Jacobi, M., & Stokols, D. The role of tradition in group–environment relations. In N. R. Feimer & E. S. Geller (Eds.), *Environmental psychology: Directions and perspectives*. New York: Praeger, 1983, pp. 157–179.

Janowitz, M. *The community press in an urban setting* (2nd ed.). Chicago: University of Chicago Press, 1967.

Kiecolt, K. J., & Nigg, J. M. Mobility and perceptions of a hazardous environment. *Environment and Behavior*, 1982, *14*(2), 131–154.

Kopf, E. Untarnishing the dream: Mobility, opportunity, and order in modern America. *Journal of Social History*, 1977, *11*, 206–227.

Kroger, J. Residential mobility and self-concept in adolescence. *Adolescence*, 1980, *15*(60), 967–977.

Long, L. H., & Boertlein, C. G. The geographical mobility of Americans: An international comparison. *Current Population Reports* (Special Studies Series P-23, No. 64). Washington, D.C.: U.S. Department of Commerce, Bureau of the Census, 1976.

Loo, C., & Mar, D. Desired residential mobility in a low-income ethnic community: A case study of Chinatown. *Journal of Social Issues*, 1982, *38*(3), 95–106.

Manchester, W. *The glory and the dream*. New York: Bantam Books, 1974.

Michelson, W. *Environmental choice, human behavior, and residential satisfaction.* New York: Oxford University Press, 1977.

Michelson, W. *Some sociological considerations on residential mobility and urban policy.* Paper presented at the Conference on Residential Mobility and Public Policy, Los Angeles, California, 1979.

Morris, R. B. *The encyclopedia of American history.* New York: Harper and Brothers, 1953.

Packard, V. *A nation of strangers.* New York: McKay, 1972.

Potter, D. *People of plenty.* Chicago: University of Chicago Press, 1954.

Rossi, P. H., & Shlay, A. B. Residential mobility and public policy issue: "Why families move" revisited. *Journal of Social Issues,* 1982, *38*(3), 21–34.

Rowland, K. F. Environmental events predicting death for the elderly. *Psychological Bulletin,* 1977, *84,* 349–372.

Schlissel, L. *Women's diaries of the westward journey.* New York: Schlocken Books, 1982.

Shumaker, S. A., & Taylor, R. B. Toward a clarification of people–place relationships: A model of attachment to place. In N. R. Feimer & E. S. Geller (Eds.), *Environmental psychology: Directions and perspectives.* New York: Praeger Publishers, 1983, pp. 219–256.

Shumaker, S. A., & Brownell, A. Toward a theory of social support: Closing conceptual gaps. *Journal of Social Issues,* 1984, *40*(4), 11–36.

Speare, A. Residential satisfaction as an intervening variable in residential mobility. *Demography,* 1974, *11,* 173–188.

Speare, A., Goldstein, S., & Frey, W. H. *Residential mobility, migration, and metropolitan change.* Cambridge: Ballinger, 1975.

Stewart, E. P. *Letters of a woman homesteader.* Lincoln: University of Nebraska Press, 1961.

Stokols, D., & Shumaker, S. A. People in places: A transactional view of settings. In J. H. Harvey (Ed.), *Cognition, social behavior, and the environment.* Hillsdale, N.J.: Erlbaum, 1981, pp. 441–488.

Stokols, D., & Shumaker, S. A. The psychological context of residential mobility and well-being. *Journal of Social Issues,* 1982, *38*(3), 149–172.

Stokols, D., Shumaker, S. A., & Martinez, J. Residential mobility and personal well-being. *Journal of Environmental Psychology,* 1983, *3,* 5–19.

Syme, S. L., Hyman, M. M., & Enterline, P. E. Cultural mobility and the occurrence of coronary heart disease. *Journal of Health and Human Behavior,* 1965, *6,* 178–189.

Taylor, R. B., & Shumaker, S. A. *Community crime prevention in review: Problems, progress, and prospects in theory, research programs and evaluation.* Paper presented at the Annual Meetings of the Law and Society Association, Toronto, Canada.

Toffler, A. *Future shock.* New York: Bantam, 1970.

Thoreau, H. D. *The Works of Henry David Thoreau* (Vol. 5). New York: Doubleday, 1906.

Unruh, J. D., Jr. *The plains across: The overland emigrants and the trans-Mississippi west 1840–1860.* Urbana: University of Illinois Press, 1979.

Webber, M. M. Order in diversity: Community without propinquity. In R. Gutman & D. Popenoe (Eds.), *Neighborhood, city, and metropolis.* New York: Random House, 1970, pp. 792–811.

11

Thinking about Home Environments

A CONCEPTUAL FRAMEWORK

AMOS RAPOPORT

THINKING ABOUT HOME ENVIRONMENTS

It is difficult to think about environments. Because theory and explicit conceptual frameworks are scarce, the numerous environment–behavior relations (EBR) studies have not been cumulative; indeed their very number has become counterproductive. In the case of home environments there is a particularly daunting amount of diverse and unintegrated work.

This profusion is to be expected. Home environments comprise most of the built environment. They also have extraordinarily high affective (and often economic and social) significance: they are the primary settings par excellence. As such they are of great interest to users. They are also of great interest to researchers, partly because funding has been available for research on home environments—generally and for various special groups.

A conceptual framework, no matter how primitive, is thus urgently needed to help think about the subject. An inductive approach is unlikely to succeed not because of any philosophical strictures against

AMOS RAPOPORT • Department of Architecture, University of Wisconsin, Milwaukee, Wisconsin 53201.

induction but on more pragmatic grounds: the sheer amount and diversity of material precludes the development of a framework through a literature review.

WHAT ARE CONCEPTUAL FRAMEWORKS?

Conceptual frameworks are neither *models* nor *theories*. Although these latter terms are used in many different and often contradictory ways, let me suggest that models *describe* how things work, whereas theories *explain* phenomena. Conceptual frameworks do neither; rather they help to think about phenomena, to order material, revealing patterns—and pattern recognition typically leads to models and theories.

Frameworks are hence more "arbitrary" than either models or theories in the sense that alternative frameworks may prove useful for different purposes. Yet they are not completely arbitrary. Some fit evidence better than others; some are simpler initially yet offer more potential for further development; some unify more material than others. Also, the gaps in most discussions of home environments suggest certain characteristics of a useful conceptual framework. For example, it should link home environments to environments more generally—natural landscapes, settlements, neighborhoods. It should apply to different cultures and periods—to preliterate societies, to vernacular design, to developing countries, and to the contemporary U.S. It should address a wide variety of conceptual issues—cross-cultural validity, the role of various mechanisms including meaning, cultural specificity, and hence differing notions of environmental quality. It should also relate widely divergent bodies of literature—research studies, the media, advertising.

WHAT PARTICULAR FRAMEWORK?

Although many frameworks could possibly meet these requirements, I will briefly discuss one simple framework. This is the notion that *choice* (which expresses preference) is important in people's interaction with all environments and is central regarding home environments. It seems characteristic of those latter that *they are chosen*. One could almost argue that *if they are not chosen they are not home*. An imposed setting is unlikely to be a home environment, although it may *become* one through ways (to be discussed later) of increasing congruence (or reducing incongruence) with needs and preferences.

The starting point of the argument (and its link to more general concepts) is what I call the three basic questions of EBR:

1. What characteristics of people, as members of a species and of various groups, or as individuals, influence (or, in design, should influence) how built environments are shaped?
2. What are the effects of the built environment on human behavior, well-being, mood, and so forth.
3. A corollary question: What mechanisms link people and environments in this mutual interaction?

Typically, all three play a role in any specific question, but they can be separated for analytical purposes. Here, the starting point is Question 2: the effect of environment on people.

THE STARTING POINT

Most studies of home environments begin with people already in them; essentially they deal with *satisfaction.* Yet there is a prior question about how people get there in the first place.

I have recently pointed out that the effect of environment on people is also addressed inappropriately, as though people were placed in environments that then have effects on them.[1] In reality the main effect of environment on people is through *choice or habitat selection:* given an opportunity, people avoid or leave some environments and seek out others (Rapoport, 1980c, 1983a). People self-select at many scales—countries, regions, cities, small towns, neighborhoods, streets within neighborhoods, and, most importantly, home environments. One can even suggest how choice operates: perceived characteristics are matched against some ideal schemata (Rapoport, 1977).

This immediately suggests variability of preferences and choices that need to be considered, and hence understood emically before etic characteristics are derived (Rapoport, 1980a). Consider just a few among the many possible examples. One (Filp, Fuentes, Donoso, & Martinic, 1983) shows clearly how different groups (peasants, skiers, and tourists in Chile) selectively perceive and evaluate different aspects of a given place. In Milwaukee, the same co-op garden generated major conflict: to some residents it was a source of pride, whereas to others it was an eyesore destroying the quality of the neighborhood and the value of

---

[1] I omit here any discussion of determinism, the relation of environment to well-being, direct versus indirect effects and many other issues.

their dwellings ("Co-op Garden," 1981). Similar differences emerged regarding the provision of a bicycle path in a Milwaukee suburb ("Residents Disagree," 1978). It is well known that major differences exist between designers and users as a whole; they are reflected in the very different preferences for home environments in the Netherlands (Jaanus & Nieuwenhuijse, 1978) or suburbs in Britain (Oliver, Davis, & Bentley, 1981). Perceived qualities may, of course, be "incorrect" (e.g., Webb, 1978), and choices in the cognized environment may have undesirable results in the operational ("real") environment (Rappaport, 1979).

Several immediate objections to this approach are possible. One might be that one cannot infer choice from behavior because choices are neither consistent nor transitive, so that microeconomic approaches are difficult to relate to aspiration levels. However, advertising and the market do seem to reflect aspirations. Also, mobility may be imposed by lack of employment, reduced income, redevelopment, flooding, mining, and the like. Choice could, however, still operate in one's response. A more serious objection is that in some cases constraints may be more important than choice (e.g., Lee, 1978); more commonly, however, constraints *limit and distort choice.*

Constraints may be of different kinds:

- *Resource constraints,* what can be afforded, that is, what is, in fact, available to the individual or group.
- *Market constraints* of supply and price.
- *Ability to cope*—apathy, fatalism, ability to plan, and so forth.
- *Willingness to move* may be minimal due to attachment, social ties, and so forth, (e.g., Cullen, Hammond, & Haimes, 1980). Also, mobility does not always follow dissatisfaction (e.g., Newman & Duncan, 1979) and is influenced by tenure, for example, ownership (Nathanson, Newman, Moen, & Hiltabiddle, 1976; Rossi, 1980).
- *Ability to move*—job, family responsibilities, and the like.
- *Knowledge and information* about alternatives and *of* alternatives— what is available or possible, objectively or subjectively; what is considered (e.g., Humphreys & Whitelaw, 1979).
- *External constraints*—prejudice, discrimination, even prohibition.

But note that (a) many of the constraints themselves reflect choices, for example, resources allocated for home environments, willingness to move, even ability to move. (b) Even when constraints are *very* tight there is usually still choice (e.g., Rapoport, 1969a), for example, the variety of choices made by "squatters." Note that spontaneous settlements themselves represent a choice among admittedly very limited and possibly undersirable alternatives. Also, if a single-family dwelling is unaffordable, a choice is still made among the remaining alternatives. (c) The constraints themselves can be studied, starting with choices made under minimal constraints, for example by wealthy people in Sydney (Rapoport, 1977) or Milwaukee (Hargreaves & Robillard, 1979). Constraints can gradually be "tightened" and changes observed. Housing games (to be discussed later) allow this. (d) Lack of choice, that is, blocked habitat selection, can be seen as a major environmental problem (Rapoport, 1979, 1980c, 1983a). Having to remain in a highly disliked environment or having to move from a liked environment are in themselves major problems (Rapoport 1977, 1978b, 1980a). Thus, housing policy issues, redevelopment, settling nomads, and participation can all fit into the framework. (e) Identical environments have very different effects when chosen or imposed. Perceived control satisfaction, then, may be as much related to the fact of having chosen as to what is chosen.

The framework proposed is an *ideal;* various constraints modify and distort, but do not eliminate, choice. Moreover, research on constraints becomes part of the framework (e.g., Smith & Thorns, 1979).

Note another very important point. Design also can be seen as a choice among alternatives: what I have called the "choice model of design" (Rapoport, 1976, 1977, 1983c); it also is modified by constraints (Rapoport, 1983b, pp. 266–267). Design-as-choice also is applicable to all kinds of environments (preliterate, vernacular, popular, high-style), to different cultures, and to different periods. *What varies are the actors, the criteria used, the time scale involved.* This view of design links it to choice; it also helps explain different built environments (e.g., pueblos and hogans) in similar milieus (e.g., Rapoport, 1969b) as a choice among alternatives. This results in the great variety of cultural landscapes (King, 1976a; Rapoport, 1984).

For most people today in the U.S., Australia, Canada, Western Europe, and increasingly elsewhere, choice is expressed through habitat selection rather than through design. Home environments already designed are chosen. In the case of new housing design-as-choice has occurred as promoters and developers attempt to meet preferences; if met, the marketing results can be extraordinarily successful (e.g., Sudjic, 1982). This links choice, design, marketing, and advertising. Once in the home, choice continues through modification, personalization, landscaping, and so forth (Rapoport, 1968, 1982a). Choice thus applies to design, to habitat selection at various scales, to modification and furnishing, and so forth.

If home environments are chosen, one can ask: *Who chooses what, where, when, and why (and possibly how)?* Answering, or even addressing these questions seems most useful; in addressing these questions constraints will be ignored, and the ideal choice situation taken as the framework.

IS THERE CHOICE?

Before proceeding one needs to ask whether choice actually occurs. No framework, however promising, is useful if not supported by evidence.

In fact, evidence seems inescapable that choice operates at all scales from international migration to consumption. The great cross-cultural and historical variety of cultural landscapes, given the relatively limited range of human behaviors, strongly suggests choice (Rapoport, 1972, 1977, 1980a, 1984). Hence the relevance of vernacular design, spontaneous settlements, and alternative environments (Rapoport, 1984). There are a variety of "nonstandard" forms of home environments even in the West (e.g., Barnett, 1977; Noble, 1973).

Changes in locational preferences over time in one place reflect changed evaluations of environments (Rapoport, 1977). In the U.S. in this century, the move from rural to urban areas (now occurring in developing countries) was followed by the decline of cities and growth of suburbs. Currently, smaller places and more "remote" areas seem to be favored over metropolitan areas, although the life-style remains urban (Rapoport, 1981a); two sets of choices are occurring. Regional shifts (e.g., the "Sunbelt" phenomenon) show choice as does the beginning of a countermigration (still small) of some elderly back to the Northeast ("Increasing Numbers," 1984). Among the elderly other clear variations in preference and choice can be seen ("Three Different Styles," 1984).

Ecological succession (decline and regeneration) in cities reflects changed choices of location and environmental quality, as in the recent revival of residence in downtown Los Angeles ("Downtown Los Angeles," 1984; cf. Gale, 1979; Golledge & Rushton, 1976; Jones, 1979). One outcome of choice is the complex social geography of the city. Significantly, what were seen as competing models of urban ecology (the zonal, sectoral, and multiple nuclei) seem to result from differential choices of groups: sectoral related to status (e.g., Backler, 1974); zonal to stage in family cycle; multiple nuclei to ethnicity (e.g., Moore, 1981). This social morphology leads to the development of particular ambiences because consistent choices based on taste influence how people live, their behavior, dress, food, furnishings, and landscaping (e.g., *American Behavioral Scientist*, 1983; Csikszentmihalyi & Rochberg-Halton,

1981; Douglas & Isherwood, 1979; Kron, 1983; Rapoport, 1980e, 1982a). Consider Australia, which was highly homogeneous in terms of both population and available home environments. Following immigration the population became more diverse. Different groups made very different choices among a very limited set of alternatives (cf. references in Rapoport, 1977). Clustering, followed by consistent modifications created a wider variety of settings—*choice increased.*

Varied settings in a given place thus not only *offer* choice—they *result* from previous choices (habitat selection and consistent modifications), for example, for particular fences or their nonuse (Anderson & Moore, 1972; Arreola, 1981) or landscaping (references in Rapoport, 1982a). A field trip through Milwaukee (part of a graduate course in housing based on this framework) reveals an extraordinary variety of home environments—different locations, neighborhood ambience and social composition, vegetation, type of housing, street lighting or its absence, sidewalks or their absence, and presence or absence of visible personalization. Choices also change with changes in social composition (e.g., "Number of Vacancies," 1984). Reflecting both pulls and pushes, and if continued long enough, they can lead to results like the "unexpected discovery" of a functioning Pathan village in the heart of Bradford, England ("Only a Heartbeat," 1982).

In this connection housing games are significant. A number have been developed, for example, by T. B. Brealy in Australia and Henry Sanoff at North Carolina State University, and used (e.g., Britten, 1977; Lawrence, 1980; Rowley & Wilson, 1975; Tipple, 1977; Whitbread, 1978). These not only demonstrate choice but allow studies impossible in real-life situations, for example, trade-offs not only among different components of home environments but also between home environments and location, travel, urban services, and proximities to various urban elements (e.g., Smit & Joseph, 1982). One can also study the willingness to pay for various additions to a basic dwelling ("So What's Wrong," 1982). These can then be compared to actual choices that they closely resemble; their effects on price and sales can also be studied. Games can also reveal clear group differences, for example, between locals and colored immigrants in Sheffield (Rowley & Wilson, 1975) or between Anglos and Hispanics in Tucson, Arizona, who choose very different locations, subdivision layouts, and dwellings (Wheeler, 1977).

It is significant that snap judgments can be made based on minimal information as in the *image game* in the set by Sanoff (1971). In several iterations during the course in housing several things significant to this chapter were found. First, based on single fairly noncommunicative photographs, 12 dwellings are easily ranked in a minute or two illustrating the global affective response to environments (Rapoport, 1977; cf. Ulrich, 1983). Second, among a small group of students there is considerable variability. Finally, many reasons are given for like or dislike. Some are based on the photographs—materials, form, landscaping; others are inferred from minimal or nonexistent information—the larger setting, interiors; others yet are associational, for example, resemblance to Grandma's house—which can lead to like *or* dislike. Choice, as we shall see later, seems to be based on many characteristics.

The fact that in a small group choices and reasons for them vary reinforces the notion of group variability: among user groups and between designers and users (Rapoport, 1977, 1982a, 1984). A striking example of the latter is the new English town of Milton Keynes (Bishop, 1983) where the very features evaluated negatively by designers were those *liked* by residents. From the residents' point of view, Milton Keynes was a success, and the remedial actions proposed by designers would destroy its desirable qualities.

In place after place, at different scales, one finds different choices being made by different groups (e.g., Beck & Teasdale, 1977; Duncan, 1973; Duncan & Duncan, 1980; references in Rapoport, 1977; Zeisel, 1973). There is not one housing market, but different submarkets (e.g., Smith & Thorns, 1978, 1979, 1980); currently as many as 47 housing market segments may be used (*Land Use Digest*, 1984).

We can thus return to the question posed earlier: Who chooses what, where, when, and why?

WHO CHOOSES?

Once one accepts that environments are group and culture specific, a major question is posed: Which are the relevant groups? This is a major unresolved research issue. Group designations as "the elderly" or "the urban poor" are not very useful, and appropriate characteristics need to be *discovered* (Rapoport, 1974, 1980d, 1983b) that define groups and link them to environments in specific ways. Although it is individuals or families that choose, the degree of choice varies. *The framework allows for different actors, time scales, and criteria for choice; the process is common. A similar statement can be made about design-as-choice.*

Individual preferences, however, add up to group preferences in the sense that differences among groups are greater than within them (Rapoport, 1980a). Because such individuals also often cluster, distinct cultural landscapes result (Rapoport, 1984). In any case, the study of groups and their characteristics can clarify and predict preferences.

How, then, could one approach the question of "who chooses?" in, say, the case of the U.S.? The following may be useful.

- *Surrounding culture* where "culture" describes characteristics of populations that are different, for example, the U.S. versus India.
- *Group membership*, that is, which subgroup within the larger population. Many potential criteria are available for perceived homogeneity. In the U.S.—subculture, stage in life cycle, age, occupation, religion, ethnicity, race, life-style, ideology, and so forth (Rapoport, 1977).

Of these, two seem particularly relevant. One, *life-style*, is possibly the most useful (Rapoport, 1977, 1980a,c) partly because it is the most applicable today, partly because it also represents a choice among alternatives (see later). Its importance has recently received support (e.g., Beattie, 1980; Weisner & Weibel, 1981). Consider one example: the unexpected defeat in Latino areas of Los Angeles of Proposition M (on rent control). The best explanation is in terms of life-style: the proposition defined family as nuclear only, whereas for Latinos the extended family is equally important ("Proposition M," 1983). Second, *stage in life-cycle*, which includes age, family composition, and the like, has received much attention (e.g., Coombs, 1981; Preston & Taylor, 1981; Rossi, 1980; Thorns, 1980). (*This can also be considered as the* when *of the question.*) An example is the concern with "child density," not only in the idea of "child-free living" for the "elderly" who seek safety and quiet but for others without children who wish to avoid their presence. This may lead to conflicts with those with children (e.g., "Downtown Becoming," 1979)—another example of conflicting choices. This is also a concern in retirement communities (on which there is a vast literature; cf. "Child-free Living," 1982) and, more recently, in preretirement communities for the affluent 48+ group ("Developing Homes," 1982). These latter, based on marketing studies, match design to life-style to encourage choice. In addition to "no children," design characteristics include smaller dwellings, privacy, maintenance, active recreation, security including special provisions for frequent travel, and a particular imagery combining a mixture of "Park Avenue" interiors and "Martha's Vineyard" exteriors ("Developing Homes," 1982)—a striking example of an environmental quality profile (see later).

- *Individual variations.* Individual past experience also plays a role. This provides a link with the literature on residential history (Ladd, 1976) and environmental autobiography (Hester, 1980). Even using a highly simplified version of those references in my housing course I quickly realized how important this is because such influences begin early (Cooper-Marcus, 1978, p. 419; cf. Lawrence, 1980; Rapoport, 1978a). These influences persist; housing consumption patterns established before age 35 strongly constrain later housing choices, which leads to cohort characteristics and cohort inertia (*Research Report*, 1979). The specific interaction of surrounding culture, life-style, stage in life cycle, and early residential history result in different "taste cultures." This provides potential links to the very large literature on marketing and consumption (Csikszentmihalyi & Rochberg-Halton, 1981; Douglas & Isherwood, 1979; Hempel, 1974; Hempel & Ayal, 1977; Kron, 1983; Rapoport, 1982a). The variety of housing markets already mentioned follows, so does the use of life-style in marketing (e.g., Mitchell, 1983). As roles, attitudes, values, occupations, family patterns, consumption, recreation, and the like change, so do (and will) choices of home environments and their environmental qualities.

Home environments, however, seem to be more than just dwellings, so that it is far from clear what people are choosing precisely. Hence the next question.

WHAT DO THEY CHOOSE?

Among different, complementary rather than conflicting answers, two are of importance. First is that people choose a particular system of settings, and second is that they choose a particular set of environmental qualities.

I have argued before (Rapoport, 1969a, 1977, 1980b, 1982b) that home environments are part of larger, culturally variable systems of settings (the house–settlement system) and are themselves best understood as *that system of settings within which a particular set of activities takes place* (disregarding the variability of activities and, specially, their latent aspects). This allows for valid cross-cultural comparisons. Also, the highly specific meanings of dwellings, e.g., as "havens" (Rainwater, 1966) or retreats from stress (Roberts, 1977), can be understood in context of the other settings in the system. Different groups choose very different combinations of elements as the home environments. The nature of a given home environment cannot be decided *a priori* but must be discovered (as must the nature of the relevant group). It may include the neighborhood (e.g., Moore, 1981) or not; it may include the street, shops, pubs, shopping centers, laundromats, recreation, workplaces, and many other settings and specialized institutions that are often non-intuitive or even counterintuitive (Rapoport, 1977, 1982b).

What happens elsewhere in the system is as important as what happens *in* the dwellings. This has implications not only for activities and changes in them but for temporal, social, and psychological aspects of home environments.[2] For example, the type of work and where (and when) it occurs influences the choice of home environment. Should work become more home centered (as many predict) the nature of home environments will also change (Rapoport, 1981a).

Instead of assuming that a "dwelling" is the home environment, one discovers where (and when) a set of activities occur (Rapoport, 1980b). More generally this is the process, for any set of activities, of *progressive contextualization* (Vayda, 1983). One thus needs to extend the notion of home environment until all the relevant activities have been accounted for. Although in principle one could include the universe, the specific location of boundaries requires research, being partly an empirical question; it varies for different groups and sets of activities (cf. Rapoport, 1980b, 1982b). Different groups make different trade-offs and choices that lead to different limits to what is considered to be the home environment.

This definition provides a way of approaching the congruence (or otherwise) of home environments with the culture, values, preferences, and needs of a given group. One can ask whether the system of settings is supportive of the life-style of the group (e.g., Bechtel, 1972); whether the system of settings appropriately expresses identity (if necessary) (Rapoport, 1981b) or status (Rapoport, 1977, 1982a). The concept of supportive environments is also useful in considering the effect of environment on people. For any given individual or group one can ask: What is being supported? By what is it being supported? How is it being supported (Rapoport, 1979, 1983b)? In this, latent aspects are as, or more, important than instrumental aspects (Rapoport, 1982a). Even for young people in Manhattan, home environments are multidimensional (Hayward, 1978) and include many latent aspects. This one would expect from their primary and affective roles as well as their great economic importance; tenure and ownership are important choice criteria both in the U.S. and in developing countries.

With these considerations, however, we reach the second answer to the question being considered. For each system of settings there will be appropriate sets of environmental quality components (a *gestalt* or pro-

[2]Given the conceptualization of *any* environment as a particular organization of space, time, meaning, and communication (Rapoport, 1977, 1980a).

file [see later]) (Rapoport, 1982a; Watson & Winchester, 1981). *One chooses a particular set of environmental qualities* to which advertisements often refer.

In making choices, perceived environmental quality, for example, topography, vegetation, appearance, newness, and the like, is matched against some norms. The particular choice depends partly on what is included in the system of settings and partly on how qualities associated with those settings are evaluated. People choose a "bundle" of qualities that define environments as "good" or "bad," suitable or unsuitable; people choose environmental quality.

ENVIRONMENTAL QUALITY

ENVIRONMENTAL QUALITY AS A CONCEPT

Environmental quality is important as the link between choice and the specifics of neighborhoods (e.g., "Series on Neighborhoods," 1980) or housing (How & Russell, 1980; Metcalf, 1977). It is also complex, comprising many components (Rapoport, 1977, chapter 2). Four things can vary: (1) The *nature* of the components; (2) the *rankings* of these components; (3) the *importance* (or magnitude) of these components vis-à-vis other things that are not part of environmental quality; and (4) components can be *positive* (pulls) or *negative* (pushes). This can be conceived as a *profile*.

When home environments are evaluated (leading to staying or leaving), or when they are chosen, altered (e.g., furnished or personalized) or designed, people are choosing, manipulating or creating a particular environmental quality profile. When people change life-styles, behaviors, or expectations they are, in effect, trying to make a particular environmental quality profile more congruent, or less incongruent, with their preferences and/or needs. Different groups may see home environments differently: primarily as settings for family life, as indications of prestige or status, or as safe havens. Each emphasis leads to a different environmental quality profile. Different profiles are associated with changes in use, for example, housing as a setting for private recreation or as a workplace.

Note again how a large and varied set of material fits into the framework, including the question of what home environments *do*, as opposed to what they are.

Such profiles become useful in understanding the success or failure, survival or decline, acceptability or otherwise of home environments.

One can so interpret variable judgments of places such as the West End of Boston (Rapoport, 1975a, 1977). Similarly, the emphasis by squatters in developing countries on education, income, or equity buildings rather than physical quality of home environments is an example of point (3) mentioned previously. Less dramatically and more generally this explains differential allocation of resources for home environments (e.g., England vs. France, blue collar vs. white collar (Rapoport, 1977). For singles in the U.S. concerning the economic aspect of dwellings, as a hedge against inflation, to build up equity and to reduce taxes are the most important environmental quality components, although control and personalization are considerations.

Profiles can help interpret studies of preference for residential environments, although group variability and associational (nonperceptual) considerations must be included (Rapoport, 1982a) particularly because perceptual characteristics are often liked for associational reasons. Environmental quality profiles are implicitly used by Michelson (1977) and help explain relative habitability, variability of standards, and changes in views about "slums" or spontaneous settlements (Rapoport, 1977) as well as the trade-offs always involved in choice. Profiles are thus useful for comparative studies—cross-cultural and over time. They are also emphasized in advertising.

I have repeatedly argued since 1969 (Rapoport, 1969c) that analyzing newspapers, novels, films, T.V., advertising, and the like are most useful forms of research. Such analyses by many students have generated interesting insights into changing or differing profiles. These are reflected in marketing (e.g., Hempel, 1974; Hempel & Ayal, 1977), in designs based on marketing analysis ("Developing Homes," 1982), associational, affective, and latent aspects tend to dominate and are reflected in advertising (e.g., Michelson, 1970; Rapoport, 1977).

Consider two examples. The first is the *Milwaukee See-for-Yourself Auto Tour* (slogan: "Discover Milwaukee, A Great Hometown"). It avoids winter photographs, and very little housing is shown. The principal images include the lake and sailboats, trees, flowers, parks, joggers, the zoo, churches, and restaurants. Clearly, these are taken to be part of the home environment. Because the positive imagery is meant to attract people, it represents a particular environmental quality profile.

This becomes even clearer in my second example of housing promotion magazines (e.g., *Living*, 1980). Its imagery also ignores actual dwellings. Verbal images include "great living," "beautiful home country," "prestige," "excellent schools," "homes that say a lot about you" (another slogan: "You Are Where You Live"). Pictorial images include elegant dinner parties, recreation in natural settings, hills, lakes, waterfalls, trees, flowers, butterflies—even beautiful sunsets. These are not atypical; other issues (e.g., *Living,* 1984a, 1984b)[3] show many more *dwellings.* There seem to be regional and temporal differences, that is, with different markets being addressed, the message is very similar. Examples include recreation in natural settings, woods, water, and recreation. A development is described as "mastering the art of living" and as a place "where living is truly a lifestyle" (this is a misuse of the term and concept of life-style very common in journalism) (*Living,* 1984b). Others emphasize "the good life," "security, serenity, friendly neighbors . . . building memories for tomorrow," (*Living,* 1984a) or suggest that you "listen with your heart, then with your head" (a perfect description of the global affective response). Generally *pride, status, dreams, memories,* and, above all, *life-style* are key terms. Clearly associational and latent considerations are primary and comprise particular environmental quality profiles. Home environments also clearly comprise much more than the dwelling itself. This is also reflected in the names of developments (cf. *Living,* 1980, 1984a,b; Rapoport, 1977, pp. 62–63).

Consider Westlake Village, California. The name is revealing, so is the story title, "Middle Class *Dream* Fulfilled" (1977) (my italics). The development is advertised as more than a "beautiful place to live . . . it's a way of life," emphasizing sociability. As in many other developments (e.g., *Living,* 1984a), varied areas are emphasized as are recreation, lakes, and a villagelike quality. Residents call it "heaven on earth," "the nicest place I ever lived," "every day here is a vacation day," and 88% want to stay there forever. A review of retirement communities describes them as "Eden" ("Retirees from State," 1979) and lists the qualities that make it such. The same point is being made about *Better Homes* magazine in a story entitled: "Better Homes: Selling Dreams" (1981).

Advertising explicitly uses specific environmental quality profiles to entice people to choose. Success is reflected in sales. Thus a particular model, very expensive by English standards, has become the best-selling house in Britain with 2,000 sold (Sudjic, 1982). Designers might be horrified (as they might be by the developments discussed here), but the success clearly reflects choice. Choice is also reflected in prices; appropriate profiles are reflected in the high prices in *Living* (1984a) and in the real estate sections of newspapers. This can also be researched more formally (e.g., Borukhov, Ginsberg, & Werczberger, 1978; cf. Rapoport, 1977, chapter 2). A student term paper found that of two identical areas of Milwaukee the area with surviving elms had significantly higher

---

[3]These were made available by my colleague Harvey Z. Rabinowitz.

house prices (Schroeder, 1976). Traffic flows can similarly influence values (e.g., Bagby, 1980). One can also specify the positive and negative monetary impact on apartment rental of location, noise, image, status, etc. which vary for different rental ranges (i.e., for different groups) (Ellis, 1976).

Choice and environmental quality profiles can be shown to be related (e.g., Backler, 1974; Burby & Weiss, 1976; Ermuth, 1974; Howard, Herold, Drisscoll, & Laperriere, 1974; cf. Rapoport, 1977, 1981b, 1982a). It is, therefore, useful to discuss components more specifically, particularly since environmental quality is too global a concept (similarly, concepts such as "culture" and "environment" benefit from such a process (Rapoport, 1977, 1980a, 1982a).

COMPONENTS OF ENVIRONMENTAL QUALITY

As in this chapter generally completeness is neither possible nor useful, the emphasis is on how these components might fit into the framework. Because architects overemphasize physical design it is useful to emphasize the wide range of components that can be "pushes" or "pulls."

1. Components Designers nor Planners Can Control

- *Taxes*—national, state, local; levels and value-for-money.
- *Climate*—macro- and microclimate.
- *Pollution levels*—real, perceived; visible or known.
- *Topography and other natural amenities* (hills, mountains, beaches, forests, lakes, oceans, etc.).
- *School quality.* This varies in different places, may be a push or pull factor, and also affects the search space (e.g., Conway & Graham, 1982; Humphrey and Whitelaw, 1979).
- *Cleanliness and maintenance* of settlement or neighborhood.
- *Urban services*, their nature, quality, proximity, or remoteness (Rapoport, 1977).
- *Perceived crime levels and safety.* This varies with place and time; concern may be at the urban scale, level of neighborhood, project, street, or dwelling.

2. Components Designers Cannot Control but Planners Might

These, like 1, involve larger societal forces and policies (i.e., other choices); they clearly could include some of the first group.

- *Ownership/tenure*—hence economic benefits.
- *Social factors*—*perceived homogeneity or heterogeneity* that occurs through self-selection, that is, choice. This can be very important (Rapoport, 1977, 1980/1981; "Number of Vacancies," 1984) or not (Weichhart, 1983); *status of area; friendliness of area; length of residence; perceived density*—discussed earlier.
- *Management*—which involves preserving maximizing or restoring qualities that are considered important. It can apply at different scales (Ahlbrandt & Brophy, 1976; Baltimore City Planning Commission, 1977; Beck & Teasdale, 1977; Francescato, Weidemann, Anderson, & Chenoweth, 1979; Sauer, 1977). Management can allow things (pets, personalization, landscaping, etc.), encourage things (trees, cleanliness, behavior, maintenance), control things (vandalism, traffic density, noise, child density). This integrates a growing literature on the importance of management for satisfaction; one can also predict that management will be most important and public in conglomerate housing and less important and personal in detached private dwellings.

3. Components Designers Can Control[4]

- *Appearance*—which is composed of many specifics and is highly subjective and variable. It is often associational, communicating social characteristics (Rapoport, 1982a).
- *Imagery generally*—for example, meaning and status (Rapoport, 1982a). It is variable among groups and over time. A rural image has traditionally been seen as negative in Latin America (Rapoport, 1977, 1982a), although that is now changing. In Britain (Bishop, 1983) or the U.S. generally (Rapoport, 1977; "Tranquil Town," 1983) a rural image is desired, although it leads to apparently "strange" environmental quality characteristics (no sidewalks, no street lighting, nothing for children to do, etc.).
- *Low perceived density* is an important aspect of rural imagery (Backler, 1974; Flachsbart, 1979; McLaughlin, 1976; Newman, 1979; Taylor, 1981). This seems important for condominia and townhouses (Beck & Teasdale, 1977; Burley & Weiss, 1976; Ermuth, 1974; Norcross, 1973, etc.).

[4]This discussion ignores issues of participation, open endedness, and the like. Also, nonvisual perceptual qualities should be included in addition to visual, social, and associational ones.

- *Privacy and perceived privacy*—These are related to the foregoing and are best understood as the control of unwanted interaction through information flows in various modalities (Altman & Chemers, 1980, Chapter 4; Rapoport, 1976, 1977). It may apply to interiors and exteriors (e.g., Coulson, 1980) and is a matter of degree; some overhearing or overviewing may be desired, for example, for safety (Cooper, 1975), whereas too much is inhibiting (e.g., Reed, 1974); all these lead to choices (e.g., Foddy, 1977; Grenell, 1972). Privacy as perceived control of information flows is related to the ability to communicate desired messages and hence to personalization. This links it to *open endedness*, generally on which there is a large literature. What one wishes to control or change varies (Rapoport, 1968) and also *when* in the design process (Becker, 1977)—another aspect of choice. Thus, again, a large body of material on privacy, open endedness, personalization, and so forth fits into the framework.
- *Trees and greenery*—often highly desired (Rapoport, 1977, 1982a) but variable (e.g., Duncan, 1973; Thorne, Diesner, Munro-Clark, & Hall, 1980; Royse, 1969).
- *House type*—detached, condominium, high-rise, or low-rise, and the like.
- *House style* (Rapoport, 1982a).
- *House details* (Rossi, 1980).
- *Nonresidential uses.* In the U.S. these are generally disliked (Rapoport, 1977). A recent case is the Park Avenue Deli, New York, which was discussed for over a month in the *New York Times;* although it was finally approved after changes in the goods and display, much opposition continues among residents: "It's a real pity, it spoils the neighborhood," said one resident ("Disputed Park Ave. Deli," 1984). Elsewhere such uses may be *preferred*.
- *Identity* (Rapoport, 1981b).

Specific preferences can be understood as a profile composed of such components. Recall that this involves matching perceived characteristics (which are variable due to "filters") against ideals, images, and schemata (which are *extremely* variable). Linkages between specific components of environments and specific groups increase understanding of what people choose and why.

REASONS FOR CHOICE

The question of why people choose involves both reasons for choice and mechanisms of choice. They will be discussed together. I have already implied that choice is a response to the environment. Animals choose habitats to which they are adapted; people choose environments supportive to both manifest and latent functions. Preference, habitat selection, migration, and choice all imply attempts to improve the congruence between people, their values, desires and needs, and perceived environmental quality. Although congruence can be achieved in other ways, choice is best (cf. Rapoport, 1968). Because choice is impossible, the existing environment can be modified (with implications for open endedness); one can adapt, changing one's life-style, behavior, clothing, and so forth (e.g., King, 1976b) (this can be destructive culturally); expectations and ideals can be changed (to the extent of "giving up"); one can reduce cognitive dissonance in other ways. The most basic mechanism is to design and build. This is the norm in preliterate and even vernacular situations and is a major component in spontaneous settlements in developing countries. As already noted, this is rare in contemporary Western countries and increasingly rare elsewhere. Hence the growing importance of choice and of modification and thus of semifixed elements (Rapoport, 1982a).

Generally, as already noted, one can distinguish between seeking out desirable qualities, that is, pull factors, and responses to stress, incongruence, misfits, and the like, that is, push factors, such as school busing (Conway & Graham, 1982), hazards and crises (Goldhaber, Houts, & DiSabella, 1983; Kiecolt & Nigg, 1982), and neighborhood change (Rapoport, 1977). Pull factors seem to be more important in the case of home environments, for example, suburbs (e.g., Guttenbock, in Schwartz, 1976; Oliver, Davis, & Bently, 1981).

Congruence is sought to obtain a supportive environment, which raises questions about what home environments *do*, in the latent as well as the manifest senses. The former plays a major role in choice and helps explain certain choices made which may seem strange to architects. Home environments support different life-styles, communicate appropriate meanings when needed (e.g., status or identity); they may even be a recreational phenomenon (Rapoport, 1977).

The variability of choices based on latent functions leads to the striking variability of home environments. Instrumental and manifest functions—what people do—are *relatively* constant, although specific activities do vary. Thus, to a nongardener, it is strange that gardening in Milwaukee is the fourth most popular summer recreation for men and the second most popular for women ("Gardening Rates," 1977). Variability increases, however, as one moves from manifest to latent aspects (corresponding to the concrete object–symbolic object distinction and the perception–evaluation sequence) (Rapoport, 1977, 1982a).

Choice, understood as the process of increasing congruence (pulls) or reducing incongruence (pushes) generally involves matching an environmental quality profile to a specific individual or group in some way. The question then becomes which characteristics of a person or group match which components of the environmental quality profile. The most useful answer is in terms of *life-style*. This seems more useful than characteristics such as age, cohort membership, class, ethnicity, race (which lead to specific life-styles) or income (which *allows* or *constrains* choice). Life-style is related to education and reflects values and attitudes to nature, life, child rearing, and so forth, which in turn are important in choosing home environments. Life-styles can be classified in different ways (e.g., *Land Use Digest*, 1984; Mitchell, 1982; Rapoport, 1977, 1980a) and there is much work on them. This is reflected in the increasing use of sociodemographics and geodemography in marketing generally and in choice of home environments specifically (Hempel, 1974; Hempel & Ayal, 1977; *Land Use Digest*, 1984). It is significant that *life-style* shares the term *style* with design: both are a result of systematic choices among alternatives (Rapoport, 1980e, pp. 288–289; 1984). In fact, I argue (Rapoport, 1977, 1980a,c) that the most useful definition of life-style (Michelson & Reed, 1970) sees it as the result of *choices* (again!) about allocating resources—economic, temporal, effort, involvement, and the like. This leads to a *life-style profile*[5] of certain components, their ranking and their importance. Life-style and environmental quality profiles can then be matched.

As far as I know, this matching has not actually been done but is potentially a very useful way of understanding the nature and characteristics of different groups, their preferences and choices, and the suitability and supportiveness of settings. Because life-style is related to activity systems, social networks, use and organization of time, home ranges, territories, meaning, and the like, it directly affects the system of settings comprising the home environment. Because life-style is also related to culture and through that to environments more generally (Rapoport, 1976, 1977, 1980a,e, 1982b, 1983b) this helps link those to home environments. Potentially, a staggering amount of material can be integrated and predictions made on how changes in life-style may change choice (and design requirements) (e.g., Hole, 1977; Hole & Taylor, 1978).

I have argued (Rapoport, 1977, p. 50) that preference is a global, affective response before analysis and evaluation of specifics occurs.

---

[5]One can have other types of profiles to help define and describe the nature of relevant groups which, as pointed out, is a major unanswered research question.

This is also the case for natural environments (Ulrich, 1983) that are important in the choice of home environments for some groups (Rapoport, 1977; Weichart, 1983), although not all (Thorne *et al.*, 1980). Because home environments are the most primary, such responses can be expected to be particularly important. This helps explain why the search process is often so minimal (e.g., Barrett, 1976). This also explains (and, indeed, predicts) the role of associational aspects and meanings in home environments as in the advertisements discussed previously, the sellings of "dreams," security, fulfillment, status, the good life, and so forth (Oliver, Davis, & Bentley, 1981, p. 33; Rapoport, 1982a; Watson & Winchester, 1981). The highly affective associational nature of choice would also be expected from our earlier discussion of how early many preferences begin.

The framework can, therefore, begin to integrate findings on wilderness and other natural environments, urban areas and suburbs, changes and reversals in preference for city versus wilderness, mountains, beaches, center versus periphery (Rapoport, 1977); inner-city revival (Gale, 1979; Lipton, 1977); changes in preference among the elderly ("Increasing Numbers," 1984; "Elderly Chose," 1984; Varady, 1980) or the return to the Bush of Australian aborigines (*Australia Bulletin*, 1978). That return, however, may be only part-time, periodic ("holiday camp"), or temporary (i.e., it could reverse again) because even the most traditional aborigines reject a fully traditional life-style (*Australian*, 1982). This return can, therefore, be interpreted as a new, syncretic environmental quality profile that emphasizes latent aspects related to reestablishing identity (cf. Rapoport, 1978b, 1981b, 1982a, 1983b). This return may also cause serious ecological problems—an example of a conflict between wants and needs. Thus, traffic noise is typically not seen as a problem in judging home environments; yet it may have undesirable effects. Different people also react differently to given traffic conditions (e.g., Anderson, Mulligan, Goodman, & Regen, 1983; Appleyard & Lintell, 1972). Reactions to airport noise, and actions against it, also seem more related to group membership and life-style than to actual noise levels (Motz, 1984). Again, the effects on noncomplaining groups may still be negative. This issue of wants versus needs will be discussed briefly later.

The renewed growth of small towns and rural areas in the U.S. makes an interesting parallel to the Aboriginal example. In this case also the life-style remains urban (Rapoport, 1981a) so that, again, a particular environmental quality profile is sought by specific groups. It may include pulls such as images of safety and low crime; cleanliness; the past and "roots"; nature; trees and the like; small size; low density; low stress; certain time rhythms; presence of vernacular; economic considerations, for example, cheaper housing and lower taxes; certain meanings; friendliness, sociability and homogeneity. There may also be pushes, for example, fleeing the opposite characteristics in metropolitan areas. New employment possibilities are an *enabling* variable. As a comparable example, different people pick planned or unplanned developments (references in Rapoport, 1977). Once in a planned new town, differential migration, that is, choice, continues (Nathanson *et al.*, 1976) as people respond to pushes and pulls (assuming no constraints [e.g., Whitelaw, 1971]).

The same elements can be pushes or pulls—they are *subjectively* defined and hence variable. For example, small towns may be picked because they are "more friendly," meaning more sociable; this can also be a reason for avoiding them. Similarly, people may both choose and avoid cul-de-sacs because they are "more friendly," although there is disagreement whether they encourage sociability (or even whether small towns do). Finally, within a cul-de-sac or block, people will choose those houses that are potentially most or least sociable.

As a result of the high value given the individual house in Anglo-American culture (among many others), one finds the use of the "triple-decker" in Massachusetts (Barnett, 1977), which is seen as a single-family dwelling. The duplexes and narrow lots of Milwaukee (Beckley, 1977) allow densities as high as townhouses while looking like single-family dwellings. The spacing of 3–4 ft is not "useful" in instrumental terms and even has disadvantages, but it has the latent function of communicating a preferred image or meaning. I have documented a Pittsburgh example where the spacing is only 18 in. (Rapoport, 1982a, p. 33).

Many other environments can be interpreted very differently.[6] Suburbs provide a good example. They are the clear choice of many users over long periods; at the same time planners and designers dislike them intensely. In England, the reasons for this conflict are, once again, latent, affective, and value laden. Architects and planners of the modern movement literally hated the suburb in an almost pathological way for such reasons. The aspirations of the users, lost on designers, were well understood by developers who were "dream builders" (Oliver *et al.*, 1981, p. 33) (cf. my previous discussion of "dreams"). The developers used names, style of dwellings, ornaments, and front gardens in responding to users who preferred and chose what builders offered.

---

[6]Note that I am ignoring the possibility of constancies and invariants—some even with an evolutionary base.

These choices formed a highly organized and coherent system, different from that of designers. In retrospect, the users' choices proved objectively much sounder than architects'—the suburbs are socially stable and well maintained and have adapted well, whereas much later architect-designed (i.e., chosen) home environments have failed and been destroyed (Oliver et al., 1981). That the choice was reasonable in spite of designers' views (cf. Taylor, 1973) is also supported by evidence in the U.S. (e.g., Donaldson, 1969); so is the view that the choice is due to pulls rather than pushes (e.g., Guttenbock, in Schwartz, 1976; "Middle Class Dream," 1979). Both, however, are clearly involved, and both can be studied (e.g., Nathanson et al., 1976). One can also study the variability of environmental quality profiles and which elements are pushes or pulls in any given case. The conflict in Milton Keynes (Bishop, 1983) discussed earlier can be interpreted in these terms. So can the housing choices, studied through gaming, with the revealing title "So What's Wrong with Little Boxes?" (1982). This shows that many people like developers' dwellings, and we have already seen that these preferences are reflected in monetary values; the English suburbs discussed by Oliver et al. (1981) have greatly increased in value.

PEOPLE IN HOME ENVIRONMENTS

I have discussed choice as though it were a one-time phenomenon; it is, of course, ongoing (e.g., Michelson, 1980). My emphasis has been on choice before people are in a given home environment; in fact all these migrating people already live *somewhere!*

After a series of choices by the various actors—about financing, design, advertising, buying or renting, the person, family, or other group (cooperative, commune, or whatever) are in their home environment. At this point most research begins: How is the home environment evaluated? How is it used? How does it work? This very large body of research also fits into the framework.

Moreover, choice still operates in the mutual interaction and adjustment processes between people and home environments; it can thus continue to serve as a framework. A series of choices are made, for example about altering, decorating, furnishing, personalizing, landscaping, and so forth within the constraints of the building type and regulations. These are important both because of instrumental and latent aspects and because they *are* choices.

Furnishings and mementos play a major role in communication of identity and status. They help take possession of space and reflect people's lives—travels, experiences, places lived, family ties. These mementos "turn a house into a home" ("Furnishings, Momentos," 1984). They both embody the past and are part of the future communicated to the next generation. Mementos and furnishings often create a home environment; in the case of the elderly a large literature testifies to the importance of mementos in new settings.

The various modifications and transformations not only represent choice; they are also ways of making home environments more congruent with the people in them. This is why issues of meaning, personalization, open endedness, and semifixed elements are centrally important. It is also why users spend much time, effort, and many resources on them (Csikzentmihalyi & Rochberg-Halton, 1981; Douglas & Isherwood, 1979; Kron, 1983; Rapoport, 1968, 1977, 1982a; Wiesner & Weibel, 1981). Yet they are disparaged and intensely disliked by designers and critics (cf. Goldberger, 1981; Rapoport, 1982a, pp. 24–25).

There is also choice about which other settings are linked to the dwelling and how to create that system of settings that is the home environment. Choices are made about work, shopping, travel, education, recreation, social relations, and entertaining. Choices are also made about uses within the dwelling and its immediate surroundings. These are expressed in rules (typically unwritten) about which spaces and areas are to be used by whom, when, and for what; about display and hiding (front and back); about privacy and penetration gradients; about inside/outside relations; about where and when one eats and many, many others. For example, half or more of many very small, traditional dwellings may be a formal living room. It was important as an indicator of status and self-dignity—like a front lawn. In the U.S. it has been suggested that the living room should be eliminated as a "useless showpiece" ("Is Living Room?" 1976) showing a complete and typical neglect of latent function. It is similarly suggested that formal dining rooms should be replaced by "informal eating areas" and "family rooms," which are clearly related to life-style. This is because of the meaning of food and eating generally (e.g., Rapoport, 1982a) so that formal family meals or their absence become very important (Rapoport, 1978a).

At this point one can most usefully pose the question: *Who does what, where, when, including/excluding whom (and why)?* It needs to be reiterated that the answer is again a result of choice, although often discussed in terms of social interactions, role relations, and the like. Behavior itself can be conceptualized in terms of a series of choices among the repertoire available, so that activity systems reflect life-style and ultimately culture (Rapoport, 1976, 1977, 1980a). The repertoire and many of the choices are constrained by culture. Activities, how they are carried out, how they are associated into systems, and what they mean represent choices and reflect (and *create*) group variability. In that sense choice still operates, as it does for individuals within the group: no members of any group behave identically, but they do behave more similarly than members of other groups. The life-style profile still describes the variable allocation of economic resources, time, effort, and the like—that is, choice.

One can try to discover whether the setting system is congruent with life-style. Satisfaction or dissatisfaction will follow. Typically, people tend to express satisfaction with their home environments, and "misfits" may be "solved" via some of the other mechanisms and strategies already discussed—modifying the home environment, changing life-style and behavior, changing expectations, reducing cognitive dissonance in other ways, moving again, and so forth. Thus an active mutual adjustment of home environments and people always occurs: there is choice about how it is achieved, although constraints may eliminate some (or most) choices. Also, as life-styles change, new choices may need to be made, want to be made—or are resisted.

Choice continues, and the framework seems useful also in accommodating material on the use of home environments, satisfaction or dissatisfaction with them, furnishings, lawns, gardens and their preferred size, plants, front/back relations, privacy, and many other topics. The framework also fits the view that people are actively trying to master the environment rather than reacting to it passively. It thus seems more in keeping with such developments in psychology, cognitive science, consumer behavior, the spatial choice literature in geography, and the housing adjustment literature in sociology. Yet in much current research on satisfaction and in the traditional way of addressing the effect of environment on people and in environment–behavior research generally, there is still an implicit view of rather passive people being acted upon by environments.

There are, of course, exceptions. I will just mention two. One is Kahana's congruence model in gerontology that emphasizes the active role of people in achieving congruence with environments. Both congruence and perceived control contribute to well-being (Lawton, Moss, & Moles, 1984; cf. Rapoport, 1977, 1978b, 1980c). This emphasis on preference receives even greater importance in another model (Kaplan, 1982) that gives it a central theoretical importance in EBR generally.[7]

---

[7]This model (Kaplan, 1982) predicts *consistency* of preference, yet the striking feature I have emphasized seems to be variability. Consistency of preference for natural landscapes

There are thus some approaches in EBS which can relate to the framework being discussed.

IMPLICATIONS FOR FUTURE RESEARCH

As already stated, this is not a theory of EBR. It is a relatively simple conceptual framework that could be elaborated much more even now. Yet it seems useful. Potentially, it can incorporate most of the literature, apply to highly varied environments cross-culturally and historically and to varied groups—designers versus users, clients versus users, different users, even different actors in the design process (Rapoport, 1983b). Eventually, of course, this framework will need to be developed, improved, and tested. It will also need to be superseded by models and theories, but even those will need to incorporate preference and choice as a major component of environment–behavior interaction. But even as discussed the framework seems helpful in addressing some basic issues.

Research is needed on how groups and their life-styles may be identified. The ways of achieving congruence with an appropriate environmental quality profile can then require study. One way is through the actual choice process. Another is to create the widest variety of home environments and observe (or simulate) the choices made. Another yet may be through appropriate open endedness in design. Other ways exist for improving congruence with environmental quality variables if those chosen are impossible (due to constraints) or are "wrong" in terms of needs as opposed to wants. Note, however, that one must be very certain indeed when wants are wrong (and why). Also, in any case, it is essential to understand wants because they often reveal needs. One can also suggest how certain cues might be used to communicate preferred environmental quality if one cannot, for whatever reasons, provide it (Rapoport, 1975a, 1980c, pp. 131–132). Moreover, the relative ranking of variables and the trade-offs made can suggest what is essential. It should be emphasized that home environments form just part of a broader set of needs, preferences, and choices; it follows that "design" forms an even smaller part. Finally, because *choice* as I have used it may

---

should be even greater, yet variability seems to be found in some cases. Lyons, however, neglects the best-developed consistency model (Appleton, 1975). The whole issue of consistency versus variability and constancy versus change, their interplay and relative impacts, are crucial and need to be investigated. They are not, however, *directly* relevant to the present discussion.

seem to be an excessively broad concept, research is needed on the specific conditions—amount of choice, types of constraints, who makes choices, the time scale involved—as well as the choices actually made.

But thinking properly about home environments, as about anything else, is the most important thing. Without a conceptual framework however elementary, such thinking is not possible. In fact, the very amount of material then becomes counterproductive, leading to accumulation rather than the growth of generalizable and replicable findings and insights.

REFERENCES

Ahlbrandt, R. S., & Brophy, P. C. Management—An important element of the housing environment. *Environment and Behavior*, 1976, *8*(4), 502–526.

Altman, I., & Chemers, M. M. *Culture and environment*. Monterey, Calif.: Brooks Cole, 1980.

American Behavioral Scientist. (Special issue, *Patterns of Cultural Choice*), 1983, *26*, 4.

Anderson, J. R., & Moore, C. K. *A study of object language in residential areas*, 1972. (Mimeographed)

Anderson, L. M., Mulligan, B. E., Goodman, L. S., & Regen, H. Z. Effects of sounds on preferences for outdoor settings. *Environment and Behavior*, 1983, *15*(5), 539–566.

Appleton, J. *The experience of landscape*. London: Wiley, 1975.

Appleyard, D., & Lintell, M. The environmental quality of city streets: the residents' viewpoint. *American Institute of Planners Journal*, 1972, *38*(2), 84–101.

Arreola, D. D. Fences as landscape taste: Tucson's barrios. *Journal of Cultural Geography*, 1981, *2*(1), 96–105.

Australia Bulletin. Australian aboriginal groups go back to their traditional bush homelands, 1978, *42*, 8.

Backler, A. L. *A behavioral study of location change in upper class residential areas (the Detroit example)*. Bloomington: University of Indiana, Department of Geography Monograph Series 5, 1974.

Bagby, D. G. The effects of traffic flow on residential property values. *American Planning Association Journal*, 1980, *46*(3), 88–94.

Baltimore City Planning Commission. *The design of neighborhood parks*. Baltimore: Department of Planning, 1977.

Barnett, P. M. *The Worcester three-decker: A study in the perception of form*. Unpublished manuscript.

Barnett, R. The libertarian suburb: Deliberate disorder. *Landscape*, 1977, *22*(3), 44–48.

Barrett, F. The search process in residential location. *Environment and Behavior*, 1976, *8*(2), 169–190.

Beattie, N. J. Perceived environmental quality: The use of linear models to approximate the environmental evaluation process. In R. Thorne & S. Arden (Eds.), *People and the man-made environment*. Sydney: Department of Architecture, University of Sydney, 1980, pp. 414–425.

Bechtel, R. B. The public housing environment: A few surprises. In W. J. Mitchell (Ed.), *Environmental design research and practice* (EDRA 3). Los Angeles: UCLA, 1972, pp. 13-1-1–13-1-9.

Beck, R. J., & Teasdale, P. *User generated program for lowrise multiple dwelling housing: Summary of a research project.* Montreal: Centre de Recherche et d'Innovations Urbaines, Universite de Montreal, 1977.

Becker, F. D. *User participation, personalization and environmental meaning: Three field studies.* Ithaca: Program in Urban and Regional Studies, Cornell University, 1977.

Beckley, R. M. *A comparison of Milwaukee's Central City residential areas and contemporary development standards: An exploration of issues related to bringing the area up to "standard."* Milwaukee: Urban Research Center, University of Milwaukee, 1977.

Better homes: Selling dreams. *New York Times,* October 22, 1981.

Bishop, J. *Will the real Milton Keynes please stand up?* Paper presented at the British Association for the Advancement of Science, annual meeting (Section E5), Aug. 22–26, 1983.

Borukhov, E., Ginsberg, Y., & Werczberger, E. Housing prices and housing preferences in Israel. *Urban Studies,* 1978, *15*(2), 187–200.

Britten, J. R. *What is a satisfactory house? A report of some nonscholars' views.* Garston: Buildings Research Establishment Current Paper, 1977.

Burby, R. J. III, & Weiss, S. F. *New communities USA.* Lexington, Mass.: Lexington Books, 1976.

Child-free living. *New York Times,* April 13, 1982.

Co-op garden: Eyesore or source of pride? *Milwaukee Journal,* November 5, 1981.

Cooper, C. *Easter Hill Village.* New York: The Free Press, 1975.

Cooper-Marcus, C. The emotional content of house/self relationships. In S. Weidemann (Ed.), *Priorities for environmental design research* (EDRA 8). Washington, D.C.: EDRA, 1978, p. 419.

Csikszentmihalyi, M., & Rochberg-Halton, E. *The meaning of things: Domestic symbols and the self.* New York: Cambridge University Press, 1981.

Cullen, I., Hammond, S., & Haimes, E. *Employment and mobility in inner urban areas—An interpretive study.* London: University College, Bartlett School of Architecture and Planning, 1980.

Developing homes for midlife. *New York Times,* April 16, 1982.

Disputed Park Ave. deli gets ready for opening. *New York Times,* April 6, 1984.

Donaldson, S. *The suburban myth.* New York: Columbia University Press, 1969.

Douglas, M., & Isherwood, B. *The world of goods.* New York: Basic Books, 1979.

Downtown becoming childless ghetto. *Toronto Star,* October 17, 1979.

Downtown Los Angeles: The new settlers. *New York Times,* April 12, 1984.

Duncan, J. S. Landscape taste as a symbol of group identity. *Geographical Review,* 1973, *63*, 334–355.

Duncan, J. S., & Duncan, N. G. Residential landscapes and social worlds: A case study in Hyderabad. Andhra Pradesh. In D. Sopher (Ed.), *An exploration of India.* Ithaca: Cornell University Press, 1980, pp. 271–286.

Elderly choose retirement living. *New York Times,* April 6, 1984.

Ellis, R. M. *Real estate investment analysis.* Report by Caldwell Banker Co., 1976. (Mimeographed)

Ermuth, F. *Residential satisfaction and urban environmental preferences* (Geographical Monographs 3). Downsview, Ont.: Atkinson College, York University, 1974.

Filp, J., Fuentes, E., Donoso, S., & Martinic, S. Environmental perception of mountain ecosystems in central Chile: An exploratory study. *Human Ecology,* 1983, *11*(3), 345–351.

Flachsbart, P. G. Residential site planning and perceived densities. *American Society of Civil Engineers, Journal of the Urban Planning and Design Division,* 1979, *105*, 103–117.

Foddy, W. H. The use of common residential area open space in Australia. *Ekistics*, 1977, *43*, 81–81.

Francescato, G., Weidemann, S., Anderson, J. R., & Chenoweth, R. *Residents' satisfaction in HUD-assisted housing: Design and management factors.* Champaign-Urbana: Housing Research & Development Program, University of Illinois, 1979.

Furnishings, momentos reflect couple's life. *Milwaukee Journal*, March 25, 1984.

Gale, D. E. Middle class resettlement in older urban neighborhoods. *American Planning Association Journal*, 1979, *45*(3), 299–304.

Gardening rates high in poll. *Milwaukee Journal*, March 27, 1977.

Goldberger, P. Transformed houses of the working class. *New York Times*, Oct. 22, 1981.

Goldhaber, M. K., Houts, P. S., & DiSabella, R. Moving after crisis. *Environment and behavior*, 1983, *15*(1), 93–120.

Golledge, R. G., & Rushton, G. (Eds.), *Spatial choice and spatial behavior.* Columbus, Ohio: Ohio State University Press, 1976.

Grenell, P. Planning for invisible people: Some consequences of bureaucratic values and practices. In J. F. C. Turner & R. Fichter (Eds.), *Freedom to build.* New York: Macmillan, 1972, pp. 95–121.

Hargreaves, P. L., & Robillard, D. A. *A comparison of two high-income group residential choices in Milwaukee.* Unpublished manuscript, Department of Architecture, University of Wisconsin, Milwaukee, 1979.

Hayward, D. G. An overview of psychological concepts of home. In R. L. Brauer (Ed.), *Priorities for environmental design research* (EDRA 8) (Part 2—Workshop Summaries). Washington, D.C.: EDRA, 1978, pp. 418–419.

Hempel, D. J. *The implications of housing choice for community planning.* Paper given at conference on Changing Values and Social Trends, British and American Marketing Associations, Oxford, June, 1974. (Mimeographed)

Hempel, D. J., & Ayal, I. Transition rates and consumption systems: A conceptual framework for analyzing buyer behavior in housing markets. In A. G. Woodside, J. D. Sheth, & P. D. Bennett, (Eds.), *Consumer and industrial buying behavior.* New York: Elsevier—North Holland, 1977, pp. 201–218.

Hester, R. T. Environmental autobiography: A tool for design education, programming and research. In R. R. Stough & A. Wandersman (Eds.), *Optimizing environments: Research practice and policy* (EDRA 11). Washington, D.C.: EDRA, 1980, p. 164.

Hole, W. V. Local housing strategies. *Building Research Establishment News*, 1977, 40, 2–5.

Hole, W. W., & Taylor, J. R. B. The housing needs of single young people and the use of older properties. *Building Research Establishment News*, Current Paper, 1978.

How, R. F. C., & Russell, A. D. Obsolete housing. *Building Research Establishment News*, 1980, *51*, 4–5.

Howard, W. A., Herold, L. C., Drisscoll, L. B., & Laperriere, L. R. *Residential environmental quality in Denver utilizing remote sensing techniques.* Denver: University of Denver, Department of Geography, Publications in Geography, Technical Paper No. 74-1, 1974.

Humphreys, J. S., & Whitelaw, J. S. Immigrants in an unfamiliar environment: Location decision-making under constrained circumstances. *Geografiska Annaler* Series B., 1979, *6*(1), 8–18.

Increasing numbers of aged return north from Florida. *New York Times*, March 15, 1984.

Is living room on way out? *Milwaukee Journal*, November 21, 1984.

Jaanus, H., & Nieuwenhuijse, B. Determinants of housing preference in a small town. In A. H. Esser & B. B. Greenbie (Eds.), *Design for community and privacy.* New York: Plenum Press, 1978, pp. 525–274.

Jones, C. Housing: The element of choice. *Urban Studies*, 1979, *16*(2), 197–204.

Journal of Social Issues. (Special Issue, *Residential mobility: Theory, research and policy*), 1983, *38*(3).

Kaplan, S. Where cognition and affect meet: A theoretical analysis of preference. In P. Bart, A. Chen, & G. Francescato (Eds.), *Knowledge for design* (EDRA 13). Washington, D.C.: EDRA, 1982, pp. 183–188.

Kiecolt, K. J., & Nigg, J. M. Mobility and perception of a hazardous environment. *Environment and Behavior*, 1982, *14*(2), 131–154.

King, A. D. *Colonial urban development (Culture, social power and environment)*. London: Routledge & Kegan Paul, 1976. (a)

King, A. D. Values, science and settlement: A case study in environmental control. In A. Rapoport (Ed.), *The mutual interaction of people and their built environment*. The Hague: Mouton, 1976, pp. 365–390. (b)

Kron, J. *Home Psych. The social psychology of home and decoration*. New York: Potter, 1983.

Ladd, F. C. Residential history: A personal element in planning and environmental design. *Urban Planning, Policy Analysis and Administration* (Policy Note P76-2), Department of City and Regional Planning, Harvard University, May, 1976.

Land Use Digest, 1984, *17*(4).

Lawrence, R. J. Meaning and the built environment: Spatial and temporal perspectives through the simulation of domestic space. In R. Thorne & S. Arden (Eds.), *People and the man-made environment*. Sydney: Department of Architecture, University of Sydney, 1980.

Lawton, M. P., Moss, M., & Moles, E. The suprapersonal neighborhood context of older people: Age heterogeneity and well-being. *Environment and Behavior*, 1984, *16*(1), 89–109.

Lee, T. Public housing, relocation and dislocation. *Town Planning Review*, 1978, *49*(1), 84–92.

Lipton, S. G. Evidence of central city revival. *American Institute of Planners Journal*, 1977, *42*(2), 136.

Living. Austin, Tex., Sept./Nov. 1980.

Living. Houston, Tex., Jan./Feb. 1984.

Living. Denver, Colo., March/April, 1984.

McLaughlin, H. Density: The architect's urban choices and attitudes. *Architectural Record*, Feb. 1976, pp. 95–100.

Metcalf, J. Standards for older housing and its surroundings. *Building Research Establishment News*, 1977, *40*, 6–9.

Michelson, W. *Man and his urban environment: A sociological approach*. Reading, Mass.: Addison-Wesley, 1970.

Michelson, W. *Environmental choice, human behavior and residential satisfaction*. New York: Oxford University Press, 1977.

Michelson, W. Long and short range criteria for housing choice and environmental behavior. *Journal of Social Issues*, 1980, *36*(3), 135–149.

Michelson, W., & Reed, P. *The theoretical status and operational usage of lifestyle in environmental research*. Toronto: Centre for Urban and Community Studies, University of Toronto, Research Paper No. 36, Sept. 1970.

Middle class dream fulfilled. *Milwaukee Journal*, March 18, 1979.

Mitchell, A. *The nine American lifestyles*. New York: Macmillan, 1983.

Moore, D. D. *At home in America (Second generation New York Jews)*. New York: Columbia University Press, 1981.

Motz, A. B. Community action and airport noise: Small communities and the Ben Gurion

International Airport. *Selected Papers on the Environment in Israel*, No. 11 (Publication No. 83-03, Jerusalem Environmental Protection Service) 1984, pp. 9–35.

Nathanson, C. A., Newman, J. S., Moen, E., & Hiltabiddle, H. Moving plans among residents of a new town. *American Institute of Planners Journal*, 1976, 42(3), 295–302.

Newman, S. J., & Duncan, G. J. Residential problems, dissatisfaction and mobility. *American Planning Association Journal*, 1979, 45(2), 154–166.

Noble, J. Contingency housing. *Architects' Journal*, October 24, 1973, pp. 976–1000.

Norcross, C. *Townhouses and condominiums: Residents' likes and dislikes*. Washington, D.C.: Urban Land Institute, 1973.

Number of vacancies at projects increasing. *Milwaukee Journal*, February 21, 1984.

Oliver, P., Davis, I., & Bentley, I. *Dunroamin' (The suburban scene and its enemies)*. London: Barrie & Jenkins, 1981.

Only a heartbeat from the Northwest frontier. *Times* (London), October 2, 1982.

Phillips, J. W. *Housing and the perception of density*. Unpublished masters thesis, Department of Architecture, University of Wisconsin, Milwaukee, 1982.

Preston, V., & Taylor, S. M. Personal construct theory and residential choice. *Annals of the Association of American Geographers*, 1981, 71(3), 437–451.

Proposition M: Minorities helped defeat measure. *Los Angeles Times*, November 10, 1983.

Rainwater, L. Fear and house-as-haven in the lower class. *American Institute of Planners Journal*, 1966 32(1), 23–31.

Rapoport, A. The personal element in housing: An argument for open-ended design. *RIBA Journal*, July 1968, pp. 302–307.

Rapoport, A. *House form and culture*. Englewood Cliffs, N.J.: Prentice-Hall, 1969. (a)

Rapoport, A. The pueblo and the hogan: A cross-cultural comparison of two responses to an environment. In P. Oliver (Ed.), *Shelter and society*. London: Barrie & Radcliffe, 1969, pp. 66–79. (b)

Rapoport, A. An approach to the study of environmental quality. In M. Sanoff & S. Cohen (Eds.) *EDRA 1*, Raleigh, N.C., 1969. (c)

Rapoport, A. People and environments. In A. Rapoport (Ed.), *Australia as human setting*. Sydney: Angus and Robertson, 1972, pp. 3–21.

Rapoport, A. Urban design for the elderly: Some preliminary consideration. In T. O. Byerts (Ed.), *Environmental research and aging*. Washington, D.C.: Gerontological Society, 1974.

Rapoport, A. Towards a redefinition of density. *Environment and Behavior*, 1975, 7(2), 133–158. (a)

Rapoport, A. An "anthropological" approach to environmental design research. In B. Honikman (Ed.), *Responding to social change*, (EDRA 6). Stroudsburg, Penn.: Dowden, Hutchinson & Ross, 1975, pp. 145–151. (b)

Rapoport, A. Socio-cultural aspects of man–environment studies. In A. Rapoport (Ed.), *The mutual interaction of people and their built environment*. The Hague: Mouton, 1976, pp. 7–35.

Rapoport, A. *Human aspects of urban forum*. Oxford: Pergamon, 1977.

Rapoport, A. The environment as an enculturating medium. In S. Weideman & J. Anderson (Eds.), *Priorities for environmental design research* (EDRA 8). Washington, D.C.: EDRA, 1978. (a)

Rapoport, A. Nomadism as a man–environment system. *Environment and Behavior*, 1978, 10(2), 215–146. (b)

Rapoport, A. An approach to designing Third World environments. *Third World Planning Review*, 1979, 1(1), 23–40.

Rapoport, A. Cross-cultural aspects of environmental design. In I. Altman, A. Rapoport,

& J. F. Wohlwill (Eds.), *Human behavior and environment: Advances in theory and research: Vol. 4. Culture and environment.* New York: Plenum Press, 1980, pp. 7–46. (a)

Rapoport, A. Towards a cross-culturally valid definition of housing. In R. R. Stough & A. Wandersman (Eds.), *Optimizing environments (Research practice and theory)* EDRA 11. Washington, D.C.: EDRA, 1980. (b)

Rapoport, A. Preference, habitat selection and urban housing. *Journal of Social Issues*, 1980, *36*(3), 118–134. (c)

Rapoport, A. Culture, site layout and housing. *Architecture Association Quarterly*, 1980, *12*(1), 4–7. (d)

Rapoport, A. Vernacular architecture and the cultural determinants of form. In A. D. King (Ed.), *Buildings and society (Essay on the social development of the built environment).* London: Routledge & Kegan Paul, 1980, pp. 283–305. (e)

Rapoport, A. Neighborhood homogeneity or heterogeneity. *Architecture and Behavior*, 1980/1981, *1*, 1.

Rapoport, A. Some thought on units of settlement. *Ekistics*, 1981, *48*(29), 447–453. (a)

Rapoport, A. Identity and environment: A cross-cultural perspective. In J. S. Duncan (Ed.), *Housing and identity: Cross-cultural perspectives.* London: Croom Helm, 1981, pp. 6–35. (b)

Rapoport, A. *The meaning of the built environment: A nonverbal communication approach.* Beverly Hills, Calif.: Sage, 1982. (a)

Rapoport, A. Urban design and human systems: On ways of relating buildings to urban fabric. In P. Laconte, J. Gibson, & A. Rapoport (Eds.), *Human and energy systems in urban planning.* The Hague: Martinus Nijhoff, 1982, pp. 161–184. (b)

Rapoport, A. The effect of environment on behavior. In J. B. Calhoun (Ed.), *Environment and population (Problems of adaptation).* New York: Praeger, 1983, pp. 200–201. (a)

Rapoport, A. Development, culture change and supportive design. *Habitat International*, 1983, *7*(5/6), 249–268. (b)

Rapoport, A. Debating architectural alternatives. *RIBA Transactions*, 1983, *3*, 105–109. (c)

Rapoport, A. Culture and the urban order. In J. Agnew, J. Mercer, & D. Sopher (Eds.), *The city in cultural context.* London: George Allen & Unwin, 1984.

Rappaport, R. A. *Ecology, meaning and religion.* Richmond, Calif.: North Atlantic Books, 1979.

Reed, P. Situated interaction: Normative and non-normative bases of social behavior in two urban settings. *Urban Life and Culture*, Jan. 1974, *2*, pp. 460–487.

Research Report. MIT–Harvard Joint Center for Urban Studies, Oct. 1979, *20*, 1–2.

Residents disagree on bicycle path. *Milwaukee Sentinel*, March 1, 1978.

Retirees from state keep busy in Eden. *Milwaukee Journal*, April 15, 1979.

Return to bush is only part-time. *Australian*, May 25, 1982.

Roberts, C. *Stressful experiences in urban places: Some implications for design.* Paper presented at EDRA 8, April, 1977.

Rossi, P. H. *Why families move.* Beverly Hills, Calif.: Sage, 1980.

Rowley, G., & Wilson, S. An analysis of housing and travel preferences. *Environment and Planning*, 1975, *7*(2), 171–177.

Royse, D. C. *Social inferences via environmental cues.* Unpublished doctoral dissertation, MIT Department of Planning, Cambridge, 1969.

Sanoff, H. *Search. A collection of games.* Raleigh, N.C.: Agricultural Extension Service, North Carolina State University/U.S. Department of Agriculture, May, 1971.

Sauer, L. Differing fates for two nearly identical housing developments. *American Institute of Architects Journal*, Feb. 1977, p. 126.

Schroeder, J. T. *The impact of tree removal on neighborhoods.* Unpublished manuscript, Department of Architecture, University of Wisconsin, Milwaukee, 1976.

Schwartz, B. (Ed.), *The changing face of the suburbs.* Chicago: University of Chicago Press, 1976.

Series on neighborhoods. *Milwaukee Journal,* December 7, 1980.

Smit, B., & Joseph, A. Trade-off analysis of preferences for urban services. *Environment and Behavior,* 1982, *14*(2), 238–258.

Smith, B. N. P., & Thorns, D. C. *Housing need and demand characteristics.* Wellington, New Zealand: National Housing Commission, Research Paper 78/1, 1978.

Smith, B. N. P., & Thorns, D. C. *Constraints, choices and housing environments.* Wellington, New Zealand: National Housing Commission, Research Paper 79/1, 1979.

So what's wrong with little boxes? *Times* (London), September 15, 1982.

Sudjic, D. The people's choice. *Sunday Times Magazine,* London, Oct. 17, 1982, pp. 70–73.

Taylor, N. *The village in the city.* London: Temple Smith, 1973.

Taylor, R. B. Perception of density (Individual differences?). *Environment and Behavior,* 1981, *13*(1), 3–21.

Thorne, R., Diesner, M., Munro-Clark, M., & Hall, R. *Consumer Survey of Housing Demand—Sydney: 18–39 Year Age Group.* Ian Buchan Fell Research Project on Housing, Faculty of Architecture, University of Sydney, 1980.

Thorns, D. C. *The role of the family life-cycle in residential mobility.* Birmingham: University of Birmingham, Center for Urban & Regional Studies, Working Paper No. 69, 1980.

Three different styles of retirement life. *New York Times,* April 12, 1984.

Tipple, G. Design a house game. *Town Planning Review,* 1977, *48*(2), 141–148.

Tranquil town is expensive. *New York Times,* October 20, 1983.

Ulrich, R. S. Aesthetic and affective response to natural environment. In I. Altman & J. F. Wohlwill (Eds.), *Human behavior and environment: Advances in theory and research. Vol. 6. Behavior and the natural environment.* New York: Plenum Press, 1983, pp. 85–125.

Varady, D. P. Housing problems and mobility plans among the elderly. *American Planning Association Journal,* 1980, *46*(3), 301–314.

Vayda, A. P. Progressive contextualization: Methods for research in human ecology. *Human Ecology,* 1983, *11*(3), 265–281.

Watson, M. K., & Winchester, D. R. Housing, social status and neighborhood gestalts. *New Zealand Geographer,* 1981, *37*(2), 49–57.

Webb, S. D. Mental health in rural and urban environments. *Ekistics,* 1978, *45*(266), 37–42.

Weichart, P. Assessment of the natural environment—A determinant of residential preference? *Urban Ecology,* 1983, *7*(4), 325–343.

Weisner, T. S., & Weibel, J. C. Home environments and family lifestyles in California. *Environment and Behavior,* 1981, *13*(4), 417–460.

Wheeler, L. Behavioral and social aspects of the Santa Cruz Riverside Project. *Man–Environment Systems,* 1977, *7*(4), 203–205.

Whitbread, M. Two trade-off experiments to evaluate the quality of residential environments. *Urban Studies,* 1978, *15*(2), 149–166.

Whitelaw, J. S. Migration patterns and residential selection in Auckland, New Zealand. *Australian Geographical Studies,* 1971, *9*, 61–76.

Zeisel, J. Symbolic meaning of space and the physical dimension of social relations: A case study of sociological research as the basis for architectural planning. In J. Walton & D. Carns (Eds.), *Cities in change: Studies on the urban condition.* Boston: Allyn & Bacon, 1973, pp. 252–263.

12

The Role of Housing in the Experience of Dwelling

SUSAN SAEGERT

INTRODUCTION

Units of housing are commodities produced and marketed within particular economic and technological constraints. For most North Americans, they are something we search for rather than produce. Home is a more elusive notion. Not only is it a place, but it has psychological resonance and social meaning. It is part of the experience of dwelling—something we do, a way of weaving up a life in particular geographic spaces. We may center our experience of dwelling in our own home, in our neighborhood, in a network of places connected by airplane routes, or in an image of our place in the world, to name but a few alternatives. The word *dwelling* is not often used in social science except to refer to dwelling units (or d.u.s., the discrete measure of housing) or to the dwellings of premodern societies, for example Hopi dwellings or the cliff dwellings of the Southwest. The notion of dwelling highlights the contrast between *house* and *home*. First it does not assume that the physical housing unit defines the experience of home. It connotes a more active and mobile relationship of individuals to the physical, social, and psychological spaces around them. It points to a spiritual and symbolic connection between the self and the physical world that was overtly recognized in

SUSAN SAEGERT • Program in Environmental Psychology, City University of New York Graduate Center, New York, New York 10036.

premodern dwellings and may now seem uselessly poetic or fanciful. It emphasizes the necessity for continuing active making of a place for ourselves in time and space. Simultaneously, it points to the way in which our personal and social identities are shaped through the process of dwelling.

Rapoport (1969) sets forth the idea that in traditional cultures the process of housing was but an aspect of dwelling. Primitive cultures endowed individuals and households with the knowledge and materials required to house themselves in ways that were compatible with the ecology of the area, the household forms of the society, and the "place" of the individual and household in the society and the cosmos. Rapoport argues that as the building of houses passes from the lay person to specialized tradesman and then to ever more distant, specialized, technologically arcane, and institutionally complex organizations, the link between a commonly ordered experience of dwelling in the world and the form of housing was lost. The focus of this paper will be on the disjunctions between housing conceived as a commodity and housing as a component of the experience of dwelling. I will argue that the disjunction arises in part because of the different participants and priorities involved in the processes of housing and of dwelling.

DWELLING

The idea of dwelling seems to me to be a basic theoretical construct for environmental psychology. It describes the physical, social, and psychological transactions by which a person maintains his or her own life, joins that life with others, creates new lives and social categories, and gives meaning to the process, thus gaining a sense of identity and place in the world. From infancy on, the individual depends on the support and viability of the physical and social environment at the same time that she or he gives a new shape and dynamic to the environment by participating in it. Dwelling is the most intimate of relationships with the environment. The extent to which a person's experience of housing shares this intimate quality depends on all the social, physical, and psychological factors that anchor people in places. Proshansky's concept of *place identity* (Proshansky, Fabian, & Kaminoff, 1983) and Stokols and Shumaker's (1982) notion of *place dependence* begin to provide conceptual frameworks for understanding the strength of a person's attachment to a particular setting though they do not specifically focus on the home.

HOME

The purpose of this paper is not to provide a definitive analysis of the meaning of *home*. However, it is necessary to distinguish between *home* and *dwelling* and between *home* and *house* (or apartment). On the one hand home is a more restrictive and place-based idea than dwelling. I will use it to mean a location in which significant activities of daily life are conducted and to which an occupant would apply this symbolically charged label. In contrast, one may tenant a house or apartment but carry out most important daily-life activities elsewhere. Or a person may distinguish between a house or apartment in which she or he lives and a "real home." Thus, one could refer to one's office or childhood residence as "my real home." Yet the idea of home will be reserved for places. Statements like "I feel at home wherever I go" or "they make foreigners feel at home" will be treated as metaphorical descriptions of experiences of dwelling. It is probably phenomenologically inaccurate to try too hard to force the distinction between a person's home and place of residence. More appropriately we might inquire into the extent to which a residence is regarded as a home. Likewise, the distinction between a home and dwelling can be approached by asking what place the home occupies in the experience of dwelling.

A second definitional distinction arises between nouns and verbs, between places and processes, thus between *home* and *house* as opposed to *dwelling* and *housing*. I will argue that the processes of dwelling and those of housing differ in terms of the focal actors, the goals, and the social meanings. These divergent processes meet and often clash in the individual and household's experience of house and home.

HOUSE AND HOME AS ANCHOR IN THE EXPERIENCE OF DWELLING

The differential constraints and opportunities presented by the social and economic structures as well as the geography and technology of an environment heavily influence the place of housing and homes in the lives of different groups and categories of people. The demographic characteristics that determine the quality and location of housing a person obtains also contribute to the experience of home. On the average, children, older people, and those with physical or mental conditions that impair mobility spend more time in their homes and are considered more place-dependent. Schorr (1964) suggests that a person's economic and social resources are limited, especially if they are inadequate for maintaining a decent standard of living; the home and neighborhood environment play a critical role in that person's life chances and identity. More women, because of their assignment to and identification with domestic duties and because of their greater fear of crime and harrassment in the world away from the home, probably experience the home as a stronger anchor in their lives than do men (Saegert, 1980; Seagert & Winkel, 1981). Culturally, general expectations about the activities and identities of men may push men physically and emotionally out of the home (Horwitz & Tognoli, 1982). Racial minorities experience the ambivalence of home as anchor in their place systems. Ghettos both restrict the space of relatively free movement and provide the setting for more experiences of social solidarity, cultural identity, and control over one's own life than the world outside (Fairchild & Tucker, 1982; Loo & Mar, 1982; Rainwater, 1970; Rivlin, 1982).

At deeper and less consciously accessible levels, being anchored in a home may always be an ambivalent feeling. When the home is considered a haven, it implies the world requires being hidden from (Rainwater, 1970; Rakoff, 1977). Rakoff has explored this ambivalence in connection with home ownership. Homeowners appear more anchored by their homes. They have a longer term financial and legal commitment even if that commitment can be abrogated by finding someone else to take it over, that is, by selling the home. Yet the strength of this anchor financially depends on the housing market, the rental market, and the job market. Psychologically, homeowners may be more anchored in the home because of the significance they attach to the act of buying a home and often to its coincidence with the establishment or growth of a family. The daily decisions and acts of maintenance may enforce the commitment or for some may make home-as-anchor into home-as-albatross. The negative qualities of being anchored through ownership in a house/home seem clear when we look at the market for selling houses in dioxin-laden Times Beach or in the shadow of the nuclear power facility at Three Mile Island.

Home As an Extension of Self

In contrast, Clare Cooper (1974) offers the vision of home as an extension of the psyche; she turns our attention to dwelling as an accomplishment, a bringing into being of a mature personality through an intense and intimate relationship with the physical world, a movement from careless or reactive use of the environment to a thoughtful, mutual nurturing of self and house.

Many criticisms of the notion of house as symbol of self come immediately to mind. What if the house houses family, boarders, unrelated individuals, servants, or regular guests? Whose self is it a symbol of? Most people do not build their own houses. How does housing bought as a commodity and possibly used for years previously by others perform this symbolic function? Cooper argues that a free-standing house on the ground serves this function best and may be related to preferences for single-family-owned dwelling units. On the other hand, many non-Western or premodern cultures provide examples of symbolically significant multifamily house forms—some cut into hillsides, some even below ground. By what processes do different housing forms come to have symbolic significance?

Cooper's (1976) paper suggests that through a multitude of choices and actions, identity comes to be symbolized both as it defines the unique person at a certain stage in life and as it expresses conformity to social norms or self-conscious challenges to those norms. An interview study of a small number of single adults by Horwitz and Tognoli (1982) illustrates the relationship between personal development and the making of a home. In a society that almost equates having a home with having a spouse and children, these single adults describe their progress after leaving their childhood homes through houses and apartments that were not homes until they establish their first real home. The study suggests that more research of this type would deepen our understanding of the psychological meaning of both housing and home.

Altman and Gauvain (1981) propose that houses express particular moments of a dialectical process. Homes reflect both the personal identity of their inhabitants and their relationship to the community. They place the individual and the household in relationship to outsiders by defining modes of access and also closing out others. Rakoff (1977), working in a Marxist framework, identifies contradictions between middle-class Americans' view of the home as private property and as a tie to a specific community and set of social relationships. Altman and Gauvain (1981) seem to locate their dialectic in universal human tensions that are handled differently in different cultures. They distinguish these from other social processes when they ask, "Does a particular home design reflect family social structure, economic values, religious values, or the dialectics discussed in this chapter?" (p. 315). Because Rakoff works within a Marxist theoretical structure he sees individual consciousness, household structure, and religious values as deriving from dialectical processes in the political and economic structures of the society. He does not address the physical form of particular homes however, leaving open how individual and household actions and choices may reflect, exacerbate, or partially resolve the contradictions he identifies.

Home and the Interdependence of Culture and Biology

The theories discussed this far place housing in the experience of dwelling through the creation of a home. However, they only partially identify aspects of the experience of dwelling that can be brought together and expressed in housing. Most attention is given to the expression of self as a psychological individual in relationship to a social structure (both rather vaguely defined). The physical existence of the self in interdependence with the environment receives little attention either at the individual level or as a primary aspect of social arrangements. That is, in most societies, housing provides a primary space for eating, sleeping, storing and cooking food, having sex, caring for children and the sick, clothing oneself, and the like. These activities are at once biologically necessary and performed in ways that have deep cultural and individual significance. Hirschon (1979) writes of the way Greek families transform the physical form of their suburban houses to regulate and support traditional relationships of men and women to each other and their symbolic relationship to culture and nature. Facilities for storing, cooking, and serving of food and the size and location of the marriage bed and dining table participate in an essential way in continuing traditional patterns of meaning and behavior.

Many more complicated questions need to be addressed to the interdependence of individual physical functioning, physical environment, and symbolic meaning in the home. We know that moving from one residence to another can endanger the health of elderly people (Rowland, 1977). Stokols and Shumaker (1982) review other studies revealing negative health effects of moving but criticize the simplistic paradigm attributing ill health effects to the stress of moving. Although they go further by calling attention to person–environment congruence in the new residence and the importance of choice, they do not suggest the deep, culturally and psychologically ingrained, and perhaps unconscious nature of intimate household activities changed for the better or worse through change in the residential environment.

The experience of dwelling links people symbolically and biologically to nature, yet relationships with the parts of the environment culturally designated as natural have been mostly neglected in social science research on housing. When they are included, the reasons natural environments might be important are not explored.

Home as Social Microcosm

The way we live in our homes reflects, expresses, and forms the social relationships among household members, kin, neighborhoods, and even more distant social partners. Anthropologists tend to view this most clearly. In addition to Hirschon's (1979) work, other authors in the same collection detail the ways that housing layout and use reflect, perpetuate, and adapt traditional relationships between women and men in Iran, the Soviet Union, Nigeria, and South Africa (Callaway, 1979; Dragadze, 1979; Ridd, 1979; Wright, 1979). We need look no further than the HUD regulations about assignment of households to units with different numbers of bedrooms. A single mother with a daughter gets one bedroom; with a son, she gets two. A married couple with a child gets two also. Callaway's (1979) piece on women in Nigeria reveals the depth of the entanglement of social forms and housing as she traces the gradual loss of home accruing to a particular woman who loses her ties with male providers. Conversely, Tognoli (1979) has written about the ways in which men's understanding of what is "masculine" in American culture today debars them from many positive identifications with domestic space.

The child growing up in a particular home learns much about appropriate relational behavior through his or her own use of space and through the use others make of it. Wolfe (1978) describes the ways children in different settings learn to understand privacy as it relates to their own and other's gender identity, social relationships, and individuality. My work with children in public housing (Saegert, 1982) reveals the impact of household density on whether children express anger by physically or verbally lashing out at others or by withdrawal. Parke (1978) develops the notion that parents facilitate the child's development at different stages by organizing the home environment to offer both engaging stimulation and available stimulus shelters. Given the strong emotional tone of most people's recollections of their childhood homes, it seems likely that the significance of the home in children's personal and social development goes much beyond the meager body of literature on the topic.

Csikszentmihalyi and Rochberg-Halton (1981) discovered an interesting relationship between the amount of affective meaning invested in domestic objects and the affective tone of family life. Families investing more meaning in the domestic environment also appeared to be warmer and closer in their style of relating. At the very least, this suggests a similarity in style of relating to objects and to people. Although for the mainly middle class, intact families studied, this continuity may simply reflect a sort of spilling over of good or bad feelings into the environment; it raises questions about the potential effects of living in a sterile, cramped, unsafe, or uncertain environment on family relations. It seems possible that conditions that block the flow of positive feelings and associations into the environment thwart the feelings themselves and put more pressure on relationships or the individual personalities. This would be especially likely if the physical and social environments outside the home were similarly unprepossessing. In the study referred to previously, these same warm, close families who invested their domestic environments with more meaning also were more involved in their communities.

In the work I have been doing with Jacqueline Leavitt on low-income tenant co-ops created out of landlord-abandoned buildings, I am becoming increasingly convinced that the sociological treatment of housing as an expression of status and group identification misses some important dynamics. Many of the people we interview seem to be struggling to make their buildings and apartments sound, viable, and beautiful as part of their effort to make the society likewise. The marble coffee table with an *Architectural Digest* lying on it in the apartment of a tenant leader in a building once reduced to an encampment of 18 households in a building of 52 mostly burned out and vandalized units could be simply interpreted as an effort to vicariously identify with a higher status group through consumption patterns. Yet whereas this aspect of the person's relationship to the environment should not be overlooked, there is another, less futile aspect to the interest in and attention to the aesthetics of the environment. The woman being interviewed described how, as they became aware of the possibility of buying the building as a cooperative, tenants started to board up the vacant apartments and reclaim them from the drug addicts. All of the co-ops we have studied have gone far beyond landlord norms of cleanliness and attractiveness in restoring apartments for habitation. Conversely, when newly painted halls are vandalized or a newly restored apartment suffers damage from a careless tenant, the blow to the active tenants is more than financial and aesthetic. They are reminded of the lack of mutual regard for each others' well-being among members of the community.

Psychological and financial investment in housing, even by very poor people, may become a central part of the experience of dwelling because social, economic, and physical aspects of the environment beyond the home preclude the intimate, caring, nurturing relationship between people and the physical environment that make the difference between dwelling in, rather than simply using, an environment. Gans's "urban villagers" may not have felt a need to "improve" their housing because their experience of dwelling extended into the physical and social fabric of the neighborhood. To some extent, the incredible effort, time, and personal expense some of the tenants invest in saving their buildings comes from a lack of alternatives. One tenant living in a frequently vandalized building stated that she would prefer to live in public housing. She wanted something new for once, having lived her adult life and raised seven children in a series of buildings in various stages of landlord abandonment. Much of her experience of dwelling involved making do in order to care for her children. She remembered most fondly the one building she lived in when her children were all at home and the other 24 children in the building treated her home as theirs also. That building burned down, and she was placed in a welfare hotel and unable to find housing because of her large family and low income until the tenant leader brought her into this building. Her commitment to nurturing still prevents her from finding the housing she wants. She did get accepted to public housing, but it was only for elderly people, and she could not take the apartment because she looks after her grandson.

Throughout these interviews, the difference between the study of dwelling and the study of housing bothered me. It bothers me the more because housing means so much to the lives of the people I am talking with. For this 83-year-old man, it is life's work that is longer and more important than any job he had. For that 70-year-old woman, it contains a social world that came together 35 years ago in this place and would be lost with the building. Even for the least involved tenants it is a home in a city increasingly full of homeless people. When I listen to the more active tenants' stories of the struggle involved in saving their buildings, I feel that their stories of struggle for a viable home are models of dwelling. But I cannot conclude that their buildings are models of housing.

HOUSING

The distance between housing and dwelling as human activities reflects not only technologically based divisions of labor, knowledge, and values. It also and perhaps primarily arises from the different places of housing and dwelling in the economic and political structures of a society. I will consider only the case of housing in the United States because these structures differ markedly among nations. Housing as a commodity is produced primarily for profit. Even when it is built under government or not-for-profit sponsorship, subsidies for the cost of land, construction, materials, debt service, management, and maintenance must conform to the same system of financial and legal constraints and opportunities as housing built for the private market. Dwelling is without economic value in any direct sense. Environmental psychologists will be confronted with the problems of understanding the joint manifestation of the two differently generated processes whenever we study house and home. These problems take center stage when we try to make our research relevant to housing development and housing policy.

COMMODITY CHARACTERISTICS

Three characteristics that are particularly important in defining house as a commodity also contribute to the weight of housing as an anchor in the experience of dwelling. These are its durability, its locational fixity, and its cost. These three factors make housing a less flexible commodity to produce and subject the industry to particular vulnerability to economic fluctuations and to large-scale changes in employment and household patterns, as well as to any changes that markedly shift the desirability of residence from one location to another (e.g., increased employment opportunities, decreased public services, the presence of environmental hazards). Changes in the routes and modes of transportation and public infrastructure investments and policies strongly influence housing investment, development decisions, and their success (Smith, 1971; Wedin & Nygren, 1976). It is widely recognized that housing is a necessity for all people and that housing needs and preferences arise from strongly held values and culturally based images of the good life. Yet, at least in the United States, the type, volume, location, and cost of available housing depend on the cost of land relative to its location, the cost of borrowing money relative to the time needed for land acquisition, construction, and marketing as well as an expected profit and the costs of materials and construction. In addition, since the 1930s federal taxation policies and government regulations of the housing finance sector have set the direction of housing investment. Housing codes, building codes, zoning regulations, subdivision regulations, and the political structure defining incorporation of separate governmental entities or inclusion in existing entities (e.g., as a separate township or as newly incorporated part of an existing city) all also strongly dictate the type and cost of housing and the land uses, amenities, and services in the housing location.

HISTORICAL FEATURES

Several long-term historical trends in housing must also be taken into account to understand the sorts of housing made available to and desired by people in the United States. These trends have been both reflected in and caused by governmental policies as well as private sector investment decisions. First of these is a commitment to home ownership in the United States. Around 65% of all households own their homes (Agnew, 1982). Surveys consistently find an overwhelming preference for home ownership (cf., Michelson, 1977; Morris & Winter, 1978). Desire to go from being a renter to being an owner figures heavily in decisions to move (Michelson, 1977; Rossi, 1980). This pattern is so historically embedded and so fully sustained by federal policies that it must be considered more than an individual or household preference (Agnew, 1982; Duncan, 1982; Wright, 1981).

The second trend characterizing American housing has been the ever-expanding dominance of suburban housing. Although much has been written relating this pattern of suburban expansion to federal policies including the establishment of the Veterans Administration and the Federal Housing Administration and the federal policy of allowing deduction of the interest on home loans from federal income taxes, Wright (1981) has established the roots of suburbanization in an ethos of individual ownership of land, flight from the corruption associated with city-dwelling migrant populations, and American idealization of nature. These attitudes have been a part of American culture since the first European settlements in North America. Tied up with these persistent social values has been a pattern of segregation of ethnic and income groups that has been particularly pervasive and discriminatory in ghettoizing blacks (Fairchild & Tucker, 1982). The equation of a good home with a single-family house fits smoothly into the ideal of homeownership and suburban living; all three form the core of the American Dream (Duncan, 1982; Wright, 1981). The dream and the economic, institutional, and technological mechanisms that produce housing form a coherent and mutually supportive structure from which individual experiences of dwelling arise as well as the context in which they are worked out.

Nancy Duncan's analysis of the relationship between consciousness and structure as they are expressed by individual's preferences for homeownership pinpoints some of the aspects of a structure that affect the experience of dwelling (Duncan, 1982). Structures are defined as reifications of human ideas and activities that become alienated from individuals as they are expressed in laws and organized institutionally. People in different classes and social worlds have different amounts of power to express their values and interests in socially binding reifications. She applies this analysis to the widespread American preference for ownership of single-family suburban housing by describing the often inescapably symbiotic relationship between supply and demand (Duncan, 1982, pp. 126–127).

DEMOGRAPHY AND HOUSING DISTRIBUTION

Demographic characteristics that significantly affect the housing
needs of a household as well as its likelihood of achieving and being
satisfied by culturally valued housing forms include household composition (including size of household, age and sex of its members, relations among members [e.g., sharing, married, parent–child], number of
members employed for pay, and stability or variability of composition);
occupations of household members; and race, income, and social resources of household members (including family, friends, religious, or
subcultural ties as well as power relations such as community influence,
political group membership, and membership in dominant or subordinate social groups). These characteristics determine many of the functions the home and location will have to serve—the resources available
for the purchase, maintenance, and elaboration of the home. They also
define what parts of the housing market a household has access to. The
residence and usually the workplace anchor individuals and households
in a system of places. Most of the anchoring goes on either out of
awareness of residents or outside the set of questions researchers have
tended to ask about housing choice. Studies of residential mobility in the
United States and Canada show that change in household composition,
particularly the birth of children, combined with a desire for ownership
of a single-family home best predict residential mobility (Michelson,
1977; Rossi, 1980; Rossi & Shlay, 1982). At the attitudinal level, households who want to move register more complaints about the housing
characteristics, especially space. Michelson (1977) argues that households moving to new housing evaluate their choices in a longitudinal
perspective. Thus, if they are moving to a high-rise apartment in a city,
they may find it relatively satisfactory so long as the option of purchasing a single-family home, probably in the suburbs, appears likely in the
future. Most of the respondents in Michelson's study reported that the
housing they chose to move to fulfilled their expectations in terms of its
characteristics (e.g., more space) and in terms of the activities it facilitated (e.g., neighboring, access to work, raising children, gardening).

As Rossi and Shlay have pointed out (1982), researchers cannot be
reminded too often that "our ideas about the way the world works
condition our analysis of the way it works" (p. 22). Most of the research
on housing choice selects populations that have the resources to move,
are not radically discriminated against in the process, and are in a stage
of household formation that makes size of dwelling unit and long-term
financial investments salient.

Michelson included only middle- and upper-middle income couples in their childbearing years. Although Rossi sampled a wider range of household types and incomes, he excluded blacks and foreign-born respondents.

Some of my own research (Saegert & Winkel, 1981) drew on the same premises: (1) a belief that the way to study what factors were important to people in housing was to study people with choice; and (2) an unacknowledged association of home and therefore housing with couples who either have children or might have them in the future. Several aspects of Rossi's work reflect this approach also. Even though two out of five households moved for reasons the researchers considered to be forced moves, the major attention in analysis was given to mobility intentions and how people went about fulfilling or not fulfilling them. From the point of view of dwelling, rather than housing choice, the experience of being forced out of one's home or changing one's life and residence through divorce, job change, and so forth would be seen as an essential part of the changed pattern of dwelling. For that matter, the birth of a child would be seen as not merely a factor that inclined a family to want more indoor space, some outdoor space, and home-ownership. Rather it would be looked at as involving major shifts in the experience of dwelling. Yet in both of these instances, the ability or inability to move to satisfactory housing and the characteristics of the new home and its location will usually have important implications for the household's whole pattern of dwelling.

HOUSING RESEARCH AND HOUSING DEVELOPMENT

Although research on housing choice and residential mobility largely accepts the commodity view of housing, researchers have also focused on activity patterns in relation to housing form, perceived satisfaction as a function of housing characteristics, and measures of well-being as a consequence of different aspects of housing (Aiello & Baum, 1979; Baldassare, 1979; Booth & Edwards, 1976; Booth & Johnson, 1975; Francescoto, Weidemann, Anderson, & Chenowith, 1978; Mackintosh, 1981; Mackintosh, Olsen, & Wentworth, 1977; Saegert, 1980, 1982). These studies either explicitly or implicitly assume that housing should be evaluated in terms of its ability to meet human needs and desires and to facilitate human development and well-being. Yet by focusing on the housing or some subset of its characteristics apart from residents' total patterns of dwelling, the research accepts a commodity-centered view. At the same time, the housing goals specified or implied have little or nothing to do with the goals of housing development. Whether or not research on these topics has an affect on housing production and regulation depends on a host of factors left unconsidered in these studies. As in other areas of applied research, studies can influence policy and production if the possibility of creating enough consensus concerning appropriate goals and actions exists among actors with control of sufficient resources to accomplish the goals and enough authority to control the actions (Saegert, 1985). This probably occurs most frequently at the scale of single residential institutions. More frequently, both consensus and the control of resources and authority cannot be brought about. Some influence of the research on policy and production can occur through a variety of channels: (1) a client or advocacy group can find out about the research and bring it to bear in appropriate contexts; (2) a political mechanism may exist that allows interested parties (for example, prisoners) to use the research to link the well-being measures to mandated rights thus obtaining legal authority to intervene in housing conditions although the control of resources may still be lacking; (3) the researcher may include an analysis of the political and financial implications of policies and production strategies in reports (Grigsby & Rosenberg, 1975); and (4) the researcher can bring the information described in Case 3 to bear on policy and production decisions through participation in the institutions and social worlds of housing constituencies, regulators, and producers. In the last two cases, assumptions and value positions that may have been merely implicit in the choice of research problems and strategies and methods will become more explicit. The researcher will have to define policy alternatives with reference to selected (even if divergent) interests. In Case 4, the personal and institutional relationships required will have entrance requirements involving demonstrated commitment to certain goals and approaches and some understanding of the institutions and frames of reference that govern housing policy and production.

The researcher confronts the disjuncture between housing policy and production and the experience of dwelling by way of an experienced difficulty in relating talk about satisfactory activity patterns, human development, and well-being to institutional pactices and conceptions of housing that govern the talk and actions of housing producers and regulators. A very partial list of the ways these conceptions and institutional practices make it difficult to incorporate these issues include the following:

1. Most of the activity and financial commitment required to produce housing aims at the production of a unit. Private market investors and developers attempt, to the extent possible over the long run, to be freed of responsibility for housing. Existing tax laws, federal debt guarantees, and the practices of finanial institutions support this limitation

of responsibility. Even if the housing is supplied as rental units, the people and institutions responsible for management are very frequently different from those who finance and own the housing.

Much housing policy concerns ways to generate money for mortgages. Recent development of a secondary mortgage market means that mortgages are held by numerous investors, many of whom buy units of mortgage securities from federally chartered agencies. These policies have, as a very general goal, the facilitation of homeownership by those who are good credit risks. Private sector housing investment decisions come about in comparison to the security and return of other investments. For the period extending from the late 1930s to the mid-1970s, federal regulations governing savings and loan associations and other aspects of housing finance partially isolated the housing finance sector from other sectors. More recently, this separation has been systematically lessened, thus merging the contingencies of housing investment with those applying to other investments.

In an effort to protect investment, both federal agencies and private lending institutions develop requirements for zoning, segregation of residential from other land uses, zoning against multifamily units, and historical refusal to underwrite loans in racially mixed or minority areas (Wright, 1981). Anti-redlining legislation partially attempted to guarantee credit to local bank customers. The recent development of a national mortgage market and a move toward nationally rather than locally based banking raise the potential for increased geographic independence of investment decisions and decrease local control of credit availability.[1]

A social scientist attempting to suggest ways to make the housing produced and its location responsive to human needs for individual and social development and well-being must address the relationship of these efforts to the system of housing finance. This task can usually best be undertaken by an interdisciplinary team. Even this type of division of labor requires that collaborators educate each other sufficiently to overcome the separate assumptions and forms of discourse employed by those who talk about housing policy and those who talk about human welfare. Few examples of this kind of collaboration can be identified in written reports.

2. The federal housing policies having the most effect on the production and location of housing no doubt center on the tax benefits

[1]Much of the information on which I rely in this section has been presented formally and informally in the Women and Housing Seminar run during 1982, 1983, and 1984, by Donna Shalala, president of Hunter College and past assistant secretary for Policy Development and Research for HUD.

associated with homeownership, other real-estate-related tax laws, and the federal role in generating and insuring mortgage credit. The effects of these policies have not been studied by social scientists who look at individual experience and behavior.

Since the 1930s the federal government has sponsored programs for publically owned or subsidized housing. These programs often involve local participation. For example, federal funds for public housing can be obtained only through establishing a local housing authority to purchase and clear property and develop and maintain the housing. For the low-income populations who are frequently studied by social scientists, the form and implementation of federally and locally subsidized housing programs has set the conditions for their experience of dwelling to a great extent. Research in this tradition has gone in two directions. Seminal studies such as Rainwater's (1970) *Behind Ghetto Walls* and Yancy's study of Pruitt Igoe (1976) document the problems of fear, negative relationships, and crime associated with large-scale public housing developments. Newman (1972) outlines design interventions directed at these problems. Others have focused on evaluating design and site-planning in subsidized and public housing (cf., Becker, 1974; Cooper, 1971, 1972, 1975; Gutman, 1966; Housing Research and Development Program, 1970, 1974a,b; Weidemann & Anderson, 1979; Zeisel & Griffin, 1975). Francescato and his colleagues (1978) identified physical, managerial, social, and psychological factors that contribute to public housing residents' satisfaction with their housing.

This body of research expands the definition of housing in several ways. Rainwater's study particularly located the experience of housing within the personal and social context of the low-income people who were trying to make up their lives in the setting. Much of the design evaluation work examines the behavior and attitudes associated with different housing forms. Various studies emphasize the notion of housing as a service. For example, Fransescato, Weidemann, Anderson, and Chenowith (1978) find management plays a critical role in relationship to satisfaction with other social and physical aspects of housing. Aside from interpretive difficulties of satisfaction measures already discussed, this approach still assumes a relatively passive relationship between people and their housing. It also fails to place that relationship either in people's broader lives or in the context of social, cultural, and economic alternatives. These studies do provide a wealth of information for the developer or manager of public housing who is committed to providing high-quality housing for low-income people.

Institutional practices often militate against the use of such information in housing development and management. Federal program housing guidelines usually aim for producing the most units for the costs involved. For example, the Department of Housing and Urban Development guidelines prohibit use of funds for community rooms or day-care centers. Most subsidy programs provide only construction-related cost, excluding maintenance, social programs, management, social services, and retrofitting over time. Well-intentioned and creative low-income housing developers and designers frequently are stopped from incorporating researchers' suggestions by these regulations and the economic context of housing development.

3. Housing production and policy decisions may not be primarily concerned with housing. Federal housing programs have often been justified as stimulants to the economy rather than as merely ways of producing housing. In this case, the quality and impact of the housing on residents are less important than the impact of programs on indicators of national economic strength. Wright (1981) and Grigsby and Rosenberg (1975) discuss the dilemmas this dual purpose of housing programs create both historically and in the context of trying to improve the housing conditions for low-income people in one city.

An important body of research documents the harm done to the purported recipients of government-sponsored slum clearance programs (Castells, 1977; Fairchild & Tucker, 1982; Fried & Gleicher, 1976; Harvey, 1973). These programs that are frequently referred to as *Negro removal programs* certainly reinforced patterns of segregation and often reduced the supply of low-income housing in an area without compensation to those displaced. Gans (1962) describes the social world of Italian-Americans in an area destined for slum clearance. Supportive social relationships and significant personal associations and identifications with the area had been held together by the sharing of a physical community. Young and Wilmott (1957) contrast the social relationships, family ties, and dominant values that characterized residents of the East End of London before and after relocation to suburban housing estates. Although crowding and difficulty in finding housing for newly formed families were problems in the old area, those who moved to housing estates found that their extensive ties with family and community members could no longer be maintained on the same basis. Couples looked to each other much more exclusively for companionship and support. Unemployed wives found themselves particularly cut off in contrast to the significant role wives and mothers had played in organizing and sustaining social life in the East End. Families in the new estates began to place much greater value on privacy and the material aspects of housing than those who stayed behind.

Many groups have attempted to fight urban renewal and slum

clearance programs in their areas, most often to no avail (Fellman &
Brandt, 1973; Hartman, 1974). These failures must play a part in the
experience of dwelling separate from the influences of the new housing
eventually obtained.

4. Political constituencies and officeholders understand that the
well-being of different groups of people is multiply determined. Thus,
although research may identify aspects of well-being associated with
particular housing conditions, the solution may not be to change the
housing conditions. Income, employment, educational, and social service programs may be seen as more efficient ways of changing the
situation.

An understanding of how housing works in the experience of
dwelling would illuminate the choice of housing- versus nonhousing-
related programs, or perhaps combined programs. Grigsby and Rosenberg (1975) describe their view of the entanglement of housing conditions with other problems of poverty. They cite the effects of substandard shelter on health and family relations, the fear and disruption
related to exposure to fires and vermin, the effect of inadequate sleep
and study arrangements on children's school performance, and relate
these to both additional expenses and loss of chances for improving
income. They argue that the visual impact of bad housing is the most
visible indicator of poverty and a cause of low self-image among the
poor. They describe the educational and opportunity deficits associated
with "the immobility of the housing product and institutional constraints, such as zoning and building codes, on the housing market."
They also note the stresses residents had to experience to achieve what
they did. Thus, they conclude that "housing deprivations can then be
viewed as a fundamental aspect of the poverty syndrome—part cause,
part consequence, and an important part of poverty itself" (p. 7).

The same argument could be made about the way housing acts in
the lives of the wealthy or the middle or working class. Research on
these issues would contribute greatly to a more fundamental understanding of how housing shapes human experiences. In studying classes of people with more power, authority, and resources, we would
probably also learn more about how people shape housing. In the process of dwelling for example, Jim Duncan's study of an elite community
in Vancouver, British Columbia, reveals the extensive activities of people sharing a residential community and a social world to determine the
social and physical forms of development in their area. Many of the
governmental controls and restriction would be viewed by the same
people in their roles as businessmen as unreasonable interference with

market forces.[2] Yet the effort to shape one's home and neighborhood environment as it shapes one is not confined to the rich and powerful. Preliminary findings in a study of low-income tenant cooperative housing in New York City disclose the unexpectedly significant role of elderly minority women in determining the success of these co-ops.[3] Both of these research programs illustrate the extent to which housing figures in peoples' lives as actively constructed and maintained settings rather than as merely something to be purchased and used or discarded for an alternative product. In fact, I would suggest that all of the obstacles to making studies of the relationship between housing and well-being relevant to policy also direct us toward the importance of studying the role of housing in the experience of dwelling rather than attempting to study housing in isolation.

IMPLICATIONS FOR FUTURE RESEARCH

The nontrivial questions about housing center on the relationship between acquiring, changing, maintaining, and otherwise living in housing and the more general process of living. These linkages arise from and are embedded in the physical, socioeconomic, and cultural milieus. They express differential access to social and economic power, cultural blessings and sanctions and individual and subgroup commitment, and solidarity and strength of purpose. The institutional mechanisms and cultural and social arrangements that produce and distribute housing cannot be ignored in any meaningful study of housing choice and satisfaction. Assessments of the impact of housing on residents must examine the places of the particular groups studied in the social, economic, and physical landscapes. It should go beyond correlations of housing type or characteristics with activity patterns and measures of satisfaction to examine the way housing comes to be inhabited over the life span in relationship to people's individual and group life projects and social standards of the good life. Research of this nature must ask some of the following questions:

[2]Presentation to Environmental Psychology Program, City University of New York Graduate School entitled *Research Report: History of the Manipulation of a Neighborhood's Image by a Particular Social Class*, by James Duncan, April 1982.

[3]This research is being conducted with Jacqueline Leavitt, associate professor of urban planning, University of California at Los Angeles. The work was begun as a collaboration during Leavitt's Postdoctoral Fellowship funded by NIMH Training Grant # 5 T32 MH16911-03.

1. How does housing fit in the lives of the populations being studied? (This question requires some historical perspective as well as an analysis of access to feasible housing alternatives. It directs our attention to looking for links [or their absence] between experiences of housing and experiences in other important life domains [work, family and social life, health, religious, and cultural values].) Methods that frame all or any of these issues in terms of commodity consumption will miss the transactional nature of the relationships being examined. Thus, new methods ranging from intensive qualitative interviewing and participant observation through the use of secondary sources and historical records should supplement our usual reliance on questionnaire measures and other standardized records like time budgets. As Glaser and Strauss (1967) point out, it is not the method but the use made of it that distinguishes between research done to validate an already formulated hypothesis and that done to discover grounded theory.

2. How do people integrate housing as a commodity into their life projects? Does the social process whereby housing is provided as a commodity have exceptions? Are some aspects of the experience of housing for different populations more or less separate from the experience of commodity choice and use? If so, how do these noncommodity or partially commodity-based relationships with housing come about, and what is their fate over time?

3. How do the social, economic, physical, political, cultural, and psychological processes and institutions that provide housing as a commodity work? How do the same individuals and groups relate to housing as a commodity in comparison to their own experiences of housing as anchor, self-expression, or social microcosm? (For social science researchers to address these questions, we must be conversant with work on housing from many different disciplines. From the vantage point of this familiarity, we can raise social and psychological questions about the constructs and social, psychological processes that structure the thinking and actions of those who participate in the production, distribution, and consumption of housing as a commodity.)

4. How do the processes of producing, distributing, and consuming housing and the integration of housing into the experience of dwelling relate to the opportunities, constraints, and meanings of neighborhoods, towns, and cities as well as larger geographic units?

5. How do the process and content of different research endeavors relate to the production, distribution, and consumption of housing as a commodity and to the experience of dwelling for ourselves and others?

Acknowledgments

I would like to thank Jacqueline Leavitt and Kathleen Christensen for commenting on drafts of this chapter. Each also deserves special thanks for other help. Jacqueline Leavitt has collaborated with me on research on low-income tenant cooperatives. Not only have we shared the work and thinking, but also I have learned much about housing policy from her. Some of my early thinking on this topic was stimulated when Kathleen Christensen brought Heidegger's use of the term *dwelling* to my attention.

REFERENCES

Agnew, J. Home ownership and identity in capitalist society. In J. S. Duncan (Ed.), *Housing and identity*. New York: Holmes & Meier, 1982, pp. 60–97.

Aiello, J., & Baum, A. (Eds.). *High density residential environments*. Hillside, N.J.: Erlbaum, 1979.

Altman, I., & Gauvain, M. A cross cultural and dialectic analysis of homes. In I. S. Liben, A. H. Patterson, & N. Newcombe (Eds.), *Spatial representation and behavior across the life span*. New York: Academic Press, 1981, 283–320.

Baldassare, M. *Residential crowding in urban America*. London, Los Angeles, and Berkeley: University of California Press, 1979.

Becker, F. *Design for living: The resident's view of multi-family housing*. Ithaca: Center for Urban Development Research, Cornell University, 1974.

Booth, A., & Edwards, J. Crowding and family relations. *American Sociological Review*, 1976, *41*, 289–308.

Booth, A., & Johnson, D. R. The effects of crowding on child health and development. *American Behavioral Scientist*, 1975, *18*, 736–749.

Callaway, H. Spatial domains and women's mobility in Yorubaland, Nigeria. In S. Ardner (Ed.), *Women and space: Ground rules and social maps*. London: Croom Helm, 1979, pp. 168–185.

Castells, M. *The urban question*. London: Edward Arnold, 1977.

Cooper, C. *Resident dissatisfaction in multi-family housing*. Berkeley: Institute of Urban and Regional Development, University of California, 1972.

Cooper, C. The house as symbol of self. In J. Lang, C. Burnette, W. Moloski, & D. Vachon (Eds.), *Designing for Human Behavior: Architecture in behavioral sciences*. Stroudsburg, Penn.: Dowden, Hutchinson, & Ross, 1974, pp. 130–146.

Cooper, C. *Easter Hill Village: Some implications of design*. New York: The Free Press, 1975.

Csikszentmihalyi, M., & Rochberg-Halton, E. *The meaning of things: Domestic symbols and the self*. Cambridge: Cambridge University Press, 1981.

Dragadze, T. The sexual division of domestic space among two Soviet minorities: The Georgians and the Tadjiks. In S. Ardner (Ed.), *Women and space: Ground rules and social maps*. London: Croom Helm, 1979, pp. 158–166.

Duncan, N. J. Home ownership and social theory. In J. S. Duncan (Ed.), *Housing and identity*. New York: Holmes & Meier, 1982, pp. 98–134.

Fairchild, H. H., & Tucker, M. B. Black residential mobility: Trends and characteristics. *Journal of Social Issues*, 1982, *38*(3), 51–74.

Fellman, G., & Brandt, B. *The deceived majority: Politics and protest in Middle America.* New Brunswick, N.J.: Transaction Books, 1973.

Francescoto, G., Weidemann, S., Anderson, J., & Chenowith, R. *Residential satisfaction in publicly-assisted housing in the United States.* Urbana: Housing Research and Development Program, University of Illinois, 1978.

Fried, M., & Gleicher, P. Some sources of residential satisfaction in a urban slum. In H. M. Proshansky, W. H. Ittelson, & L. G. Rivlin (Eds.), *Environmental psychology: People and their physical settings* (2d ed.). New York: Holt, Rinehart & Winston, 1976, pp. 550–563.

Gans, H. J. *The urban villagers.* New York: The Free Press, 1962.

Glaser, B. G., & Strauss, A. L. *The discovery of grounded theory: Strategies for qualitative research.* Chicago: Aldine, 1967.

Grigsby, W. G., & Rosenberg, L. *Urban housing policy.* New York: APS Publications, 1975.

Hartman, C. *Yerba buena.* Berkeley, Calif.: National Housing and Economic Development Law Project, 1974.

Harvey, D. *Social justice and the city.* London: Edward Arnold, 1973.

Hirschon, R. Essential objects and the sacred: Interior and exterior space in an urban Greek locality. In S. Ardnew (Ed.), *Women and space: Ground rules and social maps.* London: Croom Helm, 1979, pp. 72–88.

Horwitz, J., & Tognoli, J. Role of home in adult development: Women and men living alone describe their residential histories. *Family Relations,* 1982, *31,* 335–341.

Housing Research and Development Program, University of Illinois at Urbana-Champaign. *A response to need: Design for family housing.* Urbana: University of Illinois, 1970.

Housing Research and Development Program, University of Illinois at Urbana-Champaign. *Site improvement handbook for multi-family housing.* Urbana: State of Illinois, Department of Local Government Affairs, Office of Buildings, 1974. (a)

Housing Research and Development Program, University of Illinois at Urbana-Champaign. *Play areas for low-income housing.* Urbana: State of Illinois, Department of Local Government Affairs, Office of Housing and Buildings, (rev. ed., 1974). (b)

Loo, C., & Mar, D. Desired residential mobility in a low income ethnic community: A case study of Chinatown. *Journal of Social Issues,* 1982, *38*(3), 95–106.

Mackintosh, E., Olsen, R., & Wentworth, W. *The attitudes and experiences of the middle income family in an urban high-rise complex and in the suburbs.* New York: Center for Human Environments, City University of New York Graduate Center, 1977.

Mackintosh, E. A. *The meaning and effects of high-rise living for the middle income family: A study of three high-rise sites in New York City.* Unpublished doctoral dissertation, City University of New York Graduate School, 1981.

Michelson, W. *Environmental choice, human behavior and residential satisfaction.* New York: Oxford University Press, 1977.

Michelson, W., & Roberts, E. Children and the urban physical environment. In W. Michelson, S. V. Levine, & A. R. Spina. *The child in the city: Changes and challenges.* Toronto: University of Toronto Press, 1979.

Morris, E. W., & Winter, M. *Housing, family and society.* New York: Wiley, 1978.

Newman, O. *Defensible space.* New York: Macmillan, 1972.

Parke, R. Children's home environment: Social and cognitive effects. In I. Altman & J. Wohlwill (Eds.), *Human behavior and environment. Vol. 3. Children and the environment.* New York: Plenum Press, 1978, pp. 32–82.

Proshansky, H. M., Fabian, A. K., & Kaminoff, R. Place-identity: Physical world socialization of the self. *Journal of Environmental Psychology,* 1983, *3,* 57–83.

Rainwater, L. *Behind ghetto walls: Black families in a federal slum.* Chicago: Aldine, 1970.

Rakoff, R. Ideology in everyday life: The meaning of home. *Politics and Society*, 1977, *7*, 85–104.

Rapoport, A. *House, form and culture*. Englewood Cliffs, N.J.: Prentice-Hall, 1969.

Ridd, R. Where women must dominate: Response to oppression in a South African urban community. In S. Ardner (Ed.), *Women and space: Ground rules and social maps*. London: Croom Helm, 1979, pp. 187–202.

Rivlin, L. G. Group membership and place meaning in an urban neighborhood. *Journal of Social Issues*, 1982, *38*, 75–94.

Rossi, P. H. *Why families move* (2d ed.). Beverly Hills, Calif.: Sage, 1980.

Rossi, P. H., & Shlay, A. B. Residential mobility and public policy issues: "Why families move" revisited. *Journal of Social Issues*, 1982, *38*(3), 21–34.

Rowland, K. F. Environmental events predicting death for the elderly. *Psychological Bulletin*, 1977, *84*, 349–372.

Saegert, S. The personal and social consequences of high density environments. In A. Baum & Y. Epstein, (Eds.), *Human responses to crowding*. Hillside, N.J.: Erlbaum, 1978, pp. 259–282.

Saegert, S. Masculine cities and feminine suburbs: Polarized ideas, contradictory realities. *Signs: An Interdisciplinary Journal of Women and Culture*. Summer 1980, pp. 96–111.

Saegert, S. Environment and children's mental health. In A. Baum & J. Singer (Eds.), *Handbook of psychology and health* (Vol. 2). Hillside, N.J.: Erlbaum, 1982, pp. 247–271.

Saegert, S. Environmental psychology and social change. In I. Altman & Stokols (Eds.), *The handbook of environmental psychology*. New York: Wiley, 1984.

Saegert, S., & Winkel, G. The home: A critical problem for changing sex roles. In G. Wekerle, R. Peterson, & D. Morley (Eds.), *New space for women*. Boulder: Westview Press, 1981.

Schorr, A. *Slums and social insecurity*. Washington, D.C.: U.S. Government Printing Office, 1964.

Smith, W. G. *Housing: The social and economic element*. Berkely: University of California Press, 1971.

Stokols, D., & Shumaker, S. A. The psychological context of residential mobility and well-being. *Journal of Social Issues*, 1982, *38*(3), 171–173.

Tognoli, J. The flight from domestic space: Men's roles in the household. *The Family Coordinator*, 1979, *28*, 599–607.

Wedlin, C. S., & Nygren, L. G. *Housing perspectives: Individuals and families*. Minneapolis: Burgess, 1976.

Weidmann, S., & Anderson, J. *Resident heterogeneity in multi-family housing*. Urbana: Housing Research and Development Program, University of Illinois, 1979.

Wolfe, M. Childhood and privacy. In I. Altman & J. Wohlwill (Eds.), *Human behavior and the environment Vol. 3. Children and the environment*. New York: Plenum Press, 1978, pp. 175–222.

Wright, G. *Building the dream*. Cambridge, Mass.: MIT Press, 1981.

Wright, S. Place and face: Of women in Poshman Ziari, Iran. In S. Ardner (Ed.), *Women and space: Rules and social maps*. London: Croom Helm, 1979, pp. 136–156.

Yancy, W. L. Architecture, interaction and social control: The case of a large-scale public housing project. In H. M. Proshansky, W. H. Ittelson, & L. Rivlin. (Eds.), *Environmental psychology* (2d ed.). New York: Holt, Rinehart & Winston, 1976.

Young, M., & Willmott, P. *Family and kinship in East London*. London: Routledge & Kegan Paul, 1957.

Zeisel, J., & Griffin, M. *Charlesview housing: A diagnostic evaluation*. Cambridge: Architecture Research Office, Graduate School of Design, Harvard University, 1975.

13

Transnational Housing Policies

COMMON PROBLEMS AND SOLUTIONS

ELIZABETH D. HUTTMAN

INTRODUCTION

This chapter focuses on the underlying social-psychological value orientations associated with housing policies in northern European countries, primarily Britain, West Germany, the Netherlands, Denmark, and Sweden, and the impact of changing government ideologies in a period of continued recession. Recession-related factors, including slowed growth and government deficits, are fostering a fiscal austerity philosophy and an increasing conservative orientation of so-called welfare state governments. Thus, governments are changing from long-term postwar Labor-Social Democrat party control to Conservative control in Britain and West Germany, to politically divided coalition rule in Denmark and the Netherlands, and to a more conservatively oriented Socialist rule in Sweden. Increasingly, conservative governmental value orientations are instrumental in reshaping housing policies, especially decreasing state subsidization of massive new housing construction.

Conservative value orientations include a belief in a *diminished state role* in provision of housing, in fact a *residual* role of providing subsidies

ELIZABETH D. HUTTMAN • Department of Sociology and Social Services, California State University, Hayward, California 94542.

only for those who cannot house themselves. This is in **sharp** contrast to the welfare state philosophy of providing basic housing needs for a large part of the citizenry. Conservative orientations include *privatization* of housing, whereby ownership, management, and financing of housing production are left to the private market, and a value on *self-help/individual effort*, whereby individuals save for their own housing, negotiate the purchase, even construct their housing, or participate in management and planning of housing projects. In the British Conservative government this theme is continually preached, but on the Continent, self-help is also encouraged in terms of user participation in cooperative housing management (Sweden), in inner-city improvement projects (West Germany), or in building one's own house (Norway) (Basel, Greiff, & Muhlich, 1978). In Britain, private effort by voluntary social service groups and private housing associations is also encouraged as the way to help house the disadvantaged.

Another emerging dominant value orientation is an emphasis on *homeownership*, which has traditionally been supported through generous tax subsidies. However, a more mixed ideological orientation to homeownership has emerged, and there has been concern that the dominance of homeowner tax relief, as the main housing subsidy, negatively affects a general policy goal of equalization of housing standard through state housing subsidies. In giving preference to homeownership status, especially in British policies, the rental status that has long been acceptable in postwar northern European countries is downgraded. Instead, new types of ownership, such as cooperatives and owner-purchased modernized units are encouraged. This is of special interest because traditional free-standing new houses are becoming so economically difficult to buy.

Because of the high cost of new housing, government interest has also shifted to modernization of inner-city housing and neighborhoods. Emphasis is on rehabilitation of houses for owner occupancy, on the assumption that owners will be more motivated to keep up the modernized units. In addition, high value is being placed on preservation of core urban areas and improvement of quality of housing and environment rather than the need to increase the quantity of new housing units. The belief is that the housing stock in most northern European countries is now near housing need and that it is cheaper to rehabilitate units than to build new ones.

This chapter explores the implications of these changes in European housing policies, especially for the poor and disadvantaged, including female-headed households, those of immigrants and transients, in terms of life-style, availability of certain kinds of residential facilities, and opportunities for home ownership versus rental.

EARLY AND RECENT POSTWAR HOUSING POLICIES

Current policies in northern Europe have been shaped by the massive postwar building of subsidized units for working and lower classes. The private market was seen as inadequate to tackle the postwar task; this factor, coupled with welfare state values, led to what Harloe (1982) called the *socialization of housing*. In some countries, more than two thirds of the housing stock was erected after World War II (Economic Commission for Europe (ECE), November 11, 1982). In Britain the Labor government subsidized the local authorities to replace tenements with new council (public) rental housing; in such housing the criteria for admission was housing need rather than income. By the 1970s one third of the country's housing stock was council-owned rental units. In addition the government built a large number of planned new towns, which were lauded throughout the world for their pleasant surroundings. In the Netherlands the welfare state government subsidized construction of appealing nonprofit housing association projects and also some new towns. Again, by the 1970s a very large part of the housing stock was housing association rentals with rents regulated by the government. In Sweden, Denmark, and Norway the Socialist-Labor governments subsidized a wide variety of housing types including local authority housing, nonprofit housing association rentals, cooperatives, and new towns, especially in Sweden. The government in Sweden took responsibility for a comprehensive housing program for the whole population.

By the late 1970s, housing shortages were limited to inner-city areas and mainly affected disadvantaged groups, such as immigrants, transients, and female-headed households. This situation was not a major political issue for working-class constituents because they were comfortably housed in either subsidized housing, much of which was a pleasant living environment or, for the more affluent, in owner-occupied units.

Both governments and the dominant citizenry saw a decreased need for continuation of large-scale subsidized house-building programs (Donnison & Ungerson, 1982; McKay, 1982). Another reason for lessened interest in building new units was the high cost of construction and land. In addition, there were decreased subsidies for new building because of the increased funds needed to manage and maintain the present subsidized housing stock.

By the 1980s the fiscal austerity orientation of these governments was also instrumental in forcing overall cuts in government housing expenditures. In Britain, West Germany, and most other northern European countries new housing stocks were a major target of budget cuts (ECE, December 14, 1983; Forrest & Murie, 1984). (However, the Netherlands in 1981 temporarily increased its building of subsidized housing as an anticyclical measure.) Available funds began to be used for modernization of subsidized housing and private housing stock, and by 1983 the *quality* rather than the *quantity* of subsidized housing stock became an issue. Problems in most countries stemmed from early pre- and postwar concepts of space saving and cost cutting. Rooms were small, insulation was poor, and there was a lack of adequate parks and playgrounds. The need for modernization was uneven, however, with older Dutch units and Swedish older new town housing being more desirable than new high-rise housing in those countries (Huttman, 1978). As described later, by the 1980s the problem of improving un- popular high-rise housing and other stigmatized estates became a major concern to several governments.

A LIMITED RESIDUAL ROLE FOR THE STATE

The Sale of Council Housing

The sale of subsidized units, mainly terraced townhouses inhabited by solid working-class families, was a major policy change that came in the late 1970s in Britain. This changed policy was based on the Thatcher government's positive orientation toward homeownership and its dis- agreement with the welfare state philosophy of massive government assistance.

The large stock of publicly owned housing was in many ways the pride of the British Liberals (Harloe, 1982), and it was this symbol and its projective costs that the Conservatives wanted to dismantle. As Forrest and Murie (1985, p. 4) reported:

> The reduction in size of public housing sector has become part of the general strategy to restructure and reduce state provisions across the whole range of social services.

By selling council housing units, the Thatcher government also attacked the welfare state ideal of *equalization* of housing provision to reduce class differences. According to Forrest and Murie (1985, p. 4),

> In the minds of the British government, the sale of council housing has been

linked to the distribution of wealth and the less tangible notion of property-owned democracy.

Sale of council housing has also been motivated by high costs of management and maintenance of the projects.

Sales of British Council housing have been moderately high; purchases on desirable estates have been considered a bargain. Tenants have been encouraged to buy with the incentive of sale price reductions up to half of market value. During the period from 1979 to 1983 over half a million units, approximately 8% of council housing stock, had been sold (Forrest & Murie, 1985, p. 5). Holding back council house sales were such factors as the financial inability of tenants to buy their units, even with government subsidies, and the reluctance to buy units on estates with unfavorable images.

Due to sales of council housing, tenants' purchase of private housing, and local housing authorities' increased use of undesirable units in the 1980s for the very poor, immigrants, and homeless, the character of rental council housing changed from the early postwar period. As Forrest and Murie (1985) stated:

> There has been a movement from a position where owner-occupation was predominantly middle class tenure, high quality council housing was used by the affluent working class, and private landlordism catered for the poorest sections of population—toward one where council housing serves the vulnerable, the low paid and marginalised population with a highly strategied and differentiated home ownership as the mass tenure. (p. 5)

HOME OWNERSHIP

The value of homeownership was also advocated in other European countries. By 1983, for example, Swedish officials were speaking of greater financial participation of residents in housing construction, and West German officials encouraged citizens to save more for their own housing (ECE, January 9, 1984, p. 5) (West German postwar policy had always encouraged some private sector developments, including private cooperatives and modernization projects [Muhlich, 1978].) The policy has been to provide little direct subsidization of social housing (only 2% of units completed in 1978) or housing associations and public cooperatives (only 8% in 1978), but considerable indirect subsidies (tax relief) (McKay, 1982).

By the 1980s other northern European countries, to varying degrees, advocated homeownership as a desirable living arrangement. In the Netherlands the government took measures to help low-income people buy homes. In Denmark the government provided financial arrangements for homeowners to buy homes and nonprofit groups to build, and stated a basic goal of the right of households to own dwellings with adequate standards and the right to a choice of housing (ECE, January 9, 1984).

These governments and an increasing citizenry in all of the northern European countries in the late 1970s saw homeownership as the preferred housing tenure. Private ownership of homes was a hedge against increasing inflation and was a prudent investment for sheltering income from taxes. People desired a detached or semidetached house surrounded by green grass, and their increasing affluence in the 1970s allowed them to pursue this preference (Den Draak, 1985; Ungerson & Karn, 1980).

The main mechanism for facilitating homeownership was indirect government subsidies, in the form of tax relief and shelter of appreciated house value. For example, Lindberg (1978) attributed the increase in homeownership in Sweden in the 1970s to government policies that allowed all interest on loans to be tax deductible, and to the lack of private rentals. Homeownership in Sweden moved from less than a third of all units built in 1961–1965 to about three fourths built in 1979–1980.

Similarly, the British government promoted ownership through tax deductions and some direct mortgage assistance. Even during the period of fiscal austerity, ownership subsidies in Britain stayed high, while council housing subsidies were severely cut. For 1982–1983 the average mortgage tax relief per household amounted to 370 pounds, whereas general housing subsidies for council housing tenants per dwelling were only 207 pounds (Forrest & Murie, 1985). Homeownership has increased from 42% of all dwellings in 1960 to 57% in 1983 for all of the United Kingdom.

Indirect subsidies to homeowners have also been high in Denmark. In 1981 the total value of tax relief on housing loan interest amounted to approximately $1,000 million (U.S. dollars), whereas all other subsidies amounted to only $600 million (U.S. dollars) (ECE, January 9, 1984, p. 5). In West Germany indirect subsidies made up a large part of total subsidies. To a lesser degree this was also true for the Netherlands. By 1978 over 90% of the homes in West Germany were privately built, compared to 79% in the 1970s (Economic Commission for Europe, 1979, 1980). In the Netherlands, by 1980, two thirds of the building of homes was done by private investors, compared to one half in 1971; public and nonprofit groups built the rest, although the Dutch temporarily increased their subsidized housing in 1981 as an anticyclical measure (ECE, December 15, 1983, p. 4).

MIXED OR DIVERSE IDEOLOGICAL ORIENTATIONS

In Denmark, the Netherlands, and Sweden, with their coalition of Labor-Social Democratic governments, some politicians and bureaucrats considered homeownership to be desirable, whereas others were still partially committed to the welfare-state type of housing policy. This mixed ideological orientation is reflected in the advocacy of government homeownership subsidies and for flexible mortgage arrangements alongside proposals for equalization in distribution of subsidies. An illustration of this split ideological orientation appeared in discussions held at a 1984 ECE Committee on Housing meeting. Criticisms were made of the dominance of homeownership tax relief subsidies (ECE, January 9, 1984). A Dutch official commented that "the present system, facilitating access of all households to homeownership, created two different cultures." And a delegate from Luxembourg spoke of the "distortion of social goals [through] the effects of current housing policy due to subsidies and tax relief" (ECE, March 6, 1984). What bothered these delegates, especially the Danes, Dutch, and Swedes, was the negative effects of tax relief on equality of households (a welfare state value) (ECE, December 19, 1983, pp. 4–5). As the Luxembourg delegate commented: "A long term goal of housing policy has been to influence redistribution of income and wealth and this conflicted with the promition of home ownership through tax relief" (ECE, March 6, 1984, pp. 5–6). Both the Swedish and Dutch housing officials stated that tax relief had negative effects on the distribution of incomes and wealth and housing (ECE, January 9, 1984, p. 4). A related complaint of welfare state-oriented housing officials was the *overconsumption* of housing by homeowners and, as a result, the misallocation of a considerable amount of the country's resources for homeowner rather than for multifamily rentals housing (ECE, December 15, 1983, p. 8). Swedish housing officials, also concerned with lopsided owner-occupied new housing investment, reported that, although "the total number of dwellings completed annually [from 1970 to 1979] decreased by one half, the number of single family houses doubled and the number of modernized dwellings increased six times" (ECE, December 15, 1983, p. 3).

The prominence of homeowner subsidies was a purposeful policy in Britain, whereas in Denmark, the Netherlands, and Sweden it was a somewhat accidental occurrence. A Swedish housing official attributed this dominance of tax relief subsidies to "a certain inertia in current housing policy which had been formulated during a period of need for higher housing production and standards accompanied by different economic circumstances." A Dutch delegate pointed out that these tax relief measures had usually originated as part of the principle of income taxation; only with inflation and increased homeownership did their position shift to that of being the major housing subsidies. (ECE, December 14, 1983, p. 5; ECE, January 9, 1984, p. 7.) In 1984, the fact that many recipients of this tax subsidy were high- and middle-income groups made it politically difficult to cut these subsidies.

In summary, homeownership has recently been promoted as a desirable situation in most northern European countries. Outside of the Conservative governments of Britain, and to some degree West Germany, there have been mixed feelings, due to split ideological orientation, about tax relief subsidies to homeowners being the *dominant* subsidy to achieve private units. There has been a desire by Dutch, Danish, and Swedish housing officials to limit the amount of subsidization of homeowners in order to improve equalization of housing subsidies to all classes.

In the early 1980s there was a sharp decrease in the building and sale of private units, due to high interest rates, high building costs, exorbitant land prices, and reduced consumer purchasing power. In West Germany the cost of living doubled from 1963 to 1983, construction costs increased three times, and the price of land increased roughly six times (ECE, December 15, 1983, p. 2). A West German housing official reported that "increasing interest rates [real terms], a slow-down in the demand for new dwellings accompanied by expectations of a lower income were developments that led to a reduction in housing output from nearly 700,000 new dwellings in 1973 down to 338,000 in 1981" (ECE, December 30, 1983, p. 3). A Dutch housing official reported "the collapse of the owner-occupied housing market in 1980, triggered by the reduced purchasing power of households and high interest rates." He added that "this marked an end of the previous interest in owner-occupied dwellings, induced by the still continuing affluence and the high inflation rate, as well as by the access to the housing market of the postwar baby boom generation" (ECE, February 6, 1984, p. 2). An 1983 ECE Working Party on Housing summarized that year's situation:

> A further worsening of the situation, as far as real incomes, employment, energy prices and public budget constraints . . . has reduced substantially the effects of this factor [homeownership]; some countries, in their national monographs, have reported a shift of demand in favor of rented dwellings, particularly those which are subsidized. Considerable decline in increments of people's real incomes has weakened housing demands in general, especially for new and expensive dwellings, whether rented or owner-occupied. . . . Various systems of subsidies [including tax relief] have helped in several countries to slow down this decline of housing demand. Nevertheless such efforts appear to have encountered barriers resulting from

public finance limitations. At the same time there is now more favorable developments in investments and other activities related to housing improvement and energy conservation. (ECE, December 14, 1983, p. 14)

The result of these economic and ideological policy factors is a serious housing shortage, especially for the poor and disadvantaged. And, as indicated in the next section, the goal of modernization and rehabilitating existing housing stock may or may not solve the problem.

REHABILITATION AND MODERNIZATION OF HOUSING

Rehabilitation can intensify the housing crisis by decreasing the number of rental units through consolidation of units or conversion to owner-occupancy status; it also increases the rents of the remaining rental units.

Although some historical preservation and some private gentrification efforts to rehabilitate inner-city areas, such as in Islington in London, started early, modernization did not become a major policy direction until the late 1970s. Previously, slum clearance, that is demolition, was more likely. By 1982 modernization was a predominant concern for many governments. In several countries the "amount of resources allocated to improvement and maintenance was level with or exceeded the resources allocated to new housing construction," according to the ECE Committee on Housing (1981). This committee also stated:

> In Sweden the activity of maintenance, improvement and modernization of housing is nowadays greater than investment in new house building; in the Federal Republic of Germany, maintenance, modernization and improvement work account for 37% of total investment in the residential sector. (ECE, April 28, 1981, p. 4)

Modernization is designed to correct the deficiencies of the postwar and earlier prewar stock, and includes installation of bathrooms, a hot water supply, insulation, central heating, elevators, and consolidation of small rooms into large ones. In other words, the increase in modernization was due above all to changing requirements for modern comfort in housing and problems of substandard housing. Other reasons for increased modernization included a belief that there were cost advantages in labor, materials, and land.

Much of the modernization effort has been directed at government-subsidized housing, although some was done on private homes, often under local government organizational efforts. Housing cooperatives and individual owner–occupiers often financed repairs and modernization out of their own funds, partly by public subsidies, subsidized credits, and loans.

The value orientations of governments supported homeownership of modernized private housing in inner cities to varying degrees. As one ECE delegate stated:

> The systems of tenure and ownership of house . . . influenced moderniza-
> tion activities in an essential way. It was reported that owner-occupied dwell-
> ings were often modernized to a good standard because of economic advan-
> tages to owners through tax relief and value increases. (ECE, November 11,
> 1982, p. 10)

On the other hand, an ideological problem of these private moderniza-
tion efforts was that subsidies again were giving unequal benefits to the middle-class private parties, in this case those involved in modernization. In most market-economy countries allowances for tax reduction of interest payment served as an important means for indirect public sup-
port of modernization. Not only were the poor shortchanged in receipt of subsidies for modernization, but they suffered from increased rents and involuntary relocation caused by modernization activities.

For example, research in Cologne, West Germany, shows that in-
creased rents in privately modernized housing and the scarcity of units due to modernization created reverberating effects on poor people (Meuter, 1982). In Cologne, housing rehabilitation was promoted by the government in the belief that the inner-city area should be revitalized, suburban sprawl halted, the homeowning class's renewed interest in inner cities should be encouraged, and inner-city populations should be provided with a class mix. This however, turned out to be a policy that cut out units for the poor and pushed them to outer estates or squatter housing.

Due to rehabilitation, rents rose dramatically, and tenants had to move out. At the same time, the government's incentive program for rehabilitation and conversion to homeownership was so successful that, in some districts, over 10% of the stock was sold between 1976 and 1980. The demand for old houses kept growing so that estate agents specu-
lated on them, modernized them with government subsidies, converted them to condominiums, and put them on the market. The price jumped almost 100% in 5 years (Meuter, 1982). Many of the poor ex-tenants moved out to new social housing built in the mid-1970s on the outskirts of Cologne. This latter estate had been unpopular because of its high rent and its distance from town as well as its bleak appearance. However, the housing shortage caused by this inner-city rehabilitation meant that the distant project was filled, with 70% to 80% of the residents being foreign workers.

The cost to the state of these two developments was considerable. As a result of the shift in housing demand to the inner-city area units, the state paid to subsidize massive rehabilitation and homeownership. It also paid to subsidize the housing needs of the displaced under-privileged sectors of the population relocated in social housing. These poor people, unable to pay the rents of the outer area new social housing, went into arrears, and the state then had the added cost of evicting them. All this was caused by the shortage of inner-city private inexpensive rentals. Although some families could move into units vacated by the Cologne households who had bought on the urban fringe (between 1970 and 1975, 5% did), the demand was so great, according to Meuter, that there were about 10,000 cases of acute housing need. Meuter (1982) concluded:

> The government made a housing policy that sounded reasonably possible to rationally carry out . . . inner city rehabilitation seemed sensible to stop the impending deterioration of areas of older housing due to the migration of the middle class to urban fringe. It cost the government less because of private capital. However, because of the housing shortage, it meant private capital was draining the city of cheap rentals to meet middle class demands. High housing costs were making it impossible to provide cheap rent social housing. (p. 111)

To varying degrees the new policy directions just described—the residual role of the state, the fiscal austerity orientation, the promotion of homeownership, and the modernization policies—have had negative effects on the housing situation of the poor. These effects, in terms of shortage of affordable private rentals, homelessness, the immigrant housing situation, and stigmatized subsidized housing, are detailed next.

THE SHORTAGE OF AFFORDABLE PRIVATE RENTAL HOUSING

The decrease in affordable private rents has resulted from several factors: costs of rehabilitation, homeownership subsidies, rent regulations and bureaucratic controls that have limited profits and discouraged landlords, and the high costs of producing new rental units.

Rent regulations have led to decreased investment in new private rentals and conversion of rental housing to owner-occupied housing. In the late 1960s and 1970s, many British landlords turned their units into owner-occupied housing, in part due to the attitude of successive British Labor governments. Donnison and Ungerson (1982) stated:

> In Britain [before 1979], landlords [were] treated by the government as parasites to be ruthlessly suppressed, and sometimes paragons of free enterprise .

> to be unleased in haphazard and unselective fashion. Not surprisingly, they
> have extricated themselves from the market. (p. 232)

One reason why landlords left the business was

> the increasing number of controls that governments had introduced in the
> price, quality, etc., of rentals, compared with the still relatively free condi-
> tions in the owner occupancy sector. (Harloe, 1982, p. 213)

Although the British Conservatives since 1980 have given landlords
more freedom to raise rents, Donnison and Ungerson (1982) concluded
that developers are leery about stepping into long-term capital investments in a rental housing market subject to political reversals.

Wienen (1982) reported a similar problem in West Germany, where
bureaucratic controls have caused landlords and investors to be reluctant to take on new properties. Wienen (1982) stated that it has been
almost impossible for private investors in rental property to obtain an
acceptable profit on investments. As a result, West German construction
of new multifamily dwellings plummeted by one third from 1970–1974
to 1978–1981. In fact, in most northern European countries the number
of newly built multifamily dwellings, many of which were rental units,
dropped sharply from the late 1970s onward. In both Britain and the
Netherlands private rentals decreased from over 50% of the housing
stock right after World War II to below 15% by 1980 (Ash, 1982; ECE,
January 19, 1984). In Denmark, West Germany, and France, private
rentals, which had made up about three quarters of the housing stock in
each country after the war, were also down sharply by 1980 (McKay,
1982).

THE HOMELESS

The decline in the availability of cheap rental units caused an increase in the number of homeless and temporarily sheltered people in
the 1980s. Transients, young singles, new immigrants, recently dis-
charged armed services personnel, the unemployed, alcoholics, and
mentally ill were the marginal groups most likely to be homeless in
many countries. They often did not live long enough in one place to
have priority on social housing lists; they were not considered to be
deserving long-term residents of the community in which they resided.
Most did not fit the categories normally housed in either public or nonprofit housing, that is, they were not the usual family unit (Donnison &
Ungerson, 1982). Female-headed households were also considered to be
unacceptable to private landlords, and in Britain, to public landlords
(Ash, 1982). Their situation as casualties of family breakups, or as house-

holds with a different cultural definition of a family, for example, West Indian female-headed households in Britain, were ignored. Extended families, such as Pakistanis and Indians in Britain, were also considered unsuitable for either private or public rental housing. Those households previously evicted or with poor rent-paying records were also considered undesirable. The situation has also been difficult for many new families. Thus, of the women in Britain who married in 1971–1975 before age 20, one-third were without a home a year later; for those age 20 and over one-tenth were homeless (Ash, 1982).

There have been many adaptations to the difficult housing situation. Many people have moved in with relatives, for example, in Britain about 200,000 units were shared units in 1977. Another solution to avoid homelessness has been to take furnished transient accommodations, such as the bed sitters found in London.

This latter solution has been used by singles whose number has greatly increased in all industrialized countries (in Britain the number of singles increased 59% from 1961 to 1971). In Sweden, Gaunt (1984) reported that almost two thirds of the households now consisted of only one or two persons. The number of small accommodations in all these countries has not increased to meet the needs. For example, in England one half of the units have been three to four bedroom units (whereas only 17% of the households consist of four persons) (Ash, 1982).

The plight of singles, newly married, immigrants, and disenfranchised has been so bad that they have used shelters supplied by welfare departments and nonprofit groups; they have taken over abandoned buildings; or, in Britain and some other European countries they have moved into the least popular, stigmatized social housing projects when given that choice.

In Britain and other European countries it has been only in the last few years (1975 onward) that even a small proportion of these groups have been given subsidized housing options. Previously, in Britain, council housing was targeted to long-term resident working-class families. The uproar in the 1970s over the plight of the homeless led to the 1977 Homeless Persons Act, which mandated that local housing authorities find housing for such persons (Donnison & Ungerson, 1982). A number of authorities then moved the homeless into older council housing. However, this act, as Donnison and Ungerson (1982) reported, said "nothing about people coming from abroad [immigrants from the British Commonwealth] and this has already been proved to be a serious omission" (p. 278).

The number of homeless has continued to grow throughout Europe. Kearns (1979) estimated that the number in London was over

150,000; Amsterdam had over 58,000 persons on housing waiting lists in 1982; and Cologne had over 10,000 awaiting assignments to homes (Meuter, 1982). This shortage has frequently led to the "squatting" of homeless people in abandoned buildings. An estimated 10,000 squatters were living in hundreds of vacant office and residential buildings in Amsterdam. In October, 1982, Dutch police had a major battle with squatters. Kearns (1979) estimated that there were 30,000 squatters in Britain in 1979, 60% of whom were young single males. He reported that squatters were treated leniently in London at that time, possibly due to the housing authorities' concerns over providing alternative housing as required in the Homeless Persons Act (Donnison & Ungerson, 1982). In both Britain and the Netherlands, squatters seemed to have acquired a semilegal status.

IMMIGRANT HOUSING

In Great Britain, although immigration has declined, those who came in the postwar flux from South Asia, the West Indies, and Kenya have become permanent residents, and a second generation has now moved into child-bearing adulthood and family situations, producing a new need for housing. A similar housing crisis has occurred in many northern continental countries with the influx in the last few decades of guest workers (immigrants holding temporary work permits) who have comprised a substantial part of the urban population. Many have now returned to their native countries because of the economic recession; however, large numbers have acquired semipermanent or permanent status in Germany, Switzerland, Denmark, and Sweden, either legally or illegally. For example, in 1982, there still were over 3 million guest workers in West Germany (Wienen, 1982).

The number of immigrants in most northern European countries has been high enough to swell the inner-city housing market. Decent housing at a cheap rent has been scarce. Immigrants have been at a disadvantage in the competition for housing because of discrimination and several features that disqualify them for subsidized housing. These include newness to the area, transient status, and nontraditional family compositions, such as extended families or unmarried cohabitating couples.

These factors have led to poor living facilities for immigrants. For example, in Britain in 1975, West Indians were the group most likely to be in housing needing essential repairs and missing basic amenities. In an analysis of three working-class areas of Mannheim, Germany, Ipsen (1978) found that foreign workers lived in housing with poor sanitary arrangements and electrical installations, overcrowded rooms and exorbitant rents. Ipsen stated that, in this sample, 70% of foreign workers took the units because there were no alternatives, and 60% of the residents wanted to move.

In Britain, some South Asian immigrants have purchased large older homes and converted them to lodging accommodations. In doing so, they have been able to house extended families and others from their home village as well as many singles in desperate need. For example, Rex and Moore (1965) reported that immigrants bought large, structurally sound houses built in the 1880s in Birmingham's inner ring. Once multioccupancy started on a street, owner–occupants panicked, and whole streets changed quickly to lodging houses and to a ghetto area.

In recent years, immigrants in Great Britain have received a somewhat better reception from housing authorities, although they still have been less likely to be admitted to council housing than white applicants (Henderson, 1983). When they have been housed, however, it is usually in the older units and in estates of bad reputation. This treatment, Henderson (1983) concluded, was due to a combination of racism and of the applicants' being a stigmatized, disadvantaged group who are poor, newcomers, female-headed households, and other groups with low priority on waiting lists. Karn (1982) found this treatment stemming from both formal criteria and informal decision making. The rules also have restricted consideration for housing owner–occupiers (Asian lodging-house owners), extended families, or, at one time, those living with relatives, or the homeless. In addition, informal criteria used by housing authority home visitors often gave immigrant applicants low-priority scores, especially those from slum clearance areas (Henderson, 1983). By the same token, immigrants often stated preferences for inner-city bad-reputation housing because it was in proximity to their own group. This was due in some cases to a fear of harassment. And, they sometimes opted for bad reputation estates because they would be housed faster. It should be noted that, in many other northern European countries, immigrants have now been placed in subsidized housing, although some frequently have been housed in the unpleasant newer towns in their unpopular long-"slab" construction housing; this is true in Sweden and the Netherlands (Newman, 1983).

A major issue has been how to distribute immigrants in subsidized housing stock. Even in the 1960s the city of Birmingham, England, made some attempt at a dispersal policy but held back because of protests by both white tenants and immigrants (Rex, 1965). In 1984 another call for dispersal in British Council housing by the Commission for Racial Equality was widely publicized. Grunfeld (1982) has also reported an attempt by some municipalities in the Netherlands to counteract segregation by dispersed dwelling assignments. Here too, those attempts were resisted by both sides. Immigrants felt that they were being deported, whereas the neighborhood population felt that minority families in their areas would lower property values.

THE STIGMATIZATION OF SUBSIDIZED HOUSING

The practice of concentrating immigrants on certain housing estates has been one of a number of factors causing stigmatization of a part of the subsidized housing stock. Other factors include the promotion of homeownership and the consequent loss of better-off tenants, the decrease of private rentals and the resulting pressure to house marginal groups in subsidized housing, and the redefinition of the role of the state to a residual one, that is, housing only those who could not house themselves.

In Britain, Forrest and Murie (1985) reported that "what was new in the present situation was the level of concentration [of the poor] in the public sector, especially as the private rented sector declined" (p. 5). This is reflected in the increased number of tenants on welfare who received rent rebates, that is, the means-tested housing allowance for poor tenants in council housing who could not meet rent increases.

This newer situation is in sharp contrast to the 1947–1970 situation, where poorer groups were excluded from council housing, and the stable working classes were given priority (Huttman, 1969). The shift has resulted from a series of events involving hard-to-rent estates, movement into them by poorer and marginal populations, further stigmatization by virtue of the concentration of disadvantaged groups in this housing, and so on.

In Britain these hard-to-let units first received their poor reputation because of location or because they were in high-rise buildings (White & Maizels, 1961). High rises had originally been praised as architectural achievements and were the pride of local authorities. By 1965 flats in high-rise buildings accounted for over half the dwellings in the annual output (Ash, 1980). However, by 1970, they were unpopular. The British disliked them because they lacked gardens and privacy. People worried about elevator failures and children falling off balconies. Mothers complained of inability to supervise children playing outdoors, lack of proper play space, and density of the child population (United Kingdom Ministry of Housing, 1970). Some early subsidized housing was also unpopular, because of condensation, water penetration, and other problems that made living conditions worse than in houses classified as slums (Ash, 1980).

As estates became somewhat unpopular, the authorities concentrated disadvantaged persons in them and then did little maintenance. By the 1970s, British high-rise housing had many vacancies. This housing represented a large part of the over 100,000 hard-to-let units vacant in 1979 (2.2% of the subsidized housing stock) and the 22,000 units vacant 1 year or more (Donnison & Ungerson, 1982). It was these hard-to-let units that were used to house marginal groups.

In other European countries the subsidized housing sector also suffered from architectural mistakes of constructing massive buildings during the 1965–1974 period. During this period, the Swedish government shifted from construction of small buildings with small units, as found in the older new towns, to the construction of high density, six-to-eight story buildings—"industrialized housing slabs," sometimes a block long (Popenoe, 1977). These new high-density developments in the outer suburbs had little landscaping and poor external appearance, although they had large apartments. These "slabs" were criticized severely by the Swedes and, by 1975, building of them ceased (Huttman, 1974). These buildings had high vacancies, and units went to those with low priority on the waiting lists (20% to 30% of the tenants were foreign workers).

In the Netherlands, a similar situation existed in regard to the isolated new town of Bijlmermeer, with its 12,000 units of high-rise machine-built slab buildings. Its unpleasant appearance was increased by the maintenance problems caused by use of cheap building materials. The unpopularity of this development was such that in 1982 it was emptying out at the rate of 100 units per month (Newman, 1983). Here again, a number of units were rented to immigrant groups.

In many countries measures are being taken to utilize, convert, or rehabilitate this high-rise housing. For example, Newman (1983) and others are planning the conversion of some of Bijlmermeer into a residential center for youth. And in Britain, Ash (1980) stated:

> Some authorities are turning such highrise housing over to universities for occupancy by students and many authorities are now prepared to let these dwellings to groups of young adults. Some are being modernized for use. Several blocks, mainly highrise, unfortunately, are in such bad condition that they are being demolished . . . altogether hundreds of millions pounds have been wasted on public housing intended to eliminate the housing shortage quickly and cheaply but without due regard either for sound methods of construction, consumer needs and preferences, or cost. (p. 115)

IMPLICATIONS FOR FUTURE RESEARCH

A central issue policymakers in northern European housing are concerned with is how to make homeownership more affordable in order to satisfy the strong political and personal desires for this tenure status. With the high costs of ownership of the traditional single- or two-family house, innovative means must be located to give some households a feeling and reality of ownership while keeping their housing bills down. Governments may, to varying degrees depending on the political party in power, provide subsidies of different types for the purchase of cooperatives and condominiums, as well as encourage innovative new forms of shared ownership (communelike arrangements). Governments may promote new types of financial structures and mechanisms, such as employee saving accounts found in Yugoslavia, or new types of lending arrangements, such as longer mortgages and/or separate mortgages for different periods. A third possible trend may be increased purchaser "sweat labor" on the new house or modernization efforts to reduce housing costs. More research is needed on the most appropriate way to carry out any of these programs and on the psychological and sociological effects of different policy options.

Even if innovative policy programs are enacted, it is still questionable whether or not, with the present economic situation, home purchase will be affordable to many. With the continued likelihood for slow economic growth, public sector deficits, and the general stagnant real income increases, there are barriers to both the capacity to produce and the ability to buy new houses. The slow economic growth rate and interest payments on the public sector deficit may lead to a crowding of mortgage market demand for money. These factors plus high mortgage interest rates may continue to make loans inaccessible and expensive. This means that more people will have to accept the rental tenure status. Yet, the future of rental housing for northern Europe is bleak (Harloe, 1982). More research is needed on the depth of the crisis in rentals, who is affected, and the way people are adapting to it (such as sharing housing).

As far as predicting government's future role in providing rental housing in northern Europe, one can guess that the effect of the recession, resulting budget cuts, and the high cost of building will mean little construction of new subsidized housing. Rents on such housing may be raised, accompanied by more use of means-tested rent rebates for poorer tenants. On the other hand, European governments, to varying degrees related to the political party in power, may encourage more building of private rental units by providing interest subsidies, tax benefits, or by giving landlords more leeway to increase rents by loosening rent control regulations (Donnison & Ungerson, 1982). Whether these governments will increase rehabilitation efforts to provide standard rental units is questionable. Governments may let private investors take the lead in rehabilitation, with units sold to the middle class, especially as these governments realize the full cost of rehabilitation. And, governments may promote, to varying degrees, the building or subdividing of units into smaller size units to meet the needs of the increasing number of singles in the population, including young people and elderly (Huttman, 1982). Some governments may increase their provision of specially designed housing for the elderly, whereas others may cut back due to past heavy provisions, for example, the Netherlands, Denmark, and Britain (Denmark Ministry of Housing, 1974; Huttman, 1982). In the Netherlands the building for the elderly has been so extensive that, in 1976, the Dutch Ministry of Housing reported that a sufficient number of places in residential homes for the elderly was available everywhere (Netherlands Ministry of Housing, 1979; Vogelaar, 1976).

Future directions of government efforts to handle the homeless and squatters are harder to gauge. It is likely that the so-called deserving homeless will be given subsidized housing units, as is now happening in Britain, whereas nonprofit welfare groups, youth organizations, and local authorities may be encouraged to provide temporary shelter to transients and so-called marginal groups. Squatters may be given semi-legal rights to the units they squat in, whereas owners of vacant units may be penalized by local authorities for keeping them vacant. Research is certainly needed on the character of the homeless and the squatter population and present shelter needs.

Placement of more homeless and immigrants in subsidized housing may increase the stigmatization process for some projects, and research is needed on methods to assess and decrease such stigmatization and to evaluate various attempts to disperse disenfranchised groups. The whole situation of racial and ethnic group segregation in both public and private housing and new efforts to decrease it in these countries needs to be studied. Another issue to research is the degree to which the second generation of immigrant families, especially in Britain, now at the marrying and child-bearing age, will integrate into the English culture and be dispersed into different housing areas. Research can also follow trends as to the ideological bases of housing policy in northern Europe. Will the welfare state philosophies lose out to conservative policies?

The study of housing in northern Europe testifies to the need to undertake nation-specific and nation-comprehensive studies, and to the need to study the problem from several analytical approaches—political, sociological, and psychological.

REFERENCES

Ash, J. The rise and fall of high rise housing in England. In C. Ungerson & V. Karn (Eds.), *The consumers' experience of housing.* London: Gower, 1980.

Ash, J. *The effects of household formation and life styles on housing need in Britain.* Paper presented at the World Congress of Sociology, Mexico City, August 1982.

Basel, A., Grieff, R., & Muhlich, E. *Resident's participation in revitalization of housing areas.* Darmstadt, West Germany: Institut Wohnen und Umwelt GMBH, 1978.

Den Draak, W. Effect of population development in Dutch towns upon social and physical structure and housing policy. In W. Van Vliet, S. Fava, & E. Huttman (Eds.), *Housing needs and policy approaches: International perspectives.* Durham, N.C.: Duke University, 1985.

Denmark Ministry of Housing. *Housing in Denmark.* Copenhagen: Author, 1974.

Donnison, D., & Ungerson, C. *Housing policy.* London: Penguin Books, 1982.

Economic Commission for Europe. Committee on housing, building and planning. *Annual Bulletin of Housing and Building Statistics,* 1979, 1980.

Economic Commission for Europe. Committee on housing, building and planning. *Seminar on the forecasting and programming of housing. Madrid Conference Report.* Geneva: ECE, April 28, 1981.

Economic Commission for Europe. Committee on housing, building and planning. Working party on housing. *Report of the eleventh session.* Geneva: Author, November 11, 1982.

Economic Commission for Europe. Committee on housing, building and planning. *The relationship between housing and the national economy* (Prague Conference Report). Geneva: Author, December 14, 1983. Addendum 1. *Relationship between housing activities and other sectors.* Geneva: Author, December 15, 1983. Addendum 2. *Relationship between housing activities and the creation of national income.* Geneva: Author, December 16, 1983. Addendum 5. IV. *Social effectiveness of housing policy.* Geneva: Author, January 9, 1984. Addendum 7. *Social effects of housing policy.* Geneva: Author, January 9, 1984. Addendum 9. *Relationship between housing activities and other economic sectors, Annex I (Federal Republic of Germany) and Annex III (Sweden).* Geneva: Author, December 30, 1983.

Economic Commission for Europe. Committee on housing, building and planning. Working party on housing. *Rent policy: Synthesis report.* Geneva: Author, January 5, 1984.

Economic Commission for Europe. Working party on housing. *General and financial economic aspects of the rent policy in Western Europe: Synthesis report.* Geneva: Author, January 19, 1984.

Economic Commission for Europe. Commission on housing, building and planning. Working party on housing. *Proposal for the future work in the field of housing forecasting and programming.* Geneva: Author, February 6, 1984.

Economic Commission for Europe. *Working party. Report.* Geneva: Author, March 6, 1984.

Forrest, R., & Murie, A. Restructuring the welfare state: Privatization of public housing in Britain. In W. Van Vliet, S. Fava, & E. Huttman (Eds.), *Housing needs and policy approaches: International perspectives.* Durham, N.C.: Duke University Press, 1985.

Gaunt, L. Family needs and housing. In W. Van Vliet, S. Fava, & E. Huttman (Eds.), *Housing needs and policy approaches: International perspectives.* Durham, N.C.: Duke University Press, 1985.

Grunfeld, F. *The problem of spatial segregation and the preservation of an urban society.* Paper presented at the World Congress of Sociology, Mexico City, August 1982.

Harloe, M. A multinational perspective on housing policies: Housing and the market. In

G. M. Hellstern, F. Spreer, & H. Wollman (Eds.), *Applied urban research: Towards an internationalization of research and learning*. Bonn: Federal Research Institute for Regional Geography and Regional Planning, 1982, pp. 11–22.

Henderson, J. *Race, class and the administrative allocation of public housing in Britain*. Paper presented at the American Sociological Association meetings, Detroit, August 1983.

Huttman, E. *Stigma in public housing: International comparisons*. Berkley: University of California, unpublished thesis, 1969.

Huttman, E. Sociological implications of living in high rise. *Sociological Abstracts*, 1975, *22*, 207. (Abstract)

Huttman, E. *Suburban and new town density and transportation fit for different types of residential populations: Observations from Sweden, Finland, Holland, Britain, and France*. Unpublished paper, October, 1978.

Huttman, E. Multi-level care facilities for the elderly in Denmark and Holland. *Housing and Society*, 1982, *9*, 20–30.

Ipsen, D. *Housing conditions and interests of foreign workers in the Federal Republic of Germany*. Paper given at World Congress of Sociology, Uppsala, Sweden, August 1978.

Karn, V. Computing the points but does the point system rule? *Housing Review*, July–August, 1982.

Kearns, L. Intra-urban squatting in London. *Annals of American Association of Geographers*, 1979, *69*, 393–398.

Lindberg, G. *Cooperative housing in Sweden*. Paper presented at the World Congress of Sociology, Uppsala, Sweden, August 1978.

McKay, D. Introduction. In G. M. Hellstern, F. Spreer, & H. Wollman (Eds.), *Applied urban research* (Vol. 3). Bonn: Federal Research Institute for Regional Geography and Regional Planning, 1982, pp. 1–10.

Meuter, H. Regional and social effects of changed conditions in housing supply. In G. M. Hellstern, F. Spreer, & H. Wollman (Eds.), *Applied urban research* (Vol. 3). Bonn: Federal Research Institute for Regional Geography and Regional Planning, 1982, pp. 141–148.

Muhlich, E. *Housing policy and housing*. Paper presented at the World Congress of Sociology, Uppsala, Sweden, August 1978.

Netherlands Ministry of Housing. *Housing in the Netherlands*. The Hague: Author, 1979.

Newman, O. *Re-using undesired assisted housing*. Conference of the Royal Surveyors Association, London, August 1983.

Pahl, R. Foreword. In M. Harloe, R. Issacharoff, & R. Minns (Eds.), *The organization of housing*. London: Heinemann, 1974, pp. 3–5.

Popenoe, D. *The suburban environment*. Chicago: University of Chicago Press, 1977.

Rex, J., & Moore, R. *Race, community and conflict*. London: Oxford University Press, 1965.

Ungerson, C., & Karn, V. (Eds.), *The consumers' experience of housing*. London: Gower, 1980.

United Kingdom Ministry of Housing and Local Government. *Families living at high density*. London: Her Majesty's Stationery Office, 1970.

Vogelaar, G. A. M. Dutch Ministry of Housing statement to ECE, 1976, *Seminar on special housing needs*. Geneva: ECE, November, 1976.

White, E., & Maizels, J. *Two to five in high flats*. London: Housing Centre, 1961.

Wienen, H. The integration of parameters of action for the local government of a big city in the Ruhr area into the economic, political and institutional environment. In G. M. Hellstern, F. Spreer, & H. Wollman (Eds.), *Applied urban research: Towards an internationalization of research and learning* (Vol. 3). Bonn: Federal Research Institute for Regional Geography and Regional Planning, 1982, pp. 83–98.

Index